'*Rethinking EU Consumer Law* offers a fresh and authoritative critical perspective on this important (and very active) area of law by leading academics in this field. It is recommended to anyone interested in the key issues of EU consumer law and policy, its practical application and its theoretical underpinnings.'

Paula Giliker, University of Bristol, UK

'Howells, Twigg-Flesner and Wilhelmsson show why EU consumer law should focus less on maximum harmonisation, why a high level of consumer protection enhances EU businesses' international competitiveness, and why the "average consumer" benchmark should take the lessons of behavioural economics to heart. A must-read for consumer and business lawyers alike!'

Marco B.M. Loos, University of Amsterdam, The Netherlands

'A must-read that provides a clear presentation of EU consumer law – understanding full harmonisation becomes intuitive when reading the chapter on unfair commercial practices, and explains why it often has not met consumers and businesses' expectations and how it could. A book every consumer law scholar would have liked to write.'

Elise Poillot, Consumer Law Clinic, University of Luxembourg

Rethinking EU Consumer Law

In *Rethinking EU Consumer Law*, the authors analyse the development of EU consumer law on the basis of a number of clear themes, which are then traced through specific areas. Recurring themes include the artificiality of the EU's consumer image, the problems created by the drive towards maximum harmonisation, and the unexpected effects EU consumer law has had on national law. The book argues that EU consumer law has the potential to enhance the protection of consumers throughout the EU and could offer a model for consumer law elsewhere in the world, but in order to unlock this potential, there needs to be a rethink with regard to the EU's approach to consumer law and policy.

Geraint Howells is Chair Professor of Commercial Law and Dean of the Law School at City University Hong Kong. His expertise covers consumer law and product liability, consumer safety and tobacco regulation, and he has written, co-authored and edited many books and journal articles.

Christian Twigg-Flesner is Professor of International Commercial Law at the University of Warwick. Previously, he was Professor of Commercial Law at the University of Hull. He has expertise in consumer law, the Europeanisation of contract law, the digital revolution and contract law, Transnational Commercial Law, and the harmonisation of commercial and contract law. He has published widely on EU consumer and contract law.

Thomas Wilhelmsson is Professor of Civil and Commercial Law at the University of Helsinki. He was Rector of the University 2008–2013 and Chancellor 2013–2017. For ten years he was member of the Finnish Market Court. His expertise covers contract and tort law, consumer law and Europeanisation of private law.

Markets and the Law

Series Editor: Geraint Howells
City University of Hong Kong

Markets and the Law is concerned with the way the law interacts with the market through regulation, self-regulation and the impact of private law regimes. It looks at the impact of regional and international organizations (e.g. EC and WTO) and many of the works adopt a comparative approach and/or appeal to an international audience. Examples of subjects covered include trade laws, intellectual property, sales law, insurance, consumer law, banking, financial markets, labour law, environmental law and social regulation affecting the market as well as competition law. The series includes texts covering a broad area, monographs on focused issues, and collections of essays dealing with particular themes.

Other titles in the series

Consumer Debt and Social Exclusion in Europe
Hans-W. Micklitz and Irina Domurath
ISBN 978-1-4724-4903-0

Codifying Contract Law
International and Consumer Law Perspectives
Edited by Mary Keyes and Therese Wilson
ISBN 978-1-4724-1561-5

The European Unfair Commercial Practices Directive
Impact, Enforcement Strategies and National Legal Systems
Edited by Willem van Boom, Amandine Garde and Orkun Akseli
ISBN 978-1-4724-2340-5

The Law and Economics of Enforcing European Consumer Law
A Comparative Analysis of Package Travel and Misleading Advertising
Franziska Weber
ISBN 978-1-4724-1704-6

Rethinking EU Consumer Law

Geraint Howells,
Christian Twigg-Flesner
and Thomas Wilhelmsson

Routledge
Taylor & Francis Group
LONDON AND NEW YORK

First published 2018
by Routledge
2 Park Square, Milton Park, Abingdon, Oxon OX14 4RN

and by Routledge
711 Third Avenue, New York, NY 10017

Routledge is an imprint of the Taylor & Francis Group, an informa business

British Library Cataloguing-in-Publication Data
A catalogue record for this book is available from the British Library

Library of Congress Cataloging-in-Publication Data
A catalog record has been requested for this book

ISBN: 978-1-138-05874-3 (hbk)
ISBN: 978-0-367-27935-6 (pbk)
ISBN: 978-1-315-16483-0 (ebk)

Typeset in Galliard
by Deanta Global Publishing Services, Chennai, India

Contents

Preface

Over 20 years ago, Geraint Howells and Thomas Wilhelmsson wrote *EC Consumer Law*. That was at an exciting time when the EU was forging ahead with the adoption of many consumer law rules inspired by the desire to strengthen the protection of the European consumer. At that time, Christian Twigg-Flesner had just embarked on his PhD. Two decades on, EU consumer law has changed beyond recognition, and it is time for a fresh assessment of this topic. Christian has joined Geraint and Thomas on the team to produce this book. This is a completely new text and not just a second edition of Geraint and Thomas's earlier work – so much has changed that we want to present a fresh analysis of these topics.

The EU has remained active in the field of consumer law, but the emphasis has changed. There is less direct concern to protect the consumer as an end in its own right. Instead, consumer law is primarily seen as a tool to promote the internal market. We comment on this change and map its impact. More generally, we see a need for a thorough rethinking of the theoretical underpinnings of consumer law, and we offer our suggestions throughout the book.

One should not be too pessimistic. By international standards the EU consumer is well protected. However, so much effort in this field deserves to be supported by strong coherent foundations. We hope our critique will encourage a debate that will strengthen the brand of EU consumer law and help its export to other jurisdictions.

We take joint responsibility for the final product. Geraint Howells took the lead on Chapters 1, 6, 7 and 8 (he wishes to thank Jonathan Watson for research support and his work was supported by a grant from City University of Hong Kong Project No.9380074), Christian Twigg-Flesner on Chapters 2, 3, 5 and 9, and Thomas Wilhelmsson on Chapter 4. The bulk of the writing was completed by late summer 2016, but we have been able to include developments up to 1 January 2017.

Geraint Howells, Hong Kong
Christian Twigg-Flesner, Hull
Thomas Wilhelmsson, Helsinki

1 The rich canvas of EU consumer law

An introduction

Introduction

This book provides the reader with a critical analysis of the development and current state of EU consumer law as well as proposals for its future development. The EU has been exceptionally active in the consumer protection field. Almost all areas of consumer law (from advertising and marketing through contract and tort law rules to enforcement and redress) have been touched by EU law. EU consumer law is a subject of broad scope and some careful selection of topics has been necessary. This text concentrates on the traditional core areas of safety, contract law including credit, commercial practices and access to justice. Some areas, such as food and financial services regulation, have been excluded because they have become so complex at the EU level that they are topics in their own right. The same might also be said of travel law. This is not considered as a specific topic in this book, but several of the measures are used to illustrate key points. Other topics beyond the scope of our analysis are the consumer effects of competition law,[1] as well as services of general interest[2] and telecommunications. The latter two fields in particular are becoming more important and may challenge the application of the traditional principles of consumer protection.

Looking forward, the consumer marketplace is likely to evolve rapidly. A subject and body of legislation formed in the era of the development of mass consumer markets for cars and white goods is developing fast and being driven by increased consumer affluence and technological developments. The service sectors are growing, and the digital revolution is likely to spawn both new products and new ways of delivering them. This is an ideal time to review the development of EU consumer law to check that its fundamental values are fit for purpose. These will be tested moving forward to see if they are appropriate

1 On the relationship between consumer and competition law, see KJ Cseres, *Competition Law and Consumer Protection* (Kluwer, 2005).
2 See E Tjong Tjin Tai, 'Services, including services of general interest' in C Twigg-Flesner, *Research Handbook of EU Consumer and Contract Law* (Edward Elgar, 2016).

for the new challenges facing the global, digital and service-oriented consumer market.

Additional scrutiny of the robustness of EU consumer law might come from the UK. Following the referendum in June 2016, the UK will cease to be a member of the EU although the details of this process and the UK's future relationship with the EU remain unclear. Depending on the outcome of the negotiations, the UK might gain the freedom to develop a more independent consumer policy. The UK has always had a strong focus on consumer protection law, evidenced by recent reforms to its consumer legislation.[3] The UK may decide to tackle emerging challenges for consumer protection differently from the EU. However, it is likely that EU law will remain highly influential on the development of UK consumer law, at least in the medium term, and this book will have continued relevance for UK readers. What is clear is that there are many reasons why the quality of EU consumer law will be under continued and probably intensified scrutiny.[4]

The starting point for the analysis in this book is our belief that European consumer law and policy in recent times have risked over-emphasising the internal market goal.[5] There is a need to develop a philosophy to underpin its consumer protection policy. This should include a continued adherence to market transparency so consumers can be confident actors in the market and so help drive up standards by being part of a competitive environment. However, the EU policy needs to have more depth and an appreciation of the social welfarism goals of consumer policy. In part this involves protecting the vulnerable. This is occasionally reflected in the current *acquis*;[6] but there is little critical analysis of the concept of vulnerability or how to address the problems it gives rise to. However, any consumer policy also needs to recognise all consumers are subject to limitations when acting on the market. There is growing recognition of the important lessons for consumer law from behavioural economics in this regard,[7] particularly in the context of applying the Unfair Commercial Practices Directive.[8] One

3 See C Twigg-Flesner, 'Some thoughts on consumer law reform – consolidation, codification, or a restatement?' in L Gullifer and S Vogenauer (eds), *English and European Perspectives on Contract and Commercial Law – Essays in Honour of Hugh Beale* (Hart, 2014).

4 The European Commission is undertaking its own review of the consumer *acquis*. Results and possible reform proposals are not expected until well into 2017. With elections to the European Parliament due in 2019, it seems unlikely that there will be major reforms until after then. For more information, see http://ec.europa.eu/consumers/consumer_rights/review/index_en.htm [last accessed 18 December 2016].

5 Norbert Reich once aptly described this as the 'Janus face' of EU consumer law: N Reich, *Europäisches Verbraucherrecht*. (Nomos, 1996), p.56.

6 L Waddington, 'Vulnerable and confused: the protection of "vulnerable" consumers under EU Law', *European Law Review* 6 (2013), p.757.

7 AL Sibony, 'Can EU consumer law benefit from behavioural insights? An analysis of the unfair commercial practices directive' (2014) 22 *European Review of Private Law* p.901, and J Trzaskowski, 'Behavioural economics, neuroscience, and the Unfair Commercial Practices Directive' (2011) 34 *Journal of Consumer Policy* p.377.

8 Directive 2005/29/EU, analysed in Chapter 2.

function of the law should be to share risks so that all consumers can expect their purchases fulfil certain legitimate expectations. An effective consumer law is also compatible with the interests of good traders and should promote the EU brand and raise its international competitiveness.

Our analysis is underpinned by a number of key themes. We develop these in this chapter. Our analysis of specific fields within EU consumer law will then develop these further.

1. The balance between internal market and consumer protection objectives has swung too much in favour of market integration by the overstatement of the case for maximum harmonisation.
2. A high level of consumer protection is desirable not only for consumers but to enhance the international competitiveness of the 'European brand'.
3. The EU approach to consumer protection risks being viewed as insufficiently protective due to its adoption of the average consumer standard and an information-based protection model which has not been developed in a sophisticated manner taking into account the lessons of behavioural economics.
4. EU consumer law should be more explicit in recognising that it has a social welfare function of redistributing risk.
5. EU legislation should be in a form which allows the EU rules to be integrated into national regimes and parallel regimes for cross-border sales should only be introduced where there are good justifications.
6. The EU needs to ensure laws are effectively enforced.

The balance between internal market and consumer protection objectives has swung too much in favour of market integration by the overstatement of the case for maximum harmonisation

There has always been a tension between the avowedly consumer protection motivations of the EU when enacting the consumer *acquis* and the more utilitarian objective of enhancing the internal market by creating a level playing field for technical, administrative and private law regulation.[9] As the next section

9 G Howells and T Wilhelmsson, *EC Consumer Law*, (Dartmouth, 1997); G Howells, I Ramsay and T Wilhelmsson, 'Consumer law in its international dimension', in G Howells, I Ramsay and T Wilhelmsson (eds), *Handbook of Research on International Consumer Law* (Edward Elgar, 2010); V Mak, 'Two levels, one standard? The multi-level regulation of consumer protection in Europe' in J Devenney and M Kenny (eds), *European Consumer Protection: Theory and Practice* (Cambridge University Press, 2012); H-W Micklitz, 'The relationship between national and European consumer policy' in C Twigg-Flesner et al. (eds), *The Yearbook of Consumer Law 2008* (Ashgate, 2008), p.49; L Miller, *The Emergence of EU Contract Law* (Oxford University Press, 2011); C Twigg-Flesner, 'EU law and consumer transactions without an internal market dimension' in D Leczykiewicz and S Weatherill (eds), *The Involvement of EU Law in Private Law Relationships* (Hart, 2013); S Weatherill, 'The links between competition policy and consumer protection' in G Howells et al. (eds), *The Yearbook of Consumer Law 2007* (Ashgate, 2007).

illustrates, this is inevitable given the legal base on which most of the *acquis* is founded. However, there have been some subtle (and other less subtle) changes in emphasis and policy in recent years.[10] This was marked most obviously by the increased preference for maximum harmonisation directives. In the early days of EU consumer law the internal market criterion was met by mainly minimum harmonisation laws that sought to give consumers the confidence to shop anywhere in the EU marketplace.[11] Nowadays, this is no longer seen as sufficient. Instead businesses are considered to need the confidence that they will not be surprised by legal provisions when selling abroad.[12] Maximum harmonisation is the order of the day. This legal policy change has been underpinned by an institutional reshuffling of the cards away from the old Directorate-General on Health and Consumer Protection (DG SANCO), with most areas of EU consumer law now being handled by DG JUST (Justice and Consumers).

This faith in the level playing field as a motor for deeper integration seems misguided. EU regulation is rarely complete. It leaves gaps either expressly (e.g. with regard to sanctions and remedies) or by default due to the limited scope of the measures. These lacunae have to be filled by national law. Moreover, many EU provisions contain open-textured clauses which allow for different national legal and cultural interpretations.[13] Indeed national traditions of enforcement and styles of interpretation mean that the cross-border trader can never be assured that the law in practice will be the same in every state whatever the law books say. A false sense of security can be created if producers and consumers are led to believe the law is identical in substance and application throughout the Community. Moreover, there are many other factors more directly influencing decisions to buy and sell across borders than the substantive law, such as language, convenience, delivery costs and access to redress.

10 A crucial turning-point concerning the shift from 'minimum harmonisation' to 'full harmonisation' was set out in Commission, *Consumer Policy Strategy (2002–2006)*, OJ [2002] C137/2 at 3.1.2. For an overview of the shift in policy see H-W Micklitz, 'The targeted full harmonisation approach: Looking behind the curtain' in G Howells and R Schulze (eds), *Modernising and Harmonising Consumer Contract Law* (Sellier, 2009).

11 For critiques of the EU's view of consumer confidence, see T Wilhelmsson, "The abuse of the 'confident consumer' as a justification for EC consumer law". *Journal of Consumer Policy* 27 (2004), p.317; and C Twigg-Flesner, 'The importance of law and harmonisation for the EU's confident consumer' in D.Leczykiewicz and S.Weatherill (eds), *The Images of the Consumer in EU Law* (Hart, 2015).

12 See, for example, Commission, *Green Paper on policy options for progress towards a European Contract Law for consumers and businesses* COM (2010) 348 final, 5; see also G Howells, 'European contract law reform and European consumer law – two related but distinct regimes'. *European Review of Contract Law* 2 (2011), pp.173, 185. In relation to standard contract terms see, for example, H Collins, 'The freedom to circulate documents: Regulating contracts in Europe' (2004) 10 *European Law Journal* p.787; S Whittaker, 'On the development of European standard contract terms' (2006) 2 *European Review of Contract Law* p.51.

13 See Chapter 2 on unfair commercial practices, and Chapter 4 on unfair contract terms.

Maximum harmonisation is seen as an attack on some higher levels of protection that historically exist in some Member States. For example, under the maximum harmonisation approach adopted in the original proposal for a Consumer Rights Directive,[14] the ability of Nordic states to control core terms, or the rights of consumers in some states immediately to reject non-conforming goods without allowing an attempt to cure, would have been lost. This was one reason why the measure was scaled back by the removal of sale of goods and unfair terms rules. This episode adversely affected the image of the EU as a champion of consumer rights.

A high level of consumer protection is desirable not only for consumers but to enhance the international competitiveness of the 'European brand'

Our view is that creating high minimum standards that lead to gradual convergence is the best way forward. It is a credit to Europe that consumer lawyers now all use a common terminology[15] and there has been a high degree of legal convergence. Maximum harmonisation seeks to push this further, but for relatively small gains and at the risk of alienating the consumer movement. This policy has undermined confidence in the EU as a legislator with concern for a high level of consumer protection running through its DNA. Consumer protection should not just be a by-product of the internal market. Moreover, consumer protection is not only a concern for consumers. Strong consumer protection is also a protection for traders against unfair competition.[16] High standards properly enforced remove any incentive to produce poor products or act unfairly.[17] The EU consumer standards are also part of a branding exercise for Europe as a region known for high quality goods that are internationally attractive.[18] An

14 Commission, *Proposal for a Directive of the European Parliament and of the Council on Consumer Rights* COM (2008) 614 final. For criticism see, amongst others, G Howells and R Schulze (eds), *Modernising and Harmonising Consumer Contract Law* (Sellier, 2009); H-W Micklitz and N Reich, "Crónica de una muerte anunciada: The Commission proposal for a 'Directive on Consumer Rights'" (2009) 46 *Common Market Law Review* p.471; C Twigg-Flesner and D Metcalfe, 'The proposed Consumer Rights Directive – less haste, more thought?' (2009) 6 *European Review of Contract Law* p.368.

15 Acquis Group (Redaction Committee), 'Position paper on the proposal for a Directive on Consumer Rights' in H Schulte-Nölke and L Tichý (eds), *Perspectives for European Consumer Law* (Sellier, 2010); G Ajani and M Ebers (eds), *Uniform Terminology for European Contract Law* (Nomos, 2005); C Perfumi, 'Theory and practice of constructing a common contract law terminology' in J Devenney and M Kenny (eds), *The Transformation of European Private Law* (Cambridge University Press, 2013); B Pozzo and V Jacometti (eds), *Multilingualism and the Harmonisation of European Law* (Kluwer, 2006).

16 Seminally, G Akerlof, "The market for 'lemons': Quality uncertainty and the market mechanism" (1970) 84 *Q J Econ* p.488.

17 Ibid.

18 Commission, *Contribution of the Internal Market and Consumer Protection to Growth* (2014), p.30.

effective high level of protection means EU products and services become more competitive globally as their quality is trusted. Indeed, the whole of Europe can benefit from the reputation of those states whose products already have high standing, as it will be assumed those states only agreed to standards that met their consumers' expectations and maintained the quality level of their key industry sectors. However, if the EU were to mandate lower standards, then over time the reputation of the best will be dragged down. In the globalised economy, high income states like those in Europe will only flourish if they can manufacture and sell high-value-added products that carry a premium for consumer confidence.

A reflection of this EU brand is the export of European legal models. If legislation is seen to promote high standards in a way that is compatible with a competitive market it is likely that other states will adopt its rules. Imitation is after all the sincerest form of flattery. Several areas of EU law have been exported; this is most notable in the product liability and safety area, but also is reflected in other aspects such as unfair terms and unfair commercial practices.

The EU approach to consumer protection risks being viewed as insufficiently protective due to its adoption of the average consumer standard and an information-based protection model which has not been developed in a sophisticated manner taking into account the lessons of behavioural economics

Various characteristics of EU consumer law and policy have been criticised for threatening to undermine traditional notions of consumer protection.[19] These may jeopardise not only consumer protection, but also the brand of European goods and services. An often-cited example is the reference to the 'average consumer' standard as a standard by which to measure the impact of trader conduct, rather than using more protective images of the consumer.[20] Indeed, despite the

19 For example, B Lurger, 'Protection of consumers in European private law' in R Brownsword, H-W Micklitz, L Niglia and S Weatherill (eds), *The Foundations of European Private Law* (Hart, 2011); I Maletić, *The Law and Policy of Harmonisation in Europe's Internal Market* (Edward Elgar, 2013); W-H. Roth, "Transposing 'pointillist' EC guidelines into systematic national codes – problems and consequences" (2002) 6 *European Review of Private Law* p.761. See also T W, 'Private law in the EU: Harmonised or fragmented Europeanisation' (2002) 6 *European Review of Private Law* p.77.

20 For example, H Unberath and A Johnston, 'The double-headed approach of the ECJ concerning consumer protection' (2007) 44 *Common Market Law Review* pp.1237, 1282; B Lurger, 'The Common Frame of Reference/Optional Code and the various understandings of social justice in Europe' in T Wilhelmsson, E Paunio and A Pohjolainen (eds), *Private Law and The Many Cultures of Europe* (Kluwer, 2007); see also the contribution by T Wilhelmsson, 'The average European consumer: A legal fiction?' in the same volume.

EU's espousal of the value of consumer behavioural economics,[21] it takes as its model the rather empirically unsupported image of an average consumer as being someone who is 'reasonably well-informed and reasonably observant and circumspect'.[22] It seems to assume a mathematical test which exposes anyone below the average to risk of manipulation in the marketplace. It also risks marginalising consumer protection by suggesting any additional protection is something not needed by the typical consumer and only necessary for some vaguely termed category of 'vulnerable consumers'.

The EU also relies heavily on a model of regulation which prioritises information over substantive regulation. Whilst consumer empowerment is to be welcomed there are concerns that this may become a replacement for some desirable substantive rights.[23] It is another example of the EU failing to heed the lesson from its own discussion of behavioural economics, by not applying those insights fully to understand the limits of information as a means of protection. Whilst policy-makers will claim to be alert to these risks, the danger is that their rhetoric favours a more liberal approach to trade practices. There is a risk that consumer protection is only seen as needed by marginalised weak consumers,[24] whereas we feel consumers should be recognised as a class who are structurally poorly positioned to protect themselves in the marketplace.

EU consumer law should be more explicit in recognising that it has a social welfare function of redistributing risk

One dimension that is lacking in EU consumer policy debates is a real advocacy of consumer law as a legitimate socialisation of risk. The same criticism could be made of national consumer policy in many Member States. Whilst part of the social welfare function involves making adequate provision for those who

21 For example, Commission, *Consumer Decision-making in Retail Investment Services: A Behavioural Economics Perspective* (2010); Policy Studies Institute, *Designing Policy to Influence Consumers: Consumer Behaviour Relating to the Purchase of Environmentally Preferable Goods* (2010). See also R van Bavel et al., *Applying Behavioural Sciences to EU Policy-making* (2013); P Lunn, *Regulatory Policy and Behavioural Economics* (OECD Publishing, 2014), pp.32–33.

22 C–216/96, *Gut Springenheide GmbH v Oberkreisdirektor des Kreises Steinfurt* [1998] ECR I–4657; C–303/97 *Verbraucherschutzverein eV v Sektkellerei G.C. Kessler GmbH und Co.* [1999] ECR I–513; C–220/98, *Estée Lauder Cosmetics GmbH & Co. OHG v Lancaster Group GmbH* [2000] ECR I–117; C–465/98 *Verein gegen Unwesen in Handel und Gewerbe Köln eV v Adolf Darbo AG.* [2000] ECR I–2297; C–3/99 *Cidrerie Ruwet SA v Cidre Stassen SA and HP Bulmer Ltd.* [2000] ECR I-8749. See also Recital 18 of the Unfair Commercial Practices Directive.

23 G Howells, 'The potential and limits of consumer empowerment through information'. *JLS* 32(3) (2005), p.349.

24 J Stuyck, 'The notion of the empowered and informed consumer in consumer policy and how to protect the vulnerable under such a regime' and T Wilhelmsson, 'The informed consumer vs the vulnerable consumer in unfair commercial practices law – a comment' in G Howells et al (eds), *Yearbook of Consumer Law 2007* (Ashgate, 2007).

are vulnerable, it should go beyond this. Consumer protection should offer all consumers protection against exposure to undue risks which are nevertheless common features in market transactions. Things go wrong in the market either through incompetence, fraud or chance. Some risks consumers might have to accept as simple lessons to be learned, but others need to be redressed either because of the harm caused or to clean up the market going forward. This socialisation of risk underpins many consumer rules. The law steps in to prevent simple market power determining where risk falls and lies. In some areas as diverse as product liability[25] and rights of delayed airline passengers[26] the allocation of risk is more obviously a factor underpinning legislative intervention. Yet, it is a policy motivation that is not spoken of too loudly for fear of accusations of paternalism.

All inalienable consumer rights could be viewed as enforced insurance as the potential liability has to be factored into the price of goods and services. Many substantive consumer rights provide inalienable standards, but the information rhetoric risks downplaying them. Indeed there are important questions about just how inalienable these rights are if business is given too much latitude to manipulate the obligations through disclosure. Consumer protection needs to take note of the vulnerabilities of all consumers and some socialisation of risk should be part of the portfolio of consumer protection tools. This is a social welfare model of consumer protection[27] and should be contrasted with the neo-liberal model which simply wants to maximise consumer preferences in an open market by enhancing decision-making.[28] The balance between personal freedom and state-mandated minimum market requirements requires careful balancing. This in turn often depends upon national traditions.[29]

25 Council Directive 85/374/EEC of 25 July 1985 on the approximation of the laws, regulations and administrative provisions of the Member States concerning liability for defective products (Product Liability Directive) (1985) OJ L210/29.

26 Regulation 261/2004/EC on compensation and assistance to passengers in the event of denied boarding and of cancellation or long delay of flights (2004) OJ L46/1.

27 M Hesselink, *CFR and Social Justice* (Sellier, 2008); H-W Micklitz (ed), *The Many Concepts of Social Justice in European Private Law* (Edward Elgar, 2011); T Wilhelmsson, *Social Contract Law and European Integration* (Dartmouth, 1995). For an overview of different approaches see N Reich, 'Diverse approaches to consumer protection philosophy' (1992) 14 *Journal of Consumer Policy* p.257; T Wilhelmsson, 'Varieties of welfarism in European contract law' (2004) 10 *European Law Journal* p.712.

28 H Eidenmüller et al., 'The Common Frame of Reference for European private law – policy choices and codification problems' (2008) 28 *Oxford Journal of Legal Studies* p.659.

29 See, in general, D Leczykiewicz and S Weatherill (eds), *The Involvement of EU Law in Private Law Relationships* (Hart, 2013). In relation to the underlying ideological tendencies of balancing freedom and regulation see, D Kennedy, 'Genealogy of proportionality in private law', in R Brownsword, H-W Micklitz, L Niglia and S Weatherill (eds), *The Foundations of European Private Law* (Hart, 2011). See also H Collins, 'European private law and the cultural identity of states' (1995) 3 *European Review of Private Law* p.353.

EU legislation should be in a form which allows the EU rules to be integrated into national regimes and parallel regimes for cross-border sales should only be introduced where there are good justifications

The sale of goods and unfair terms provisions were removed from the proposal for a Directive on Consumer Rights.[30] The successor initiative for a Common European Sales Regulation[31] was more overtly internal market-focused. It sought to create a tailored regime expressly for cross-border sales. This focus on solutions for exclusively cross-border problems was first adopted in the area of access to justice where sensitivity about interferences with national procedural autonomy was the rationale. The Common European Sales Regulation attempted to promote cross-border sales without threatening national substantive law by limiting its scope to cross-border sales. However, it is hard to find any objective justification[32] for different substantive rules depending upon whether one buys locally, on the internet, or from other Member States.[33] The proposal was withdrawn, but instead a new set of proposals were brought forward including one establishing a mandatory regime adopting maximal harmonisation for online sales.[34] This is unlikely to be adopted and the criticism is again the complexity created by having different regimes for online and offline contracts.

The Common European Sales Regulation proposal is also illustrative of an increasing preference for regulations over directives.[35] This ensures more uniformity in the laws of the Member States as the same laws become directly applicable in all Member States.[36] It can also be seen as more honest in many respects as the strict way the Commission and CJEU monitors Member States' implementation leaves little latitude for national diversity of legal culture and terminology.[37] Indeed, the use of regulations makes particular sense in situations

30 COM (2008) 614 final.

31 Commission, *Proposal for a Regulation of the European Parliament and of the Council on a Common European Sales Law* COM (2011) 635 final.

32 Although see C Twigg-Flesner, 'Time to do the job properly – the case for a new approach to EU consumer legislation' (2010) 33(4) *Journal of Consumer Policy* p.355; C Twigg-Flesner, 'CESL, cross-border transactions and domestic law – why a dual approach could work (although CESL might not)' (2015) 23 *European Review of Private Law* p.231.

33 Clearly the internal market dimension may give impetus to making some law reforms: liability of franchisors and producer's liability is one such issue. M Ebers, A Janssen and O Meyer (eds), *European Perspectives on Producers' Liability* (Sellier, 2009).

34 *Proposal for a Directive on Certain Aspects Concerning Contracts for the Online and Other Distance Sales of Goods* COM (2015) final.

35 On a shift from directives to regulations see C Twigg-Flesner, *A Cross-border-only Regulation for Consumer Transactions in the EU: A Fresh Approach to EU Consumer Law* (Springer, 2012); also M. Monti, *A New Strategy for the Single Market – at the Service of Europe's Economy and Society* (Brussels, 2010), p.93.

36 Art. 288 TFEU.

37 For example, see in relation to the Product Liability Directive, Case C–52/00 *Commission v France* [2002] ECR I–3827; Case C-154/00 *Commission v Greece* [2002] ECR I–3879; and the Unfair Contract Terms Directive, Case C–478/99 *Commission v Sweden* [2002] ECR I-4147.

where new EU rules are adopted that can operate in isolation from national rules. They make sense when a particular EU institution is created such as the Online Dispute Resolution (ODR) platform[38] or an additional European procedure is adopted as in the case of small claims.[39] The move to maximum harmonisation makes the use of regulations more tempting given the lack of national discretion. However, directives should not be too readily abandoned as they allow the law to be framed in national terminology. This is particularly important where the EU rules interact or sit alongside national rules.

The EU needs to ensure laws are effectively enforced

The effectiveness of any consumer protection regime is a combination of the quality of the substantive rules, the extent of their enforcement and the effectiveness of any sanctions. Consumer law enforcement models typically involve both public (through government- or state-sponsored agencies) and private (individual or consumer organisations) bodies. The exact mix of public/private models varies between Member States.

As important to overall effectiveness as the mechanisms of enforcement, is ensuring the resources are available within Member States to make use of those means. Some state agencies are well-resourced; others are not. Some states have consumer organisations that can undertake significant litigation; other consumer groups in Europe simply do not have the expertise or resources to engage in such activity. Some court systems function efficiently; others have such long backlogs that they cannot deliver timely justice.

The EU has recently become more engaged in access to justice issues.[40] This is to be welcomed. It also recognises the need to address the challenges posed by increased cross-border sales. The borders between Member States should not be used as cloaks by disreputable traders to avoid their legal liabilities. The EU also has an important role in promoting the exchange of ideas and development of best practice particularly in states where enforcement mechanisms have been lacking or weak.

Summary

In summary, the drive to use substantive law harmonisation as an engine for increased cross-border sales has taken the focus off defining the key elements

38 Regulation 524/2013/EU on online dispute resolution for consumer disputes (2013) OJ L 165/1.

39 Regulation 861/2007/EC establishing a European Small Claims Procedure (2007) OJ L 199/1.

40 For example in the area of alternative dispute resolution, Regulation 524/2013/EU on online dispute resolution for consumer disputes (2013) OJ L 165/1; Directive 2013/11/EU on alternative dispute resolution for consumer disputes (2013) OJ L165/63. See also Commission, *Towards a European Horizontal Framework for Collective Redress* COM (2013) 401 final.

of consumer protection. Information provision has become the dominant tool of protection, because it fits well into this internal market dialogue since it does not challenge basic standards. Substantive standards risk creating fissures between states that have different ideas of risk-sharing. Such risk-sharing is, however, at the core of a social welfare model of consumer protection. There is likely to be diversity in how states want to allocate risks between consumers and producers. Europe has a role to keep these divergences within tolerable limits. The internal market objective needs to be balanced against national consumer protection values to foster convergence in a manner which is sympathetic to consumer expectations of protection. In some areas of regulation there may be good reasons why EU standards need to be imposed on a maximal harmonisation basis, for example, as regards technical harmonisation. However, EU consumer policy should not be about imposing uniform values where these are not reconcilable with national social and cultural standards.

These features of EU consumer law will be developed using examples from particular areas of EU consumer law in subsequent chapters. First, some background information is provided.

What is the EU's motivation for regulating consumer law?

Legal base

Any critique of the EU's consumer protection policy has to take account of the legal base for EU legislative activity, which essentially requires that consumer protection be an adjunct of internal market policy. This might be an excuse for a rather limited approach to consumer protection, focusing on cross-border dimensions. At least until recently that has not been a key criticism of EU consumer policy. Indeed, even in the early days when legislative powers in the consumer field were even more limited, the EU felt confident to legislate on doorstep sales[41]; this was no doubt a pressing consumer concern, but was hardly the most obvious topic to tackle from an internal market perspective. Moreover, the internal market legal base should not be an excuse for a weak consumer protection policy, for the Treaty provisions dictate that a high level of consumer protection be adopted.

The original Treaty made sparse reference to consumer protection. A role for consumer protection could be viewed as implicit in general statements about living conditions[42] and it formed an element in the Common Agricultural Policy[43]

41 Council Directive 85/577/EEC to protect the consumer in respect of contracts negotiated away from business premises (1985) OJ L372/31.

42 The Preamble to the Rome Treaty talked of 'the constant improvement of the living and working conditions of their people' being an objective and Art. 2 made 'an accelerated raising of the standard of living' one of the Community's tasks.

43 One of whose objectives was 'to ensure that supplies reach consumers at reasonable prices'; Art. 39(1)(e) TFEU.

and competition policy.[44] This did not prevent the Commission developing a consumer policy with legislation being based on Article 100 (now Article 115 TFEU) which permitted directives to be adopted for the approximation of matters directly affecting the establishment or functioning of the internal market.

Article 100 required unanimity and the first significant liberalisation of powers came under the Single European Act in 1986 where under Article 100a (now Article 114 TFEU) a qualified majority procedure was introduced to allow for 'measures', not just directives, affecting the establishment and functioning of the internal market. Significantly, Article 100(a)(3) EC provided that proposals concerning consumer protection would take as a base a high level of protection.[45]

The Maastricht Treaty provided that the Community's activities should include 'a contribution to the strengthening of consumer protection'.[46] Consumer protection was therefore recognised as an explicit objective of the Community in its own right. The Treaty of Amsterdam included a specific provision on consumer protection, on which the current provision concerning consumer protection, in Article 169 TFEU, is still modelled.

In the current treaties there are several specific mentions of consumer protection as well as provisions promoting economic and social progress and other provisions that relate to consumer interests such as public health[47] and the environment.[48] The rules of judicial co-operation on civil matters are also relevant for access to justice and enforcement measures.[49] Those provisions specifically on consumer protection are:

- i The Charter of Fundamental rights demands that Union policies shall ensure a high level of consumer protection (Article 38);
- ii Consumer protection is listed as an area of shared competence (Article 4(2)(f) TFEU);
- iii Consumer protection requirements should be taken into account in defining and implementing other Union policies and activities (Article 12 TFEU);
- iv Consumer protection is listed in competition provisions as potentially exempting otherwise illegal agreements allowing consumers a fair share of benefit (Article 101(3) TFEU) and defining abuse of dominant position as including developments prejudicial to consumers (Article 102(b) TFEU);

44 Agreements could be exempted if they contribute 'to improving the production or distribution of goods or to promoting technical and economic progress, while allowing consumers a fair share of the resulting benefit' (Art. 101(3) TFEU) and an abuse of dominant position consisted of 'limiting production, markets or technical development to the prejudice of consumers' (Art. 102(b) TFEU).

45 Art. 2(15) Treaty of Amsterdam added that 'account should be taken of new developments based on scientific facts'.

46 Art. (3)(s).

47 Art. 168 TFEU.

48 Art. 191 TFEU.

49 Art. 81 TFEU.

v Requiring a high level of consumer protection to be taken as a baseline when approximating laws to improve the internal market by qualified majority (Article 114(3) TFEU);

vi Art. 169 TFEU provides a specific provision on consumer protection. This provides as follows:

> 1 In order to promote the interests of consumers and to ensure a high level of consumer protection, the Union shall contribute to protecting the health, safety and economic interests of consumers, as well as to promoting their right to information, to education and to organise themselves in order to safeguard their interests.
>
> 2 The Union shall contribute to the attainment of the objectives referred to in Paragraph 1 through:
>
> a measures adopted pursuant to Article 114 in the context of the completion of the internal market;
>
> b measures which support, supplement and monitor the policy pursued by the Member States.
>
> 3 The European Parliament and the Council, acting in accordance with the ordinary legislative procedure and after consulting the Economic and Social Committee, shall adopt the measures referred to in paragraph 2(b).
>
> 4 Measures adopted pursuant to paragraph 3 shall not prevent any Member State from maintaining or introducing more stringent protective measures. Such measures must be compatible with the Treaties. The Commission shall be notified of them.

This Article sets out the broad range of consumer interests the EU is concerned with in paragraph 1. It then provides two ways in which this can be met – paragraph 2(a) does not provide a new legal base but rather just refers to Article 114. Paragraph 2(b) is a separate legal base, but is limited to measures which support, supplement or monitor Member State policies. Given the subordinate nature of these rules, it is not surprising that paragraph 4 ensures these are of a minimum character and do not interfere with Member States' autonomy.

The Treaty has conferred powers on the Union to be competent with respect to consumer protection, but as it is an area of shared competence its powers are governed by the principles of subsidiarity and proportionality.[50] Subsidiarity means that the Union shall only act:

> if and in so far as the objectives of the proposed action cannot be sufficiently achieved by the Member States, either at central level or at regional or local level, but can rather, by reasons of the scale or effects of the proposed action, be better achieved at Union level.[51]

50 Art. 4(2)(f) TFEU.
51 Art. 5(3) TEU.

The proportionality principle requires that neither the content nor form of measures shall exceed what is necessary to achieve Treaty objectives.[52] Thus in the consumer context substantive controls might not be justified if information rules could achieve the same objective. As regards form, it implies a hierarchy with binding rules such as Regulations and Directives being a last resort. Protocol (No. 2) on the application of the Principles of Subsidiarity and Proportionality provides various procedural safeguards, including consultation especially with national Parliaments. It also has requirements for reasoned justifications including the need to provide qualitative and where possible quantitative indicators.

These constitutional controls have only rarely been an impediment to the development of consumer protection policy. The striking down of the Tobacco Advertising Directive[53] in *Germany v Parliament and Council*[54] was based on the Union exceeding its powers with regard to public health, but could have been the start of a closer scrutiny of legislation. In reality it is best viewed as a response to mute the concerns of the German Constitutional Court.[55] To a certain extent the *Tobacco Advertising* judgment's emphasis on the measures promoting free movement has assisted calls for maximum harmonisation measures. The Commission is diligent in ensuring impact assessments are undertaken, but their methodology and the implications that can be derived from these have not always been convincing. One can see a tendency to see the jurisdictional issues as a reason for limiting measures to cross-border situations, but whether it is desirable to have different rules for domestic and inter-state consumer matters is a matter for discussion. Certainly such limited rules seem more a response to political pressures than to constitutional controls.

Consumer policy

The consumer policy of the Commission has been fashioned through policy statements. In the early years (1975–1990) these were described as programmes,[56] in the middle years as action plans (1990–2001)[57] and in more recent times as strategy documents.[58] They often set out policy for prescribed periods. The latest

52 Art. 5(4) TEU.
53 Directive 98/43/EC (1998) OJ L213/9.
54 Case C-376/98 *Germany v Parliament and Council* [2000] ECR I-8419.
55 As expressed in *Brunner v The European Union Treaty* [1994] 1 CML Rev 57.
56 Council Resolution of 14 April 1975 on a preliminary programme of the European Economic Community for a consumer protection and information policy [1975] OJ C92/1; Council Resolution of 19 May 1981 on a second programme of the European Economic Community for a consumer protection and information policy [1981] OJ C133/1.
57 Commission, *Three Year Action Plans of Consumer Policy in the EEC (1990–1992)* COM (90) 98 final; *Priorities for Consumer Policy 1996–1998* COM (95) 519 final and *Consumer Policy Action Plan 1999–2001* COM (98) 696 final.
58 Commission, *Consumer Policy Strategy 2002–2006* COM (2002) 208 final; *EU Consumer Policy Strategy 2007–2013* COM (2007) 99 final.

document is *A European Consumer Agenda – Boosting Confidence and Growth*,[59] which does not have any fixed dates attached to it.

In the early stages the Community was concerned simply to establish the basic principle that consumer protection was a matter it had jurisdiction over. The 1975 Preliminary Programme[60] set out five basic consumer rights:

i the right to protection of health and safety;
ii the right to protection of economic interests;
iii the right of redress;
iv the right to information and education;
v the right of representation (the right to be heard).

There has never been any serious questioning of the Union's involvement in health and safety. A focus of the early programmes and action plans was to expand the scope of EU consumer policy to encompass a range of economic interests affecting consumers. This era included the push to create the Single Market and consumer protection became part of that initiative.[61] The urgency was reflected in document names, such as the Commission internal communication on *A New Impetus for Consumer Protection Policy*[62] in 1985 and Council resolutions in 1989 on *Future Priorities for Relaunching Consumer Protection Policy*[63] and in 1992 on *Future Priorities for the Development of Consumer Protection Policy*.[64] There was much talk of integrating consumer protection into other policies.[65] This was understood to extend beyond simply integrating consumer policy into the internal market to include its integration in other policies such as environment[66] and telecommunications.[67] The 1999–2001 action plan felt confident in talking about consumer policy 'coming of age'.[68] This was an important element in creating the

59 COM (2012) 225 final.
60 (1975) OJ C92/2.
61 Council Resolution of 19 May 1981 on a second programme of the European Economic Community for a consumer protection and information policy (1981) OJ C 133/1. See also (1979) OJ C218/4 at 9 for a list of early legislative proposals e.g. product liability.
62 COM (85) 314 final.
63 (1989) OJ C294/1.
64 (1992) OJ C186/1.
65 Council Resolution of 15 December 1986 on the integration of consumer policy in the other common policies (1987) OJ C3/1.
66 E.g. Regulation 66/2010/EC on the EU Ecolabel (2010) OJ L27/1; Directive 2012/27/EU on energy efficiency (2012) OJ L315/1. See also Commission, *Sustainable Consumption and Production and Sustainable Industrial Policy Action Plan* COM (2008) 397 final.
67 E.g. Regulation 531/2012/EU on roaming on public mobile communications networks within the Union (2012) OJ L172/10. See also Commission, *Telecommunications Single Market* COM (2013) 634.
68 COM (98) 696 final, p.1. For assessments of the truth of this see J Stuyck, 'European consumer law after the Treaty of Amsterdam: Consumer policy in or beyond the internal market?' (2000) 37 *Common Market Law Review* p.367; G Howells and T Wilhelmsson, 'Consumer law – has it come of age?' (2003) 28 *European Law Review* p.370.

image of Europe with a social face granting rights to its citizens and detracting from criticism that Europe was just benefiting capital.[69]

The new century saw a fresh change of emphasis. If consumer law had reached maturity, it was in a very different form from that espoused by many of the early advocates of consumer law.[70] Substantive regulation was still an important part of the EU framework, but the rhetoric of consumer empowerment by providing consumers with information to protect their own interests was taking hold.[71] The 2002–2006 Strategy talked of measures giving 'consumers the means to protect their own interests by making autonomous, informed choices'. Empowering consumers was in the title of the 2007–2013 Strategy and empowerment runs through the 2012 European consumer agenda.[72] Empowerment is admittedly broader than merely providing information about products and services and includes general consumer education as well as building up knowledge of legal rights and the capacity to enforce them. Undoubtedly promoting confident consumers is a valuable goal. However, it is unclear to what extent education can assist consumers. Moreover, it is potentially dangerous to believe that even well-educated consumers can always protect themselves as the structural weakness they face in the marketplace often demands a need for minimum enforced standards ensuring they can benefit from a high level of protection in the market.

The debate on the integration of consumer law into Single Market policy has been recast. Instead of promoting consumer protection by instilling the consumer protective ethic into other policies, consumer protection has itself become the vehicle for establishing the internal market.[73] Harmonising consumer laws has become the vehicle for both promoting more confident consumers and giving businesses the confidence to shop across borders.[74] This has led to

69 See, for example, Commission, *Action Plan for the Single Market* CSE (91) 1 final, 9, in which the Commission recognised that 'failure to ensure adequate enforcement of social rules [...] can lead to negative reactions and damage to public confidence in the Single Market'. See also H-W. Micklitz and S Weatherill, 'Consumer policy in the European Community: Before and after Maastricht' (1993) 16 *Journal of Consumer Policy* p.285 who noted that the Single European Act exhibited tendencies to favour free trade over social protection.

70 Se e.g, T Bourgoignie, 'Characteristics of consumer law' (1992) 14 *Journal of Consumer Policy* pp.293–315; J Calais-Auloy and F Steinmetz, *Droit de la consummation,* 7th ed (Dalloz-Sirey, 2006).

71 *Consumer Policy Strategy 2002–2006* COM (2002) 208 final.

72 Commission, *A European Consumer Agenda – Boosting Confidence and Growth* COM (2012) 225 final. On the subject of empowerment, see also S Weatherill, *EU Consumer Law and Policy*, 2nd ed, (Edward Elgar, 2014), pp.310–315.

73 V Mak, 'Two levels, one standard? The multi-level regulation of consumer protection in Europe' in J Devenney and M Kenny (eds), *European Consumer Protection: Theory and Practice* (Cambridge University Press, 2012); L Miller, *The Emergence of EU Contract Law* (Oxford University Press, 2011) pp.45–50; J Rinkes, 'European consumer law: Making sense' in C Twigg-Flesner et. al. (eds), *Yearbook of Consumer Law 2008* (Ashgate, 2008). Of course the positive dimension of integration of consumer values also remains: see COM (2007) 99 final, 8.

74 For example COM (2002) 208 final, para 2.3.3.

a preference for maximum harmonisation measures. It reflects an ideology that consumers benefit from more competition as consumers move across borders or businesses offer their goods and services in more Member States. Any marginal losses in national protective rules are considered insignificant in the light of the constitutional guarantee that EU consumer rules would take as their base a high level of protection. The ability of consumer rules to promote greater trade is itself disputable given the importance of other factors, such as language, ease of delivery and ability to resolve problems, in determining the amount of cross-border trade. Certainly it can be questioned whether consumer confidence is increased by consumers knowing they can have no protection beyond that set by the European legislator.

The *Green Paper on Consumer Protection*[75] paved the way for the Unfair Commercial Practices Directive[76] and the adoption of the *Communication on European Contract Law*.[77] The Unfair Commercial Practices Directive was the zenith in the maximum harmonisation strategy, perhaps because it focused on trade practices and provided much greater clarity on permissible marketing strategies. Maximum harmonisation of consumer contract law has proven less successful as opposition from consumer groups and some Member States forced the Commission away from ambitious plans in the original proposal for a Consumer Rights Directive[78] or from other plans for a form of European Civil Code[79] or even from the more focused measure limited to cross-border sales in the proposed Regulation on a Common European Sales Law.[80]

The meaning, effect and value of the maximal harmonisation process are returned to shortly below. However, it is important to recognise a couple of other features of EU consumer policy. One is the promotion of consumer organisations as a voice for consumers. This has been a consistent strand of EU policy. Of course, it is diplomatic for the Commission to have good relations with consumers. It is advised by a European Consumer Consultative Group[81] that meets three times a year in Brussels. It is unclear what effective influence the Group has as typically this format it is more about imparting information rather than real engagement. Real engagement comes through consultations on specific proposals

75 COM (2001) 531 final.

76 Directive 2005/29/EU. See Chapter 2.

77 COM (2001) 398 final.

78 COM (2008) 614 final.

79 European Parliament, *Resolution on Action to Bring into Line the Private Law of the Member States* (1989) OJ C158/401; European Parliament, *Resolution on the Harmonization of Certain Sectors of the Private Law of the Member States* (1994) OJ C205/519.

80 COM (2011) 635 final.

81 And comprises one representative per state from national consumer organisations; one member from each European consumer organisation (BEUC – The European Consumer Organisation that acts as an umbrella group for national organisations and ANEC, which co-ordinates representation in standardisation); with two associate members (EUROCOOP and COFACE) and two EEA observers from Iceland and Norway.

with the umbrella organisation for national consumer organisations, the European Consumer Organisation, BEUC, playing an important role. In recent times relations have been strained as BEUC has not supported the Commission's policy of maximal harmonisation and the optional regime for cross-border sales under the proposed Regulation on a Common European Sales Law. The link with consumer organisations seems to have weakened as the Commission has come to see consumer law as increasingly a dimension of the internal market policy and has promoted competition sometimes at the expense of traditional forms of protection.

Another increasing trend has been the desire to increase the effectiveness of consumer law enforcement and redress. This is covered in detail in Chapter 8, but there is an increased realisation that the substantial *acquis* which has been built up needs to be effective in practice to achieve its objectives. There has of course always been a concern for good enforcement, but it is becoming more prevalent in policy documents in this century. What is not so often written about, but is a very real concern in practice, is the differential level of application between Member States. As a rough rule of thumb the further South and East one goes the harder it is for consumers and governments effectively to utilise the law to control business. There are fewer resources to regulate or litigate and courts are more overburdened. However, in all states there is a gap between the law in books and the law in practice – if for no other reason than many consumer cases are of too small a value to justify individual action.[82] Individuals taking on such actions need to have 'super-spite'.[83] One response is to simplify procedures so that costs are brought down and more claims are worth bringing. However, there is also a need for some sort of public interest regulation and whether this is through public administration or private collective actions is a major contemporary debate.[84]

Institutional structures

Originally, the Commission dealt with consumer affairs in D-G XI which had responsibility for the environment, consumer protection and nuclear safety. An independent Consumer Policy Service was established in 1989, which was given Directorate-General status in 1995 (D-G XXIV). It subsequently became known as DG SANCO. However, there have been frequent reshuffles, and responsibilities for contract law and consumer and marketing law were transferred to DG Justice in 2009. Its current incarnation is DG JUST with the responsibility for most aspects of consumer law. Other Directorate-Generals also interact with

82 M Olsen, *The Logic of Collective Action*, (Harvard University Press, 1971).

83 A Leff, 'Injury, ignorance and spite – the dynamics of coercive collection'. *Yale Law Journal* 80 (1970), p.1.

84 See, for example, D Fairgrieve and G Howells, 'Collective redress procedures: European debates' in D Fairgrieve and E Lein (eds), *Extraterritoriality and Collective Redress* (Oxford University Press, 2012), pp.15–41; C Hodges, *The Reform of Class and Representative Actions in European Legal Systems: A New Framework For Collective Redress in Europe* (Hart, 2008).

consumer policy, for instance, DG GROW (internal market and industry), DG FISMA (financial services) and DG SANTE (health and food safety).

Since 1973 the Commission has been assisted by a consumer consultative group. As already noted, today this body comprises the European Consumer Consultative Group[85] and involves one representative per state representing national consumer organisations and one from each European consumer organisation – BEUC (the European Consumer Organisation), and ANEC (European Association for the Co-ordination of Consumer Representation in Standardisation). This Group was intended to be smaller and more streamlined than its predecessor the Consumers' Consultative Council, which it replaced in 2003. It meets three times a year, but it seems mainly to be a forum for explaining EU policy to consumer groups rather than for critical reflection on that policy and interrogation of the Commission. The same point could be made about the far larger annual Consumer Forum which the Commission has now ceased to host. Most of the critical input into EU consumer policy discussions from the consumer perspective comes during specific consultations from the engagement of BEUC and those national organisations which are sufficiently well funded and organised.

The European Parliament has also been active in consumer affairs through in particular its Internal Market and Consumer Protection[86] and Legal Affairs committees and the European Economic and Social Council has also pushed the consumer agenda.[87]

Maximum harmonisation

Traditionally, many of the consumer directives, at least in the contract and unfair commercial practices fields, were minimum harmonisation directives. This meant the EU law created a foundation on which national law could build, but all consumers throughout the Community were assured of a common minimum set of rights. This was modelled on an image of the confident consumer,[88] who was to be the engine for greater cross-border sales which would in turn lead to a more competitive market as traders became sensitive to the loss of sales to more consumer-friendly shopping environments. Whether this would really increase cross-border sales became questionable as it became obvious that consumers' legal

85 Commission Decision 2009/705/EC of 14 September 2009 setting up a European Consumer Consultative Group [2009] OJ L244/21.

86 See, for example, European Parliament, Report of 21 October 2011 on a new strategy for consumer policy (2011/2149 (INI)).

87 See the ECSC's Consumer Portal at http://www.eesc.europa.eu/?i=portal.en.consumers [last accessed 17 December 2016]. It also organises the Annual *European Consumer Day* conference, held since 1999.

88 S Weatherill, 'The evolution of European consumer law and policy: From well informed consumer to confident consumer' in H-W Micklitz (ed), *Rechtseinheit oder Rechtsvielfalt in Europa?* (Nomos, 1996); T Wilhelmsson, "The abuse of the 'confident consumer' as a justification for EC consumer law". *Journal of Consumer Policy* 27 (2004), p.317.

rights were only part of the picture – other factors such as distance, transport and delivery costs, language, and access to redress all influence the decision on where to purchase.[89] The ability to use the internal market provision (now Article 114 TFEU) combined with a minimum harmonisation clause was also questioned in the *Tobacco Advertising*[90] judgment, because it was doubted whether the effects on the internal market could be achieved by measures that did not guarantee access to all the internal market for products that complied with the EU rules. However, it might be questioned whether private law rules with more indirect effects on market access will be scrutinised as carefully. There is after all a direct call for minimum harmonisation on Article 169 TFEU, but the use of that Treaty provision has not been well developed. Nevertheless, the legal uncertainty combined with a new policy direction to favour maximum harmonisation. The way to increase cross-border sales was seen to be by encouraging more businesses rather than more consumers to trade across borders. Under this policy ideally the only protection allowed to be granted to consumers would be at the level set down in EU laws. Confident businesses were now the object of consumer law.[91] It was hoped they would trade across borders using the internet or set up subsidiaries in other Member States. The obvious risk is that whilst confident consumers would demand high protection, businesses if anything would favour lower levels. The Commission points to its commitment to a high level of protection, which is also written into the Treaty, but it seems willing to sacrifice some of the highest levels of protection in some Member States for the sake of promoting greater competition. Nevertheless, a high level of protection is relevant to promote the brand of 'Europe'.

The Commission finds current levels of cross-border trade unsatisfactory (e.g. in 2012 only 25% of retailers sold cross-border and only 15% of consumers made online cross-border purchases).[92] It is not entirely clear why it finds this level unsatisfactory as there is nothing inherently better about a cross-border sale than a domestic sale. Indeed all things being equal one would have thought domestic sales in most cases were preferable on environmental grounds, which is another concern of the

89 C Twigg-Flesner 'The importance of law and harmonisation for the EU's confident consumer' in D.Leczykiewicz and S.Weatherill (eds), *The Images of the Consumer in EU Law* (Hart, 2015).

90 C-376/98 *Germany v Parliament and Council* [2000] ECR I-8419. See also, for example: P Rott, 'Minimum harmonization for the completion of the internal market? The example of consumer sales law' (2003) 40 *Common Market Law Review* p.1107; S Weatherill, 'Harmonisation: How much, how little?' (2005) 3 *European Business Law Review* p.553.

91 G Howells, 'European contract law reform and European consumer law – two related but distinct regimes' (2011) 2 *European Review of Contract Law* pp.173, 186.

92 Commission, *Consumers' Attitudes to Cross-Border Trade and Consumer Protection* – Flashbarometer 358 (2013); Commission, *Retailers' Attitudes to Cross-Border Trade and Consumer Protection* – Flashbarometer 359 (2013). Reports available online under: http://ec.europa.eu/consumers/archive/strategy/facts_eurobar_en.htm. Indications of dissatisfaction with the results can be seen in the presentation of the 'negative' results, for instance the emphasis on the increase of consumers who made a domestic purchase (as opposed to the dramatic increase of cross-border purchases since 2006), see Flashbarometer 358 (2013), p.16.

Community.[93] Certainly, cross-border sales can make enforcement more difficult and undoubtedly complicate legal redress as the disputes involve questions of private international law as well as substantive law. Nevertheless, the Commission has become frustrated sitting in Brussels and possessing relatively few levers to achieve its objective of increasing cross-border sales. Adopting maximum harmonisation is one of the few ways in which it can show it is seeking this objective. This policy has unsettled many who have traditionally supported consumer rights, because, in some instances, it requires the removal of long-standing consumer remedies. Whether this is justified due to the overall gains is questionable, though the answer may vary from state to state. The more limited competition there is currently in a state (typically those to the East and South of the EU) the greater impact on consumer welfare there may be from any new entrants as a result of the policy.

Leaving aside concerns about whether the Commission is right to be pressing so hard on this matter, there is a risk that maximum harmonisation will in any event have a relatively low impact on encouraging cross-border sales. The extent to which legal rules really affect traders' decisions to sell beyond their home jurisdiction is uncertain.[94] Whilst traders may voice concerns about disparities and suggest that more harmonised rules would give them greater confidence, this is not the same as evidence demonstrating that varying rules actually affect decisions on whether to trade cross-border. There are plenty of examples of states with internal legal systems (UK, US and Spain being just three) where the differences in law seem to have little impact on sales. For some legal rules, it is clear that having EU laws which guarantee access to all EU markets for all compliant products is important. Technical harmonisation rules and those concerning labelling and presentation of products are clearly examples where disparate laws would make market integration difficult. It is less clear that private law rules or general commercial practice rules have such a strong impact. EU harmonised rules may not provide the legal security the trader desires in any event.

Stuyck has noted that the Commission and Court prefer the terms full or total harmonisation to maximum harmonisation.[95] In fact, 'maximum' is preferable, for rarely does an EU law achieve full or total harmonisation of the field.[96]

93 Art. 191 TFEU.

94 A Schwartze, 'Design for an empirical data investigation into the impact of existing contract law harmonisation under the White Paper of 1985' in S Grundmann and J Stuyck (eds), *An Academic Green Paper on European Contract Law* (Kluwer Law International, 2002). Although statistical evidence from European Commission surveys does show that compliance with national legal rules is a concern for some traders, regional variations do not allow for a broad generalisation, see Flashbarometer 359 (n 92) p.31.

95 J Stuyck, 'Unfair terms' in G Howells and R Schulze (eds), *Modernising and Harmonising Consumer Contract Law* (Sellier, 2009).

96 See O Cherednychenko, 'Full harmonisation of retail financial service contract law: A success or a failure?' in S Grundmann and YM Atamer (eds), *Financial Services, Financial Crisis and General European Contract Law* (Kluwer Law International, 2011); L Miller, *The Emergence of EU Contract Law* (Oxford University Press, 2011), pp.83–84. See also R Sefton-Green, 'Multiculturalism, Europhilia and harmonization: Harmony or disharmony?' *Utrecht Law Review* 6 (2010), p.50, who discusses the impact of multiculturalism on harmonisation objectives.

EU law in areas of shared competence, such as consumer law, only pre-empts national law where it has entered the field. Thus matters outside the scope of the EU law remain covered by national competence; so, for instance, damage caused by a defective product to non-consumer goods remains a matter for national law.[97] There may in some areas be partial exemption from the EU rules, so the full impact of EU law does not apply, for example, as regards the application of consumer credit rules to social lending.[98] Member States may be given discretion as to how to implement rules, for example, in relation to the scheme for early repayment of loans. Even in directives, such as the Product Liability Directive, which are understood to be maximum harmonisation directives, certain measures are made optional or left to national law.[99] It also expressly left some existing regimes in place. It is also not uncommon for a directive to have a main maximum harmonisation clause, but then to expressly provide certain provisions are subject to minimum harmonisation.[100] Some of these partial harmonisation outcomes result from political compromises; others from the reality that the law is a mass of regulations and any one measure only covers part of the legal terrain affecting particular issues. Even a proposal as broad as that for a Common European Sales Law[101] did not provide a full code governing all private law or even all contract law obligations.[102]

These reasons should be enough to deter traders from relying on EU assurances of uniform consumer law. This is even before one moves on to the difference in practical application of the laws between states. For example, studies have shown different national traditions affecting the application of the Unfair Commercial Practices Directive.[103] The concept of good faith has also been interpreted differently in the Member States.[104] At a very practical level the differences between enforcement approaches will also affect businesses. What is governed by state regulation in one state might be dealt with by private law in another, and self-regulation will mean different things in different contexts. Even the enforcement mechanisms, tools available to regulators, and civil and criminal law procedures will differ. These factors can be as perplexing to enterprises as differences in the substantive law.

97 See Chapter 7, p.266.
98 See Chapter 6, p.227.
99 See Chapter 7, p.265.
100 E.g. Art. 5 of the Consumer Rights Directive (2011/83/EU). See Chapter 3, p.119.
101 COM (2011) 635 final (n 21).
102 The proposal for a Common European Sales Law does not cover areas such as capacity, illegality or change of parties, see Recital 27. See also Max Planck Institute for Comparative and International Private Law, *Policy Options for Progress Towards a European Contract Law* 75 (2011) *RabelsZ* pp.371, 427–429.
103 B Duivenvoorde, *The Consumer Benchmarks in the Unfair Commercial Practices Directive* (Springer, 2015).
104 For comparative studies see S Whittaker and R Zimmermann (eds), *Good Faith in European Contract Law* (Cambridge University Press, 2000).

European motivations – some conclusions

The initial activity by the EU in the consumer field seemed motivated by a genuine desire to promote consumer rights and give Europe a social dimension. In recent times, the internal market has been to the fore and consumer welfare has been promoted through greater competition spurred on by a more business-friendly legal environment. The risk that this will bring with it lower standards should be mitigated by the constitutional requirement to take as a base a high level of consumer protection. There is also a business case for Europe setting high consumer standards. Not only will this assure high value for European consumers, but will also promote the quality of European products and Europe as a purchasing destination (in person or at a distance, for example over the internet). Europe should be a brand that resonates with consumer quality and protection. There are some examples that might indeed reflect EU consumer policy is a brand used for the benefit of traders and consumers. For example, the CE marking,[105] even if placed on products in say China, is using EU laws as a designation of quality. The idea behind the 'blue button'[106] approach to persuading consumers to contract under a distinctly EU law of consumer sales again has the message that consumers should trust the European brand.

What kind of consumer policy does the EU want?

General observations

One consequence of the maximum harmonization policy is that it places the substantive content of EU consumer laws under greater scrutiny.[107] So long as the EU only provided a minimum level of protection, Member States which were concerned to better protect their consumers could be agnostic about the EU level of protection. They were free to offer higher protection than the minimum mandated by the EU. Once these rules become the maximum permitted – thereby ousting existing national rules and barring any new additional rules – the quality of the protection provided by the EU rules becomes crucial.

First, the formal scope of the EU rules is considered. This reveals that the EU has a relatively restricted definition of who counts as a consumer. Several groups that might benefit from protective rules for similar reasons as consumers are excluded from the protection of EU law. Thus a professor buying a laptop to write his book would not be protected, but the same person would be protected when buying a computer to play games on. However, this can have the ironic effect that

105 See Chapter 7, p.259.

106 H Schulte-Nölke, "EC law on the formation of – from common frame of reference to the 'blue button'". *European Review of Contract Law* 3 (2007), p.332.

107 G Howells and T Wilhelmsson, 'EC and US approaches to consumer protection - should the gap be bridged?' (1997) *Yearbook of European Law* p.207; L Miller, *The Emergence of EU Contract Law* (Oxford University Press, 2011), p.82.

those outside the scope of the EU rules can benefit from national laws which are allowed to offer higher levels of protection.[108] There is, however a double irony, for this narrow definition of the consumer should have allowed the EU to develop a rather high level of protection. Indeed, one criticism of attempts to generalise consumer law to include broader groups such as small and medium-sized enterprises (SMEs) is that it can tempt legislators to adopt a relatively low level of protection with a view to the rules being generalised. The blandness of much current EU consumer law makes it relatively easy to call for this generalisation.

Next, the type of consumer laws the EU has adopted is explored. The EU's image of the consumer is reflected on. This informs the content of the laws. The nature of protective rules will be conditioned by the extent to which consumers are assumed to be capable of protecting themselves. Like most national laws, EU consumer law contains a mix of rules – some fix minimum required levels of protection before traders and their products and services are permitted entry to the market (safety, quality, contract terms, and marketing practices). Others are information rules to enable consumers to make informed choices within the sphere of permitted competition. The EU has tended to favour information rules as these are more conducive to the internal market. This in turn is because it has a rather robust image of the consumer. Vulnerability is seen as an exception only to be taken into account in particular instances.[109] Consumers generally are expected to act in a very prudent manner that does not map on to real-life experience and is actually irrational; for instance, few consumers would rationally read every contract term! We also discuss the EU right of withdrawal, which has been a key element and also can be seen as supporting an informed consumer policy.

Finally, the crucial issue of what drives consumer law and policy is considered. We find, as in national systems, a mixture of motives that are not always well articulated. Certainly driving out rogue traders is one objective. The notion that the average trader is oppressive towards consumers has perhaps become less commonplace. Instead the relative strength of both parties in terms of bargaining power, investment in the contract and asymmetry of information have come to the fore. It is not totally clear to what extent the EU accepts all consumers suffer from these disadvantages or whether protection should be focused more

108 S Whittaker, 'Unfair contract terms and consumer guarantees: the proposal for a directive on consumer rights and the significance of full harmonisation'. *European Review of Contract Law* 3 (2009), pp.223, 231; F Zoll, 'The remedies for non-performance on the proposed Consumer Rights Directive and the Europeanisation of private law' in G Howells and R Schulze (eds), *Modernising and Harmonising Consumer Contract Law* (Sellier, 2009). With regard to product liability see also V Mak, 'Degree of harmonisation in the proposed Consumer Rights Directive: A review in light of liability for products' in G Howells and R Schulze (eds), *Modernising and Harmonising Consumer Contract Law* (Sellier, 2009).

109 M Friant-Perrot, 'The vulnerable consumer in the UCPD and other provisions of EU law' in W van Boom, A Garde and O Akseli, *The European Unfair Commercial Practices Directive* (Ashgate, 2014); N Reich, 'Vulnerable consumers in EU law' in D Leczykiewicz and S Weatherill, *The Images of the Consumer in EU Law* (Oxford, Hart, 2015).

on only the vulnerable consumers. A criticism of the EU policy is that it fails to fully articulate that consumer law should be about a sharing of risks and that all consumers (and indeed fellow traders) need the 'insurance' of good consumer law. A high level of consumer protection is in fact necessary for Europe if it wants to maintain its international trading competiveness.

The consumer concept

Legal definition of 'consumer'

The definition of consumer found in most EU legislation is fairly formal and given in a negative form, excluding business and professional activities.[110] In some particular contexts legislation uses analogous concepts which are broader in scope. Thus, in the Package Travel Directive,[111] the term traveller (which is used instead of consumer) is defined more widely to include any person who is seeking to conclude a contract, or is entitled to travel on the basis of a contract concluded, within the scope of the Directive.[112] The Overbooking Regulation[113] uses the term passenger without defining it. Again this would seem to cover any one flying in any capacity, including business people. Equally, although financial services are outside the scope of this book, the Markets in Financial Instruments Directive (MIFID)[114] refers to clients rather than consumers and distinguishes between professional and retail clients, with the criteria being set out in Annex II. Those criteria allow certain high-net-worth individuals with experience of financial markets to opt to be treated as professionals. This is not the case for most consumer laws under which consumers cannot opt out of their consumer status or the protection afforded them in EU law and are also protected from the choice of a non-EU law that would reduce protection.[115] Typical of the standard

110 The Product Liability Directive is more than a consumer protection measure as it covers death and personal injury caused by any defective product (not only consumer products), irrespective of whether the injured person used the product or was confronted by it as a consumer and regardless of whether it was a consumer product. However, damage to products is limited to products intended for private consumption.

111 Directive 2015/2302/EU on package travel and linked travel arrangements (2015) OJ L326/1.

112 Art. 3(6).

113 Regulation No 261/2004/EC establishing common rules on compensation and assistance to passengers in the event of denied boarding and of cancellation or long delay of flights (2004) OJ L46/1.

114 Directive 2004/39/EC on markets in financial instruments (2004) OJ L145/1, Art. 4(1), pp.10–12.

115 For example, a series of EU consumer directives provide that the 'Member States shall take the necessary measures to ensure that consumers are not deprived of the protection afforded by this Directive as a result of opting for the law of a non-member State as the law applicable to the contract where the contract has a close connection with the territory of the Member State'. Such directives include Directive 93/13/EEC on Unfair Contract Terms (1993) OJ L95/29, Art. 6(2); Directive 1999/44/EC on the Sale of Consumer Goods and Associated Guarantees (1999) OJ L171/12, Art. 7(2); Directive 2008/48/EC on Credit Agreements for Consumers (2008) OJ L 133/66, Art. 22(4).

definition of 'consumer' is Art. 2(1) of the Consumer Rights Directive,[116] according to which "'consumer' means any natural person who, in contracts covered by this Directive, is acting for purposes which are outside his trade, business, craft or profession."

There has been much discussion about whether consumer protection should be extended to small and medium-sized enterprises, which often face similar difficulties in the marketplace to consumers. Indeed, the proposal on a Common European Sales Law[117] would have encompassed small and medium-size enterprises.[118] As the typical EU consumer definition refers to natural persons only, it clearly excludes legal entities.[119] Some business entities may still formally qualify as natural persons if formed as partnerships or associations, but when acting for commercial purposes these will still be outside the scope of consumer law directives. The notion of 'consumer' has been given an abstract definition based on the status of the purchaser. The opinion of Advocate General Mischo in *di Pinto* that the concrete experience of the person (in that case the seller of a business) should be relevant was not followed.[120] As the Court said some time ago in the context of interpreting the Brussels Convention on Jurisdiction and Enforcement of Judgments, 'only contracts concluded for the purpose of satisfying an individual's own needs in terms of private consumption come under the provisions designed to protect the consumer as the party deemed to be the weaker party economically'.[121]

The CJEU, in the *Gruber* case, has also been restrictive as regards mixed purposes contracts, excluding from consumer protection any contract where there is a business element unless the trade or professional purpose is so limited as to be negligible in the overall context of the supply. It was even considered irrelevant that the private element was predominant.[122] That decision was made in the context of a jurisdiction issue raised by a farmer who bought tiles for his farm where the farm buildings, were used for farming and as his private quarters. It had been wondered whether this rather strict interpretation was unique to private international law where certainty as to jurisdiction might be considered paramount or

116 Directive 2011/83/EU on consumer rights (2011) OJ L304/64.

117 COM (2011) 635 final.

118 Art. 7(2) of the proposal defines a small- and medium-sized enterprise on the basis of the number of employees (less than 250) and its annual turnover (less than 50 million euro). Recital 13 of the Consumer Rights Directive allows Member States to decide to apply the rules of the Directive to non-governmental organisations, start-ups or small- and medium-sized enterprises. In relation to EU policy considerations concerning SMEs see also Commission, *Think Small First – a 'Small Business Act' for Europe* COM (2008) 394 final.

119 C–541/99 *Cape Snc v Idealservice Srl.* [2001] ECR I–9049.

120 C–361/89 *Criminal Proceedings against Patrice di Pinto* [1991] ECR I–1189.

121 C–269/95 *Francesco Benincasa v Dentalkit Srl.* [1997] ECR I–3767, para 17.

122 C–464/01 *Johann Gruber v Bay Wa AG* [2005] ECR I–439.

should be applied more broadly across the substantive EU consumer *acquis.*[123] The Consumer Rights Directive in recital 17 states:

> in the case of dual purpose contracts, where the contract is concluded for purposes partly within and partly outside the person's trade and the trade purpose is so limited as not to be predominant in the overall context of the contract, that person should also be considered as a consumer.

This clearly resolves the issue for that Directive in favour of allowing contracts to be consumer contracts so long as the business element does not predominate. Probably in other substantive consumer legislation the Court will feel able to distinguish a private international law case like *Gruber* and also apply this more generous test.

The Court has also been strict in not allowing consumer protection rules to apply to related contracts if the main contract is not a consumer contract. So in one case the rules on doorstep-selling did not apply to a son, who was not in business, but who had guaranteed his father's business loan.[124]

Undoubtedly, even with the more generous rules in the Consumer Rights Directive, the EU concept of 'consumer' is limited to those who in large measure are furthering their private consumption needs. These actors benefit from a substantial consumer *acquis.* As maximum harmonisation increases its reach they are coming to rely more and more solely on the quality of EU law to afford them protection as the scope for national intervention is reduced. The next section begins to investigate the quality of these rules.

Images of consumers

It is well known that European law uses the average consumer as its benchmark. This started in internal market law as a reaction, in particular, against the rather over-protective German unfair commercial practices law which focused on protecting the uneducated, stupid or otherwise weak consumers.[125] The Court's average consumer standard may have served a useful purpose in that context, but it went on to be rather uncritically applied expressly in the Unfair Commercial

123 See M Ebers, 'Wer ist verbraucher? – Neuere entwicklungen in der rechtsprechung' in G Ajani and M Ebers (eds), *Uniform Terminology for European Contract Law* (Nomos, 2005).

124 C–45/96 *Bayerische Hypotheken- und Wechselbank AG v Edgar Dietzinger* [1998] ECR I–1199.

125 For example in C–315/92 *Verband Sozialer Wettbewerb eV v Clinique Laboratoires SNC and Estée Lauder Cosmetics GmbH.* [1994] ECR I–317; C–470/93 *Verein gegen Unwesen in Handel und Gewerbe Köln e.V. v Mars GmbH.* (1995) ECR I–1923; *Gut Springenheide* (n 22); *Sektkellerei* (n 22); *Estée Lauder* (n 22). For an overview of the formerly restrictive nature of the German unfair commercial practices law see R de Vrey, *Towards a European Unfair Competition Law: A Clash between Legal Families* (Brill, 2005), pp.172–173.

Practices Directive[126] and by the Court when assessing the fairness of terms.[127] It has been suggested that despite concerns about the standard it is best to apply the standard consistently across the EU *acquis*.[128]

There are, however, several concerns about the use of the average consumer test in substantive consumer law.[129] First, it separates consumers into the average and the vulnerable, and makes the need for additional consumer protection a statement of weakness. Some consumers may be unwilling to label themselves as vulnerable to obtain protection. Moreover, it fails to underline that in some situations all consumers need protection.[130]

Second, this approach means that all less-than-average consumers are left without protection under that rule unless they can be deemed vulnerable. However, it is not clear they do not need protection. There is a continuum between protecting all consumers and protecting no consumers, with the average consumers being somewhere on that line. It is not always clear that the average standard reflects the correct protective level. One might well wish to intervene at a standard different from that needed to protect the average consumer where the consequences of a practice are severe and its utility small. Protective levels may well fall above or below this arbitrary line depending on what policy choices are made. There is clearly a sense from the EU that in advertising and marketing, the welfare of the majority should dominate, but this is not fully articulated. Indeed, it may well depend on how many below-average consumers are harmed and to what extent, compared to the gains of the above-average consumer. For example, an advertisement that most people find mildly amusing, but actually confuses a significant number of consumers and causes them serious loss, may be worth controlling even if it does not affect the average consumer.

Third, this approach at best requires a careful policy as regards vulnerability. EU law does protect the vulnerable in some instances,[131] but it is unclear how

126 Unfair Commercial Practices Directive, Recital 18.

127 C–453/10 *Jana Pereničová and Vladislav Perenič v SOS financ spol. s r. o.* ECLI:EU:C:2012:144. See also B Keirsblick, 'The interaction between consumer protection rules on unfair contract terms and unfair commercial practices: Pereničová and Perenič' (2013) 50 *Common Market Law Review* p.247; C Willet, *Fairness in Consumer Contracts* (Ashgate, 2007), p.114, who, at an earlier stage, indicated the potential use of the average consumer test in relation to the fairness of terms.

128 M Djurovic, 'The Apple case: The commencement of pan-European battle against unfair commercial practices' (2013) 9 *European Review of Contract Law* p.253; M Durovic, *European Law on Unfair Commercial Practices and Contract Law* (Hart Publishing, 2016), p.191.

129 See also the discussion in Chapter 2, pp.66–73, in the context of the Unfair Commercial Practices Directive.

130 P Cartwright, 'Understanding and protecting vulnerable financial consumers' (2015) 38 *Journal of Consumer Policy* p.119.

131 For example the protection of 'vulnerable consumers' in relation to the supply of energy (Directive 2009/72/EC on common rules for the internal market in electricity (2009) OJ L211/55, Directive 2009/73/EC on common rules for the internal market in natural gas (2009) OJ L211/94) and the protection of minors (Directive 2010/13/EU on the provision of audiovisual media services (2010) OJ L95/1).

extreme the vulnerability has to be and whether all categories of vulnerability are covered.[132] There is now a wealth of literature on consumer vulnerability, but this seems not to have informed EU policy.[133] It implies that consumer protection of the vulnerable is an exception that has to be justified and is not derived from any structural weaknesses of consumers as a class.

Fourth, the average standard is a rather arbitrary line to draw. Indeed the calculation of average is well known to be subject to different calculations. The median consumer may be different from the mean.

Fifth, even if it is justified to strip out protection of the vulnerable from the protection of the average consumer, the image of the average consumer as 'a reasonably well informed and reasonably observant and circumspect' person is not truly reflective of actual consumer behaviour. The EU law's average consumer could indeed be labelled the prudent or careful consumer. Empirically, the average consumer is likely to be closer to the Nordic law image of the passive glancer, rather that the active and critical information-seeker which dominates EU thinking.[134] Although the EU mentions behavioural economics frequently[135] it does not seem to appreciate in legislative practice that consumer behaviour is not always in accordance with rational expectations.[136] More details will be given in the next section when the information policy approach is critiqued. However, at a very basic level it has to be questioned whether the consumer image of the average is the right one. Behavioural science has itself been criticised for focusing on 'weird' (Western, educated, industrialised, rich, and democratic) people, but even within that set optimistic assumptions seem to be made. Although the

132 Defining vulnerability is, however, a complex task. See J Stuyck, 'The notion of the empowered and the informed consumer in consumer policy and how to protect the vulnerable under such a regime' in Howells et al., *Yearbook of Consumer Law 2007* (Ashgate, 2007); BIS, *Better Choices: Better Deals, Consumers Powering Growth* (2011), which refrains from defining 'vulnerable' and also refers to 'disadvantaged consumers'; See also Commission, *Consumer Empowerment – Special Eurobarometer* 342 (2011) which bases vulnerability on a combination of marketing and individual circumstances.

133 P Cartwright, *The Vulnerable Consumer of Financial Services: Law, Policy and Regulation* (2011); FCA, *Consumer Credit and Consumers in Vulnerable Circumstances* (April 2014); OFGEM, *Consumer Vulnerability Strategy* (July 2013); European Parliament, *Resolution of 22 May 2012 on a Strategy for Strengthening the Rights of Vulnerable Consumers* (2013) OJ CE264/11.

134 T Wilhelmsson, 'Consumer images in East and West' in H-W Micklitz, *Rechtseinheit oder Rechtsvielfalt in Europa?* (Nomos, 1996).

135 For example, *Consumer Decision-Making in Retail Investment Services: A Behavioural Economics Perspective* (November 2010), available online under: http://ec.europa.eu/consumers/archive/strategy/docs/final_report_e n.pdf.

136 But see the more optimistic view with regard to the CJEU's attitude noted by H Schebesta and K Purnhagen, 'The behaviour of the average consumer: A little less normativity and a little more reality in the court's case law? Reflections on Teekanne' (2016) *European Law Review* p.590.

standard takes account of social, cultural and linguistic factors,[137] in practice linguistic issue are the most likely to be taken seriously into consideration. [138] That said the Court has at times shown itself open to protecting vulnerable categories of consumers.[139]

In sum, the policy of selecting the average consumer as the standard for protection has not been fully articulated and justified.[140] Even if the average consumer is the one used to judge the appropriate level of protection, establishing who that average consumer is empirically is not an easy matter. It is clear that underpinning some of the statements by courts and legislators is a belief that consumers should be given more space to protect themselves. This was in the free movement cases a reaction against national laws whose main achievement had been to prevent fair competition by too easily condemning practices as unfair competition. This is also seen as a theme of many of the post-Unfair Commercial Practice Directive cases, which have sought to liberalise trade practices laws.[141] However, one can sympathise with that objective and still not want a law of consumer protection which is only there for the benefit of consumers who are always reasonably well-informed and reasonably observant and circumspect. Indeed there are examples where the Court has been willing to support genuine cases of consumer protection[142] and the legislation has shown at times a concern to not exclude those needing protection.[143] There is scope for reconsidering the dominant image of the consumer in EU law and finding a better way to express legislative policy which recognises that all consumers can be vulnerable, whilst also ensuring those that are acutely vulnerable are given particular protection to the extent appropriate. Possibly inspiration might be found in the New Zealand case of *Godfrey Hirst v Cavalier*[144] that would treat as average "all the consumers in the class targeted except the outliers.

137 C-313/94 *F.lli Graffione SNC v Ditta Fransa* [1996] ECR I-6039, para 22; C-220/98 *Estee Lauder Cosmetics GmbH & Co. OHG v Lancaster Group GmbH* [2000] ECR I-117, para 29.

138 B Duivenvoorde, *The Consumer Benchmarks in the Unfair Commercial Practices Directive* (Springer, 2015).

139 C-382/87 *R. Buet and Educational Business Services (EBS) v Ministère Public* [1989] ECR 1235; C-441/04 *A-Punkt Schmuckhandels GmbH v Claudia Schmidt* [2006] ECR I-2093 and C-195/14 *Bundesverband der Verbraucherzentralen und Verbraucherverbände eV v Teekanne GmbH & Co KG* EU:C:2015:361.

140 S Weatherill, "Who is the 'average consumer'?" in S Weatherill and U Bernits, *The Regulation of Unfair Commercial Practices under EC Directive 2005/29 – New Rules and New Techniques* (Oxford, Hart, 2007), p.135.

141 See Chapter 2, pp.67–73.

142 See, for example, Case 286/81 *Oosthoek's Uitgeversmaatschappij*, [1982] ECR 4575 and Case 382/87 *R. Buet and Educational Business Services (EBS) v Ministère Public* [1989] ECR 1235.

143 The Unfair Commercial Practices Directive on vulnerability is one example, but see also General Product Safety Directive 2001/95/EC, Art. 2(b)(iv), which refers to the categories of consumers at risk when using the product, in particular children and the elderly.

144 *Godfrey Hirst NZ Limited v Cavalier Bremworth Limited* [2014] NZCA 418.

The 'outliers' encompass consumers who are unusually stupid or ill equipped, or those whose reactions are extreme or fanciful."[145] The consumer is then expected to act with the 'care to be expected of reasonable consumers. Or, to put it accurately, by a reasonably careful consumer'.[146]

Information policy

One of the key debates in modern consumer policy is the extent to which consumers can protect themselves through information. This links back to the previous discussion on the average consumer. If the image of the person being protected is an average consumer, defined as having a good ability to consume and process information, one will naturally see information as an effective protective tool. It certainly enhances the autonomy of the consumer, at least in a formal sense, whilst imposing limited demands and constraints on the trader. The modern approach is to use information, sometimes alongside other techniques such as default options based on favoured consumer behaviour, to guide or 'nudge' consumers to make the 'right decisions'.[147] It is seen as more acceptable politically than regulation that mandates minimum standards for products and services. These risk threatening to remove perceived 'risky' products from the market and thereby reducing consumer choice and competition between producers. Information has a role to play in allowing consumers to make better choices. However, EU policy-makers seem on occasions to unduly favour information regulation as promoting market-driven decisions.[148] Whereas, the structural vulnerability of consumers as a class tends to suggest that consumers' real autonomy can best be exercised once the law has screened out dangerous and poor-quality goods and services, and unfair terms and practices. Nevertheless, in the European context information is an appealing strategy for the EU as it makes less formal demands on producers to change their basic product designs which may be based

145 Para [20].

146 Para [53], citing the Australian High Court in *Parkdale Custom Built Furniture Pty Ltd v Puxu Pty Ltd* [1982] HCA 44.

147 See C Sunstein and R Thaler, 'Libertarian paternalism is not an oxymoron' (2003) 70 *University of Chicago Law Review* 1159. C Sunstein and R Thaler, *Nudge: Improving Decisions about Health, Wealth and Happiness* (Penguin, 2012). They argue that it is possible to affect behaviour whilst respecting freedom of choice. However, their example from consumer protection seems to be wrong. They identify cooling-off periods and note that rather than block choices, regulators ensure a period of reflection. However, this is not a true example of residual free choice. Free choice would require consumers to be given the option of a contract with or without a cooling-off period. Once the law requires such a cooling-off period, the cost will be factored into the product and the consumer will have no option but to buy this right.

148 C.Twigg-Flesner and R.Schulze, 'Protecting rational choice: information and the right of withdrawal' in G Howells, I Ramsay and T Wilhelmsson (eds) *Handbook of Research on International Consumer Law* (Edward Elgar, 2010).

on national traditions and regulation. Instead many consumer concerns can be addressed by providing information.

The EU has long had rules preventing misinformation.[149] This is now reflected in the Unfair Commercial Practices Directive.[150] EU laws have also been used to support the right of traders to give factual information.[151] However, the heart of EU consumer information policy lies in the positive obligations it places on traders to provide information about goods and services. This has grown from the very modest obligation in the Doorstep Selling Directive to mention the right of withdrawal[152] to far more extensive obligations. Doorstep- and distance-selling rules have now been combined in the Consumer Rights Directive.[153] There are numerous directives following this duty to provide information model, such as the directives on distance selling of financial services,[154] consumer credit,[155] timeshare,[156] and package travel.[157]

These rules seek to redress the balance between trader and consumer caused by the asymmetry of information. This formal balancing of access to information, however, often fails to take account of the insights of behavioural economics literature.[158] This teaches us that consumers have limited ability to handle information and even when they have the information they may process it in ways that do not lead to the expected outcomes if the consumer acted economically rationally.[159] Moreover, if there is little choice for even the perfectly informed consumer its impact is naturally of limited utility.

The EU has engaged at a theoretical level with behavioural economics, but putting them into practice is harder. Thus concentrating on ensuring consumers

149 As an example of early EEC legislation see Council Directive 84/450/EEC on misleading advertising (1984) OJ L250/17.

150 Unfair Commercial Practices Directive, Art. 6(1). See Chapter 2.

151 Directive 97/55/EC on comparative advertising (1997) L290/18. See also C–362/88 *GB-INNO-BM v Confédération du Commerce Luxembourgeois* [1990] ECR I–667; S Weatherill, 'The role of the informed consumer in EC law and policy'. *Consumer Law Journal* 2 (1994), p.49.

152 Directive 85/577/EEC of 20 December 1985 to protect the consumer in respect of contracts negotiated away from business premises (1985) OJ L372/31, Art. 4.

153 Consumer Rights Directive, Arts. 6–16. See Chapter 3.

154 Directive 2002/65/EC on the distance marketing of consumer financial services (2002) OJ L271/16.

155 Directive 2008/48/EU on credit agreements for consumer (2008) OJ L133/66.

156 Directive 2008/122/EC on the protection of consumers in respect of certain aspects of timeshare, long-term holiday products, resale and exchange contracts (2009) OJ L33/10.

157 Directive 2015/2302/EU on package travel and linked travel arrangements (2015) OJ L326/1.

158 For a summary, see See C Busch, 'The future of pre-contractual information: From behavioural insights to big data', in C Twigg-Flesner (ed), *Research Handbook on EU Consumer and Contract Law* (Edward Elgar, 2016).

159 AL Sibony, 'Can EU consumer law benefit from behavioural insights? An analysis of the unfair Commercial Practices Directive' (2014) 22 *European Review of Private Law* p.901.

are aware of key information may well be a good policy, but often comes up against the political imperative of needing to please states that are keen to allow national information rules to be maintained. The need to placate national sentiment explains why the Distance Selling of Financial Services Directive allows for over 30 potential pieces of information to be provided.[160] The difficulties of fully implementing the behavioural economics insights should not be underestimated. It is hard to get consensus on which are the key pieces of information or to agree which information can safely be left out or given less profile. It is understandable that it is easier to reach a consensus that over-includes information obligations. Consumer groups themselves even tend to argue for more information, even if they know less might mean more effective information.[161] It is hard to decide which pieces of information should be left out.

Consumers have limited ability to understand and process information. This is not just an issue for those with literacy, numeracy or financial skill deficits.[162] All consumers have limited ability to process information. The human mind handles data by breaking it down into manageable chunks. It has been estimated that roughly seven chunks of information is the most the human mind can handle at any one time.[163] Less can mean more when it comes to information disclosure.[164] Moreover, as consumers have only limited time, it is only to be expected they glance at advertisements or decide it is not practical to read standard terms and conditions.[165] Many consumers will not take full notice of information provided.[166] This need not be a problem on a macro-scale as a margin of active information-seeking consumers can have a healthy impact on the market.[167] However, it would be wrong to assume that all information was actually being read so that all consumers were making fully informed decisions. Indeed there is

160 See Chapter 3.
161 O Ben-Shahar and CE Schneider, *More Than You Wanted to Know: The Failure of Mandated Disclosure* (Princeton, 2014).
162 J Hanson and D Kysar, 'Taking behaviouralism seriously: The problem of market manipulation' (1999) 74 *New York University Law Review* pp.630, 633.
163 G Miller, 'The magical number seven, plus or minus two: Some limits on our capacity for processing information' (1956) 63 *Psych Rev* p.81.
164 Better Regulation Executive and National Consumer Council, *Warning: Too Much Information Can Harm* (2007).
165 See, for example, O Ben-Shahar, "The myth of the 'opportunity to read' in contract law" (2009) 5 *European Review of Contract Law* p.1.
166 W Kip Viscusi, 'Individual rationality, hazard warnings and the foundations of tort law'. *Rutgers Law Rev* 48 (1996) p.625, at 632 citing studies showing only 25% of consumers recall the sodium content listing on food labels, only 40% recalled the ingredient listing at all. Only 69–74% of patients read patient package insert for prescription drugs, and, although 73% of Utah residents drank alcohol only 35% recalled the alcohol beverage warning.
167 A Schwartz and L Wilde, 'Intervening in markets on the basis of imperfect information: A legal and economic analysis' (1979) 127 *University of Pennsylvania Law Review* p.630.

a social equity issue as it is typically better-off consumers who tend to make use of information.[168]

There are ways in which information can have a greater impact. Focus can be placed on a limited range of key sets of information; these can be chosen for the relevance to consumers and presented using language and visual images in ways that attract the consumers' attention.[169] We shall see the unfair terms rules on intelligibility have been interpreted to demand that consumers are presented with information in a manner that enables them to understand its consequences.[170] However, just as regulators can seek to ensure information helps consumers make rational decisions, industry is also aware of the human psychology and can use this to promote its desired outcomes. This may potentially include limiting the impact of mandatory disclosures and warnings.[171] Consumer choices can also be manipulated by the way information is provided[172] or by the use of visceral factors to deflect consumer preferences.[173] Standardised formats that take account of these factors may be required. This is well-illustrated by the controls on tobacco product presentation and warnings.[174]

However, even if the consumer receives the information it may be processed in ways that limit its impact. Consumers do not view all information equally. They will tend to prefer information confirming their view and to discount information that does not sit easily with their opinion.[175] In other words there is a tendency to anchor assessments around initial judgments, effectively discounting the value of experience and subsequent knowledge.[176] Equally consumers may not be well

168 WC Whitford, 'The functions of disclosure regulation in consumer transaction' (1973) *Wisconsin Law Rev* p.400.

169 E.g. J Clement, 'Visual influence on in-store buying decisions: An eye-track experiment on the visual influence of packaging design' (2007) 23 *Journal of Marketing Management* p.917; M Kim and S Lennon, 'The effects of visual and verbal information on attitudes and purchase intentions in internet shopping' (2008) 25 *Psychology & Marketing* p.146.

170 See Chapter 4, pp.152–3.

171 J Hanson and D Kysar, 'Taking behaviouralism seriously: Some evidence of market manipulation' (1999) 112 *Harvard Law Review* p.1420.

172 D Kahneman and A Tversky, 'Choice, values, and frames' (1984) 39 *Am Psychologist* p.341; I Simonson, 'Choice based on reasons: The case of attraction and compromise effects' (1989) 16 *Journal of Consumer Research* p.158.

173 G Lowenstein, 'Out of control: Visceral influences on behaviour' (1996) 65 *J Org Behav & Hum Dec Proc* p.272.

174 G Howells, *The Tobacco Challenge* (Ashgate, 2011), pp.272–275. With regard to EU legislation see Directive 2014/40/EU on the manufacture, presentation and sale of tobacco and related products (2014) OJ L127/1.

175 J Bruner and M Potter, 'Interference in visual recognition' (1964) 144 *Science* p.424; C Lord, L Ross and M Lepper, 'Biased assimilation and attitude polarisation: The effects of prior theories on subsequently considered evidence' (1979) 37 *J. of Pers. and Soc. Psych.* p.2098; M Rabin, 'Psychology and economics' (1998) 36 *J. of Econ. Lit.* p.11; L Ross and M Lepper, 'Perseverance in self-perception and social perception: Biased attributional processes in the debriefing paradigm' (1975) 32 *J. of Pers. and Soc. Psych.* p.880.

176 C Lord, L Ross and M Lepper, 'Biased assimilation and attitude polarisation: The effects of prior theories on subsequently considered evidence' (1979) 37 *J. of Pers. and Soc. Psych.* p.2098

placed to process the information about risk as their perception of risk may be affected by how much they value the product or service.[177] Classically warnings may go unheeded as the desire to use the product is strong. Moreover, it is natural to tend to downplay everyday risk and exaggerate the risk of major harm.[178] Also immediate benefits may be emphasised and delayed costs downplayed.[179] This is typical for health risks for consumer products or the need to repay loans at high interest rates. Even if a risk is understood in a general sense, consumers may be too optimistic about their own ability to avoid a risk, especially when they feel they have some control over the situation.[180]

Finally, information only helps if consumers have choices. If there are no alternatives – for instance, for low-income consumers of credit – then understanding the only choice you have only promotes your autonomy to the limited extent of allowing you to decide whether to make that particular purchase. In a similar way if all the products are clearly understood, but the comparison between them is hard to make because there are too many variables then again the information has limited utility.[181] Indeed if the information illustrates there is a better deal, but the switching costs create impediments, again the information is of limited value.[182]

There have been instances of the consumer having been assisted, on the basis of information rules, by the development of a strong principle of transparency.[183] This has often been used to alleviate the position of a consumer in an indirect way. The lack of transparency allows relief to be given without reviewing the substantive fairness of the transaction. However, though useful in the instant cases, such solutions do not address the underlying problem. The same transaction could take place if the terms had been more transparent; it would rely on that transparency affecting consumer behaviour. That is by no means a certain outcome.

The challenge for Europe is to find the appropriate role for information policy and to then apply lessons of behavioural economics to ensure the information

177 P. Sloviv, 'Smokers: Rational actors or rational fools?' in P Slovic (ed) *Smoking: Risk, Perception and Policy* (Sage, 2001).

178 People may be very afraid of terrorist attack or a plane crash, but expose themselves without care to more likely harm from smoking, or over-consumption of alcohol or sugary or fatty food.

179 For example, when enjoying tobacco, alcohol, sugary or fatty food the immediate satisfaction can be obvious and the future risks easily discounted. K Kirby and R Herrnstein, 'Preference reversals due to myopic discounting of delayed reward' (1995) 6 *Psyc. Sci.* p.83. In a similar vein see the poetic words of JK. Galbraith, *The Affluent Society*, 3rd ed, (Houghton Mifflin, 1976) p.148: 'The legacy of wants, which are themselves inspired, are the bills which descend like winter snow on those who are buying on the instalment plan'.

180 N Weinstein, 'Optimistic biases about personal risks' (1989) 246 *Science* p.1232.

181 I Simonson, 'Choice based on reasons: The case of attraction and compromise effects' (1989) *Journal of Consumer Research* p.158

182 TA Burnham, JK Freis and V Mahajan, 'Consumer switching costs: A typology, antecedents and consequences' (2003) 31 *Journal of the Academy of Marketing Science* p.109.

183 I Ramsay, 'Framework for regulation of the consumer marketplace' (1985) *Journal of Consumer Policy* p.353.

enhances consumer autonomy. Information is important, but it also has its limitation as a consumer protection technique.[184]

Right of withdrawal

Another way in which EU consumer law seeks to enhance autonomy is by granting consumers a right of withdrawal.[185] This is a rather remarkable right when set against the traditional contract law doctrine of *pacta sunt servanda*. Consumers in some circumstances, based either upon the type of goods or services or the circumstances in which they were sold, are given a right of withdrawal within a limited period without having to give any explanation.[186] This is done to enhance autonomy in case undue pressure was placed on the consumer or they were rushed into making a decision. Another factor in some cases is to allow the consumer to be fully informed about the product by actually being able to use it, before being irrevocably committed. This is of course particularly important in sales where the product is not seen, such as those made at a distance.

The modalities of exercising this right can be complex and are discussed below. For now we simply want to note the limitations of this approach.[187] Consumers may be reluctant to take advantage of the right. They may not want to admit they made a mistake; may not realise what a bad deal they have struck, or may not have realised that within the withdrawal period; may not have sufficient incentive to make use of the right or be worried that they may not actually recover any sums paid over.[188] The incentive to make use of the right of withdrawal reduces if deductions can be made for the fact they have used the product for a period or delivery costs cannot be recovered or high return costs need to be incurred. Despite the information obligations about the right, many consumers may still be unaware of the right. Traders may well negotiate with them when they seek to exercise the right. All of this does not mean that rights of withdrawal are bad for consumers. On the contrary, they can provide a rather simple self-help remedy in many circumstances. However, they should not be seen as a panacea for all ills. Consumer law should seek to minimise the likelihood that anyone would want to change their mind by ensuring products and services of good quality are fairly marketed.

184 G Howells, 'The potential and limits of consumer empowerment by information' (2005) *Journal of Law and Society* p.349.

185 See Chapter 3, pp.113–125.

186 For example, the purchase of goods via distance means (e.g. via the internet) or in 'off-premises' situations (e.g. doorstep sales) (see Directive 2011/83/EU), timeshare contracts (see Directive 2008/122/EU) and consumer credit contracts (Directive 2008/48/EC).

187 P Rekaiti and R Van den Bergh, 'Cooling-off periods in the consumer laws of the EC Member States. A comparative law and economics approach' (2000) 23 *Journal of Consumer Policy* p.371.

188 O Ben-Shahar and EA Posner, 'The right to withdraw in contract law' (2011) 40 *Journal of Legal Studies* p.115.

Goals beyond enhanced autonomy

Arguments to enhance consumer autonomy by enhancing information and giving rights of withdrawal seem a painless means of promoting consumer welfare. There may be a few complaints that they restrict the freedom of traders, but these are rather mild.[189] There may also be concerns that they impose unnecessary costs, but again these criticisms though occasionally voiced are not strongly forced; this is probably because the costs are relatively low and seen as a price worth paying to avoid more interventionist regulatory approaches. However, their effectiveness in achieving enhanced consumer welfare and protection needs to be questioned. Indeed information obligations have become in many respects a defence for industry; whether it be warnings against the risk of tobacco (described by the main lawyer for the tobacco industry as the best achievement he gave the industry[190]) or the open disclosure of extraordinary high-interest rates adding to their apparent legitimacy. The open-hands policy provides legitimation of industry practices. It makes those goods or services seem acceptable even if their implied acceptance by consumers in the market is often a mirage.

However, going beyond promoting autonomy provides challenges to justify any interventions. The interventions are seen to limit choice – something which is highly prized in Western economies[191] – and have the potential to be anti-competitive. There is certainly a risk that established players participate in the rule-making process and so can skew it in their favour. There is a danger of pricing poorer consumers out of the market if the standards are set too high.[192] This can lead to criticism that consumer protectionism benefits the upper classes.[193] The poor are left out because legal rules cannot normally alter market realities and traders are normally, discrimination laws aside, allowed the freedom to decide with whom to contract and on what conditions. This is, of course, a familiar criticism of paternalism. The greater the formal legal requirements for entry to the market the less role there is for autonomous freedom of contracting. It can be argued that consumer contracts are not a pure form of contract anymore, but

189 For example, P Mankowski, 'Formation of contract and pre-contractual duties to inform' in S Grundmann and M Schauer (eds), *The Architecture of European Codes and Contract Law* (Kluwer, 2006), p.332. For a general discussion on the relationship between party autonomy and information see, e.g. S Vogenauer, W Kerber and S Weatherill (eds), *Party Autonomy and the Role of Information in the Internal Market* (de Gruyter, 2001).

190 G Howells, *The Tobacco Challenge – Legal Policy and Consumer Protection* (Ashgate, 2011), p.280.

191 Cf. C Sunstein, *Choosing Not to Choose – Understanding the Value of Choice* (Oxford University Press, 2015).

192 Seminally, D Caplovitz, *The Poor Pay More* (Free Press, 1963). On its continuing relevance, see E Mierzwinski, 'Colston E. Warne lecture: Consumer protection 2.0 – protecting consumers in the 21st century' (2010) 44 *Journal of Consumer Affairs* p.578.

193 For recent evidence, see F D'Acunto and AG Rossi, *Ditching the Middle Class with Consumer Protection Regulation*. Robert H. Smith School research paper no. RHS 2833961. Available at SSRN: https://ssrn.com/abstract=2833961.

rather a form of regulation.[194] However, this is only within limits. There is still plenty of scope in most contexts for a wide choice to be offered to consumers within the broad scope of what is legally permissible.

The state has a duty to regulate the market. It can of course impose limits of what can be bought and sold. So bans on sale of human body parts are widely viewed as appropriate in Europe.[195] Forms of marketing that mislead or offend taste and decency are also widely accepted as wrong. There would be horror if the state did not prevent the sale of dangerous goods. In the economic sphere, there is arguably more room to allow consumers freedom to make mistakes, but consumers have come to have legitimate expectations of quality and contractual fairness. Even in the UK despite many years of ideological opposition, a conservative government has recognised the need for interest and fee caps to deal with problematic payday loans.[196] Some rationales will be suggested to support these interventions. It is also noticeable that often good traders benefit as much as consumers from consumer laws. The real winner of the EU adopting a progressive and enlightened consumer policy is the EU itself. The right policy should generate higher consumer welfare within the EU and a better reputation globally for EU products and services.

Certainly one easy justification for consumer rules is to prevent rogue traders. The dodgy second-hand car salesperson has probably been replaced by a remote unscrupulous internet seller as the most obvious source of consumer detriment. Such practices often involve fraud and their regulation needs little justification. It is when the trading practices of legitimate businesses are questioned that the rationales for intervention become more complex. Early justifications for controlling standard-form contracts were indeed still driven by the notion that a powerful trader would seek to use its power to abuse consumers.[197] This may have been true in the 1960s and 70s, but in Europe is less so today – though some of the mandatory arbitration clauses in the United States suggest that legacy may be alive there and the Apple warranty cases might have traces of such behaviour.[198] In Europe, one often-advanced argument in favour of regulation is that traders will seek to make small advantages that can go under the radar of consumers. There will not be gross abuses but rather techniques to squeeze extra profit at the margin, for

194 R Brownsword, 'Regulating transactions: Good faith and fair dealing' in G Howells and R Schulze (eds), *Modernising and Harmonising Consumer Contract Law* (Sellier, 2009); see also R Brownsword, 'The theoretical foundations of European private law: A time to stand and stare' in R Brownsword, H-W Micklitz, L Niglia and S Weatherill (eds), *The Foundations of European Private Law* (Hart, 2011); H Collins, *Regulating Contracts* (OUP, 1999).

195 M Trebilcock, *The Limits of Freedom of Contract* (Harvard University Press, 1997).

196 Consumer Credit (Cost Cap) Instrument 2014 (FCA 2014/56).

197 Anthony Kronman, 'Paternalism in the law of contracts' (1982) 92 *Yale L.J.* p.763.

198 M Djorovic, 'The Apple case: The commencement of pan-European battle against unfair commercial practices' (2013) 9 *European Review of Contract Law* p.253.

example by placing terms that marginally favour traders in the small print.[199] The unfairness is that consumers are taken by surprise, but an equally important reason for controlling such terms is to make sure that traders that seek to use them do not have an unfair advantage over traders that want to provide a straightforward honest deal to consumers. This same rationale of being fair between traders is again seen in terms of laws fixing minimum quality standards. This goes back to the famous piece by Akerlof on the market for lemons.[200] If traders were allowed to sell sub-standard products without sanction there would be no incentive to produce goods of the appropriate quality. Again consumer laws are seen to be as much for the benefit of preventing unfair competition as consumer welfare. Consumers do, however, benefit as they have the insurance that they will have redress, in sales or product liability law if they suffer loss because a product fails to meet legitimate expectations prescribed by law. There is actually no regressive effect on the poor as the rules only seek to ensure the goods meet the standards that were promised and presumably that had already been reflected in the price. It might be contended that the mandated standard might have been pitched too high, but in fact it is hard to understand how anyone would want to accept goods which were non-conforming or defective. Moreover, those standards are framed as minimum standards of acceptable quality and safety, and are sufficiently flexible to be adapted by disclosure on the trader's part.[201] In this sense the liability rules are an insurance that reflects a socialisation of risks to ensure that the consumer obtains what has been bargained for. This risk might be because the design of the product fails to meet the expected standard, but it can of course be the case that the product is a true 'lemon', in the sense where something has gone wrong in the production of that particular product or batch of products.

The socialisation of risk is recognised expressly in the Product Liability Directive which talks about the 'fair apportionment of risk inherent in modern technological production'.[202] Unfortunately, the meaning given to that has been restricted and the full impact of strict liability has been diluted so that there has only been a limited sharing of risks. In the most obvious cases, such as rogue products, the insurance principle undoubtedly applies and indeed its impact has been felt in contexts as emotive as the supply of contaminated blood. However, there has not been a strong interpretation of strict liability to

199 H Beale, 'Legislative control of fairness: The Directive on Unfair Terms in Consumer Contracts' in J Beatson and D Friedman (eds), *Good Faith and Fault in Contract Law* (Clarendon Press, 1995).

200 See Akerlof (n 16).

201 K Riesenhuber, 'Party autonomy and information in the Sales Directive', in S Grundmann, W Kerber and S Weatherill (eds), *Party Autonomy and the Role of Information in the Internal Market* (De Gruyter, 2001); S Hedley 'Quality of goods, information, and the death of contract' (2001) *Journal of Business Law* p.114; C Twigg-Flesner, 'Information disclosure about the quality of goods – duty or encouragement?' in G Howells, A Janssen and R Schulze (eds), *Information Rights and Obligations* (Ashgate, 2005).

202 Directive 85/374/EEC (1985) OJ L210/29, Recital 2.

ensure consumers are compensated for all unexpected product-related injuries. Although not express, the socialisation of risk is also inherent in compensation for non-conforming poor quality goods. One area where it is very clear to see a choice has been made in favour of the socialisation of risk is as regards the duties to provide assistance and possibly compensation for denied boarding, cancellation and delay of flights.[203] Indeed this is contentious because the socialisation of risk is very evident in that it imposes an active obligation to meet consumers' needs, rather than a mere liability. It is fiercely opposed by the low-cost carriers as the compensation is not linked to the price of the ticket. The Eyjafjallajökull volcano explosion in 2010 brought widespread calls for limitations on the obligations from a wider range of carriers. It is likely that this Regulation will be revised to moderate the obligations of carriers[204] and it is only right that the extent of the insurance is reviewed. However, the basic principles are likely to remain intact. There will always be problems in air transit and the policy reflects that airlines are better placed to deal with the issues than passengers. If those on low-cost flights tend to be relatively poorer they are even less well placed to deal with the emergency.

Brand Europe

Promoting the competitiveness of Europe is a key part of the European agenda.[205] A strong consumer protection policy that empowers consumers to make choices and enforce their rights can be an important driver in promoting good standards and hence enhancing competitiveness.[206] The importance of branding is well known in commerce.[207] But just as companies benefit from brand recognition so do states. Just think of the connotations associated with German engineering,

203 Regulation (EC) No 261/2004.

204 Commission, *Proposal for a Regulation of the European Parliament and of the Council Amending Regulation (EC) No 261/2004 Establishing Common Rules on Compensation and Assistance to Passengers in the Event of Denied Boarding and of Cancellation or Long Delay of Flights and Regulation (EC) No 2027/97 on Air Carrier Liability in Respect of the Carriage of Passengers and Their Baggage by Air* COM (2013) 130 final.

205 For example, Commission, *An Integrated Industrial Policy for the Globalization Era, Putting Competitiveness and Sustainability at Centre Stage* COM (2010) 614 final; Regulation 1287/2013/EU establishing a Programme for the Competitiveness of Enterprises and small- and medium-sized enterprises (COSME) (2014–2020) (2013) OJ L347/33.

206 M Porter, *The Competitive Advantage of Nations* (1990); DTI, *Modern Markets, Confident Consumers* (1999); COM (2007) 99 final (n 44).

207 The importance is relation to consumer behaviour was recognised at an early stage e.g. B Render and TO'Connor, 'The influence of price, store name, and brand name on perception of product quality' (1976) 4 *Journal of the Academy of Marketing Science* p.722; J Jacoby, GJ Szybillo and J Busato-Schach, 'Information acquisition behavior in brand choice situations' (1977) 3 *Journal of Consumer Research* p.209. In relation to the impact on modern transactions see e.g. M Ward and M Lee, 'Internet shopping, consumer search and product branding' (2000) 9 *Journal of Product & Brand Management* p.6.

Japanese electronics or Finnish vodka! If consumer protection is at a high level in the EU, it will encourage consumers to have trust in those markets. This was, after all, the original idea behind the *consumer acquis*, which by setting minimum standards sought to promote consumer confidence to shop anywhere within the EU. Those who advocated the Common European Sales Law believed consumers would press the 'blue button' to contract under EU law because it would represent a high level of protection.[208] Strong and effective EU consumer laws should attract global consumers to shop from EU traders with confidence and make EU goods attractive wherever they are sold in the world. In part the CE marking, signifying conformity to new-approach technical harmonisation directives, can be viewed as a brand mark for the EU.[209]

In summary, there should be a role for consumer protection in setting standards that socialise some of the risks in the market. Consumers will benefit, but so will traders who avoid unfair competition and generally the EU brand will gain strength. Of course there are debates about the extent to which risks should be socialised and the boundaries between interventionist regulation and free choice guided by information.

The EU should develop a consumer protection regime which pays more attention to the limits of information policy as a protective tool and recognises that there are risks faced by all consumers in the marketplace that need to be socialised. The rules are fair to traders as they will only kick in when standards, which they agreed to either expressly or which were imposed on all traders by law as the price for the right of entry to the market, are not met. Obviously they will help consumers. The risk of any negative impact caused by the increased associated costs is also negligible given the nature of those standards. Strong consumer protection rules are good for EU consumers, but also for traders who are not undermined by unfair competition and the improved image of European goods and services.

Those who argue that the EU does not have the mandate for developing such a policy are right to the extent that the EU could usefully amend its constitution to provide an independent base for consumer protection. In practice, by using its internal market powers it has already addressed almost every aspect of consumer protection; therefore it should take responsibility for the content of those laws. If the EU cannot provide a strong consumer protection content to its laws, then that is a reason for opposing its deeper involvement. However, the EU already has a mandate to develop a strong consumer protection policy along the lines

208 H Beale, 'The CESL proposal: An overview'. *Juridica International* (2013), pp.20, 30; H Schulte-Nölke, 'Scope and function of the optional instrument on European contract law' in R Schulze and J Stuyck (eds), *Towards a European Contract Law* (Sellier, 2011).

209 G Howells 'Co-regulation's role in the development of European fair trading laws' in H Collins (ed), *The Forthcoming Directive on Unfair Commercial Practices* (Kluwer, 2004). On the economic function of standardisation in general see Regulation 1025/2012/EU on European standardisation (2012) OJ L316/12, Recital 3.

advocated because of the obligations in the Treaty to provide a high level of consumer protection when legislating.

What tools does EU use to achieve its objectives?

What form should EU intervention take? This very much depends upon what is sought to be achieved. If the goal is uniformity then a regulation achieves that better than a directive.[210] Indeed given the lack of leeway the court has allowed states when implementing directives,[211] one can well understand why there have been moves to use regulations rather than directives. Equally if improving cross-border trade is the concern, limiting measures to cross-border contracts is a potentially useful way forward and can avoid opposition from those who want the EU intervention to leave their domestic law intact. However, it might be questionable whether it is wise to develop dual regimes for domestic and cross-border goods, given the need for consumer law to be understood with ease by consumers and traders. These two policy drivers – uniformity and cross-border sales – came together neatly in the Proposal for a Regulation on a Common European Sales Law.[212] More recently, they are reflected in the proposal for a directive on online sales of tangible goods.[213]

However, a top-down model may not be the best way forward. EU law should work with, not against, national law. Directives and other instruments that allow the integration of the EU rules into national law should be favoured. The continued use of national legal terminology is to be preferred as this normally makes the law simpler to understand and promotes coherence with non-harmonised legal areas. Calls to have a European consumer code[214] miss the point that a neat and tidy EU law is not what is needed. It is a coherent and simple national law that is important. Achieving that requires instruments that proscribe the ends to be reached without dictating the means. Of course regulations may still be appropriate where entirely new regimes are being established or there is a need to set up institutions or methods of co-operation between states. They may therefore have a continued role in enforcement and access to justice policy. However, their role in private and trade practices law should be limited.

210 C Twigg-Flesner, *A Cross-border-only Regulation for Consumer Transactions in the EU – a New Approach to EU Consumer Law* (New York, Springer, 2012).

211 C-59/89 *Commission v Germany* [1991] ECR I-2607; C-144/99 *Commission v Netherlands* [2001] ECR I-3541; C-70/03 *Commission v Spain* [2004] ECR I-7999.

212 COM (2011) 635 final.

213 *Proposal for a Directive of the European Parliament and of the Council on Certain Aspects Concerning Contracts for the Online and Other Distance Sales of Goods* COM (2015) 635 final.

214 Commission, *A More Coherent Contract Law – Action Plan* COM (2003) 68 final, Annex 4.3.5. See also several contributions to S Grundmann and J Stuyck (eds), *An Academic Green Paper on European Contract Law* (Kluwer, 2002).

There are clearly some areas that need to be fully harmonised if the internal market is to work. In other fields only minimum harmonisation may be required for internal market reasons to ensure the differences between systems are not so great that they affect competitiveness. The EU should become a torchbearer for a progressive consumer protection policy grounded in strong theoretical underpinnings. This theoretical support is needed as the EU protectionist philosophy is coming under a strong challenge from US scholars and reformers who favour a more market-based consumer policy.[215] Just as some states may feel the current EU policy is too limited, others might be reluctant to embrace a more radical base that promotes more fully the socialisation of risk doctrine. Within bounds this is a reflection of national cultures and traditions which should be respected. However, the EU should advocate for its preferred approach. The 'Open Method of Co-ordination' (OMC) can be a valuable approach to seek to educate states to accept the value of the EU's favoured approach.[216] This may rely on framework directives that in addition to fixing minimum rights set out goals and procedures for developing strong consumer protection. These may be fleshed out in soft law instruments like recommendations or codes.

Finally, the CJEU merits particular mention. The Court has been called upon a perhaps surprisingly high number of times to adjudicate on consumer matters. Many of its judgments will be mentioned in the following pages. What is striking is that lots of the decisions are on constitutional issues relating to legal base,[217] implementation,[218] and the relationship between EU and national measures.[219] Relatively few address substantive matters and in the recent glut of unfair contract terms cases many were treated as involving procedural law.[220] Indeed the CJEU has been criticised for lack of expertise in private law matters as many of the judges have a public law background.[221]

215 See the American Law Institute's forthcoming *Restatement of the Law, Consumer Contracts* (2017).

216 L Miller, *The Emergence of EU Contract Law* (Oxford University Press, 2011), p.199; J Smits, 'Plurality of sources in European private law' in R Brownsword, H-W Micklitz, L Niglia and S Weatherill (eds), *The Foundations of European Private Law* (Hart, 2011); W van Gerven, 'Harmonisation of private law: Do we need it?' (2004) 41 *Common Market Law Review* p.505.

217 For example, *Germany v Parliament and Council* (n 39); C–491/01 *R v Secretary of State for Health, ex parte British American Tobacco (Investments) Ltd and Imperial Tobacco Ltd* [2002] ECR I–11453. See also S Weatherill, 'The Commission's options for developing EC consumer protection and contract law: Assessing the constitutional basis' (2002) *European Business Law Review* p.497, and *Contract Law of the Internal Market* (Intersentia, 2016).

218 E.g. C-312/03 *Commission v Belgium* [2004] ECR I-1975 (consumer sales); C-282/08 *Commission v Luxembourg* [2009] ECR-13 and C-421/12 *Commission v Belgium* ECLI:EU:C:2014:2064 (UCPD).

219 See e.g. the cases discussed in the context of the UCPD in Chapter 2, pp.57–63.

220 Discussed in Chapter 4 at pp.154–162.

221 W Wurmnest and C Heinze, 'General principles of tort law in the jurisprudence of the European Court of Justice' in R Schulze (ed), *Compensation of Private Losses – the Evolution of Torts in European Business Law* (Sellier, 2011).

One particular development in the CJEU's jurisprudence needs to be noted here: the development of an *ex officio* doctrine which focuses on the role national courts can play in ensuring the effective application and enforcement of EU consumer law.[222] This principle has evolved principally in the context of the Unfair Contract Terms Directive.[223] It started with *Oceano*,[224] where the CJEU held that a domestic court could decide, of its own motion, that a term in a consumer contract is unfair and refuse to apply it. Subsequently, in *Mostaza Claro*,[225] the CJEU held that a national court hearing an action for the annulment of an arbitration award must determine of its own motion whether the arbitration clause is unfair, even though the consumer has not raised this argument himself. In *Pannon v Győrfi*,[226] the Court confirmed that if a national court has all the factual and legal information available to it to assess the unfairness of a term, it is required to do so of its own motion. This went beyond recognising a mere power to do so, which was the approach in *Oceano*. However, the CJEU also said that a consumer, aware of the court's assessment on unfairness, can decline the non-application of the term.[227] This doctrine initially developed in the field of unfair contract terms, but it has since extended to many other areas of consumer law, including consumer credit,[228] consumer sales,[229] and doorstep-selling.[230] It is potentially a very consumer-friendly doctrine because it should ensure the application of consumer law even where a consumer omits to plead this before a national court. However, it does create concerns too. The full extent of the national court's duties is unclear; sometimes, the CJEU speaks of a power to act of its own motion, and at other times (particularly after *Pannon*[231]) as an obligation. This, in turn, raises the question whether the failure by a national court to apply a relevant provision of consumer law of its own motion could form the basis of a claim for state liability.[232] This issue was considered in *Tomášová v Slovenia*.[233] Here, the CJEU confirmed that an action for state liability is available against the final court of appeal in

222 For an excellent analysis, see the PhD thesis by A Beka, *The ex Officio Doctrine in European Consumer Law. A Procedural Tool Reinvigorating Individual Consumer Litigation* (University of Luxembourg, 2015).

223 See Chapter 4, pp.150–160 for a fuller discussion.

224 C-240-244/98 *Oceano Grupo Editorial SA v Rocio Quintero and others* [2000] ECR I-4941.

225 C-168/05 *Elisa María Mostaza Claro v Centro Móvil Milenium SL* [2006] ECR I-10421.

226 C-243.08 *Pannon GSM Zrt. v Erzsébet Sustikné Győrfi* [2009] ECR I-4713.

227 Ibid., para [35].

228 C-429/05 *Max Rampion and Marie-Jeanne Godard, née Rampion v Franfinance SA and K par K SAS* [2007] ECR I-8017.

229 C-32/12 *Soledad Duarte Hueros v Autociba SA and Automóviles Citroën España SA* ECLI:EU:C:2013:637 and C-497/13 *Froukje Faber v Autobedrijf Hazet Ochten BV* ECLI:EU:C:2015:357. See P Rott, 'Improving consumers' enforcement of their rights under EU consumer sales law' (2016) 53 *Common Market Law Review* p.509.

230 C-227/08 *Eva Martín Martín v EDP Editores SL* [2009] ECR I-11939.

231 C-243/08 *Pannon GSM Zrt. v Erzsébet Sustikné Győrfi* [2009] ECR I-4713.

232 The possibility that actions by a national court could result in Member State liability was established in C-224/01 *Gerhard Köbler v Republik Österreich* [2003] ECR I-10239.

233 C-168/15 *Milena Tomášová v Slovenská republika* ECLI:EU:C:2016:602.

national jurisdiction for an infringement of EU Law. In this case, a national court had failed to consider the unfairness of a contract term of its own motion. The consumer eventually brought a claim for state liability. The national court had given its ruling in the original dispute in 2008. This pre-dated the CJEU's ruling in *Pannon*,[234] which established the full obligation on national courts to raise the unfairness of a contract term of their own motion. In *Tomášová*, the breach of EU Law therefore was not sufficiently serious to form the basis of a claim for state liability, although the CJEU seems to have reached that conclusion because the *Pannon* obligation to act *ex officio* had not been established at the time of the national ruling. Nevertheless, *Tomášová* is an important warning call to national courts to take seriously their obligation under the *ex officio* principle.

On the whole the CJEU has shown itself willing to understand the concerns of consumers, but national court systems are often better-placed to handle consumer matters as domestic litigation can generate sufficient cases to allow some specialisation and expertise. If minimum harmonisation measures are the norm, the CJEU will only be responsible for determining the core obligations required by EU law. States that are not satisfied with the EU's approach will be allowed to maintain or introduce more protective rules. If the protective ethic of consumer protection is more clearly spelt out, it will assist the CJEU to follow the EU's consumer protection philosophy. Hopefully, the justifications will be convincing so that a high level of consumer protection becomes accepted as the EU norm with Member States retaining the freedom to experiment within the broad framework established at the EU level.

Next steps

This chapter has provided the context for the discussion of specific areas of EU consumer law in the subsequent chapters. Each chapter will develop one or more of the themes discussed above in analysing a particular topic. The topics chosen for this book are the mainstream areas of EU consumer law: the regulation of unfair commercial practices, pre-contractual information and the right of withdrawal; unfair contract terms; sales contracts; consumer credit; product liability and safety; and enforcement and redress. A number of more specialist areas are not covered in-depth in this volume,[235] although reference is made to these where appropriate. The final concluding chapter will draw together the main strands of our discussion, and offer a number of pointers for the future development of EU consumer law, both in the context of its short-term focus on the challenges of the digital agenda and beyond.

234 C-243.08 *Pannon GSM Zrt. v Erzsébet Sustikné Győrfi* [2009] ECR I-4713.

235 Such as travel law (see e.g. JM Bech Serrat, 'Consumer travel law' in C Twigg-Flesner (ed) *Research Handbook on EU Consumer and Contract Law* (Edward Elgar, 2016)) or specialist financial services (see e.g. V Mak, 'Financial services and consumer protection' in the same *Research Handbook*).

2 Regulation of unfair commercial practices

Introduction

General

This chapter focuses on the way EU law regulates unfair commercial practices, i.e. the behaviour of traders towards consumers as regards the marketing of goods and services. This aspect of EU consumer law has had a lengthy gestation period, developing from the early case law of the CJEU in the context of the free movement of goods and the first directive on misleading advertising into the landmark directive on unfair commercial practices (UCPD) adopted in 2005.[1] Prior to the adoption of the UCPD, the EU had adopted directives on misleading[2] and comparative[3] advertising. Together, these directives had provided a good basis for the regulation of advertising throughout the EU. This had been done using minimum harmonisation. At the national level, there had been considerable variation in the way advertising, and fair trading generally, had been regulated.[4] The advertising directives were a first step towards a common set of rules, but fell short of the broader approach to fair trading rules found in some Member States.

In 2001, the European Commission published a *Green Paper on EU Consumer Protection*.[5] Its primary focus was on whether there should be broader regulation of trade practices at the EU level. In particular, the *Green Paper* mooted the possibility of a framework directive based around a general clause on fair commercial practices. Subsequently, the Commission confirmed its intention to proceed with such a framework directive,[6] and duly put forward its proposal for a directive on unfair commercial practices.[7] Alongside this proposal, the Commission also put

1 Directive 2005/29/EC on business-to-consumer unfair commercial practices (2005) OJ L149/22.
2 Directive 84/450/EEC on misleading advertising (1984) OJ L250/17.
3 Directive 97/55/EC on comparative advertising, amending Directive 84/450/EEC (1997) OJ L290/18.
4 For a useful summary, see G Howells, H-W Micklitz and T Wilhelmsson, *European Fair Trading Law* (Ashgate, 2006), Chapter 1.
5 COM (2001) 531 final.
6 European Commission, *Follow-up Communication on EU Consumer Law* (2002) 289 final.
7 COM (2003) 356 final.

forward a proposal for a regulation on sales promotions.[8] This overlapped with aspects of the proposal for the UPCD. The UCPD prevailed, and the sales promotion regulation was ultimately withdrawn.[9] The UCPD is noteworthy for several reasons. First, it is one of the first consumer law directives which is based on a maximum harmonisation standard. Second, at its heart is a broad general clause outlawing unfair commercial practices. This is supplemented by more specific clauses as well as a list of practices prohibited outright. Third, the UCPD explicitly utilises the average consumer concept which had already developed in the case law of the CJEU in the context of the free movement provisions,[10] albeit with modifications where commercial practices target specific groups of consumers or are likely to have detrimental impact on vulnerable consumers. These features of the UCPD make it a good example of EU consumer law to explore several of the themes considered in this book.[11]

Chapter themes

Maximum harmonisation

The UCPD is based on maximum harmonisation, and seeks to establish a single set of European rules for combatting unfair commercial practices. It came at a time when the EU was changing its philosophy to one in which consumer protection *per se* was less emphasised, and instead the role of consumer law harmonisation driving the single market came to the fore. Its success in this measure encouraged the Commission to start with the maximum harmonisation objective in other subsequent areas, but with mixed success. In contrast to many prior key EU consumer law directives, therefore, the UCPD removed the scope for the Member States to adopt or retain domestic legislation offering a higher level of consumer protection. In particular, as the UCPD contains a list of commercial practices prohibited outright, the ability of the Member States to prohibit other commercial practices has been pre-empted by the Directive. Non-prohibited practices need to be challenged under the general standards in the UCPD instead. Moreover, the maximum harmonisation nature of the UCPD has prompted a number of references to the CJEU to determine the compatibility of national legislation with the UPCD's maximum harmonisation standard. In particular, whilst the UCPD is intended to cover only business-to-consumer commercial practices, this does not mean that only those national laws concerned exclusively

8 COM (2001) 546 final.

9 See statement at (2006) OJ C64/3. The objective of the proposed sales promotion regulation was deregulatory in that it would have precluded Member States from introducing a range of restrictions.

10 Cf. A Johnston and H Unberath, 'The double-headed approach of the ECJ concerning consumer protection' (2007) 44 *Common Market Law Review* p.1237.

11 For a detailed analysis of the UCPD and its impact on key national laws, see B Keirsblick, *The New European Law of Unfair Commercial Practices and Competition Law* (Hart, 2011).

with business-to-consumer commercial practices are affected; several CJEU rulings have made it clear that the maximum harmonisation effect of the UCPD also touches national measures regulating commercial practices more generally, to the extent that these apply to business-to-consumer commercial practices. This consequence might not have been anticipated at the time of adopting the UCPD, and might be described as the Directive's 'Jack-in-the-box' effect. These issues will be explored fully in light of the body of case law which has been handed down by the CJEU. Despite this approach, the use of broad standards to ensure that the UCPD can be applied to newly-emerging practices means that questions arise as to how consistency of interpretation and application can be ensured across the EU. One tool deployed by the European Commission is a very detailed guidance document.[12]

Consumer – average consumer and vulnerable consumer

A second feature is that the UCPD is the first Directive which explicitly incorporates the average consumer yardstick into its provisions. Thus, whether a commercial practice is unfair depends on the effect, or likely effect, on the average consumer. This is, of course, a concept familiar from the CJEU's case law, particularly in the context of the free movement of goods provisions of the TFEU. The average consumer concept has been defined as a 'reasonably well-informed and reasonably observant and circumspect'[13] consumer, 'taking into account social, cultural and linguistic factors'.[14] This concept has not gone without criticism,[15] particularly because it seems to be a rather different image from the majority of consumers. It is doubtful whether empirical testing of the characteristics of an average consumer would conform to this norm. This has been recognised by the EU's legislature, and the UCPD therefore contains two modifications of the average consumer test: first, if a commercial practice is targeted at a particular group of consumers, then the average consumer is to be taken from that group; second, if a commercial practice is likely to affect consumers who are particularly vulnerable, then the fairness of the practice is to be assessed with reference to its impact on such vulnerable consumers. The explicit recognition of vulnerable consumers is an important feature of the UCPD, although it will be seen that the particular instantiation of the vulnerable consumer in this Directive is rather more limited: only a small number of categories of vulnerability are recognised.

12 Commission staff working document, *Guidance on the Implementation/Application of Directive 2005/29/EC on Unfair Commercial Practices* SWD (2016) 163 final, 25 May 2016.

13 Recital 18, UCPD, reflecting CJEU cases such as C-210/96 *Gut Springenheide GmbH and Rudolf Tusky v Oberkreisdirektor des Kreises Steinfurt – Amt für Lebensmittelüberwachung* (1998) ECR I-4657.

14 Recital 18, reflecting e.g. C-220/98 *Estee Lauder Cosmetics GmbH & Co. OHG v Lancaster Group GmbH* [2000] ECR I-117.

15 See discussion in Chapter 1, pp.27–31, and also below, pp.66–73.

Relationship with rest of acquis

The UCPD is a full-harmonisation directive which has both links and overlaps with other directives making up the EU's consumer *acquis*. In particular, there is some duplication with regard to the provision of information, relevant both under the UCPD and other directives.[16] However, there has been insufficient co-ordination between these directives and the UCPD, with the consequence that overlapping information duties are presented in different and not always consistent ways. Moreover, whilst the UCPD does not directly affect individual consumer contracts,[17] the existence of an unfair commercial practice can have a bearing both on contract formation and performance, but this has also not been considered appropriately by the EU legislature. This issue has arisen e.g. in the context of contract terms which could be regarded as both unfair under the Unfair Contract Terms Directive and qualify as unfair commercial practice.[18] The UCPD does not grant individual consumers any immediate rights to individual redress; instead, this is a matter left to domestic law. However, the overlap between the UCPD and other directives carves out some instances where individual redress might be available, albeit in an uncoordinated fashion. Greater alignment of the UCPD with other directives could certainly improve the overall coherence of EU consumer protection.

Role of the CJEU

Finally, the CJEU's role in the interpretation of the UCPD is interesting.[19] It is trite law that the CJEU's role is to interpret the law but not to apply it, but with the UCPD based on a full-harmonisation standard and utilising broad clauses to catch as many commercial practices as possible, there may be both a desire on the part of national courts for greater guidance from the CJEU and a temptation for the Court to stray into the application of the UPCD's rules to the facts of the particular case which has given rise to a reference under Art. 267 TFEU. There have been instances where the line between the respective responsibilities of the national courts and the CJEU has become blurred, with the CJEU providing a very strong steer to national courts as to how the relevant provisions of the UCPD could be applied to the facts of the case which led to a reference. On the one hand, there is a benefit in this in that it may be possible to extrapolate general points regarding the scope and application of the UCPD which could be of assistance to other courts and therefore promote greater consistency across the EU. On the other, it leaves the CJEU open to criticism that it has exceeded its responsibilities. If obtaining greater guidance from the CJEU is felt desirable,

16 See Chapter 3 on 'Information and withdrawal rights'.
17 Cf. Art. 3(2) UCPD.
18 Discussed more fully below.
19 J Stuyck, 'The Court of Justice and the Unfair Commercial Practices Directive' (2015) 52 *Common Market Law Review* pp.721–752 reviews the case law of the CJEU up to 2015.

then this should lead to a more fundamental reconsideration of the CJEU's role – whether limited to the field of consumer law, or more generally.

Overview of the UCPD

This section will present a general overview of the main provisions of the UPCD,[20] and will take into account relevant rulings by the CJEU on the interpretation of particular provisions.[21]

Commercial practices

The UCPD only applies to 'business-to-consumer commercial practices' which are defined in Art. 2(d) as 'any act, omission, course of conduct or representation, commercial communication including advertising and marketing, by a trader, directly connected with the promotion, sale or supply of a product to consumers'. There are a number of points to note about this definition. First, it covers both acts and omissions by a trader,[22] i.e. it can extend to a failure by a trader to do something. Second, whatever action or omission occurs has to relate to the promotion, sale or supply of the product, but it is not necessary that the trader who undertakes the commercial practice is the one who then supplies the product to the consumer – this can be someone further below in the supply chain.[23]

Third, the commercial practices must be 'directly connected with the promotion, sale or supply of a product'. 'Product' is defined broadly as 'any good or service, including immovable property, rights and obligations' (Art. 2 (c)). There is, however, some difficulty with the fact that the trader's commercial practice must be 'directly connected with the promotion, sale or supply' of the product. It clearly covers any actions or omissions leading up to the conclusion of a contract (or the decision not to conclude a contract), but it is not entirely clear from this definition whether it extends to matters arising after a contract has been concluded, i.e. during its performance or at the time of renewal. However, in light

20 See also J Stuyck, E Terryn and T van Dyck, 'Confidence through fairness? The new Directive on Unfair Business-to-Consumer Commercial Practices in the Internal Market' (2005) 43 *Common Market Law Review* p.107.

21 See also W van Boom, 'Unfair commercial practices' in C Twigg-Flesner (ed), *Research Handbook on EU Consumer and Contract Law* (Cheltenham, Edward Elgar, 2016).

22 'Trader' is defined as 'any natural or legal person who, in commercial practices covered by this Directive, is acting for purposes which are outside his trade, business, craft or profession' (Art. 2(b)). The definition extends to public law bodies charged with a task of public interest: C-59/12 *BKK Mobil Oil Körperschaft des öffentlichen Rechts v Zentrale zur Bekämpfung unlauteren Wettbewerbs eV.* ECLI:EU:C:2013:634.

23 In commenting on a draft of the UCPD, the UK's Law Commissions highlighted the significance of the comma after 'trader' in this regard: see Law Commission, *Simplifying Consumer Legislation – a Response from the Law Commission to the DTI's Consultative Document on Consumer Strategy* (October 2004), p.21 and note 24.

of Art. 3, which states that the Directive applies to commercial practices 'before during and after a commercial transaction in relation to a product', it seems that the UCPD applies to all stages of a transaction.

It will be obvious that the notion of 'commercial practice' is extremely broad, essentially covering the full range of ways in which a trader deals with a consumer. As will be explained below, the UCPD includes a list of commercial practices which are always regarded as unfair, as well as broad prohibitions against misleading and aggressive practices. However, despite the broad and flexible notion of 'commercial practice', there may still be doubt at times whether a particular type of conduct by a trader qualifies as a commercial practice. Since the UCPD became law, there have been a significant number of requests for a preliminary ruling on the interpretation of the Directive to the CJEU. Although the role of the CJEU in the context of Art. 267 TFEU proceedings should be confined to providing guidance on the *interpretation* of the various provisions of the UCPD, the court has adopted a tendency towards applying the definition of commercial practice from Art. 2(d) in considering whether in the case before it, the UCPD would be applicable at all. Many of these cases were concerned with the compatibility of national rules prohibiting specific commercial practices with the maximum harmonisation standard of the UCPD.

In *VTB-VAB NV v Total Belgium NV*,[24] the CJEU noted the 'particularly wide definition to the concept of commercial practice' in Art. 2(d).[25] That definition covers 'commercial acts which clearly form part of an operator's commercial strategy and related directly to the promotion thereof and its sales development'.[26] Crucially, the practices 'must be commercial in nature, that is to say, they must originate from traders and they must be directly connected with the promotion, sale or supply of their products to consumers.'[27] There has to be a clear link between the trader's commercial practice and the products supplied by that trader. In *RLvS Verlagsgesellschaft mbH v Stuttgarter Wochenblatt GmbH*.[28] a newspaper had included several sections, which had been sponsored by another trader to advertise that trader's products. They had not been identified clearly as advertisements by the newspaper, as required under state law in Germany. Another newspaper publisher complained about this, and the question arose whether the state law was compatible with the UCPD. The CJEU concluded that the UCPD was not applicable, because the newspaper itself had not engaged in a commercial practice in this

24 Joined cases C-261/07 *VTB-VAB Belgium NV v Total Belgium NV* and C-299/07 *Galatea BVBA v Sanoma Magazines Belgium NV* ECLI:EU:C:2009:244.

25 Ibid., para [49].

26 Ibid., para [50].

27 C-391/12 *RLvS Verlagsgesellschaft mbH v Stuttgarter Wochenblatt GmbH*, ECLI:EU:C:2013:669, para [37].

28 C-391/12 *RLvS Verlagsgesellschaft mbH v Stuttgarter Wochenblatt GmbH* ECLI:EU:C:2013:669

instance – the sponsored pages were not promoting the newspaper itself. The various promotional activities by third parties found inside a newspaper are, in the CJEU's view, unlikely to affect a consumer's decision whether to acquire the newspaper itself.[29]

Moreover, the notion of 'commercial practice' does not envisage a particular course of conduct; it is sufficient that the action of a trader takes place once and only affects one consumer to be regarded as a commercial practice.[30]

From the various preliminary rulings handed down, it can be seen that the following are regarded as commercial practices which fall within the scope of the UCPD:

- combined offers (where the right to acquire goods or services on certain conditions depends on the purchase of other goods or services, such as buying petrol to obtain free breakdown cover[31] or a magazine containing a discount voucher for a store[32]);[33]
- participation in a lottery or prize draw which is conditional on buying goods or services;[34]
- sales with free advantages/bonuses;[35]
- price reductions;[36]
- announcements of price reductions during periods preceding specific sales periods;[37]
- selling goods at a loss;[38]
- announcement of a clearance sale;[39]
- a travel agency advertising the exclusive availability of certain hotels;[40]

29 Ibid., para [41].

30 C-388/13 *Nemzeti Fogyasztovedelmi Hatosag v UPC Magyarorszag Kft.* ECLI:EU:C:2015:225.

31 C-261/07 *VTB-VAB NV v Total Belgium NV* ECLI:EU:C:2009:244.

32 C-299/07 *Galatea BVBA v Sanoma Magazines Belgium NV* ECLI:EU:C:2007:484.

33 See also C-522/08 *Telekomunikacja Polska SA w Warszawie v Prezes Urzedu Komunikacji Elektronicznej* ECLI:EU:C:2010:135.

34 C-304/08 *Zentrale zur Bekämpfung unlauteren Wettbewerbs e V v Plus Warenhandelsgesellschaft* ECLI:EU:C:2010:12.

35 C-540/08 *Mediaprint Zeitungs- und Zeitschriftenverlag GmbH & Co. KG v 'Österreich'-Zeitungsverlag GmBH* ECLI:EU:C:2010:660.

36 C-13/15 *Cdiscount* ECLI:EU:C:2015:560.

37 C-288/10 *Wamo BVBA v JBS NV, Modemakers Fashion NV* ECLI:EU:C:2011:443 . Belgian law stipulated specific sales periods for January and July for the clothing, fine leather and footwear sectors and prohibited price reductions during the seven weeks before these periods. See also C-126/11 *INNO NV v Unie van Zelfstandige Ondernemers and others* ECLI:EU:C:2011:851, dealing with the same issue.

38 C-343/12 *Euronics Belgium CVBA v Kamera Express BV* ECLI:EU:C:2013:154.

39 C-206/11 *Georg Köck v Schutzverband gegen unlauteren Wettbewerb* ECLI:EU:C:2013:14.

40 C-435/11 *CHS Tour Services GmbH v Team4 Travel GmbH* ECLI:EU:C:2013:574.

- communication of information in the context of after-sales service relating to a subscription;[41]
- indicating an APR on a loan lower than the real rate.[42]

All of these are instances where the CJEU has applied the definition of 'commercial practice' to the particular practice in issue in the case which prompted a reference. This was done because the national courts had referred questions about the relationship of the UCPD with national legislation addressing particular practices. In order to consider whether there was a conflict between the UCPD and national law, the CJEU first had to establish whether the practice dealt with in the national legislation fell within the UCPD's definition of commercial practices. Once this had been established, the CJEU proceeded to consider the compatibility of national law with the maximum harmonisation mandate of the UCPD.

Outright prohibitions

The UCPD approaches the prohibition of unfair commercial practices in three stages, which are best understood as moving from particular to general assessment; there are some practices which are prohibited outright, and these are listed in Annex I of the Directive.[43] There are then specific prohibitions of misleading actions and omissions as well as aggressive commercial practices, and finally a general clause which effectively operates as a safety net to catch unfair commercial practices neither listed in the Annex nor the more specific prohibitions.

The commercial practices listed in Annex I are regarded as unfair in all circumstances,[44] and there is no need to consider the additional requirements for establishing unfairness which are relevant to the specific or general prohibitions. If a trader engages in a practice which is listed in Annex I, then the mere fact that the action has been undertaken will be sufficient. As will be explored more fully later, the maximum harmonisation nature of the UCPD means that Member States are precluded from prohibiting outright any commercial practices not listed in Annex I, a matter which has prompted a high volume of CJEU cases.

Annex I lists 31 unfair commercial practices, grouped into 'misleading commercial practices' and 'aggressive commercial practices', which corresponds with the specific treatment of misleading and aggressive behaviour in Arts. 6–9 UCPD, discussed below. There are 23 misleading practices, and 8 aggressive practices. The classification of particular commercial practices under these headings is not always convincing – for example, item 27 regards as an aggressive commercial practice 'requiring a consumer who wishes to claim on an insurance policy to

41 C-388/13 *Nemzeti Fogyasztovedelmi Hatosag v UPC Magyarorszag Kft.* ECLI:EU:C:2015:225.
42 C-453/10 *Jana Pereničová and Vladislav Perenič v SOS financ spol. s r. o.* ECLI:EU:C:2012:144.
43 See also the appendix to this chapter.
44 Art. 5(5) UCPD.

produce documents which could not reasonably be considered relevant as to whether the claim was valid ...' – certainly a frustrating practice, but not particularly aggressive. One might wonder whether it matters that a practice listed in Annex I has been classified as misleading or aggressive or whether the fact that the practice listed is to be regarded as inherently unfair and therefore always prohibited without requiring examination on a case-by-case basis is crucial. However, the CJEU's ruling in *Purely Creative v OFT*[45] suggest it may be. This case was concerned with the prohibition in point 31 of Annex I which prohibits:

> Creating the false impression that the consumer has already won, will win, or will on doing a particular act win, a prize or other equivalent benefit, when in fact either:
>
> - there is no prize or other equivalent benefit,
>   or
> - taking any action in relation to claiming the prize or other equivalent benefit is subject to the consumer paying money or incurring a cost.

Purely Creative (and others) had run various promotional activities in which consumers received various forms of communications stating that they were entitled to claim a prize from a range of low-value to one prize of considerable value. These prizes were genuinely available but in order to claim a prize, a consumer had to call a premium telephone line, use reverse SMS text messaging or use the ordinary post. Consumers were encouraged to use the premium-rate phone line, and phone calls took several minutes; in addition, consumers also had to incur additional charges for delivery and insurance. Action was taken by the OFT and the Court of Appeal requested a preliminary ruling on two issues: first, whether the prohibition was infringed even if the cost to the consumer is *de minimis*; and second, whether the word 'false impression' is an additional requirement to the obligation to pay money or incur a cost to claim the prize. On the second point, the CJEU swiftly explained that 'false impression' was not a separate requirement and that the false impression arose from the fact that a prize was not truly free when the consumer had to make a payment. The CJEU referred to the classification of the prohibition in point 31 as 'aggressive' as rendering irrelevant whether the commercial practice had a misleading character, and that the aggressive features of the particular practice were the result of the 'psychological effect created in the mind of the consumer by the perspective of having won something and to cause him to take a decision which is not always rational'.[46] This suggests that the way commercial practices have been grouped in Annex I does have a bearing on how these should be interpreted. On the first issue, the

45 C-428/11 *Purely Creative Ltd and Others v Office of Fair Trading* ECLI:EU:C:2012:651.
46 Ibid., para [49].

CJEU's conclusions were that any payment or cost, even if *de minimis*, was prohibited. This was so even where a consumer had a range of options for claiming the prize, one of which was free of charge, because the psychological effect is such that a consumer is more likely to choose the quickest method for discovering which prize has been won, even if that method is the most expensive.[47] The CJEU further explained that the way the prize is described is important and that it is necessary to distinguish between information about the prize itself and the steps needed to claim it.[48] The prohibition in point 31 only relates to the latter, which means that prize should not be described as 'free' if the consumer has to incur expenses in claiming it. However, by making it clear what the prize entails, a trader can avoid falling foul of point 31. The onus is on the trader to ensure that the description of the prize is unequivocal and that it must be clear what is included in the prize and what is not.[49] Otherwise some costs may be deemed to be costs related to claiming the prize. The CJEU gave the following example to illustrate this: 'a prize defined as an 'entrance ticket' for a certain football match does not include the transport of the consumer from his home to the football stadium where the match takes place. On the other hand, if the prize is stated simply to be 'attendance' at that sports event, the trader must bear the costs of the consumer's travel'.[50] The clarity of this information is tested against the average member of the group of consumers targeted by the practice. The assumption here is that a consumer should be able to tell from the prize description which costs are covered and which costs need to be incurred, e.g. in the case of a cruise, the need to travel to the port of departure.

A number of observations can be made on this case. First, it illustrates that the prohibition of certain commercial practices throughout the EU brings with it the risk that traders might seek to circumvent the prohibition, unless the prohibition is clear and comprehensive. The traders in this case sought to do so by having one *de minimis* or free way of finding out about the prize, but this option was firmly closed-off by the CJEU. It underlines how important it is that any outright prohibitions are clear and do not leave any room for debate about what is covered. This might not prevent some traders from deploying arguments that their actions do not quite fall within the prohibitions (as the traders in *Purely Creative* attempted), but that CJEU decision and general approach should make it easy to dismiss such arguments.

The need for clarity of such outright prohibitions also necessitates careful translation of the UCPD into the various official languages of the EU to ensure that the requirements of the prohibition are consistent. A variation between different language versions was an issue in *'4finance' UAB*,[51] a case involving a pyramid

47 Ibid., para [50].
48 Ibid., para [51].
49 Ibid., para [53].
50 Ibid., para [52].
51 C-515/12 *'4finance' UAB v Valstybinė vartotojų teisių apsaugos tarnyba and Valstybinė mokesčių inspekcija prie Lietuvos Respublikos finansų ministerijos* ECLI:EU:C:2014:211.

scheme prohibited by point 14 of Annex I. The English language version, with which most other language versions were consistent, prohibits

> Establishing, operating or promoting a pyramid promotional scheme where a consumer *gives consideration* for the opportunity to receive compensation that is derived primarily from the introduction of other consumers into the scheme rather than from the sale or consumption of products. (italics added)

The German version, with which the Lithuanian version corresponds, says

> Einführung, Betrieb oder Förderung eines Schneeballsystems zur Verkaufsförderung, bei dem der Verbraucher die Möglichkeit vor Augen hat, eine Vergütung zu erzielen, die hauptsächlich durch die Einführung neuer Verbraucher in ein solches System und weniger durch den Verkauf oder Verbrauch von Produkten zu erzielen ist.

The words in italics in the English version do not have an equivalent in the German version. The CJEU was therefore asked whether the provision of consideration by consumers participating in the scheme was essential. In the CJEU's view, three cumulative conditions are required: (i) there is a promise that a consumer will receive a commercial advantage; (ii) the realisation of the promise requires that more and more consumers join the scheme; and (iii) the greater part of the payments made to consumers are not the result of an economic activity.[52] The Court noted that such schemes are based on money being contributed by new entrants which is used to pay compensation to earlier members, and that consequently some financial contribution (consideration) is required.[53] However, there was no minimum amount required – even 1 cent would suffice. In the case itself, the payments made to existing members were only in a very small part based on financial contributions made by new entrants (and therefore not 'derived primarily from the introduction of other consumers into the scheme'),[54] which meant that the particular scheme was not caught by point 14 at all and instead had to be assessed under the general prohibition in Art. 5. The CJEU has subsequently added to this by holding that there will be a pyramid scheme even if there is only an indirect link between the contributions paid by new members and any payments made to existing members ('compensation').[55]

Both *Purely Creative* and *'4finance' UAB* demonstrate that the outright prohibitions in Annex I are given a literal interpretation. This means that no additional

52 Ibid., para [20].

53 Ibid., para [22].

54 As required by point 14 of Annex I, or the third element mentioned in the CJEU's judgment at para [20].

55 C-667/15 *Loterie Nationale – Nationale Loterij NV van publiek recht v Paul Adriaensen and Others* ECLI:EU:C:2016:958. This case concerned a pyramid scheme which enabled

elements other than those in the wording of each prohibition itself may be considered before concluding that there has been an infringement; on the other hand, such literal interpretation also entails that practices which do not satisfy all of the elements in an outright prohibition will not automatically be unfair and need to be assessed on a case-by-case basis. This matter is particularly important when it comes to the extent of UCPD's maximum harmonisation standard.

The specific prohibitions

The specific clauses on misleading and aggressive practices and the general clause raise a number of issues which are briefly explored at this stage. The most complex provision is the general clause prohibiting unfair commercial practices in Art. 5. Before these prohibitions are examined further, it needs to be emphasised that a number of factors have no bearing on whether a commercial practice falls to be considered as unfair. Thus, Article 11 UCPD which deals with enforcement (see below) states that it is irrelevant whether the trader acted intentionally or negligently in engaging in an unfair commercial practice (to which one can add 'innocently'). The mere fact that the practice satisfies the criteria to be considered as unfair suffices. Similarly, it is not necessary to show that consumer(s) have suffered any loss or damage as a result of the unfair commercial practice. This can in some instances be unfortunate where a commercial practice qualifies as unfair at a technical level; for example, in *Nemzeti Fogyasztovedelmi Hatosag*,[56] a trader provided the wrong date on which a subscription agreement was due for renewal (typing '02' rather than '01' for the month) which caused a consumer to be liable for an additional charge. This was deemed to be an unfair commercial practice. The CJEU emphasised that there is no minimum threshold in terms of the frequency of the action or number of consumers affected,[57] and that it is irrelevant that it was unintentional.[58] In short, the UCPD operates with a strict liability approach which is only concerned with the fact that a particular commercial practice is caught by the criteria for unfairness.

The following discussion will first explain the elements of the general clause in Art. 5, before turning to the specific clause on misleading actions, omissions and aggressive practices. In most cases, a particular commercial practice is likely to be covered by the specific clauses, and the general clause will be a safety net to cover

participants to play the Belgian national lottery together. Any payments made to members would depend on winnings received by the scheme, rather than contributions made by new participants. The chances of winning increased with the numbers of participants introduced. This could constitute an indirect link sufficient for the scheme to be caught by point 14 (cf. para [32] of the judgment).

56 C-388/13 *Nemzeti Fogyasztovedelmi Hatosag v UPC Magyarorszag Kft.* ECLI:EU:C:2015:225.

57 Ibid., para [45]. For a critical discussion of this very broad reading, see B Keirsblick, 'The UCPD's notion of commercial practice' (2016) 53 *Common Market Law Review* p.527.

58 Ibid., para [47].

all the remaining commercial practices. However, as the general clause underpins the whole of the UCPD, it is appropriate to consider this first.

The general clause (Article 5)

The core of the UCPD is the general clause in Art. 5, which contains the general prohibition of unfair commercial practices as well as the criteria to be applied in assessing the fairness of a particular commercial practice. Article 5 is supplemented by more specific prohibitions in Arts. 6–8. Consequently, the main function of Art. 5 is to act as a safety net for commercial practices which are not caught by Arts. 6–8 nor by the list of prohibited practices in Annex I. A number of elements make up the prohibition in Art. 5 but, as discussed below, these elements are not relevant to applying the more specific prohibitions in Arts. 6–8.

Art. 5(1) opens with the straightforward statement that unfair commercial practices are prohibited, but this raises the question of how one determines when a commercial practice should be regarded as unfair. Art. 5(2) therefore sets out the criteria for establishing unfairness. The first is that the commercial practice is 'contrary to the requirements of professional diligence'. The notion of professional diligence is defined in Art. 2(h) as the 'the standard of special skill and care which a trader may reasonably be expected to exercise towards consumers, commensurate with honest market practice and/or the general principle of good faith in the trader's field of activity'.

In order to consider whether a trader's practices fail to meet this standard, several matters have to be considered; generally, it refers to a 'standard of *special* skill and care' which presumably merely stresses the fact that a trader's actions are measured against the particular skills and care expected of a trader rather than persons generally, i.e. a higher threshold. Moreover, the reference point is what would be regarded as honest market practice in the trader's field of activity. Although one might fear that this could set a low expectation for traders in sectors where standards are low, the emphasis on 'honest' practices provides a normative point against which to assess a trader's conduct. The explicit inclusion of 'good faith' adds a further normative element to the notion of 'professional diligence'. A trader deliberately treating a consumer unfairly cannot be acting in good faith, but even inadvertent unfair treatment might be regarded as contrary to good faith. Although the scope of the good faith criterion is left vague, one may assume that it covers both the need for a trader to be transparent in his dealings with a consumer, and to take the interests of a consumer into account. For instance, in *Deroo Blanquart v Sony*,[59] the CJEU mentioned as relevant considerations the fact that 'the consumer was correctly informed'[60] and that the trader's actions 'met the expectations of a significant proportion

59 Cf. C-310/15 *Vincent Deroo-Blanquart v Sony Europe Ltd.* ECLI:EU:C:2016:633.
60 Ibid., para [37].

of consumers'.[61] These factors relate to both transparency and regard for the consumer's interests.

If the actions of a trader are found to be contrary to professional diligence, then the second element to show is that the commercial practice in question materially distorts (or is likely to materially distort) the economic behaviour of the average consumer who is subject to the commercial practice. This is defined in Art. 2(e) as appreciably impairing a consumer's ability to make an informed decision which causes a consumer to take a transactional decision he would not have taken otherwise. 'Transactional decision' is defined in Art. 2(k) as a decision to act or not to act with regard to making a purchase or payment, keeping or disposing of a product or exercising a contractual right in respect of a product – in other words, any decision which is connected to a product. The CJEU has confirmed that a transactional decision is any decision 'directly related to the decision whether or not to purchase a product',[62] something which includes 'in particular, the decision to enter into a shop'.[63]

The consumer notion in the UCPD is discussed below. For present purposes, it should be noted that the inclusion of the average consumer standard makes this an objective test: the economic behaviour of an average consumer determines whether the commercial practice is unfair, rather than the fact that a particular individual consumer was affected adversely by the trader's practices. This standard can be modified where a particular group of consumers is targeted by the practice, or where the commercial practice is likely to affect only a group of consumers who are particularly vulnerable.

The nature of this general prohibition in Art. 5 is such that it is rather open-ended as it needs to cover a wide range of situations. National courts handling a case which cannot be dealt with under more specific general provisions (discussed below) might therefore be concerned that their view on how the prohibition should apply to a specific practice might not be shared by the CJEU and other national courts. This could be seen to reduce the maximum harmonisation effect of the UPCD, a matter explored more fully later in this chapter. Here, it is important to recall that the CJEU's role is to provide guidance on the interpretation of the various components of the prohibition, rather than to advise a national court as to the application of the law to the specific case before it.[64] Although many of the cases involving the UCPD decided by the CJEU contain clear statements requiring national courts to form a final view on the facts of the case, there are instances where the CJEU has offered quite detailed guidance.

61 Ibid.

62 C-281/12 *Trento Sviluppo srl, Centrale Adriatico Soc. Coop. arl v Autorita Garante della Concorrenza e del Mercato* ECLI:EU:C:2013:859.

63 Ibid., para [36].

64 Cf. the case law under the Unfair Contract Terms Directive, dealing with the fairness test. Chapter 4.

This was particularly so in *Deroo-Blanquart v Sony*.[65] In this – somewhat strange – case a consumer, who had bought a laptop with pre-installed software, argued that the fact that the laptop was not available without preinstalled software was an unfair commercial practice. The French Cour de Cassation referred a number of questions on the UCPD to the CJEU, including whether the sale of a laptop combined with pre-installed software would be an unfair commercial practice under Art. 5(2). Rather than merely offering general guidance on the notions of 'professional diligence' and 'material distortion', the CJEU provided rather detailed guidance on the factual elements that might need to be considered in this case. Thus, with regard to professional diligence, the CJEU noted that market analysis indicated that most consumers prefer computers with pre-installed software, that the consumer was informed that there was pre-installed software on the laptop, and that the consumer was given the choice to cancel the purchase when he did not wish to accept the licence conditions of the pre-installed software.[66] Taken together, these factors 'are likely to satisfy the requirements of honest market practices or of the principle of good faith in the field of the manufacturing of computer equipment for the general public'.[67] Although the CJEU acknowledges that the final decision is for the national court, there is a very clear steer coming from the CJEU in applying Art. 5(2) to the facts of the particular case. Similarly, the CJEU considered whether the fact that a laptop was offered for sale only with pre-installed software had the effect of undermining the ability of a consumer to make an informed decision. Again, the Court provided strong guidance to the national court, observing that the court should consider:

> in circumstances such as those at issue in the main proceedings, namely when a consumer has been duly informed, prior to the purchase, that the model of computer that is the subject matter of the sale was not marketed without pre-installed software and that he was therefore, in principle, free to choose another model of computer, or another brand, with similar technical specifications, sold without software or used with different software, the ability of that consumer to make an informed transactional decision was appreciably impaired.[68]

Perhaps the reason why the CJEU gave such a strong steer to the national court was due to the fact that the consumer's claim seemed to lack sufficient merit to have gone this far. Whilst this might be acceptable in this particular instance, it is important for the CJEU not to stray too far into applying the provisions of the UCPD to the particular facts of the case giving rise to a reference, not

65 C-310/15 *Vincent Deroo-Blanquart v Sony Europe Ltd.* ECLI:EU:C:2016:633.
66 At para [35]. This information was provided to the CJEU by the national court as part of the request for a preliminary ruling.
67 Para [37].
68 Para [41].

least because the national court's order for reference might not contain sufficient information to do so (although in *Deroo-Blanquart*, this was not an issue).

The specific prohibitions

As will be apparent, the general clause in Art. 5 is very broad and its various ingredients comprise multiple open-ended standards. There are therefore more specific prohibitions which deal with the most common types of unfair commercial practices:[69] misleading actions and omissions, as well as aggressive commercial practices.

Before considering these further, it can be noted that, unlike Art. 5, the specific prohibitions in Arts. 6–9 do not require that the trader must be acting contrary to the 'professional diligence' test. The European Commission, in its Explanatory Memorandum to the proposal for the Directive, stated that misleading (and aggressive) practices are contrary to professional diligence which made it unnecessary to show explicitly that the actions by a trader breached the professional diligence requirement.[70] This was confirmed by the CJEU in *CHS Tour Services v Team4 Travel*.[71] Team4 Travel, an Austrian company selling skiing trips for schoolchildren from the UK, had negotiated an exclusive arrangement with several hotels. Those hotels subsequently entered into agreements for accommodation with *CHS*, a company providing the same service as Team4, and these agreements were a breach of contract between the hotels and Team4. CHS subsequently complained that Team4's brochure claiming exclusivity in respect of these hotels was an unfair commercial practice because that information was misleading by virtue of Art. 6(1)(b) UPCD.[72] Team4 argued that it had acted with due professional diligence at the time the brochures were printed and published as it was not aware at that time of the breach of contract by the hotels. The lower courts agreed with Team4, but the Austrian Supreme Court requested a preliminary ruling on whether it was permissible to consider professional diligence when applying the specific prohibitions. The CJEU noted that a commercial practice which fulfils the criteria in Arts. 6–9 is categorised as unfair by virtue of Art. 5(4) UCPD, rendering the general criteria in Art. 5(2) irrelevant.[73] Furthermore, the misleading nature of a commercial practice arises once the criteria in Art. 6 are met, with no consideration of any other factors.[74]

The CJEU's ruling in *CHS Tour Services* is not surprising and is consistent with the overall scheme of the UCPD – the broad general clause in Art. 5 is supplemented by more specific prohibitions in Arts. 6–9 which deal with particular

69 Art. 5(4) UCPD.
70 COM (2003) 356 final, para 56.
71 C-435/11 *CHS Tour Services GmbH v Team4 Travel GmBH* ECLI:EU:C:2013:574.
72 This Article stipulates that information about the main characteristics of a product includes its availability.
73 At para [39].
74 Para [42]. See also C-388/13 *Nemzeti Fogyasztovedelmi Hatosag v UPC Magyarorszag Kft.* ECLI:EU:C:2015:225.

kinds of commercial practice. However, on the facts of this particular case, the outcome could be detrimental to a trader who has done everything reasonable to ensure that no unfair commercial practice has been committed.[75] It is possible for national law to take this into account when determining how to respond to a finding that the trader's commercial practice is unfair – for example, the severity of any sanctions might be reduced in light of the trader's care in trying to avoid the fact that an unfair commercial practice has been committed. Moreover, national law might treat a claim such as the one brought by CHS with a degree of disdain – e.g. by applying general requirements of good faith (where available) or abuse of process rules. Indeed, the fact that the UCPD leaves the conditions of enforcement to the Member States (see below) places the onus on each Member State to consider the range of appropriate sanctions when it is established that an unfair commercial practice exists. In this regard, the CJEU has stated clearly that

> it is for the Member States to provide for an appropriate system of sanctions…while ensuring that those sanctions comply, in particular, with the principle of proportionality. It is in this context that due account could be taken of factors such as the frequency of the practice complained of, whether or not it is intentional, and the degree of harm caused to the consumer.[76]

On the other hand, as explained above, the UCPD operates with a strict liability approach which does not allow for inadvertence or the fact that there was only a single infringement to affect a finding of unfairness. This will be the case even where, for instance, a consumer could have discovered that the information was incorrect.[77] Perhaps at national level, the strictness of this approach could be mitigated by making available a defence to a trader that he had acted with all the necessary care in conducting the commercial practices. This would not affect the finding that the trader's conduct amounted to an unfair commercial practice, but could reduce or eliminate the application of the penalties otherwise envisaged under national law.[78] The CJEU's emphasis on proportionate sanctions would certainly indicate that a low penalty or a purely notional sanction might be imposed in instances such as that giving rise to *CHS Tour Services*.

75 Stuyck has described the ruling as 'severe': J Stuyck, 'The Court of Justice and the Unfair Commercial Practices Directive' (2015) 52 *Common Market Law Review* pp.721–752, at p.737.

76 C-388/13 *Nemzeti Fogyasztovedelmi Hatosag v UPC Magyarorszag Kft.*, ECLI:EU:C:2015:225 para [58].

77 Cf. C-388/13 *Nemzeti Fogyasztovedelmi Hatosag v UPC Magyarorszag Kft.*, ECLI:EU:C:2015:225 para [54].

78 For example, UK law makes available a 'due diligence' defence as part of its provisions on criminal enforcement of the national legislation giving effect to the UCPD. See Reg. 17 of the Consumer Protection from Unfair Trading Regulations 2008 (S.I. 2008/1277).

PROHIBITION OF MISLEADING COMMERCIAL PRACTICES (ARTICLES 6 AND 7)

Two types of misleading actions are prohibited by Art. 6(1): (i) a commercial practice containing false information which is therefore untruthful; or (ii) a commercial practice which in any way, including overall presentation, deceives or is likely to deceive the average consumer, even if the information is factually correct, in relation to a number of specified categories of information. There are seven categories of information referred to in Art. 6(1): the existence or nature of the product; its main characteristics;[79] the extent of trader's commitments, motives for the commercial practices and the nature of the sales process as well as any statement or symbol in relation to direct or indirect sponsorship or approval of the trader or the product; price or the manner in which the price is calculated, or the existence of a specific price advantage;[80] need for service, part, replacement or repair; nature, attributes and rights of the trader or his agent; and consumer's rights or risks he may face.

For either type of misleading action, the information must cause, or be likely to cause, the average consumer to take a transactional decision he would not have taken otherwise.[81]

In addition to these broad types of misleading actions there are more specific types of misleading actions in Art. 6(2). These practices which, in their factual setting, cause or are likely to cause a consumer to take a transactional decision he would not have taken otherwise are:

a Marketing, including comparative advertising, creating confusion with products, trade marks, trade names and other distinguishing marks of a competitor
b Non-compliance with commitments in a code of conduct the trader has undertaken to follow, provided that:

 i The commitment is not aspirational but firm and verifiable; and
 ii The trader has indicated in a commercial practice that he is bound by the code.

In addition to these types of misleading action, Art. 7 also regards as an unfair commercial practice an omission to provide information. This applies, where, in the factual context and taking account of limitations of the means of communication used, material information which the average consumer needs to take an informed transactional decision is not provided. If the consumer takes, or is likely to take, a transactional decision he would not have taken otherwise, then this constitutes a prohibited practice. An 'omission' includes circumstances where the

79 See Art. 6(1)(b) for relevant aspects.

80 See also C-611/14 *Criminal proceedings against Canal Digital Danmark A/S* ECLI:EU:C:2016:800, where the CJEU suggested that it would be misleading to separate a price into several components and focus marketing on one of those (here, a monthly fee of DKK 99 was given prominence but a half-yearly DKK389 charge was barely mentioned).

81 This was confirmed by the CJEU in Case C-281/12 *Trento Sviluppo srl, Centrale Adriatico Soc. Coop. arl v Autorita Garante della Concorrenza e del Mercato* ECLI:EU:C:2013:859.

information is hidden, or provided in an unclear, unintelligible, ambiguous or untimely manner or fails to identify the commercial intent of the practice if not apparent from the context (Art. 7(2)). One qualification is that the information in question must be 'material'. Greater precision of what is 'material' is given in two instances. It includes information that has to be provided in accordance with existing EU legislation (a non-exhaustive list of which is in Annex II).[82] Where the commercial practice qualifies as an invitation to purchase, Art. 7(4) specifies the information that is regarded as material (primarily about the characteristic of the product, details relating to the trader, price, payment and delivery, and the existence of a right of withdrawal).[83] An 'invitation to purchase' is defined as 'a commercial communication which indicates characteristics of the product and the price in a way appropriate to the means of the commercial communication used and thereby enables the consumer to make a purchase.'[84]

The meaning of this definition was considered by the CJEU in *Konsumentombudsmannen v Ving Sverige AB*,[85] which concerned an advertisement in a Swedish newspaper for trips to the USA. The advertisement only indicated the starting price and did not provide full details of the trip. The Konsumentombudsmannen argued that this was a breach of the national rules implementing Art. 7(4) UCPD. The CJEU first considered the point at which a commercial communication should be treated as an invitation to purchase and consequently be subject to the requirements of Art. 7(4), in particular, whether such a commercial communication had to include an actual opportunity to place an order or whether the fact that information about the product and its price was sufficient for a consumer to make a decision on whether to purchase was enough for it to qualify as an invitation to treat. The CJEU held that the definition should be given a 'non-restrictive'[86] interpretation to ensure a high level of consumer protection. Moreover, the word 'thereby' in the definition was to be interpreted not as adding an additional requirement. Rather, the information about the product and its price was sufficient to allow a consumer to make a decision. Consequently, the inclusion of an actual opportunity to make a purchase was not required for the commercial communication to be regarded as an invitation to treat. The CJEU further commented on the amount of detail about the price and product required, holding that it could be sufficient to provide the entry-level price where a product was available at different prices for different versions of the product. Similarly, a visual or verbal reference to indicate a product's main characteristics (such as a close-up picture) could be sufficient to meet the

82 Art. 7(5) UCPD.
83 However, compliance with Art. 7(4) UCPD does not preclude a finding that a commercial practice is misleading under Art. 6(1) or Art. 7(2) UCPD: C-611/14 *Criminal proceedings against Canal Digital Danmark A/S* ECLI:EU:C:2016:800.
84 Article 2(i) UCPD.
85 C-122/10 *Konsumentombudsmannen v Ving Sverige AB* ECLI:EU:C:2011:299.
86 Ibid., para [30].

requirements of the definition of 'invitation to purchase'. However, in respect of both, this depended on the medium of communication used as well as whether the information provided was sufficient to enable a consumer to make a transactional decision. From this ruling, it seems that a commercial communication qualified as an 'invitation to purchase' as soon as the information about price and characteristics of the product were sufficient for a consumer to decide on whether to make a purchase. For a trader, it is important therefore to consider how much detail to include in a commercial communication, because once it is regarded as an 'invitation to purchase', the requirements of Art. 7(4) must be complied with.

The CJEU was further asked about the detail of information that needs to be included in the 'invitation to purchase' to comply with Art. 7(4). For example, Art. 7(4)(a) requires information about the main characteristics of a product, which, depending on the nature of the product, might have to be quite detailed. The CJEU accepted that it could be sufficient if certain main characteristics were given in the communication together with a reference to the trader's website where all the required information was provided, taking into account the context of the invitation to purchase, the medium of communication used and the nature and characteristics of the product.[87] Similarly, it might be sufficient to comply with the requirements as to price in Art. 7(4)(c) if an entry-level price only is given, but again, this would depend on the nature of the product and also require consideration of whether the omission of any indication of how the final price would be calculated would prevent a consumer from taking an informed transactional decision.[88] On the other hand, where a subscription payment includes both a monthly charge and a six-monthly charge, giving undue prominence to the former and barely mentioning the latter is likely to be misleading.[89]

One thing that becomes immediately apparent from considering this particular ruling is a seeming desire on the part of the CJEU to balance the need for a high level of consumer protection with a recognition that applying the various rules of the UCPD could impose too tight a straightjacket on traders. In particular, the CJEU refrained from stating firm requirements for complying with the particular obligations in Art. 7(4) in respect of 'invitations to purchase', requiring instead that national courts consider each situation on a case-by-case basis taking account of a range of variables in determining whether a trader is guilty of a misleading omission. It might be argued that this leaves the law too uncertain; yet, with broad and inherently flexible requirements such as those in Art. 7, it is important to take a much more context-sensitive approach. This would seem to be the

87 At paras. [50]–[59].

88 Paras. [60]–[72]. Cf. C-310/15 *Vincent Deroo-Blanquart v Sony Europe Limited* ECLI:EU:C:2016:633, where the CJEU held that providing only the final price of a combined offer of a laptop and pre-installed software, rather than a breakdown of the price for each component was not a misleading practice because the price of each item of software was not material (see para [51] of that ruling).

89 C-611/14 *Criminal proceedings against Canal Digital Danmark A/S* ECLI:EU:C:2016:800.

trade-off between imposing sweeping obligations on traders and the realism of the huge variety in which business and marketing is conducted.

PROHIBITION OF AGGRESSIVE COMMERCIAL PRACTICES (ARTICLES 8 AND 9)

Article 8 prohibits aggressive commercial practices. There are three aspects to this prohibition: (i) there has to be harassment and/or coercion and/or undue influence; (ii) this must significantly impair the average consumer's freedom of choice (or be likely to do so); and (iii) an average consumer will, or is likely to, take a transactional decision he would not have taken otherwise. In applying these criteria, the factual context of the practice and its features and circumstances need to be taken into account.

Only undue influence is defined (in Art. 2(j)) and requires that the following is established: (i) the trader is in a position of power in relation to a consumer; (ii) the trader uses this position to put pressure on the consumer; and (iii) this significantly limits the ability of the consumer to make an informed decision. Duress and coercion are not defined separately, but Article 9 provides a list of factors that should be taken into account in establishing whether there has been harassment, coercion or undue influence. They are: (i) timing, location, nature or persistence of the practice; (ii) whether there was threatening or abusive language/behaviour; (iii) exploitation of a specific misfortune or circumstance of such gravity as to impair the consumer's judgement, of which the trader is aware; (iv) onerous or disproportionate non-contractual barriers to the exercise of contractual rights and (v) any threat to take action that cannot legally be taken.

It is not entirely clear whether this list is exhaustive so that domestic courts are precluded from considering additional factors. Bearing in mind that the UCPD is a maximum harmonisation measure, it is plausible that only those factors listed in Art. 9 can be considered. Alternatively, the list in Art. 9 could be seen as providing factors which must be considered in every case where it is alleged that a commercial practice is aggressive, i.e. a court would only be permitted to conclude that a practice is not aggressive if it has considered all of these factors. On this latter view, Art. 9 would not be exhaustive and other factors could also be considered by a national court.

As with the other prohibitions, the effect of the trader's practice on the average consumer's freedom of choice and the fact that a transactional decision would be taken by an average consumer as a result is a determining factor. This behaviour will only constitute an unfair commercial practice within Art. 8 if it would have a *significant* impact on the *average* consumer's freedom of choice.

The consumer image: Average, targeted and vulnerable

The summary of the various prohibitions in the UCPD above repeatedly mentioned that the effect of the trader's actions on an 'average consumer' need to be considered. This means that the UCPD is not designed to assist individual consumers who have reason to complain about the actions of a trader, but rather to police the way traders behave in the market. In that regard, it is as much about protecting competitors as it is about protecting consumers. However, the consumer image in the UCPD is not straightforward,[90] because it not only focuses on the 'average consumer', but can also be modified in certain instances to focus on the average consumer within a group specifically targeted by a commercial practice, as well as on certain categories of vulnerable consumers particularly susceptible to a commercial practice.[91]

The 'average consumer' benchmark

The benchmark for establishing that the behaviour of a trader constitutes an unfair commercial practice is the impact on the average consumer. It is important to explore this notion more fully. The concept is familiar from the case law of the CJEU,[92] where it has been developed in the context of assessing whether advertising is misleading,[93] as well as in determining the compatibility of national rules with the free movement provisions. The UCPD adopts this test and treats the average consumer as someone 'who is reasonably well-informed and reasonably observant and circumspect, taking into account social, cultural and linguistic factors'.[94]

The shortcomings of this concept were already discussed earlier in this book[95] and are relevant in this specific context.[96] A key concern about the use of the 'average consumer' yardstick is whether focusing on whether an artificial average consumer is sufficiently protected is likely to fail those consumers who fall below that standard who probably are more in need of protection from the law. This is because the average consumer test might be set at too high a level of competence which does not reflect the majority of consumers. The CJEU's guidance on this concept has been rather limited, with judgments generally repeating the same explanations.[97]

90 For a detailed analysis, see B Duivenvoorde, *The Consumer Benchmarks in the Unfair Commercial Practices Directive* (Springer, 2015).
91 See also P Cartwright, 'The consumer image within EU law' in C Twigg-Flesner (ed), *Research Handbook on EU Consumer and Contract Law* (Cheltenham, Edward Elgar, 2016).
92 E.g. C–216/96 *Gut Springenheide GmbH v Oberkreisdirektor des Kreises Steinfurt* [1998] ECR I–4657; C–303/97 *Verbraucherschutzverein eV v Sektkellerei G.C. Kessler GmbH und Co.* [1999] ECR I–513; C–220/98 *Estée Lauder Cosmetics GmbH & Co. OHG v Lancaster Group GmbH* [2000] ECR I–117; Case C–465/98 *Verein gegen Unwesen in Handel und Gewerbe Köln eV v Adolf Darbo AG.* [2000] ECR I–2297; C–3/99 *Cidrerie Ruwet SA v Cidre Stassen SA and HP Bulmer Ltd.* [2000] ECR I-8749, and many others.
93 Under the old Directive on misleading advertising (84/450/EEC).
94 Recital 18 UCPD.
95 See Chapter 1, pp.27–31.
96 See also R Incardona and C Poncibo, 'The average consumer, the Unfair Commercial Practices Directive and cognitive revolution' (2007) 30 *Journal of Consumer Policy* p.21.
97 See e.g. C-611/14 *Criminal proceedings against Canal Digital Danmark A/S* ECLI:EU:C:2016:800, para [39].

One possible way forward which is beginning to emerge is to draw on modern research about consumer behaviouralism.[98] This might reveal a number of guiding criteria which could be attached to the concept of the 'average consumer' to give it a normative component. Research from behavioural economics and consumer psychology offers valuable insights into how individuals react to certain techniques or triggers. This could be utilised in defining objective criteria to determine which actions will have a misleading effect, i.e. certain practices will always have a particular effect.[99] There are early indications of how this could work in practice: In commenting on *Tekanne*,[100] Schebesta and Purnhagen[101] note that the reasoning by the CJEU indirectly reflected behavioural economics research. In *Teekanne*, packaging for teabags contained pictures of raspberries and vanilla but these were not present in the tea, as the list of ingredients clarified. The CJEU held that packaging should not give the impression that there are ingredients which the product does not in fact contain, even where this is made clear on the list of ingredients. Applying the traditional 'average consumer' concept, one would have expected the information from the list of ingredients to provide all the relevant information to that consumer. By taking into account the pictorial depiction, the CJEU reflected the fact that consumers process visual information quickly, whereas textual information required more deliberative processing.[102]

Concerns about the substance given to the 'average consumer' test are particularly pertinent in the context of the UCPD, which seeks to regulate the behaviour of traders towards consumers generally. Depending on how the 'average consumer' is ultimately understood, this might result in a threshold for compliance which is set at a rather generous level for traders. This might be welcome from a business perspective in that it makes cross-border trading more attractive, but it does run the risk of many commercial practices being found to be fair despite their negative impact on a proportion of consumers. Even if taking behaviouralism into account might mitigate this, it might not suffice: some practices might affect only certain categories of consumers adversely (e.g. children, or elderly or disabled consumers), or be understood differently as between consumers from different Member States.[103] To some extent, this is recognised in

98 J Trzaskowski, 'Behavioural economics, neuroscience, and the Unfair Commercial Practices Directive' (2011) 34 *Journal of Consumer Policy* p.377.

99 For a fuller discussion, see AL Sibony, 'Can EU consumer law benefit from behavioural insights? An analysis of the Unfair Commercial Practices Directive' (2014) 22 *European Review of Private Law* p.901.

100 C-195/14 *Bundesverband der Verbraucherzentralen und Verbraucherverbände eV v Teekanne GmbH & Co KG* EU:C:2015:361.

101 H Schebesta and K Purnhagen, 'The behaviour of the average consumer: A little less normativity and a little more reality in the court's case law? Reflections on Teekanne' [2016] *European Law Review* p.590.

102 Ibid., pp.595–596.

103 T Wilhelmsson, 'The average European consumer: A legal fiction?' in T Wilhelmsson, E Paunio and A Pohjolainen, *Private Law and the Many Cultures of Europe* (Kluwer, 2007).

the UCPD through the modification of the average consumer standard in two instances, discussed below.

Weatherill has rightly observed that using the average consumer standard familiar from CJEU case law 'is an attempt to navigate a course between the rich diversity of actual consumer behaviour and the need for an operational regulatory benchmark'[104] in order to ensure that harmonisation can proceed at all.[105] In that context, it must be borne in mind that the average consumer will rarely, if ever, be at the same level across the EU. Indeed, the explicit recognition of 'social, cultural and linguistic factors'[106] will usually mean that the average will be drawn from a regional, national or local context. This means that the objective concept of the 'average consumer' – perhaps supplemented by established findings from the research on consumer behaviouralism – is the starting point for setting a general standard, with recognition of specific social or cultural factors as appropriate. Additional mitigation to reflect the impact on particular (groups of) consumers is achieved through the variations to the average consumer concept, discussed next.

The average targeted consumer

The average consumer is generally regarded as the representative consumer of the entire body of consumers. This standard is therefore appropriate to consider the fairness of commercial practices which are directed at consumers generally (subject to the discussion of vulnerable consumers in C, below). However, some commercial practices will have a narrower target group in mind, e.g. new parents, people about to retire or the recently bereaved. In the UCPD, the average consumer standard can therefore be modified in circumstances where a commercial practice is directed at a particular group of consumers; in that case, the average consumer will be an average consumer from within the group at which the practice is directed (the 'targeted average consumer'). This permits a more focused assessment of the fairness of targeted commercial practices – if assessed against the average consumer, it might be more likely that such a practice will be regarded as fair, whereas seen from the perspective of an average consumer from within the targeted group, it might not. However, the use of this standard does raise questions about which of the attributes of the average consumer are modified or to be disregarded altogether. At the very least, the expectations with regard to the features of the average consumer (reasonably informed, observant and circumspect) must be reduced in view of the general characteristics of the

104 S Weatherill, "Who is the 'average consumer'?" in S Weatherill and U Bernits, *The Regulation of Unfair Commercial Practices under EC Directive 2005/29 – New Rules and New Techniques* (Oxford: Hart, 2007), p.135.

105 Note the approach taken in *Godfrey Hirst v Cavalier* [2014] NZCA 418 – see Chapter 1, p.30.

106 As was the case in C–220/98 *Estée Lauder Cosmetics GmbH & Co. OHG v Lancaster Group GmbH* [2000] ECR I–117.

targeted group.[107] This will be particularly the case where one of the characteristics of the group being targeted is that it is less observant and able to identify information which might be misleading.

Vulnerable consumers

However, in addition to the average consumer test, the UCPD also recognises a different category of consumer: the vulnerable consumer. Explicit reference to this idea is made in the context of the general prohibition in Art. 5 only. This raises the question whether the vulnerable consumer test could also be applied in the context of Arts. 6–8, or whether the specific prohibitions are only assessed as against the average consumer test. However, it would be more coherent if the vulnerable consumer test could be deployed in the context of the specific prohibitions, too.[108]

According to Art. 5(3), where a commercial practice, or the product to which the practice relates, is likely only to materially distort the economic behaviour of a group of consumers which is clearly identifiable and these consumers qualify as vulnerable, the average consumer standard is modified to reflect the average vulnerable consumer, provided that this is reasonably foreseeable by the trader.[109] The introduction of this category seems to reflect the obvious concern that some commercial practices such as advertising or cold-calling directed at consumers generally could have a particularly detrimental effect on some consumers because of their vulnerability. Thus, a commercial practice which would not distort the economic behaviour of an average consumer could nevertheless be tackled if its detrimental impact on vulnerable consumers can be demonstrated.[110]

However, this possibility is limited by the proviso that 'this is without prejudice to the common and legitimate advertising practice of making exaggerated statements or statements which are not meant to be taken literally'.[111] This could be seen as taking away much of the special protection granted to vulnerable consumers as swiftly as it was provided. However, it may only exclude matters which are so obvious that even vulnerable consumers should realise that these statements are not serious. Either way, the proviso raises many questions as to its scope:[112] for example,

107 Interestingly, the European Commission's database on Unfair Commercial Practices does not include any cases where this issue appears to have been considered.

108 This point is considered more fully in G Howells, H-W Micklitz and T Wilhelmsson, *European Fair Trading Law* (Ashgate, 2006), pp.131–133.

109 See generally G Howells, H-W Micklitz and T Wilhelmsson, *European Fair Trading Law* (Ashgate, 2006), esp. pp.111–116.

110 Cf. S Weatherill, "Who is the 'average consumer'?" in S Weatherill and U Bernits, *The Regulation of Unfair Commercial Practices under EC Directive 2005/29 – New Rules and New Techniques* (Hart, 2007), p.136.

111 Final sentence of Art. 5(3) UCPD.

112 Cf. J Stuyck, 'The notion of the empowered and informed consumer' in G Howells, A Nordhausen, D Parry and C Twigg-Flesner (eds), *The Yearbook of Consumer Law 2007* (Ashgate, 2007), p.178.

when is it common and legitimate to make exaggerated statements? And how can one determine which statements are not to be taken literally? This seems particularly difficult if one bears in mind that one of the instances of vulnerability in Art. 5(3) is 'credulity' – i.e. a tendency to believe rather too readily that something is true.

Indeed, the approach to defining who qualifies as a vulnerable consumer for the purpose of Art. 5(3) is questionable.[113] Only three types of vulnerability are covered: (a) mental or physical infirmity; (b) age; and (c) credulity. All of these categories of vulnerability can be described as person-focused vulnerability – they are attributes which attach to individuals who form a distinct group because of this attribute.[114] Generally speaking, these attributes are also long-term or permanent (although mental and physical infirmities can be both short-term and long-term/permanent). There is no recognition in the UCPD that most consumers can be vulnerable not because of a long-term personal attribute but rather because of a particular situation in which they find themselves. Indeed, the category-based classification rather than a situational one in the UCPD invites the criticism that it is liable to stigmatise certain consumers.[115] Moreover, even if a categorisation using person-focused attributes is appropriate, the UCPD is open to challenge for taking insufficient account of other key instances of vulnerability, such as low educational attainment, ethnicity, or income.[116]

Cartwright developed a different taxonomy of vulnerability which seeks to avoid classifying consumers as vulnerable based purely on person-focused attributes and instead focuses on vulnerability created by particular circumstances.[117] He proposes the following instances of vulnerability:

i informational vulnerability, both with regard to the ability to obtain and to process information;
ii pressure vulnerability, arising from individual characteristics, temporary individual circumstances, or the physical situation they find themselves in;
iii supply vulnerability – the inability to access and/or afford essential goods and services;
iv redress vulnerability – difficulties in being able to seek redress;

113 See also the discussion in L Waddington, "Vulnerable and confused: The protection of 'vulnerable' consumers under EU law" (2013) *European Law Review* p.757.

114 See M Friant-Perrot, 'The vulnerable consumer in the UCPD and other provisions of EU law' in W van Boom, A Garde and O Akseli, *The European Unfair Commercial Practices Directive* (Ashgate, 2014).

115 Cf. T Wilhelmsson, 'The informed consumer vs the vulnerable consumer in European unfair commercial practices law – a comment', in Howells et al., *Yearbook of Consumer Law 2007*, op. cit., pp.212–213.

116 S Weatherill, "Who is the 'average consumer'?" in S Weatherill and U Bernits, *The Regulation of Unfair Commercial Practices under EC Directive 2005/29 – New Rules and New Techniques* (Oxford: Hart, 2007), p.136.

117 P Cartwright, 'Understanding and protecting vulnerable financial consumers' (2015) 38 *Journal of Consumer Policy* p.119.

v impact vulnerability – a consumer who suffers more severely from the impact of making a bad choice with regard to a particular product or service.

The advantage of this taxonomy is that it avoids categorising consumers into vulnerable or non-vulnerable purely on their membership of a particular class (children, elderly, disabled etc.) and instead considers whether in a given context an individual consumer is likely to be vulnerable because of one or more of the factors set out above. This kind of approach offers a much more sophisticated approach to the question of vulnerability, although it should not preclude consideration of person-focused attributes as well. Admittedly, it would be more difficult to reflect in legislation. Relying on clear categories has the advantage of a higher degree of certainty, whereas recognising vulnerability based on situational factors would require flexible legal standards to define vulnerability.

A question that might be asked is whether it would be permissible for Member States to recognise additional categories of vulnerability, or, indeed, adopt a situational approach such as that suggested by Cartwright. Whilst such a move might be welcome from a consumer protection perspective, it seems that the ever-present clash with the overarching objective of a fully harmonised level playing field for traders throughout the EU would rule this out. This is yet another of the many detrimental aspects of maximum harmonisation. If the EU continues to persist with a maximum harmonisation approach, then it seems essential to develop a better understanding of vulnerable consumers.[118] In the meantime, the only route for recognising other vulnerabilities might be on the basis of the 'targeted average consumer' concept for instances where a commercial practice is directed at a particular category of consumers that could be described as vulnerable.[119] One example might be a leaflet with information about memorial headstones for graves sent to someone recently bereaved ("targeted" due to the bereavement which is a situational factor).

Scope of the targeted average consumer and vulnerable consumer standards

Although there are questions about the precise interpretation of the two modified consumer standards in Arts. 5(2)(b) and (3), the fact that there is recognition in the legislation that vulnerable consumers, in particular, need special protection has been a welcome development. However, the precise scope of these modified standards is also not clear; the recognition of the 'average targeted' and 'average vulnerable' consumers in Art. 5 appears to be confined to the context of the general prohibition in

118 For a useful survey of the different approaches to vulnerable consumers in EU Law, see N Reich, 'Vulnerable consumers in EU law' in D Leczykiewicz and S Weatherill, *The Images of the Consumer in EU Law* (Oxford: Hart, 2016).

119 Cf. J Stuyck, 'Consumer concepts in EU secondary law' in F Killick and K Riesenhuber, *Verbraucherleitbilder* (De Gruyter, 2015), p.121.

that Article only. It is unclear from the UCPD itself whether the vulnerable consumer standard can also be deployed in the context of the specific prohibitions in Arts. 6–9.

The specific prohibitions are not merely an amplification of the general prohibition in Art. 5, but operate as free-standing specific prohibitions. The absence of any reference to the vulnerable consumer here suggests that the specific prohibitions might only operate with reference to the standard average consumer test. However, if the effect of a commercial practice on a group of vulnerable consumers could only be challenged on the basis of Art. 5, then it would potentially be more cumbersome because of the need to show that the practice in question is contrary to the requirement of professional diligence. This question has not been considered directly by the CJEU. However, in *CHS Tour Services v Team4 Travel*[120] and *Nemzeti Fogyasztovedelmi Hatosag*,[121] the CJEU held that the professional diligence requirement in Art. 5(2) was irrelevant when applying the provisions in Arts. 6–9, and one might assume that this would also be the case with regard to the modified consumer standards. However, that would significantly limit the opportunities for considering the effect of commercial practices on targeted and/or vulnerable consumers and strengthen criticism of the UPCD as being insufficiently protective of consumers.

Maximum harmonisation

The UCPD was adopted as a maximum harmonisation measure at a time in the development of EU consumer law when there was a strong desire on the part of the European Commission to shift from minimum to maximum harmonisation, ostensibly with the desire to create a single set of rules on commercial practices applicable throughout the Single Market.[122] The intention behind the UCPD is therefore to create a single set of rules for the regulation of unfair commercial practices which harm consumers' economic interests.[123] In short, this means that Member States cannot regulate commercial practices in a manner which deviates from the standard of regulation adopted in the UCPD, a matter underlined by Art. 4 which makes it clear that the free movement of goods or services cannot be restricted 'for reasons falling within the field approximated by this Directive'. In other words, national authorities in a Member State cannot challenge the conduct of a trader whose commercial practices are not unfair within the meaning of the UCPD – whether that trader is based in that or another Member State.

There are several exceptions to this, which are listed in Art. 3:

- rules on the validity, formation and effect of a contract (Art. 3(2));
- health and safety aspects of products (Art. 3(3));

120 C-435/11 *CHS Tour Services GmbH v Team4 Travel GmBH* ECLI:EU:C:2013:574.
121 C-388/13 *Nemzeti Fogyasztovedelmi Hatosag v UPC Magyarorszag Kft* ECLI:EU:C:2015:225.
122 See Chapter 1, pp.16–18.
123 Art. 1.

- specific Community rules regarding specific aspects of unfair commercial practices prevail in respect of those aspects (Art. 3(4));[124]
- until 12 June 2013, it was possible to maintain stricter national provisions where these national provisions implemented directives based on a minimum harmonisation standard (Art. 3(5));
- conditions of establishment or authorisation regimes for regulated professions (Art. 3(8));
- in respect of financial services (as defined in Directive 2002/65/EC) and immovable property, Member States may impose more restrictive or prescriptive requirements than the UCPD.

So, although the UCPD has a broad scope and its maximum harmonisation standard makes deep inroads into national law, there are several areas where this does not apply. However, the leeway given to the Member States to derogate is monitored closely by the CJEU. For example, in *Commission v Belgium*,[125] it was argued that a Belgian rule requiring that any announcement of a price reduction had to refer to the lowest price charged in the month prior to the reduction was incompatible with the UCPD. The Belgian government, somewhat disingenuously, argued that it could rely on the derogation in Art. 3(5) because Directive 98/6/EC on unit pricing was only a minimum harmonisation measure. This was rejected swiftly by the CJEU because Directive 98/6 dealt with price indications with reference to unit prices only and was not concerned with rules on pricing generally.[126] In the same case, it was emphasised that the derogation in Art. 3(5) was only available in respect of national rules already in force on the date the UCPD entered into force (para [73]). Consequently, Belgian rules prohibiting certain forms of itinerant trading which entered into force after that date were not compatible with the UCPD, despite the fact that they would have been permissible by virtue of Art. 3(5) and Art. 8 of Directive 85/577/EEC on contracts negotiated away from business premises, had they already been in force when the UCPD became law.

Nevertheless, the wide reach of the maximum harmonisation standard raises a number of issues for further consideration: first, the extent to which the UCPD curtails the ability of individual Member States to regulate commercial practices aimed at consumers and respond to unfair commercial practices of particular concern to that Member State. As will be seen shortly, there are several cases concerning the compatibility of national rules prohibiting particular commercial

124 E.g. Directive 98/6/EC on the 'selling price' of goods: see C-476/14 *Citroën Commerce GmbH v Zentralvereinigung des Kraffahrzeuggewerbes zur Aufrechterhaltung lauteren Wettbewerbs eV (ZLW)* ECLI:EU:C:2016:527.

125. C-421/12 *European Commission v Kingdom of Belgium* ECLI:EU:C:2014:2064.

126 Although see the CJEU's ruling in C-476/14 *Citroën Commerce GmbH v Zentralvereinigung des Kraffahrzeuggewerbes zur Aufrechterhaltung lauteren Wettbewerbs eV (ZLW)* ECLI:EU:C:2016:527, suggesting that a 'selling price' is governed solely by Directive 98/6/EC.

practices with the UCPD. Second, it is clear that the UCPD fully harmonised the manner in which the national laws of the Member States can regulate unfair commercial practices and therefore effectively displaced any national rules regarding such practices. However, it was unclear as to the extent to which the maximum harmonisation nature of the UCPD also affected national legislation which was not exclusively or primarily intended to regulate unfair business-to-consumer commercial practices, but could be deployed in that context. This was especially controversial where the objective pursued by that national legislation did not focus on business-to-consumer practices. Third, as was explained above, the UCPD combines clear outright prohibitions with a number of flexible prohibitions requiring case-by-case application by national enforcement authorities. In this regard, there may be concerns over potential divergences in the way national authorities in different ways interpret and apply these prohibitions. There is at least a theoretical risk that a commercial practice may be regarded as unfair by the authorities in one Member State, but not in another. Such an outcome might be seen as undermining the maximum harmonisation objective pursued in the UCPD. It also invites discussion about the role of the CJEU in the application of these prohibitions, in particular whether it should offer its views on particular commercial practices in the context of Art. 267 TFEU preliminary reference rulings. In the context of the Unfair Contract Terms Directive (93/13/EEC),[127] there has been much debate about whether the CJEU should express its opinion as to whether a particular term is unfair, or whether this matter should be left to the national courts. Furthermore, there might be alternative means of facilitating greater consistency in the decisions taken at national level, such as databases recording national decisions or detailed guidance based on such case law. These issues will now be considered in turn.

Ability of Member States to regulate unfair business-to-consumer commercial practices

The UCPD prohibits outright only those specific commercial practices listed in Annex I. However, there are many more commercial practices which will only then be unfair if they are caught by the prohibitions in Arts. 5–8 UCPD. This means that Member States are no longer able to prohibit outright any commercial practices not listed in the Annex. It was seen earlier that the outright prohibitions in Annex I are interpreted strictly and that only those commercial practices which satisfy all the elements of a practice included in Annex I can be prohibited outright.[128]

127 See Chapter 4.

128 C-428/11 *Purely Creative Ltd and Others v Office of Fair Trading* ECLI:EU:C:2012:651; C-515/12 *'4finance' UAB v Valstybinė vartotojų teisių apsaugos tarnyba and Valstybinė mokesčių inspekcija prie Lietuvos Respublikos finansų ministerijos* ECLI:EU:C:2014:211.

However, whilst this position would appear to be simple enough to state, there have nevertheless been a noticeable number of cases which concerned the compatibility of national rules which prohibit certain practices with the UCPD.

Indeed, this was the main issue in the first-ever Art. 267 TFEU reference regarding the UCPD, *VTB-VAB NV v Total Belgium NV*.[129] Belgian law prohibited the use of combined offers. Having established that combined offers constitute a commercial practice within the scope of Art. 2(d), the CJEU went on to consider how such offers are treated in the UCPD. As combined offers are not listed in Annex I of the UCPD, they are not prohibited outright. Had the UCPD been a minimum harmonisation measure, it would have been possible for individual Member States to prohibit other commercial practices, but the maximum harmonisation nature of the UPCD precludes such action. The presumption of unlawfulness of combined offers in Belgian law was therefore not compatible with the Directive.[130] This outcome cannot have come as a surprise – the effect of maximum harmonisation is to curtail significantly the ability of Member States to take action which derogates from the approach taken in a directive, and so the prohibition of commercial practices not included in Annex I to the UCPD was clearly not possible. However, the CJEU did not go so far as to say that Member States are precluded from singling out certain types of commercial practice as giving rise to particular concern. The Court noted that the incompatibility of the Belgian law related only to the general and pre-emptive nature of the prohibition. Had the national provisions incorporated the criteria from Arts. 5–9 UCPD in determining whether a combined offer was unlawful, then this would have been compatible with the UCPD.[131] Including these criteria would entail the need for a case-by-case analysis of whether combined offers constitute an unfair commercial practice and would not result in their prohibition in all circumstances. The CJEU's judgment offers helpful pointers for working out the extent of the maximum harmonisation principle – on the one hand, it can have a very restrictive effect on the ability of the Member States to take action in respect of most commercial practices. On the other hand, it does not make it impossible for individual Member States to include prohibitions of specific commercial practices in addition to those listed in the Annex, provided that such additional prohibitions need to be applied on a case-by-case basis and by taking into account the criteria for this in Arts. 5–9 UCPD. In other words, it would be permissible to have national rules targeting specific practices, provided that the criteria establishing a violation

129 Joined cases C-261/07 *VTB-VAB Belgium NV v Total Belgium NV* and C-299/07 *Galatea BVBA v Sanoma Magazines Belgium NV* ECLI:EU:C:2009:244.

130 See B Kersblick, 'Pre-emption of national prohibitions on sale below cost: Some reflections on EU law between the past and the future' in W van Boom, A Garde and O Akseli, *The European Unfair Commercial Practices Directive* (Ashgate, 2014), who also notes how the withdrawn proposal for a Sales Promotion Regulation would have preserved the option for Member States to prohibit sales below cost.

131 See para [62].

of that prohibition require consideration of the factors from Arts. 5–9 (such as the transactional decision and professional diligence requirements). Although this is a long way from being able to respond to concerns about commercial practices at a domestic level in a way which derogates from the UCPD, the ability to list specific commercial practices could have a signalling function which will make it clear to traders that there are suspicions about certain practices, and it might also make the task of enforcement bodies slightly easier.

This approach to national provisions which prohibit commercial practices not listed in Annex I outright without requiring the criteria in Arts. 5–9 UCPD to be considered has been followed repeatedly in subsequent rulings, such *Plus Warenhandelsgesellschaft mbH*,[132] *Euronics Belgium CVBA*,[133] and *Cdiscount*.[134] In these cases, there were some exceptions to the outright prohibitions in the national laws in issue. However, the CJEU has consistently held that as such exceptions are both limited and pre-defined rather than depending on a case-by-case analysis taking full account of the individual fact situations, they cannot justify an otherwise outright prohibition of a commercial practice not included in Annex I.[135]

However, it is compatible with the UCPD's maximum harmonisation standard for a Member State to prohibit commercial practices to the extent that they fall within exceptions in Art. 3 (see above). In *Citroën Belux NV v FvF*,[136] the national prohibition in issue concerned combined offers of which at least one component was a financial service. In *VTB-VAB*, the CJEU had declared outright prohibitions of combined offers as incompatible with the UCPD; however, in *Citroën*, the CJEU referred to the exclusion of financial services from the maximum harmonisation standard of the UCPD in Art. 3(9), which permits more restrictive requirements with regard to financial services. The CJEU notes that this permission to derogate is not subject to any 'limit as regards how stringent national rules may be in that regard',[137] so outright prohibitions are permissible. The prohibition of combined offers in the national law in issue was not restricted to a combination of different financial services, nor an instance where the financial services component was dominant. The CJEU gave the derogation in Art. 3(9) a generous interpretation, which had the effect of upholding the national prohibition in this instance. The CJEU concluded that the intention of the EU legislature had been to 'leave it to the Member States themselves to assess how restrictive they wish to make those measures and to allow them freedom of action in that

132 C-304/08 *Zentrale zur Bekämpfung unlauteren Wettbewerbs eV v Plus Warenhandelsgesellschaft mbH* ECLI:EU:C:2010:12.

133 Case C-343/12 *Euronics Belgium CVBA v Kamera Express BV* ECLI:EU:C:2013:154.

134 C-13/15 *Cdiscount SA* ECLI:EU:C:2015:560.

135 Ibid., para [53] and e.g. C-540/08 *Mediaprint Zeitungs- und Zeitschriftenverlag GmbH & Co. KG v 'Österreich'-Zeitungsverlag GmBH* ECLI:EU:C:2010:660, para [40].

136 C-265/12 *Citroën Benelux v Federatie voor Verzekerings – en Financiële Tussenpersonen (FvF)* ECLI:EU:C:2013:498.

137 Para [25].

connection, enabling them to go so far as to prohibit certain arrangements'.[138] However, even though this particular commercial practice was not incompatible with the UCPD, it might still be in conflict with the Treaty provisions on free movement of services (Art. 56 TFEU). The CJEU therefore also considered whether the prohibition of combined offers involving at least one financial service was compatible with Art. 56 TFEU. Although such a prohibition could impede the free movement of services, the restriction pursued the legitimate objective of ensuring a high level of consumer protection and was not disproportionate. So on this occasion, the national prohibition was also compatible with the TFEU. Overall, the approach in *Citroën* to the derogation in Art. 3(9) appears unusually generous, particularly in view of the CJEU's generally restrictive approach when determining the scope of any derogating provisions, although in this particular instance, this might be explained because of the broad wording of Art. 3(9) and sensitivity to the need for financial service regulation.

Another instance where the UCPD was not found to affect the freedom of Member States to regulate certain practices was *RLvS Verlagsgesellschaft v Stuttgarter Wochenblatt*.[139] State press law required that pages sponsored by a trader as part of their promotional activities were identified clearly as advertisements. RLvS published two features of sponsored content which had not been clearly identified as such, and this was challenged by a competitor, Stuttgarter Wochenblatt. Point 11 of Annex I to the UCPD prohibits advertorials, i.e. a trader paying for editorial content in the media to promote a product without clearly identifying that content as an advertisement. The CJEU held that this prohibition relates to the trader whose products are being promoted, rather than imposing an obligation on newspaper publishers to ensure that advertisers clearly identity the advertisements as such where the content is linked to the promotion of their products. The only direct obligation in EU Law arises in the audiovisual field,[140] which requires a broadcaster to identify sponsored content clearly as such,[141] but a similar obligation has not been introduced in respect of print media. Consequently, the obligation to identify sponsored content in a newspaper as an advertisement was not covered by EU Law, but lay within the power of the Member States.[142]

Reach of maximum harmonisation

The maximum harmonisation standard of the UCPD only extends to prohibiting 'business-to-consumer commercial practices', i.e. prohibitions which concern

138 Para [27].

139 C-391/12 *RLvS Verlagsgesellschaft mbH v Stuttgarter Wochenblatt GmbH* ECLI:EU:C:2013:669.

140 Directive 2010/13/EC concerning the provision of audiovisual media services (2010) OJ L95/1.

141 Ibid., Art.10(1)(c).

142 *RLvS Verlagsgesellschaft*, para [48].

the way a trader acts in dealings with a consumer. This is underlined by Recital 6, which includes the qualification that the UCPD 'neither covers nor affects the national laws on unfair commercial practices which harm only competitors' economic interests or which relate to a transaction between traders'. If there is national legislation prohibiting commercial practices which clearly does not relate to the protection of the economic interests of *consumers*, then the maximum harmonisation standard of the UCPD does not preclude Member States from maintaining or adopting such legislation. However, this possibility might encourage a Member State facing a challenge to legislation prohibiting particular commercial practices outright to claim that this legislation is not primarily concerned with the protection of the economic interests of consumers. This issue was first raised in *Zentrale zur Bekämpfung unlauteren Wettbewerbs eV v Plus Warenhandelsgesellschaft mbH*[143] in the context of a German law provision which prohibited tying participation in a lottery with the purchase of goods or services. Following its approach in *VTB-VAB*, the CJEU held that this provision was incompatible with the UCPD. One of the arguments before the court was that the principal aim of the German law was not to protect consumers, but competitors of the business in question, and therefore, following Recital 6,[144] it was not affected by the UCPD's maximum harmonisation standard. The CJEU rejected this argument, not least because the relevant German law included clear references to consumer protection as one of its objectives.[145]

The determination of whether a particular national law has consumer protection as one of its objectives is for the national court to make – especially where this is not obvious from the legislation itself.[146] Once it is established that the protection of consumers' economic interests is at least one objective of the national law in issue, then the maximum harmonisation standard of the UCPD precludes any deviation, except where the UCPD itself permits such derogation. The derogations in Art. 3 were set out above, and if a Member State claims that a national measure that affects consumers pursues an objective not included in Art. 3, then it is not permissible to introduce additional restrictions without making an assessment based on the general criteria found in the UCPD. For example, in *Mediaprint v 'Österreich' Zeitungsverlag*,[147] the Austrian government's claim that a prohibition of sales with bonuses had the objective of preserving pluralism of the press was rejected, because this was not a permissible ground of derogation.

143 C-304/08 *Zentrale zur Bekämpfung unlauteren Wettbewerbs eV v Plus Warenhandelsgesellschaft mbH* ECLI:EU:C:2010:12.

144 See above.

145 Gesetz gegen den unlauteren Wettbewerb (UWG), paragraphs 1, 3 and 4 (cited at paras. [9]–[11] of the judgment in *Plus Warenhandelsgesellschaft*).

146 C-288/10 *Wamo BVBA v JBS NV, Modemakers Fashion NV* ECLI:EU:C:2011:443; C-126/11 *INNO NV v Unie van Zelfstandige Ondernemers and others* ECLI:EU:C:2011:851; C-13/15 *Cdiscount SA* ECLI:EU:C:2015:560.

147 C-540/08 *Mediaprint Zeitungs- und Zeitschriftenverlag GmbH & Co. KG v 'Österreich'-Zeitungsverlag GmBH* ECLI:EU:C:2010:660.

On the other hand, where it is clear that the national provision in issue is not concerned with the protection of consumers' economic interests (such as a national law requiring shops to close for a 24-hour period each week[148]), it falls outside the ambit of the UCPD.

Dealing with the risk of divergent application

A third aspect of the UCPD's maximum harmonisation nature is how the consistent application of the Directive's open-ended clauses and the average consumer standard[149] by the national courts of the Member States can be assured. It was seen earlier that there are multiple elements of the UCPD's provisions which require application on a case-by-case basis, and this leaves scope for divergence between the courts of the Member States in the way similar situations might be addressed. Some degree of variance at national level is inevitable, but if this becomes too pronounced, then this would undermine the objective pursued by full harmonisation. In that situation, although the formal legal rules are the same in all the Member States, the practical operation of these rules would not be sufficiently harmonised.

There are a number of ways of addressing this. Perhaps ideally, the CJEU would have a much stronger role in monitoring the application of the UCPD at national level, but this would be inconsistent with the constitutional role ascribed to it by Art. 267 TFEU. This has not stopped the CJEU from offering very detailed guidance at times (cf. the discussion of *Deroo-Blanquart v Sony*[150] above), but relying on this alone would not address this issue sufficiently.

The challenge of ensuring consistent application of harmonised laws is not unfamiliar, and a solution used in several contexts is to create a mechanism for recording and making accessible decisions by national courts, to allow lawyers and other national courts to discover how the rules implementing a harmonising measure in a particular domestic law have been applied by the national courts in that jurisdiction.[151] In the context of the UCPD, the European Commission has utilised two tools to provide information about how the Directive operates throughout the EU. The first of these is a database which records national and CJEU case law applying the domestic provisions implementing the Directive.[152]

148 C-559/11 *Pelckmans Turnhout NV v Walter van Gastel Balen NV and others* ECLI:EU:C:2012:615.

149 See B Duivenvoorde, *The Consumer Benchmarks in the Unfair Commercial Practices Directive* (Springer, 2015), who identifies variations in the application of the consumer benchmarks in a number of Member States.

150 C-310/15 *Vincent Deroo-Blanquart v Sony Europe Ltd* ECLI:EU:C:2016:633.

151 For example, in the context of the UN Convention on the International Sale of Goods 1980 (CISG), the United Nations Commission on International Trade Law has established its CLOUT database to record cases involving the CISG, and has published two editions of a digest which summarises the relevant case law to provide additional guidance on the scope of each Article of the Convention.

152 This database can be accessed at https://webgate.ec.europa.eu/ucp/ [last visited 17 October 2016].

There are several options for navigating this database. For example, if someone wishes to find out if there are any cases on the application of Art. 5 UCPD, the database allows a user to navigate to the text of Art. 5 and access a pop-up menu offering a number of options, including 'cases'.

Databases such as this are potentially very useful in that they could provide detailed information about the way in which the UCPD works at national level, and also help to identify aspects where there is a danger of significant divergence in the approaches taken between several Member States. However, the usefulness of this database will depend on the accuracy and clarity of the information fed into it, as well as on its comprehensiveness. It requires that decisions handed down at national level (whether by courts or administrative authorities) are notified to the European Commission (or the contractor managing the database on its behalf) for inclusion in the database. In addition, the information about the case has to be clear about the essential facts of the case, the legal issues considered and the reasoning for reaching a particular conclusion. Moreover, there will be the need to ensure the accurate translation of this information. At the present time, the database is only available in English, so the information about many of the reported cases will have to be translated prior to inclusion. This could make this database a costly endeavour, and might mean that there could be selectivity in the information to be included, as well as limited opportunities for updating the database.[153] Also, one needs to bear in mind the experiences encountered with the CLAB database in the context of the Unfair Contract Terms Directive[154] which was ultimately abandoned.[155]

A second tool provided by the European Commission is a detailed guidance document on the UCPD.[156] This is a lengthy document (175 pages in total) which provides article-by-article guidance on the application of the UCPD, with examples taken from national and CJEU case law. As such, it provides both a more detailed explanation of how the provisions of the UCPD should be understood and a digest of significant cases applying the Directive.

Taken together, both the database and the guidance are designed to facilitate the enforcement of the UCPD and to enable national authorities and courts to take a more consistent approach. It will be interesting to see if empirical evidence can be gathered to gauge the effectiveness of these initiatives.

There is a more fundamental question: to what extent ought divergence in the application of the UCPD at national level be regarded as problematic at all? One might be tempted to dismiss this question – the purpose of maximum

153 At the time of writing, the database had last been updated on 1 October 2015.

154 See H-W. Micklitz and M Radeideh, '*CLAB Europa* – the European database on unfair terms in consumer contracts' (2005) 28 *Journal of Consumer Policy* p.325.

155 See Chapter 4 on unfair contract terms.

156 Commission staff working document, *Guidance on the Implementation/Application of Directive 2005/29/EC on Unfair Commercial Practices* SWD (2016) 163 final, 25 May 2016.

harmonisation is to have uniform rules in the interest of legal certainty,[157] and surely that must entail also the necessity of uniform application. However, uniform application is much easier to achieve with more technical and straightforward provisions such as the duration of the period during which a right of withdrawal can be exercised than with the flexible and open-textured general clauses in the UCPD.[158] De Vries argues that one should not be too concerned with consistency of outcomes, because the effect of the UPCD is that the same legal criteria will be deployed in assessing the fairness of commercial practices, and that uniformity in application might take much longer to emerge.[159] Stuyck, on the other hand, bemoans the fact that the CJEU cannot give clearer guidance to national courts on the application of the UCPD.[160] But perhaps it is right to suggest that there should be less concern with ensuring consistent application than with clarity about the criteria which national authorities and courts should apply.

For example, should the 'average consumer' test be applied as meaning the average *European* consumer, or should it be possible to reflect peculiarities of national consumer cultures? The maximum harmonisation standard of the UCPD, which entails maintaining consistent standards across the Member States so as to enable traders to operate on the same basis throughout the Single Market, might suggest not. However, the average consumer standard developed in CJEU case law reveals some recognition of variations in consumer culture; in the famous *Lifting* case,[161] the CJEU acknowledged that, in applying the average consumer test, particular variations could mean that consumers in one country may understand particular terms differently from consumers in another country. This could have the effect that something might be regarded as misleading in that country whereas consumers elsewhere have not complained about being misled. The reference to 'social, cultural or linguistic factors'[162] from this judgment is part of the UCPD average consumer concept already,[163] which seems to reinforce the fact that national variations in applying the average consumer test are fully expected. The 'average consumer' is unlikely to be the average European consumer, but will in most cases relate to 'the average of a certain national or local market'.[164] It is well-known that there are cultural variations among the consumers of Europe,

157 Cf. Recital 5 UCPD.
158 A De Vries, 'The aim of complete uniformity in EU private law: An obstacle to further harmonization' (2012) 20 *European Review of Private Law* pp.913–931.
159 Ibid., at 929/930.
160 J Stuyck, 'The Court of Justice and the Unfair Commercial Practices Directive' (2015) 52 *Common Market Law Review* pp.721–752 at p.751.
161 C-220/98 *Estee Lauder Cosmetics GmbH & Co. OHG v Lancaster Group GmbH* [2000] ECR I-117.
162 Ibid., para [29].
163 Cf. Recital 18 and discussion above.
164 G Howells, H-W Micklitz and T Wilhelmsson, *European Fair Trading Law* (Ashgate, 2006),

and the ability to take this into account when applying the 'average consumer' test is important.[165]

In the same vein, therefore, one might also expect some national variation in the way other flexible concepts, such as the 'professional diligence' requirement in Art. 5(2), are applied. This offers a degree of counter-balance to the pre-emptive effect of the maximum harmonisation standard of the Directive. Whilst no additional outright prohibitions are possible at national level, there is at least the possibility to take into account national consumer cultures in applying the 'average consumer' standard, and perhaps also the 'professional diligence' test.

Maximum harmonisation – evaluation

The effect of the maximum harmonisation approach seems to have been underestimated by some Member States, if the number of cases concerning a clash between the UCPD and national prohibitions is taken as a measure. The CJEU's interpretation of the scope of the UCPD's maximum harmonisation standard demonstrates just how far-reaching this approach can be. It also shows that consumer protection becomes a subsidiary issue to the maximum harmonisation principle because it is no longer possible for Member States to introduce outright prohibitions of commercial practices beyond the list in Annex I. There is, as the CJEU has noted several times, still the possibility for a case-by-case assessment on the basis of the criteria in Art. 5. However, the drawback of this approach is that it requires enforcement bodies to take specific action, which could be resource-intensive.

The UCPD suffers from one major gap: the possibility for Member States to derogate from the maximum harmonisation standard where there is a specific need to do so at national level. It is not inconceivable that some commercial practices will be particularly prevalent in one Member State (or in a small number of Member States). For that Member State, it would be much more effective to introduce an outright prohibition, but the UCPD does not permit this. A procedure for derogating from the maximum harmonisation standard to deal with particular circumstances of concern for a Member State should have been considered for inclusion in the UCPD.[166] Such a procedure could have allowed a Member State to prohibit a specific commercial practice on its territory. The European Commission would have had to monitor the use of this procedure and publish information about any such prohibitions. In order to minimise the

165 For a detailed analysis of this, see T Wilhelmsson, 'The average European consumer: A legal fiction?' in T Wilhelmsson, E Paunio and A Pohjolainen, *Private Law and the Many Cultures of Europe* (Kluwer, 2007).

166 Admittedly, this might have been in conflict with the derogation procedure in Art. 114 TFEU, which does not envisage consumer protection as a permissible ground of derogation from a harmonising measure adopted on the basis of that Article. However, derogations from a maximum harmonisation standard are found in other directives such as the Consumer Rights Directive (2011/83/EU).

derogation from the UCPD's maximum harmonisation standard, a national provision adopted on this basis could be time-limited and subject to regular review. Such an approach could have ensured a better balance between the needs of the Single Market and of consumer protection. It is unfortunate that this has not been done.[167] It is worth noting that the European Commission included a similar procedure in its proposal for the Consumer Rights Directive to update the list of contract terms which would have been deemed unfair in all circumstances as well as the indicative list of terms presumed to be unfair.[168] This would have been subject to a maximum harmonisation standard. However, the final version of the CRD does not affect the minimum harmonisation status of the unfair contract terms rules,[169] and so this procedure was not enacted.

Enforcement

One important feature of the UCPD is that it does not envisage a right of action for individual consumers in circumstances where they have been the victims of an unfair commercial practice. Instead, the UCPD merely requires 'adequate and effective means to combat unfair commercial practices'.[170] However, at the time when the UCPD was adopted, the CJEU had indicated that the principle of effectiveness might entail that individual rights of redress needed to be provided so as to ensure the adequate and effective application of EU Law.[171] This resulted in the recognition of individual rights in the context of directly applicable provisions of EU Law, such as competition law.[172] The UCPD, as a directive, is not directly applicable, and this case law would not be sufficient as a basis for allowing individual consumers to bring individual claims against traders. However, the CJEU's jurisprudence does indicate[173] that Member States should consider a private right of redress for individual consumers as part of its 'adequate and effective means' to prevent unfair commercial practices.[174] Some Member States already provided a private right of redress for unfair commercial practices and this is not

167 Note the possibility for deviation from a harmonised rule provided for in Art. 114 TFEU.

168 COM (2008) 614 final, Arts. 39 and 40.

169 Discussed in Chapter 4.

170 Art. 11(1).

171 Notably Case C-453/99 *Courage v Crehan* [2001] ECR I-6297 and Case C-253/00 *Antonio Munoz Cia SA v Frumar Limited* [2002] ECR I-7289.

172 In *Courage*, the individual right related to Art. 101 TFEU on competition law, and in *Munoz*, a directly applicable regulation.

173 See G. Betlem, 'Torts, a European *ius commune* and the private enforcement of Community law' (2005) *Cambridge Law Journal* p.126.

174 C Twigg-Flesner and D Parry, 'The challenges posed by the implementation of the Directive into domestic law – a UK perspective'; in S.Weatherill and U.Bernitz (eds), *The Regulation of Unfair Commercial Practices under EC Directive 2005/29: New Rules and New Techniques* (Hart, 2007); D Poelzig, 'Private or public enforcement of the UCP Directive?' in W van Boom, A Garde and O Akseli, *The European Unfair Commercial Practices Directive* (Ashgate, 2014).

affected by the Directive. Indeed the UCPD's implementation has caused some states to introduce such a private right.[175]

However, the UCPD is purely concerned with regulating the conduct of traders in their dealings with consumers. Consequently, the enforcement of the prohibitions in the UCPD is viewed as primarily a matter for public bodies and other organisations with an interest in combating unfair commercial practices to take legal action and/or complain to a relevant administrative authority.[176]

Member States must empower courts or administrative authorities (i) to order the cessation of unfair commercial practices or (ii) to prohibit a practice which is imminent but before it is carried out.[177] Such powers may only be exercised where they are necessary, taking all the interests involved into account, as well as the overall public interest, although it is not necessary to prove that there has been any actual loss or damage, or that the trader intended to commit an unfair commercial practice, or was negligent. Moreover, Art. 13 requires Member States to specify the penalties for infringements of the provisions implementing the UCPD, which must be effective, proportionate and dissuasive.

The CJEU has supplemented these provisions in its ruling in *Köck v Schutzverband gegen unlauteren Wettbewerb*.[178] This case involved an Austrian provision which required prior authorisation before a trader could announce a clearance sale. Having concluded that such announcements would constitute a commercial practice, the CJEU held that the criteria used by the relevant authority in determining whether to authorise such sales should be those which determine whether a commercial practice is unfair (something the Austrian authorities had not been required to do). The CJEU therefore confirmed that a requirement of prior authorisation of particular commercial practices is permissible and in accordance with the discretion given to the Member States in determining how to tackle unfair commercial practices, because 'anticipatory or preventive measures...may in certain circumstances prove more adequate and more appropriate than subsequent measures'.[179] The UCPD precludes a prohibition of a commercial practice without prior authorisation where the refusal not to authorise the commercial practice does not involve an assessment of its fairness on the basis of the criteria in the UCPD, but where the authority does undertake such an assessment before refusing to authorise the commercial practice, there is no infringement of the UCPD.

175 Ireland introduced a right for damages in s. 74 of the Consumer Protection Act 2007. In the UK, the Law Commission recommended a limited private right of redress (see Law Commission, *Report 332*/Scottish Law Commission, Report No 226 – *Consumer Redress for Misleading and Aggressive Practices* (TSO, 2012)), which was given effect through the Consumer Protection (Amendment) Regulations 2014 S.I. 2014/870.

176 Art. 11.

177 Art. 11(2).

178 C-206/11 *Georg Köck v Schutzverband gegen unlauteren Wettbewerb* ECLI:EU:C:2013:14.

179 Ibid., para [45].

Relationship with the rest of the *acquis*

The UCPD is an important component of the consumer *acquis*, but it is also distinct from most of the other directives because it does not envisage any individual rights or remedies for consumers who have been the victims of an unfair commercial practice. Indeed, as already noted, Art. 3(2) UCPD makes it clear that it is 'without prejudice to contract law and, in particular, the rules on the validity, formation or effect of a contract'. This proviso does not preclude any influence of the UCPD on domestic or EU contract law rules, and one might expect that EU rules, in particular, would be more clearly aligned with the UCPD. As will be seen, this does not yet seem to be the case. Moreover, although the UCPD is 'without prejudice' to contract law, it could still have an indirect effect on contract law,[180] e.g. with regard to the interpretation of directives in the consumer contract law *acquis*.[181]

Focusing on the first issue: a key instance where there seems to be insufficient alignment between the UCPD and the rest of the *acquis* is the field of pre-contractual information duties. As was seen earlier, Art. 7 on misleading omissions could effectively be regarded as an obligation on a trader to disclose certain items of information, with particular items specified in Art. 7(4) as being 'material' in the context of an invitation to treat. In comparison, Arts. 5 and 6 of the Consumer Rights Directive (CRD) contain duties to provide a list of items of information before a consumer decides to enter into a contract. There are strong similarities between the lists in the UCPD and the CRD, but they are not identical. Those items which are required in both directives are not set out in the same way, and some are more detailed than others (e.g. information about price in Art. 6(1)(d) CRD compared to Art. 6(d) or 7(c) UCPD). Art. 6 CRD also contains several additional items of information. It is clear that, by virtue of Art. 7(5) UCPD, the information required by the CRD is regarded as material for types of transactions the CRD covers (primarily off-premises and distance contracts), and so there is no direct conflict. However, it seems unnecessary to have such variations in the requirements to provide information, and greater consistency between the various directives would make the law both clearer and more certain.

Second, the potential overlap between the UCPD and the Unfair Contract Terms Directive was considered in *Pereničová*.[182] In this case, a loan agreement had stated that the APR was fixed at 48.63%, but the national court had

180 S Whittaker, 'The relationship of the Unfair Commercial Practices Directive to European and national contract laws' in S.Weatherill and U.Bernitz, *The Regulation of Unfair Commercial Practices under EC Directive 2005/29* (Oxford: Hart, 2007).

181 For a useful survey of the relationship of the UCPD with contract law, see M Durovic, 'The subtle Europeanization of contract law: The case of Directive 2005/29/EC on Unfair Commercial Practices' (2015) 23 *European Review of Private Law* p.715; also M Durovic, *European Law on Unfair Commercial Practices and Contract Law* (Bloomsbury, 2016).

182 C-453/10 *Jana Pereničová and Vladislav Perenič v SOS financ spol. s r. o.* ECLI:EU:C:2012:144.

calculated the true APR as being 58.76%. On the basis that this amounted to a misleading commercial practice, the national court asked the CJEU whether a finding that a contract term constituted an unfair commercial practice was relevant to a finding of whether this was also an unfair contract term for the purposes of the Unfair Terms Directive (93/13/EEC). As explained elsewhere,[183] Art. 4(1) UTD states that the assessment of unfairness requires *inter alia*, 'all the circumstances attending the conclusion of the contract' to be taken into account. The CJEU held that the fact that a term in a contract amounted to an unfair commercial practice could be such a relevant factor, but this would not be sufficient to lead to the automatic conclusion that the term was also unfair.[184] The CJEU based its reasoning on the fact that Art. 3 (2) UCPD is without prejudice to the validity of a contract: a finding that a term constitutes an unfair commercial practice can therefore not lead to the automatic conclusion that the term is unfair, because that could, in turn, affect the validity of the contract as a whole by virtue of Art. 6(1) UTD. The indirect approach[185] adopted by the CJEU in this regard seems to strike the right balance.[186] Conversely, it has been argued that the use of an unfair contract term should also be regarded as constituting an unfair commercial practice because such a term could mislead a consumer about their rights and obligations.[187]

Then there is the relationship of the consumer concept of the UCPD[188] with that in other directives. For example, are the provisions of the Unfair Contract Terms Directive to be applied with reference to the same average consumer test, including, possibly, an average targeted consumer or vulnerable consumer? Stuyck has argued that the yardstick for all EU consumer law is the average consumer but that individual directives compensate for instances where a consumer might be at risk of not being sufficiently well-informed.[189] Thus, the Unfair Contract Terms

183 See Chapter 4.
184 *Pereničová*, para [44].
185 Such an indirect approach can also be utilised where information about the goods creates expectations as to quality which are subsequently not met. In that case, it might be possible to argue that the goods are not in conformity with the contract (Art. 2(2)(d) of the Consumer Sales Directive – see Chapter 5). See T Wilhelmsson, 'Contract law enforcement of provisions on marketing: The solution of the Consumer Sales Directive' in H Collins (ed), *The Forthcoming EC Directive on Unfair Commercial Practices* (Kluwer, 2004).
186 Although see H-W Micklitz, 'A common approach to the enforcement of unfair commercial practices and unfair contract terms' in W van Boom, A Garde and O Akseli, *The European Unfair Commercial Practices Directive* (Ashgate, 2014). Micklitz argues that the *Pereničová* judgment is the start of a much closer alignment between the two directives, which 'demonstrates a certain inclination to a common approach of the two fields of law' (at p.198).
187 S Orlando, 'The use of unfair contractual terms as an unfair commercial practice' (2011) 7 *European Review of Contract Law* p.25.
188 See above.
189 J Stuyck, 'Consumer concepts in EU secondary law' in F Killick and K Riesenhuber, *Verbraucherleitbilder* (De Gruyter, 2015), p.132.

Directive assumes that the consumer is a weaker party in contractual relations with a trader, but the aim of the rules of that Directive is to restore a consumer to the position of the average consumer.[190] The CJEU referred to the average consumer test in *Kásler*[191] in the context of the duty of a national court to determine whether a term is in plain and intelligible language, showing an explicit recognition of the average consumer standard in that Directive. Moreover, the notion of the 'vulnerable consumer' has found its way into the preamble of the Consumer Rights Directive (2011/83/EU). When providing information to a consumer,[192] a trader should take into account the 'specific needs of consumers who are particularly vulnerable because of their mental, physical or psychological infirmity, age or credulity in a way which the trader could reasonably be expected to foresee'[193] to ensure information is provided in a clear and comprehensible manner. So, for example, if a consumer is visually impaired, a trader should provide information in a format which the consumer can utilise, such as braille. However, it is important to note that the UCPD's notion of the vulnerable consumer has only founds its way into the preamble, but not into the substantive articles of the Consumer Rights Directive.

A further instance where the UCPD and the *acquis* might overlap is in respect of directives which regulate certain types of commercial practices but do so subject to a minimum harmonisation standard. One such instance was the issue in *Commission v Belgium*.[194] Belgian law prohibited door-to-door sales of goods or services exceeding €250, which was compatible with the minimum harmonisation standard of the old Doorstep-selling Directive (85/577/EEC). Following the adoption of the UCPD, such a prohibition would only be permitted if it was compatible with the UCPD, and as Annex I does not list door-to-door sales as a commercial practice always regarded as unfair, the prohibition in Belgian law could no longer be maintained.[195]

Similarly, a difficulty arises where a directive contains rules on a specific matter which can also be of broad application. For example, Directive 98/6/EC on price indications requires the provision of a 'selling price',[196] defined as the

190 Ibid.

191 C-26/13 *Árpád Kásler and Hajnalka Káslerné Rábai v OTP Jelzálogbank Zrt.* ECLI:EU:C:2014:282, para [74].

192 For a detailed discussion of these obligations, see Chapter 3, pp.193–106.

193 Recital 34.

194 C-421/12 *European Commission v Kingdom of Belgium* ECLI:EU:C:2014:2064.

195 Member States were given a grace period until 12 June 2013 before they had to align national legislation on commercial practices which had taken advantage of a minimum harmonisation clause in another directive (cf. Art. 3(5) UCPD). There was, therefore, a period of time during which the Member States were required to revise their national legislation to ensure that it was compatible with the UCPD. In *Commission v Belgium*, Belgium could not avail itself of Art. 3(5) UCPD, because the prohibition of door-to-door sales only entered into force *after* the UCPD had become law.

196 Art. 3(1) of Directive 98/6/EC.

'final price for a unit of the product, or a given quantity of the product, including VAT and all other taxes'.[197] This obligation extends to advertisements mentioning the selling price. In *Citroën Commerce*,[198] the CJEU held that the final selling price of a car includes the costs of transfer from the manufacturer to the dealer where this is payable by the consumer (so-called 'Überführungskosten'). An advertisement by Citroën had failed to include this cost in the overall selling price. The referring court put questions to the CJEU in respect of both Directive 98/6/EC and the UCPD, notably Art. 7(4) on invitations to purchase.[199] The CJEU determined that the UCPD was not applicable to the extent that Directive 98/6/EC governed the way the final selling price of a product is presented in advertisements. This ruling reveals a difficulty regarding the overlap between Directive 98/6/EC and the requirements as regards the price in Art. 7(4) UCPD. Insofar as Directive 98/6/EC deals with the selling price, Art. 7(4) UCPD cannot apply. However, Art. 7(4) UCPD requires more detailed information about the price (e.g. delivery charges), so will still be applicable to those other aspects.

Outside the immediate consumer *acquis*, there are other EU directives which overlap with the UCPD. For example, Directive 2001/83/EC relating to medicinal products for human use[200] contains provisions in Arts. 86–100 dealing with the advertising of such products. These provisions overlap with those in the UPCD, as acknowledged in Annex II to the UCPD according to which the requirements in Directive 2001/83/EC are regarded as material information for the purposes of Art. 7 UCPD. However, as noted earlier, Art. 3(3) UCPD clarifies that it is 'without prejudice to [EU] or national rules relating to health and safety aspects', and Art. 3(4) provides that EU directives containing rules on specific aspects of unfair commercial practices prevail to that extent over the UCPD. From this, one can see a clear hierarchy between specific rules and the UCPD. Specific rules such as those in Directive 2001/83 apply to the extent that they overlap with the UCPD, but all other aspects regarding commercial practices with regard to medicinal products for human use are subject to the UCPD.[201]

It is apparent that there are as-yet-unresolved issues regarding the relationship between the UCPD and the rest of the consumer *acquis*. There are inconsistencies which would benefit from being ironed out, and there is need to verify to what extent the UCPD and other directives are still at risk of clashing on specific issues. The no-prejudice rule in Art. 3(2) with regard to contract law does not

197 Art. 2 of Directive 98/6/EC.

198 C-476/14 *Citroën Commerce GmbH v Zentralvereinigung des Kraffahrzeuggewerbes zur Aufrechterhaltung lauteren Wettbewerbs eV (ZLW)* ECLI:EU:C:2016:527.

199 See above, p.64.

200 (2001) OJ L311/67, as amended.

201 Cf. the discussion of this point in joined cases C-544/13 and C-545/13 *Abcur AB v Apoteket Farmaci AB and Apoteket AB and Apoteket Famaci AB* ECLI:EU:C:2015:481.

offer a complete screen between the UCPD and the contract law directives (even if it had been intended as such), as the *Pereničová* case illustrates.

Conclusions

More than a decade has passed since the UCPD was adopted, and there is now considerable experience of how the Directive operates across the Member States.[202] As the discussion in this chapter has shown, there has been particular interest in the way the UCPD utilises the average consumer concept, but also recognises the needs of (some) vulnerable consumers. An aspect of the directive which is likely to give rise to further debate is the relationship between the UCPD and the directives on consumer contract law, as well as the wider effect of the UCPD on national contract laws.

A considerable volume of CJEU case law has built up during this time. A substantial number of cases have been concerned with the extent to which the UCPD pre-empts the possibility for national law to prohibit specific types of unfair commercial practices. The CJEU's line has been consistent in precluding this possibility except where national legislation does not impact at all on consumer protection. In all of these decisions, the CJEU has upheld the maximum harmonisation mandate of the UCPD. This neatly illustrates the tension between maximum harmonisation and effective consumer protection, with maximum harmonisation having the upper hand in this context. Perhaps the reason for this success is that the UCPD had a more regulatory aim, and did not have a direct impact on private law rules. This is in contrast to the experience with the CRD, where maximum harmonisation of core areas of private law was rejected. As a consequence of the UCPD's maximum harmonisation standard, the interests of a level playing field in the Single Market outweigh particular – and often justified – concerns at national level about particular unfair commercial practices. One important lesson to be drawn from the experience under the UCPD thus far is that maximum harmonisation is best regarded as the default position, but that there needs to be a procedure to allow Member States to take action in derogation from a harmonised standard where peculiarities at national level so demand. Such a procedure could be managed by the Commission and could ensure transparency about any specific action taken at national level. It could also be designed to be time-limited.

The UCPD is also the focus of the ongoing debate about developing a more realistic conception of the consumer image in EU consumer law. The average consumer test is well established but equally well criticised. With a commitment towards incorporating behavioural economics into policy-making, and a growing body of scholarship to apply behavioural economics and consumer psychology

202 See e.g. the country reports published in (2015) 4(5) *Journal of European Consumer and Market Law.*

research to the average consumer notion, the time for a rethink of the consumer concept has come.

Annex – List of unfair commercial practices

Commercial practices which are in all circumstances considered unfair

Misleading commercial practices

1 Claiming to be a signatory to a code of conduct when the trader is not.
2 Displaying a trust mark, quality mark or equivalent without having obtained the necessary authorisation.
3 Claiming that a code of conduct has an endorsement from a public or other body which it does not have.
4 Claiming that a trader (including his commercial practices) or a product has been approved, endorsed or authorised by a public or private body when he/it has not or making such a claim without complying with the terms of the approval, endorsement or authorisation.
5 Making an invitation to purchase products at a specified price without disclosing the existence of any reasonable grounds the trader may have for believing that he will not be able to offer for supply or to procure another trader to supply, those products or equivalent products at that price for a period that is, and in quantities that are, reasonable having regard to the product, the scale of advertising of the product and the price offered (bait advertising).
6 Making an invitation to purchase products at a specified price and then:

    a refusing to show the advertised item to consumers;
    or
    b refusing to take orders for it or deliver it within a reasonable time;
    or
    c demonstrating a defective sample of it,

    with the intention of promoting a different product (bait and switch)
7 Falsely stating that a product will only be available for a very limited time, or that it will only be available on particular terms for a very limited time, in order to elicit an immediate decision and deprive consumers of sufficient opportunity or time to make an informed choice.
8 Undertaking to provide after-sales service to consumers with whom the trader has communicated prior to a transaction in a language which is not an official language of the Member State where the trader is located and then making such service available only in another language without clearly disclosing this to the consumer before the consumer is committed to the transaction.
9 Stating or otherwise creating the impression that a product can legally be sold when it cannot.
10 Presenting rights given to consumers in law as a distinctive feature of the trader's offer.

11 Using editorial content in the media to promote a product where a trader has paid for the promotion without making that clear in the content or by images or sounds clearly identifiable by the consumer (advertorial). This is without prejudice to Council Directive 89/552/EEC.
12 Making a materially inaccurate claim concerning the nature and extent of the risk to the personal security of the consumer or his family if the consumer does not purchase the product.
13 Promoting a product similar to a product made by a particular manufacturer in such a manner as deliberately to mislead the consumer into believing that the product is made by that same manufacturer when it is not.
14 Establishing, operating or promoting a pyramid promotional scheme where a consumer gives consideration for the opportunity to receive compensation that is derived primarily from the introduction of other consumers into the scheme rather than from the sale or consumption of products.
15 Claiming that the trader is about to cease trading or move premises when he is not.
16 Claiming that products are able to facilitate winning in games of chance.
17 Falsely claiming that a product is able to cure illnesses, dysfunction or malformations.
18 Passing on materially inaccurate information on market conditions or on the possibility of finding the product with the intention of inducing the consumer to acquire the product at conditions less favourable than normal market conditions.
19 Claiming in a commercial practice to offer a competition or prize promotion without awarding the prizes described or a reasonable equivalent.
20 Describing a product as 'gratis', 'free', 'without charge' or similar if the consumer has to pay anything other than the unavoidable cost of responding to the commercial practice and collecting or paying for delivery of the item.
21 Including in marketing material an invoice or similar document seeking payment which gives the consumer the impression that he has already ordered the marketed product when he has not.
22 Falsely claiming or creating the impression that the trader is not acting for purposes relating to his trade, business, craft or profession, or falsely representing oneself as a consumer.
23 Creating the false impression that after-sales service in relation to a product is available in a Member State other than the one in which the product is sold.

Aggressive commercial practices

24 Creating the impression that the consumer cannot leave the premises until a contract is formed.
25 Conducting personal visits to the consumer's home ignoring the consumer's request to leave or not to return except in circumstances and to the extent justified, under national law, to enforce a contractual obligation.
26 Making persistent and unwanted solicitations by telephone, fax, e-mail or other remote media except in circumstances and to the extent justified under national

law to enforce a contractual obligation. This is without prejudice to Article 10 of Directive 97/7/EC and Directives 95/46/EC and 2002/58/EC.

27 Requiring a consumer who wishes to claim on an insurance policy to produce documents which could not reasonably be considered relevant as to whether the claim was valid, or failing systematically to respond to pertinent correspondence, in order to dissuade a consumer from exercising his contractual rights.

28 Including in an advertisement a direct exhortation to children to buy advertised products or persuade their parents or other adults to buy advertised products for them. This provision is without prejudice to Article 16 of Directive 89/552/EEC on television broadcasting.

29 Demanding immediate or deferred payment for or the return or safekeeping of products supplied by the trader, but not solicited by the consumer except where the product is a substitute supplied in conformity with Article 7(3) of Directive 97/7/EC (inertia selling).

30 Explicitly informing a consumer that if he does not buy the product or service, the trader's job or livelihood will be in jeopardy.

31 Creating the false impression that the consumer has already won, will win, or will on doing a particular act win, a prize or other equivalent benefit, when in fact either:

- there is no prize or other equivalent benefit,
  or
- taking any action in relation to claiming the prize or other equivalent benefit is subject to the consumer paying money or incurring a cost.

3 Pre-contractual information duties and the right of withdrawal

Introduction

This chapter examines two key instruments of EU consumer law: the provision of information before a contract is concluded, and the right to withdraw from (or 'cancel') a contract for a short period of time after it has been concluded. Both these tools have been integral parts of the EU's consumer law toolbox from the very beginning – indeed, the Doorstep-selling Directive (85/577/EEC) was the first to introduce both the right to withdraw from a contract concluded away from business premises and the obligation to provide information (albeit limited to information about the right to withdraw). Both instruments have been deployed in several other contexts since, and the rules on both have become progressively more detailed as EU consumer law has continued to evolve. The culmination of this development has been the enactment of the Consumer Rights Directive which now contains the most detailed sets of rules on both pre-contractual information duties (PCIDs) and the right of withdrawal.

Chapter themes

In this chapter, two particular themes from those set out in the introductory chapter are pursued in more depth: the impact of a gradual shift from minimum to maximum harmonisation, and the information-based approach to consumer protection as a hallmark of EU consumer law.

The move towards maximum harmonisation

The evolution of both pre-contractual information duties and the right of withdrawal provides an interesting lesson of what happens when an area of law initially subject to minimum harmonisation is converted into one of maximum harmonisation. It will be seen in this chapter that this tends to have the effect of creating both more legal rules and an increase in their technical and complex nature. The drive towards maximum harmonisation is usually underpinned by concerns that allowing too much legal fragmentation would be detrimental to the operation of the internal market. In order to remove discrepancies, there has to be more detailed regulation at the EU level of areas subject to maximum harmonisation. The need to satisfy different national traditions with regard to the provision of information has resulted in lists of information which have become longer and longer. The invariable consequence of this is that EU consumer law has increasingly become a straightjacket, with inflexible information duties and an over-regulated set of rules on the right of withdrawal. A fundamental review of the way information duties are used is overdue.

At the same time, one can also trace some inconsistencies in this context. For example, there has been a strong desire to move towards maximum harmonisation. This entailed the need for a more coherent set of legal rules, which was attempted as part of the reform process in the early years of the new millennium.[1] However, this has not always been successful; for example, the rules on the right of withdrawal are not all identical in all of the directives providing for this. Similarly, there are still discrepancies in the treatment of pre-contractual information duties. The Consumer Rights Directive, which was intended to be a consolidating directive for much of the consumer *acquis*, has fallen short of providing consistency across EU consumer law.

Information-based consumer protection

One of the themes of this book is that the approach of EU consumer law could be criticised as being insufficiently protective, especially for those consumers who are in particular need of protection. Much of EU consumer law takes as the notional consumer who is to benefit from protection the 'average consumer'. That average consumer is said to be reasonably well-informed, reasonably observant and reasonably circumspect.[2] As a result, there is a general focus on enhancing the position of consumers by ensuring they receive information to enable them to be reasonably well-informed. However, it is by now a rather uncontroversial statement to say that there is a gap between the focus on information and withdrawal rights in EU law on the one hand and the growing body of scholarship, particularly from the field of behavioural economics, about the limited value of these instruments on the other.[3] Although the EU has committed to making better use

1 A considerable amount of work was undertaken by the *Acquis* Group on this: See Research Group on Existing EC Private Law, *Contract II: General Provisions, Delivery of Goods, Package Travel and Payment Services* (Sellier, 2009). See also R Schulze (ed), *CFR and Existing EC Contract Law*, 2nd ed (Sellier, 2009).

2 Seminally, case C-216/96 *Gut Springenheide v Oberkreisdirektor des Kreises Steinfurt* [1998] ECR I-4657 and recent applications, e.g. C-195/14 *Teekanne* EU:C:2015:361 and C-75/15 *Viiniverla Oy V Sosiaali- ja terveysalan lupa- ja valvontavirasto* ECLI:EU:C:2016:35; see also Chapter 2, pp.66–73.

3 See e.g. AL Sibony and G Helleringer, 'EU consumer protection and behavioural sciences: Revolution or reform?' in A Alemanno and AL Sibony, *Nudge and the Law* (Bloomsbury, 2015).

of behavioural economics in policy-making,[4] there is little evidence that this has filtered down into the design of EU consumer legislation. Our discussion of the development of pre-contractual information duties neatly illustrates how there has been a steady increase in the volume of information to be given to consumers before they enter into a contract, despite a clear message from the behavioural economics literature that too much information will have little or no beneficial effect and may even confuse the consumer.

Pre-contractual information duties

Why have pre-contractual information duties?

The introduction of contractual information duties is often justified on the basis that this would be preferential to substantive regulation of consumer transactions.[5] Early case-law by the CJEU in the context of the free movement of goods laid the foundations for the EU's strong focus on information duties, particularly in the pre-contract setting.[6] The provision of information by the stronger party to the weaker party (i.e. by the trader to the consumer) is also said to promote the exercise of a consumer's freedom of contract because a fully-informed consumer can be said to be able to truly consent to any contract they wish to conclude. On that basis, rather than regulating the substance of the contract, as well as the conduct of the parties, the provision of information is deemed sufficient to enable a consumer to take a fully-informed decision. This will mean that contractual freedom and the ability to give informed consent to a contract are preserved. In addition, the provision of information by a trader could facilitate the process of shopping-around by a consumer and thereby enable him/her to compare what a number of traders are offering, before deciding where and what to purchase.

A related feature of pre-contractual information duties, particularly where these require the provision of information by durable means, will ensure that essential information regarding the contract is recorded and can be referred to throughout the lifetime of the contract. A similar objective is pursued by rules which require the confirmation of information once a contract is concluded, and the provision of contract documentation.

Going beyond the transaction-supporting function of pre-contractual information duties, there are additional benefits which may flow from the requirement to provide information about the various aspects of a transaction. For example, if information has to be provided about after-sales support offered to a consumer, a trader who does not offer a great deal of such support might be encouraged

4 E.g. European Commission, *Behavioural Insights Applied to Policy* (European Union, 2016).

5 See S Grundmann, W Kerber and S Weatherill (eds), *Party Autonomy and the Role of Information in the Internal Market* (De Gruyter, 2001).

6 See Case 120/78 *Rewe v Bundesmonopolverwaltung für Branntwein (Cassis de Dijon)* [1979] ECR 649.

to develop this so as not to appear to be likely to be unsupportive once a consumer has concluded a contract. In other words, the requirement to provide pre-contractual information can have an indirect standard-raising effect, because consumers might be expected to prefer to buy from a trader who will generally treat them better than a trader who is less likely to support a consumer after a contract has been concluded. And finally, pre-contractual information duties may be one element in the law reflecting a broader objective of securing transparency and honesty in the way contracts are made and performed.

In light of this, one can distinguish between two broad purposes of information duties; the first focuses on the disclosure of information which the party required to provide might prefer not to reveal. Such a duty encourages both the protection of informed consent and promotes honesty. The extent to which such a duty is imposed varies considerably throughout the European legal systems, with the common law jurisdictions tending to be less demanding when it comes to the disclosure of information than e.g. the Continental civilian and Nordic jurisdictions. In general terms, disclosing information allows a consumer (at least in theory) to decide more carefully whether to conclude a contract and on what terms. At the same time, it prevents a trader from hiding information from the consumer.

The second purpose primarily seeks to ensure that transparency in the contracting process is enhanced by requiring the provision of a range of items of information about the transaction to the consumer. Whilst this purpose also facilitates the exercise of real consent by the consumer, it is much more concerned with seeking to enable a consumer to act rationally in the market.

Related to both purposes is also a duty not to omit information. Disclosure and transparency duties ensure that a consumer has access to all the relevant information, and this can be expressed also as a duty not to omit relevant information rather than merely being a positive duty which stipulates all the information that has to be provided.

These general observations prompt the question of how useful the use of information is as a tool for protecting consumers. There can be little doubt that it is a widely used tool, but despite its popularity, the effectiveness of information provision as an effective consumer protection tool has been doubted in recent years, not least as a result of findings in the field of behavioural economics.

The classic reason for consumer protection measures focusing on the provision of information is that consumers are generally insufficiently informed about all the relevant aspects of any particular contract. Iain Ramsay seminally commented that 'imperfect consumer information is a fundamental rationale for consumer protection measures'.[7] As a result, a requirement to provide consumers with pre-contractual information sounds superficially very attractive; starting from the assumption that a trader is better informed than a consumer, pre-contractual information duties have the effect of correcting such an imbalance in

7 I Ramsay, 'Framework for regulation of the consumer marketplace' (1985) *Journal of Consumer Policy* pp.353, 359.

the distribution of information. However, this approach presupposes that (i) the trader is able to provide all the information required by pre-contractual duties, and (ii) that a consumer is both able and willing to process such information.

With regard to the latter, a number of points can be made: first, the ability to comprehend and process information will vary significantly from consumer to consumer, with some more likely to utilise information than others. For example, it has been suggested that 'affluent, well-educated, middle-class consumers'[8] might be better placed to utilise information than less-educated consumers. But well-educated consumers will probably also in any event generally be able to evaluate the benefits and drawbacks of any given transaction prior to making any decisions, and so any pre-contractual information duty may have a limited effect. More significantly, those consumers who would need greater protection are also less likely to be able to process huge amounts of information and might therefore be left without any *de facto* protection.

In addition, the cognitive ability of consumers to deal with information generally is restricted and the notion of the rational consumer taking full account of all available information does not reflect reality. Thus, consumers are described as having 'bounded rationality'[9] which means that they can only process a limited amount of information.

Moreover, even if consumers do pay attention to pre-contractual information and are able to understand it, this does not mean that they will also be aware of all the implications which flow from that information.[10] For example, telling a consumer that a car emits a certain amount of greenhouse-gas emissions might be clear on its own, this does not mean that a consumer will immediately understand how environmentally (un)friendly the car really is.

Finally, as will be seen below, one of the hallmarks of current pre-contractual information duties is that consumers will be given information at a time when that information will not be relevant and is therefore less likely to be considered properly.[11] So whilst pre-contractual information duties offer some assistance to consumers, their effectiveness is often over-stated and insufficiently reflects the way consumers really act in the market-place. There are solutions to this: in some instances, it might be possible to tailor the information to the particular needs of a consumer and therefore provide more personalised information.[12] Additionally,

8 See G Howells, 'The potential and limits of consumer empowerment by information' (2005) *Journal of Law and Society* p.349.

9 See e.g. London Economics, *Consumer Detriment under Conditions of Imperfect Information – OFT Research Paper 11* (Office for Fair Trading, 1997).

10 MJ Trebilcock and S Elliot, 'The scope and limits of legal paternalism' in P Benson (ed), *The Theory of Contract Law* (Cambridge: Cambridge University Press, 2001).

11 Seminally, WC Whitford, 'The function of disclosure regulation in consumer transactions' (1973) 68 *Wisconsin Law Review* pp.400–470.

12 C Busch, 'The future of pre-contractual information: From behavioural insights to big data', in C Twigg-Flesner (ed), *Research Handbook on EU Consumer and Contract Law* (Edward Elgar, 2016).

the provision of some information which will not be of immediate relevance for a decision to enter into a contract could be moved into the post-contractual stage. This could be done by supplying this information with the goods, or even later.

Moreover, in some instances, it would be rational for a consumer to decide to limit the amount of information to be considered before concluding a contract. Invariably, processing information in order to make a better-informed decision takes time, which is a form of transaction cost, and a consumer might decide to reduce that cost by limiting the information considered. This is particularly pertinent for small-value transactions.

The use of pre-contractual information duties in EU consumer law

The Consumer Rights Directive

Pre-contractual information duties were first introduced in the Doorstep-selling Directive and then developed in the Distance-selling Directive. Both were repealed by the Consumer Rights Directive (CRD). The CRD introduced the most detailed set of pre-contractual information obligations yet – not only for doorstep and distance contracts, but also for face-to-face in-store contracts.

The CRD was initially intended to be a more wide-ranging directive than it eventually became,[13] but its provisions on pre-contractual information duties are of broad application. However, there are different provisions for different contracting situations, and the CRD operates with three types of contracts: off-premises contracts, distance contracts, and contracts which are neither of the previous two types. Before examining the rules on information duties, the definitions for these contracting types are examined. 'Business premises' are '(a) any immovable retail premises where the trader carries out his activity on a permanent basis; or (b) any movable retail premises where the trader carries out his activity on a usual basis' (Art. 2(9)).

Whereas the old Doorstep-selling Directive only applied to unsolicited visits by a trader, the CRD covers all contracts concluded in an off-premises situation. Although this might seem overly generous to consumers, it eliminates a tactic deployed by some traders of artificially creating a solicited visit.[14]

An off-premises contract is a contract between trader and consumer 'concluded in the simultaneous physical presence of the trader and the consumer, in a place which is not the business premises of the trader.'[15] This could be at the consumer's

13 See generally, S Weatherill, 'The Consumer Rights Directive: How and why a quest for coherence has (largely) failed' (2012) 49 *Common Market Law Review* p.1279.

14 This problem prompted the UK to extend the legislation which had implemented the Doorstep-selling Directive to cover solicited visits, as well. At the time, this required a special enabling power in s.59 of the Consumers, Estate Agents and Redress Act 2007 in order to adopt the Cancellation of Contracts made in a Consumer's Home or Place of Work etc. Regulations 2008 (S.I. 2008/1816).

15 Art. 2(8)(a) CRD. Art. 2(8)(b) extends this to cover the situation where an offer was made by the consumer in an off-premises setting.

home, or perhaps the consumer's place of work, or even just somewhere in the street. The crucial element is that both trader and consumer are present at the same time, but not on the trader's business premises. Furthermore, the definition also includes excursions which were organised by the trader in order to promote or sell goods or services to consumers.[16] These situations are familiar from the earlier Doorstep-selling Directive with the extension to all off-premises situations. The definition of an 'off-premises' contract in the CRD deals with a potential avoidance tactic in Art. 2(8)(c), which applies the definition to contracts 'concluded on the business premises of the trader or through any means of distance communication immediately after the consumer was personally and individually addressed in a place which is not the business premises of the trader in the simultaneous physical presence of the trader and the consumer'. For example, a consumer might be stopped in the street by a trader offering particular goods or services, and after some discussion, the consumer is persuaded to sign a contract. He is then invited into the trader's shop nearby. The contract is then formally concluded on the business premises, but the negotiations leading up to it were conducted off-premises.

A 'distance contract' is 'any contract concluded between a trader and a consumer under an organised distance sales or service-provision scheme without the simultaneous physical presence of the trader and the consumer, with the exclusive use of one or more means of distance communication up to and including the time at which the contract is concluded' (Art. 2(7)). There is no definition of 'organised distance-selling scheme,' although one may assume that it is directed as traders who regularly conclude contracts at a distance and as an integral part of their business activities. This definition specifies three elements for a contract to be regarded as a distance contract: (i) the trader must operate an organised distance-selling scheme; (ii) consumer and trader do not have face-to-face contact during the process of contract formation; and (iii) the contact between trader and consumer has to be entirely through means of distance communication until the contract has been concluded. The basic definition is supplemented by the following explanation in Recital 20:

> [The definition] should also cover situations where the consumer merely visits the business premises for the purpose of gathering information about the goods or services and the subsequent negotiation and conclusion of the contract takes place at a distance. By contrast, a contract which is negotiated at the business premises of the trader and finally concluded by means of distance communication should not be considered a distance contract. Neither should a contract initiated by means of distance communication, but finally concluded at the business premises of the trader be considered a distance contract. Similarly, the concept of distance contract should not include the reservations made by a consumer through a means of distance

16 Art. 2(8)(d) CRD.

communications to request the provision of a service from a professional, such as in the case of a consumer phoning to request an appointment with a hairdresser. The notion of an organised distance sale or service-provision scheme should include those schemes offered by a third party other than the trader but used by the trader, such as an online platform. It should not, however, cover cases where websites offer purely information on the trader, his goods and/or services, and how the trader can be contacted.

This Recital provides clarification with regard to one potential grey area: where a consumer visits the trader's premises to browse goods but then negotiates and concludes the entire contract at a distance. Such a situation has features of both a 'distance' and an 'on-premises' contract, and this clarification illustrates where the line between both should be drawn. A key aspect is whether the consumer has merely been a passive browser before an order is placed online (in which case, it is a distance contract), or has actively discussed the prospective contract with the trader. In the latter situation, the contract would not be treated as a distance contract. This distinction could be justified on the basis of fairness – in the latter situation, the trader has provided some effort and it might seem inappropriate to then make that trader subject to the rules on distance contracts. However, it is not clear what sort of distance communication is envisaged here. A simple follow-up telephone call to confirm that a consumer wishes to go ahead should clearly not turn an in-store contract into a distance contract. On the other hand, if the actual order is placed through the trader's website after an in-store negotiation, the case for not treating this contract as a distance contract might be weaker. At the very least, it might be difficult to prove that a particular order based online was preceded by in-store negotiations. As it might be difficult to distinguish between orders only placed online and orders based on in-store negotiations, in purely practical terms both instances are better treated as distance contracts.

Such a precise explanation is probably necessary in view of the maximum harmonisation character of the CRD. However, even seemingly helpful clarifications such as those in Recital 20 raise further questions. This is an inevitable problem of trying to provide an indication of how definitions should be understood in specific contexts. As soon as some explanations are given, further questions arise. For example, one gap in this Recital is a situation where a trader provides an in-store computer terminal to order goods from the trader's online service, e.g. clothing where the size desired by the consumer is not available in-store. It would seem that such a contract could be regarded as a distance contract if the consumer had been a passive browser, but might not be so if the consumer had been advised by a sales assistant.

There is a fairly lengthy list of contracts which are excluded from the scope of the CRD in Article 3. Some of these are contracts for specific situations (social services or health care), contracts relating to real estate, and contracts which are governed by other EU directives requiring information provision (package travel and timeshare).

Content of information

The detail of the information which has to be provided before a contract is concluded has gradually grown in detail. In the old Doorstep-selling Directive, the only information which had to be given was about the right of withdrawal. By the time the Distance-selling Directive was enacted 12 years later, the list of information to be given had grown, and a consumer had to be given information about (Art. 4): (a) the supplier's identity, and, where prepayments are required, his address; (b) main characteristics of the goods or services; (c) price, including all taxes; (d) delivery costs, where appropriate; (e) arrangements for payment, delivery or performance; (f) where available, the existence of the right of withdrawal; (g) the cost of using the means of distance communication if it varied from the basic rate; (h) period during which the offer/price remained valid; and (i) the minimum duration of the contract, where the goods or services were to be supplied permanently or recurrently. Also, where a consumer was contacted by telephone, it was additionally required that the supplier make clear his identity and the commercial purpose of the call.[17] However, in comparison to the information requirements in the CRD, this list was still relatively short.

The CRD has separate information requirements for contracts off-premises/ distance contracts and then for other contracts. Article 5(1) CRD requires of these other contracts that a range of items of information is given before a consumer is bound by a contract (or any corresponding offer).[18] Broadly speaking, this information relates to the main characteristics of the goods or services; the trader; the price and other charges; payment, delivery and after-sales support; contract duration; and, in the case of a contract for the supply of digital content, functionality and interoperability of the digital content. This information has to be given in a clear and comprehensible manner.[19] However, this information is only required to the extent that it is not 'already apparent from the context'.

Also, as far as 'day-to-day transactions', which are 'performed immediately at the time of their conclusion' are concerned, an option is given to the Member States not to require the provision of the information under this Article.[20] Which transactions are covered by this is not defined further. There is already an exclusion in Art. 3(3) of contracts under which a trader regularly delivers 'foodstuffs, beverages or other goods intended for current consumption in the household'. One may assume that this derogation covers e.g. groceries purchases in a supermarket, or drinks or food bought in cafes and restaurants.

Finally, Member States retain the freedom to provide additional pre-contractual information duties with regard to contracts covered by Art. 5, so could

17 Art. 4(3). Note that the Distance Marketing of Financial Services Directive (2002/65/EC) had a much more detailed list – see below.

18 The full list is set out in Appendix I.

19 See discussion under the heading 'form', below.

20 Art. 5(3) CRD.

introduce additional requirements. In this regard, Art. 5 deviates from the maximum harmonisation character of the CRD.

There is an even more detailed list of items of pre-contractual information for distance and off-premises contracts.[21] This list contains 20 paragraphs on different categories of information, and many of these paragraphs go into considerable detail about the various elements of information to be provided.[22] Broadly speaking, the categories in respect of which information has to be given are the main characteristics of the goods or services; details about the trader; price and additional charges, as well as any deposits or financial guarantees to be provided by the consumer; arrangements for delivery, payment and performance; right of withdrawal; conformity requirement with regard to goods; after-sales support; functionality and interoperability of digital content; contract duration and minimum contract period; existence of relevant codes of conduct; and availability of out-of-court dispute settlement procedures. All this information has to be given in a clear and comprehensible manner. This seems somewhat ironic in view of the volume and detail which Art. 6(1) requires.

Although this is a very extensive list the provision of some of this information is facilitated through model instructions on the right of withdrawal,[23] use of which is deemed as compliance with items (h), (i), and (j). However, these model instructions only cover a small fraction of the overall information to be provided.

The extent of the information obligation in Art. 6(1) is bewildering. It is possible to view this list as the high-water mark in the development of pre-contractual information duties in EU consumer law. Every time a new directive containing obligations to provide information was adopted, the list of information grew. The CRD covers a wide range of contracts, and combined with its maximum harmonisation nature, it is not surprising that there are both a large number of different categories of information and a lot of prescriptive detail about the various facets of those categories. This development shows an obvious drawback with this particular kind of maximum harmonisation pursued in EU consumer law. This has focused on technical and quite detailed provisions, rather than broad principles. It might be asked why broad headings did not find favour over very detailed requirements. It seems to have been an inevitable development that more detail would be added to the list of information to ensure that almost anything conceivable was covered.

The fact that maximum harmonisation would bring with it ever more detailed lists of information was already evident from the Directive on the Distance Marketing of Financial Services.[24] This Directive had very detailed pre-contractual information obligations. It divided these into broad categories: supplier (five items), financial service (seven items, including the main characteristics of the

21 Art. 6(1) CRD.
22 The full list is set out in Appendix II.
23 This is included in Annex I of the Consumer Rights Directive.
24 Directive 2002/65/EC.

financial service, and various items relating to cost), contract (seven items, including details of the right of withdrawal and the minimum duration of a contract to be performed permanently or recurrently), and redress.[25] The volume of information reflects both the complex nature of financial services contracts and the maximum harmonisation standard of that Directive.[26] However, by grouping this information into categories, the volume of information seems to have been made more manageable. It is unfortunate that this approach was not adopted for the CRD.

In this regard, it is instructive to consider Art. II.-3:103 of the Draft Common Frame of Reference,[27] which had originally been intended as a toolbox to be tested when preparing the Consumer Rights Directive.[28] That provision only identifies the broad categories of information to be provided rather than going into fine detail. Some additional detail in respect of price[29] and the identity of the business[30] is set out in subsequent articles, but overall, there is much less detail in these provisions.[31] Unfortunately, the CRD as adopted shows little evidence of having been inspired by the DCFR.

In this context, it is also important to note that the CRD has not been sufficiently aligned with the Unfair Commercial Practices Directive.[32] The UCPD also contains pre-contractual information requirements (particularly through its provisions on misleading actions and misleading omissions). There is some overlap between the items of information required in the UCPD and CRD, but they are not fully congruent. Although the UCPD does not affect contract law directly,[33] it nevertheless seems that both the UCPD and the CRD require the provision of

25 Ibid., Art. 3(1).

26 However, derogations from these pre-contractual information obligations are permitted (i) where there are existing EU rules on financial services which impose pre-contractual duties beyond those in the Distance Marketing Directive; and (ii) where Member States wish to maintain or introduce more stringent provisions, provided that these are compatible with EU law (Article 4).

27 Study Group on a European Civil Code/Research Group on the Existing EC Private Law (Acquis Group), *Principles, Definitions and Model Rules on European Private Law – Draft Common Frame of Reference* (Oxford University Press, 2009). See generally, C Twigg-Flesner, *The Europeanisation of Contract Law*, 2nd ed (Routledge, 2013), ch.5.

28 Commission, *European contract law and the revision of the acquis: The way forward* COM (2004) 651 final, 11 October 2004. See D Staudenmeyer, 'The way forward in European contract law' (2005) *European Review of Private Law* p.95.

29 Art. II.-3:107 DCFR.

30 Art. II.-3:108 DCFR.

31 The DCFR provisions were based on Arts. 2:203 (general list), 2:205 (address and identity) and 2:206 (price) of the Acquis Principles. These were developed on the basis of the then-existing EU rules on pre-contractual information. See C Twigg-Flesner, 'Pre-contractual duties – from the *acquis* to the Common Frame of Reference' in R Schulze (ed), *CFR and Existing EC Contract Law*, 2nd ed (Sellier, 2009).

32 See Chapter 2.

33 Cf. Art 3(2) UCPD.

pre-contractual information, and there should therefore have been more joined-up thinking.[34]

One further point about can be made about the CRD: although it is concerned with distance selling, the pre-contractual information duties in the CRD have not been combined with the specific information duties in respect of contracts concluded electronically from the E-Commerce Directive.[35] Where contracts are concluded by electronic means (with the exception of those concluded exclusively by electronic mail or equivalent individual communications[36]), information has to be given about (a) the different technical steps that need to be followed in order to conclude the contract; (b) whether the contract will be filed by the service provider, and whether it will be accessible; (c) how input errors can be identified and corrected before an order is placed[37]; and (d) the languages in which the contract may be concluded.[38] Also, information about relevant codes of conduct must be given,[39] and, where applicable, the terms of the contract and general conditions have to be provided in a way that will allow the recipient to store and reproduce them.[40]

Pre-contractual information duties in other directives

Although the CRD contains a very extensive list of pre-contractual information obligations, it does not apply to all types of contracts. In particular, there are certain other directives which contain separate pre-contractual information requirements. In the field of travel law, the Package Travel Directive[41] contains a long list of pre-contractual information duties in Art. 5. In particular, the requirement to provide information about '(a) the main characteristics of the travel services', is broken down into 8 elements of information specific to a package travel contract, and there are other information requirements of particular relevance to this type of contract (e.g. para (c) and (d) on aspects of costs and payment, or (g) on visa and health requirements). In the Timeshare Directive,[42] there are different requirements for the marketing stage and the immediate pre-contractual phase. Article 4(1) specifies the information to be provided, with detailed standardised information forms for the various types of contract (timeshare, long-term holiday product, resale, and exchange contract) provided in the annexes to the Directive.

34 Cf. C Busch, *Informationspflichten im Wettbewerbs- und Vertragsrecht* (Mohr Siebeck, 2008).
35 Directive 2000/31/EC.
36 Art. 10(4).
37 In this regard, Art.11(2) requires that 'appropriate, effective and accessible technical means' are provided to enable the identification and correction of input errors before an order is placed.
38 Art. 10(1).
39 Art. 10(2).
40 Art. 10(3).
41 Directive 2015/2302/EU.
42 Directive 2008/122/EU.

This information becomes an integral part of the contract.[43] Changes to this information may be agreed by the parties, and other changes are only permitted where these result from circumstances beyond the trader's control.[44]

In order to manage the volume of information required for contracts falling within the scope of the Consumer Credit Directive,[45] also a maximum harmonisation Directive, a template has been designed. The Directive requires that all the information is provided by using the standard 'European Consumer Credit Information' (SECCI) form.[46] Article 5 specifies no fewer than 19 items of information for this form, such as basic information about the credit provider and details of the proposed credit agreement, including the APR, total amount borrowed and repayable, details of repayments, penalties for failing to maintain regular payments and information about early repayment. All of these directives show that maximum harmonisation brings with it very detailed information obligations.[47] In each of these, there are attempts to make this information seem less complex, although the extent to which it has become easier for consumers to comprehend and act upon this information remains a matter of debate.

Form

A further feature of the requirement to provide pre-contractual information in EU consumer law are rules on form and presentation, as well as language. Once again, the Consumer Rights Directive contains detailed rules on form in respect of off-premises contracts in Art. 7[48] and for distance contracts in Art. 8. These reflect the continuous evolution towards more and more detailed (and technical) rules. In the CRD, there are different requirements as to form depending on the type of the contract.

The default position is that the information required under Art. 6(1) has to be given on paper, but, if the consumer agrees, it may instead be provided on another 'durable medium'. This term has been utilised for some time in EU

43 Ibid., Art. 5(2).
44 Ibid., Art. 5(2).
45 Directive 2008/48/EU, discussed in-depth in ch.6.
46 See Annex II of the Consumer Credit Directive.
47 See also Article 22 of the Services Directive (2006/123/EC), which lists 11 items of pre-contractual information: the main characteristics of the service; price and related costs; the identity of the service provider; contract terms, especially choice of law and jurisdiction clauses; any applicable redress procedures; and – in respect of service providers required to have professional indemnity insurance, details of that insurance. A service recipient can request information about the professional rules applicable to the regulated professions; multidisciplinary activities and partnerships and measures taken to avoid conflicts of interest; and any relevant codes of conduct, including dispute resolution mechanisms available under a code or through membership of a trade association.
48 These are exhaustive and Member States cannot impose any additional formal requirements: Art. 7(5).

consumer law directives, although it was not always defined clearly. Early directives only required 'written notice'.[49] This then developed into the possibility that the requirement for a contract to be in writing could be met by providing the contract in 'another form which is comprehensible and accessible to the consumer'.[50] Since then, the requirement found in most directives (including the CRD) is that information should be provided on paper or on another durable medium.[51] The phrase 'durable medium' is intended to cover the alternative ways of providing information electronically in the context of the digital environment. However, it is not easy to determine when the provision of information by electronic means qualifies as 'durable', and so the definition of this term is crucial. Surprisingly, the old Distance-selling Directive used the phrase but provided no definition. A definition was first provided in the Distance Marketing of Financial Services Directive. According to this, a durable medium 'means any instrument which enables the consumer to store information addressed personally to him in a way accessible for future reference for a period of time adequate for the purposes of the information and which allows the unchanged reproduction of the information stored.'[52] This definition is essentially the same in the CRD, with the addition of the words 'or trader' after 'consumer'.[53]

From the perspective of the digital environment, the most difficult question is how information provided via websites or e-mail should be treated. In the Insurance Mediation Directive,[54] the definition of 'durable medium' was supplemented with an additional sentence, which states that 'durable medium covers floppy disks, CD-ROMs, DVDs and hard drives of personal computers on which electronic mail is stored, but it excludes Internet sites, unless such sites meet the criteria specific in the first paragraph'.[55] This definition is a product of its time, and 15 years later, most of the tangible mediums are less common. Moreover, emails are now frequently stored on remote servers and no longer downloaded onto the consumer's hard-drive. In the CRD, it is suggested that durable medium 'should include in particular paper, USB sticks, CD-ROMs, DVDs, memory cards or the hard disks of computers as well as e-mails'.[56] At least with regard to emails, this suggests a more flexible approach, and it may be assumed that information supplied in an email will qualify as having been provided on a durable medium, irrespective of where this is stored. However, websites are unlikely to satisfy this requirement. The CJEU said as much in *Content Services* in the context of the old

49 Art. 4(1) of the Doorstep-selling Directive on information about the right of withdrawal.
50 Cf. the old Package Travel Directive (90/314/EEC), Ar. 4(2)(b).
51 E.g. in the Directives on Consumer Credit (Arts. 5(1) and 6(1)) or Distance Marketing of Financial Services (Art. 5(1)).
52 Art. 2(f) of Directive 2002/65/EC.
53 Art. 2(10) CRD.
54 Directive 2002/92/EC [2003] O.J. L 9/3.
55 Ibid., Art. 2(l).
56 Recital 23 CRD

Distance-selling Directive,[57] because information stored on a website could be modified at any time and therefore could not assure the unchanged reproduction of that information. However, the CJEU left open whether emerging website designs ('sophisticated websites') might qualify as a durable medium.[58] In any event, the CJEU also held that allowing a consumer to access this information via a hyperlink would not satisfy the requirement that the information is 'given to' or 'received' by the consumer. This is so because clicking on a hyperlink would require an active step by the consumer, such as clicking on the link.[59] This seems to be a rather strict approach – in practical terms, there is little difference between clicking on a hyperlink and opening an email message. However, the CRD uses the word 'provided', which entails that a consumer cannot be required to take an active step to access this information.

Information must be in plain and intelligible language, and be legible. The explicit reference to legibility is a requirement introduced by the CRD, and it will be interesting to see how this will be interpreted by the CJEU.[60] A second formal requirement is that the consumer must receive a copy of the signed contract, or the confirmation of the contract – again on paper as a default obligation, but another durable medium can be used if the consumer so agrees.

Finally, there is a modified formal requirement in respect of off-premises contracts where the consumer has called out a trader to carry out repairs or maintenance and where the payment to be made by the consumer does not exceed €200. The trader only has to provide information about his identity and address together with the price or an estimate of the total price on paper (or another durable medium if the consumer agrees). Information about the main characteristics of the service, and the fact that a right of withdrawal is not available, can be given orally if the consumer so agrees.[61]

Article 8 CRD stipulates the formal requirements for distance contracts.[62] Again, information has to be provided in plain and intelligible language, but instead of specifying that it be given on paper or another durable medium, the information has to be given in 'a way appropriate to the means of distance communication used'.[63] Where information is provided on a durable medium, the information must be legible.

57 C-49/11 *Content Services Ltd v Bundesarbeitskammer* ECLI:EU:C:2012:419. See C Twigg-Flesner, 'Information requirements and the internet' in E Terryn, G Straetmans and V Colaert, *Landmark Cases of EU Consumer Law – in Honour of Jules Stuyck* (Intersentia, 2013).

58 Ibid., paras. [47]–[49].

59 Ibid.

60 See 'style', below.

61 Art. 7(4).

62 Again, these are exhaustive and Member States cannot impose any additional formal requirements: Art. 8(10).

63 Art. 8(1).

An additional requirement is introduced by the CRD in respect of contracts concluded by electronic means, where the contract places the consumer under an obligation to pay. Before the consumer places his order, information about the main characteristics of the goods/service, price, contract duration and the minimum contract period has to be given in a clear and prominent manner. The consumer must acknowledge explicitly that there is an obligation to pay once the order is placed. Art. 8 (2) states that if the consumer has to activate a button to place the order, this has to be labelled with the words 'order with obligation to pay' or words to that effect. If the trader does not comply with this requirement, the consumer is not bound by the contract/order.

There are also a number of rather technical requirements. Thus, trading websites have to specify any delivery restrictions and accepted methods of payment at the start of the ordering process.[64] Further, where the means of distance communication used for concluding the contract allows limited space or time to display information (e.g. text messages or short communication on social media ('Twitter')), then only some items of information have to be given.[65] Also, a trader who contacts a consumer by telephone has to disclose his identity and the commercial purpose of the call at the start of the conversation.[66]

Finally, there is a confirmation requirement: a trader has to provide confirmation of the pre-contractual information on a durable medium (if not already so provided).[67] Also, Member States are given the option of requiring that where a distance contract is concluded by telephone, the consumer has to receive a confirmation of the offer, and the consumer will only be bound once he has signed the offer or sent his written consent.

Also, as is the case with off-premises contracts, if the supply of a service is to commence during the withdrawal period, the trader must require the consumer request this expressly.[68]

A general observation which can be made about the formal requirements in the CRD is that these are rather prescriptive and quite technical. This is undoubtedly one of the effects of the full harmonisation approach adopted in the Directive.

Style and language

As already noted, the CRD requires that any information given must be in plain and intelligible language.[69] It must also be given in a 'clear and comprehensible manner'.[70] The 'plain and intelligible language' requirement is also used in the

64 Art. 8(3)
65 Art. 8(4)
66 Art. 8(5)
67 Art. 8(7).
68 Art. 8(8).
69 Cf. Art. 7(1) and 8(1) CRD.
70 Art. 6(1) CRD.

Unfair Contract Terms Directive.[71] In that context, the CJEU has held that this requirement had to be understood in a broad sense and was not limited to considering whether a contract term is 'formally and grammatically intelligible'.[72] Rather, a consumer must be able to evaluate on the basis of clear, intelligible criteria, the economic consequences resulting from the term in question.[73] If this approach were applied in the context of the CRD, it would make its pre-contractual information duties even more onerous, because it might be necessary to provide additional clarification in respect of some items of information. Moreover, the additional requirement in the CRD that the information must be given in a comprehensible manner could suggest that the CJEU would treat this requirement in the CRD in the same way.

Some directives contain provisions on the use of a particular national language. For example, the Timeshare Directive requires that both the information document and the contract itself should be in writing and drafted in the language of the Member State where the consumer is a resident, or the language of which the consumer is a national (provided it is an official language of the Union). However, the Consumer Rights Directive does not contain a specific language requirement of this kind. Member States have the option of introducing a language requirement in their domestic law,[74] but the CRD is not intended to harmonise language requirements.[75] A decision on whether to introduce a language requirement for contracts within the scope of the CRD is therefore a matter for the Member States. This is yet another instance where EU legislation can be criticised for not addressing an issue which is of high significance for consumers from a Single Market perspective. Some consumers might be deterred from buying goods or services from another Member State because of language barriers rather than out of concerns over variations in the levels of consumer protection. Consumers and traders need to be able to communicate in order to conclude a contract, so language is crucial. It is regrettable that the EU continues to shy away from dealing with issues such as this. It might be a controversial issue from a political perspective, but it would be an issue of particular relevance to the Single Market.[76]

Burden of proof

The Consumer Rights Directive contains a specific provision on the burden of proof for showing that the information duties under Art. 6 have been complied

71 See Chapter 4, p.152.
72 C-26/13 *Árpád Kásler, Hajnalka Káslerné Rábai v OTP Jelzálogbank Zrt* (2014) ECR I-n.y.r., para [71].
73 Ibid., para [73].
74 Art. 6(7) CRD.
75 See Recital 10 CRD.
76 Cf. G Howells, B Marten and W Wurmnest, 'Language of information, contract and communication' in G Dannemann and S Vogenauer, *The Common European Sales Law in Context* (Oxford University Press, 2013).

with. This burden falls on the trader,[77] rather than on the consumer, i.e. the trader has to show that the information was provided, rather than the consumer having to show that it was not.

Sanctions

Despite the widespread use of information requirements in various EU consumer law measures, the consequences of failing to comply with such requirements have not been regulated consistently. Generally, the question of sanctions was left to domestic law, resulting in a range of different responses at Member State level.[78] However, in some directives, one sanction for failing to provide pre-contractual information was to extend the period during which a consumer could exercise the right of withdrawal, where available.[79] However, in the CRD, this particular sanction has been limited to a failure to inform a consumer about the existence of the right of withdrawal.[80]

The Consumer Rights Directive attempts to deal with this, but only does so up to a point. All the items of information are part of the contract between trader and consumer,[81] which means that a failure to provide information as required could give rise to an action for breach of contract. Also, information which has become part of the contract by virtue of this provision cannot be amended without the express agreement of the parties.[82] Furthermore, where information about additional charges or costs payable, or the costs of returning goods, is not provided, then the consumer will not have to bear those costs.[83]

Whilst this creates a route for a potential sanction for at least for some instances of non-compliance, it still falls a long way short of a clear set of remedies/sanctions for non-compliance.

Pre-contractual information: Conclusions

The preceding pages have demonstrated how crucial the provision of pre-contractual information is for EU consumer law, and how the rules on this have become more and more detailed as time has progressed. In part, the ever-increasing detail will have been shaped by the desire progressively to move to a maximum harmonisation standard for aspects of EU consumer law. The popularity of this tool is perhaps less well explained on the basis of any convincing theoretical rationale (pure economic theory with the image of the rational consumer acting

77 Art. 6(9) CRD.
78 H Schulte-Nölke, C Twigg-Flesner and M Ebers (eds), *EC Consumer Law Compendium*, pp.482–496.
79 See discussion below, and see e.g. Art. 6(1) of the Distance-selling Directive (97/7/EC).
80 Art. 10 CRD.
81 Art. 6(5) CRD.
82 Art. 6(5) CRD, final sentence.
83 Art. 6(6) CRD.

with the benefit of full information is on rather shaky foundations these days) than the rather more pragmatic reason that requiring information interferes less with national laws than rules which would substantively regulate consumer contracts. Although information duties raise some issues about how these relate to national doctrines on matters such as pre-contractual liability, duties of disclosure or requirements of honesty and transparency, they are still more easily absorbed into national law than more substantive rules. The difficulties with the latter are well-illustrated by the problems encountered with reforming the rules on consumer sales over recent years.[84] However, even though information duties might be perceived as less intrusive than substantive rules, it also has to be noted that the volume of information now required seems excessive, leading us to ask whether providing all this information will really equip consumers to make better decisions.[85] Indeed, it has been argued that the direct provision of information should be abandoned as a regulatory tool altogether, with compromise alternatives to be found in intermediaries who mine all the information to provide focused guidance to consumers.[86]

There are also cost-based arguments against the current approach to information: the cost for a trader of having to comply with all these obligations might be rather high. One can therefore question whether the value gained from improving the information available is not outweighed by the associated costs. From a consumer perspective, the volume of information is often meaningless,[87] at least to the extent that it is simply generic information and not personalised to the consumer's circumstances. In respect of the latter, there might be a solution. Not so long ago, the idea of personalising information might have seemed far-fetched; however, the possibilities offered by 'big data', i.e. the extensive accumulation of data about individuals online, could one day be harnessed in providing information in a more tailored and personalised fashion.[88] However, this would undoubtedly raise concerns over privacy and data protection.[89]

84 See Chapter 5, p.201.

85 G.Howells, 'The potential and limits of consumer empowerment by information'. *Journal of Law and Society* 32 (2005), p.349; also see e.g. C.Twigg-Flesner and R.Schulze, 'Protecting rational choice: Information and the right of withdrawal' in G Howells, I Ramsay and T Wilhelmsson (eds), *Handbook of Research on International Consumer Law* (Edward Elgar, 2010).

86 O Ben-Shahar and CE Schneider, *More than you Wanted to Know – the Failure of Mandated Disclosure* (Princeton, 2014).

87 Cf. O Ben-Shahar, "The myth of the 'opportunity to read' in contract law" (2009) 5 *European Review of Contract Law* p.1.

88 See C Busch, 'The future of pre-contractual information: From behavioural insights to big data', in C Twigg-Flesner (ed), *Research Handbook on EU Consumer and Contract Law* (Edward Elgar, 2016).

89 C Kuner, FH Cate, C Millard and DJ Svantesson, "The challenge of 'big data' for data protection" (2102) 2 *International Data Privacy Law* p.47.

Right of withdrawal

As already mentioned, the second major instrument frequently used in EU consumer law is the 'right of withdrawal' (this has also been called a right of cancellation in some directives, but by now, the term 'right of withdrawal' is the norm). A right of withdrawal permits a consumer to declare themselves as being no longer bound by a contract they have concluded, and perhaps performed,[90] without having to give any reason for this. Crucially, there is no requirement that the trader must somehow be in breach of contract; it suffices that the consumer has decided that he no longer wishes to proceed with the performance of the contract. The existence of such a right seems to conflict with a fundamental principle of contract law in all European jurisdictions (and beyond): the notion of *pacta sunt servanda*, which means that a contract, once concluded, cannot be set aside unless a party was in default or there was some defect in the process of contract formation which vitiated the consent of either party.[91] Where available, a right of withdrawal therefore provides a route for a consumer to escape from a contract for no reason other than that he has changed his mind.

Contrary to what consumers might often assume, a right of withdrawal does not exist in respect of every consumer contract; instead, it is only made available in specific instances. In the context of EU consumer law, it is possible broadly to identify 3 such instances:[92]

1. Where a contract has been concluded in circumstances where a consumer might have been caught by surprise and/or felt under some degree of pressure to sign without having the opportunity properly to consider the nature of the transaction and possible alternatives;
2. Where the consumer is unable to inspect or evaluate the goods or services offered by the trader in advance;
3. Where the transaction is complex and/or has potentially very significant implications for the financial position of the consumer.

The classic example for the first category is contracts concluded away from the trader's business premises (off-premises or doorstep contracts), particularly where

90 The right of withdrawal exists for a period of time after the delivery of goods.

91 R Sefton-Green (ed), *Mistake, Fraud and Duties to Inform* (Cambridge University Press, 2004).

92 There are other rationales for introducing a right of withdrawal. For an economics-based perspective, see O Ben-Shahar and EA Posner, 'The right to withdraw in contract law' (2011) 40 *Journal of Legal Studies* p.115; P Reikati and R van den Berg, 'Cooling-off periods in the consumer laws of the EC Member States' (2000) 23 *Journal of Consumer Policy* p.371, and H Eidenmüller, 'Why withdrawal rights?' (2011) 7(1) *European Review of Contract Law* pp.5–18; for an assessment of the behavioural science arguments, see JA Luzak, 'To withdraw or not to withdraw? Evaluation of the mandatory right of withdrawal in consumer distance selling contracts taking into account its behavioural effects on consumers' (2013) 37 *Journal of Consumer Policy* pp.93–100.

the trader appears without prior arrangement. A consumer may be caught unawares. As a consequence, a consumer might decide to buy something without due reflection, or even just to get the trader to leave, even though the purchase was neither contemplated nor necessary.

As for the second category, the main example is goods bought through distance or online contracts. In these circumstances, there is usually less of a pressure element (although cold-calls do have a pressure element). Instead, the consumer will not be able to see the goods, for example, by inspecting a display model, or try on the goods. Colours might for instance look different on a screen than in reality. This opportunity to examine will only arise once the goods have been delivered. Finally, many financial services contracts, such as consumer credit agreements, fall in the third category, as do timeshare contracts.

It is important to appreciate that the three instances listed above provide the rationales for the introduction of a withdrawal right in the various contexts in which it is found; however, as will become clear, once a particular situation has been earmarked as meriting the availability of a right of withdrawal, it is not necessary for a consumer to demonstrate an underlying rationale was present. It sufficient that the contract from which the consumer seeks to withdraw was entered into in the circumstances specified in the rules. So whilst a right of withdrawal in the context of online shopping is generally justified on the basis that a consumer cannot inspect goods until they are delivered, it is often the case that a consumer might already have seen the goods in a store but has chosen to find them at a better price online. Similarly, in a doorstep setting, it is not necessary that the consumer was surprised or felt under pressure – the right of withdrawal is made available for the particular type of contract, irrespective of the precise circumstances in which it was concluded.[93]

Moreover, whilst the three factors set out above are the most commonly advanced reasons for the adoption of a right of withdrawal in EU law, there are other justifications for this.[94]

The right of withdrawal in EU consumer law

First introduced in the Doorstep-selling Directive in 1985, the right of withdrawal became increasingly heavily regulated in subsequent directives, culminating in the full harmonisation provisions in the Consumer Rights Directive. The evolution of the right of withdrawal can be tracked through a number of directives, starting with the Doorstep- and Distance-selling Directives which provided for this

93 Seminally, C-423/97 *Travel Vac SL v Sanchis* [1999] ECR I-2195, paras [43]–[44].

94 O Ben-Shahar and EA Posner, 'The right to withdraw in contract law' (2011) 40 *Journal of Legal Studies* p.115. For example (p.134), the availability of a right of withdrawal could have an insurance function in that consumers can make a purchase in case their economic situation changes after a contract was made (e.g. because unexpected expensive house repairs suddenly need to be paid for). However, the short duration of the withdrawal periods limits this function.

right on a minimum harmonisation basis. The revised Timeshare and Consumer Credit Directives (which replaced earlier directives in these areas[95]) also contain provisions on a right of withdrawal, but on a maximum harmonisation basis. In the Consumer Rights Directive, also a maximum harmonisation directive, a set of detailed rules on the right of withdrawal was included.[96]

The evolution of the right of withdrawal

Initially, there were not many rules about the right of withdrawal other than the fundamental requirement that such a right should be made available for certain contracting situations or contract types, as well as a duty on a trader to provide clear information about the existence of this right. The early instantiations of the right of withdrawal were all of a minimum harmonisation character, which resulted in considerable variation between the laws of the Member States,[97] and the partial regulation of the various aspects of providing and exercising such a right also prompted several requests for preliminary rulings to the CJEU, whose determinations added complexity to the legal rules on the right of withdrawal.

This is seen very clearly in the Doorstep-selling Directive ('contracts negotiated away from business premises'), which was enacted in 1985. According to Article 5 of the Doorstep-selling Directive, a consumer had a right to withdraw from a contract for a period of not less than seven days[98] from the day on which the consumer was given information about the right of withdrawal. As the Directive said nothing about the consequences of failing to inform the consumer about this right, it was arguable that the withdrawal period could not start until this information was given. This would effectively mean that there would be an unlimited period of time for exercising this right. This view was endorsed by the CJEU when it ruled that national law could not impose a restriction of, e.g. one year from the date of concluding the contract for exercising the right of withdrawal.[99] As will be seen below, more recent directives now provide an outer time-limit for this situation, rather than permitting an unlimited extension of the

95 The old Consumer Credit Directive (87/102/EEC) did not provide for a right of withdrawal. The old Timeshare Directive (94/47/EC) provided for a right of withdrawal within 10 days.

96 See also J Watson, 'Withdrawal rights' in C Twigg-Flesner (ed), *Research Handbook on EU Consumer and Contract Law* (Edward Elgar, 2016).

97 See H Schulte-Nölke, 'The right of withdrawal' in H Schulte-Nölke, C Twigg-Flesner and M Ebers (eds), *EC Consumer Law Compendium* (Sellier, 2008), pp.471–482.

98 Assuming Art. 2(b) of Regulation 1182/71 determining the rules applicable to periods, dates and time limits (1971) O.J. L124/1 applied, this was 'calendar days' rather than 'working days'.

99 C-481/99 *Heininger v Bayerische Hypo- und Vereinsbank AG* [2001] ECR I-9945. National law could, however, provide that this 'unlimited' right of withdrawal would cease to be available one month after both parties have performed fully their obligations under the contract: see C-412/06 *Annelore Hamilton v Volksbank Filder eG* [2008] ECR I-2383.

withdrawal period. The CJEU also held that a national court is able to raise the lack of appropriate notice of its own motion, without the consumer raising this, and determining that the contract is void as a result.[100] This is another instance of the CJEU's endorsement of an *ex officio* approach by national courts to the enforcement of consumer law. In this instance, the CJEU merely accepted the possibility for a national court to act, rather than imposing an obligation.[101]

To exercise the right of withdrawal a consumer had to give notice before the period had expired (Art. 5(1)), and once given, the consumer was released from all the obligations under the contract (Art. 5(2)). No charge could be made to the consumer for withdrawing from a contract in this context.[102]

There was nothing in the Doorstep-selling Directive about the consequences of a consumer exercising the right of withdrawal. This matter was left to the Member States. This eventually prompted several references to the CJEU about the compatibility of national provisions with EU law. For example, in the context of a loan agreement, an obligation to repay a loan in full and immediately, together with interest at the market rate, would not be incompatible with the Directive.[103] That obligation applied whether or not the consumer was aware of his right of withdrawal. However, where the consumer had not been made aware, Member States had to ensure that consumers who were exposed to a risk because they were not informed about their right of withdrawal could avoid 'bearing the consequences of the materialisation of those risks'.[104] The context for these rulings was loan agreements to finance the acquisition of a property to be made available for rent, but the rental returns fell well below what had been promised. The CJEU seemingly tried to equate this situation with that of a consumer who had withdrawn from the contract after having been informed correctly about the right of withdrawal, but the precise meaning and consequences of its ruling are unclear.[105]

In the same context the CJEU held that a national rule which provided that a consumer's decision to withdraw from a loan agreement had no effect on the supply contract.[106] In the case itself, the main contract was for the transfer of an interest in immovable property and such contracts fell outside the scope of the Directive. The CJEU rejected the argument that both contracts should be treated as an economic unit.[107]

100 C-227/08 *Eva Martín Martín v EDP Editores SL* [2009] ECR I-11939.
101 Contrast this with the case law in the context of the Unfair Contract Terms Directive. See ch.4.
102 C-423/97 *Travel Vac SL v Sanchis* [1999] ECR I-2195. See E Ioriatti, 'Annotation' (2001) *European Review of Private Law*, pp.441–448.
103 C-350/03 *Schulte v Deutsche Bausparkasse Badenia AG* [2005] ECR I-9215.
104 C-350/03 *Schulte*; C-229/04 *Crailsheimer Volksbank v Conrads and others* [2005] ECR I-9273.
105 See P Rott, 'Linked contracts and doorstep selling' in G Howells, A Nordhausen, D Parry and C Twigg-Flesner, *Yearbook of Consumer Law 2007* (Ashgate, 2007).
106 C-350/03 *Schulte v Deutsche Bausparkasse Badenia AG* [2005] ECR I-9215.
107 Para [78]. See also Chapter 6.

The Distance-selling Directive provided a right of withdrawal from a distance contract for a period of at least seven *working* days.[108] Unless agreed otherwise between the parties, there was no right of withdrawal for contracts for services where performance had begun with the consumer's agreement before the withdrawal period had expired, and there were various other excluded contracts.[109] The seven-day withdrawal period only started once the pre-contractual information required by Art. 5(1) had been given. Failure to do so resulted in an extension of the period during which the right of withdrawal could be exercised for up to three months. If the information was provided within the three-month period, the seven-working-day withdrawal period started from that point.[110] Once the consumer had exercised his withdrawal right, all sums which the consumer had paid to the supplier had to be refunded as soon as possible and within 30 days at the latest, although the consumer could be charged for the direct cost of returning the goods.[111] In addition, the Directive dealt with the question of certain linked contracts: if the purchase of the goods or service by the consumer had been financed at least in part with a credit arrangement (whether with the same supplier, or under a separate agreement with a third party), the decision to withdraw from the supply contract would also bring the credit agreement to an end without penalty to the consumer.[112] The precise rules for the cancellation of the related credit agreement were to be determined at Member State level.

Both Directives were of a minimum harmonisation standard, which left some freedom to the Member States to adopt more generous rules for consumers, e.g. by extending the duration of the period during which the right of withdrawal could be available. This brought with it inevitable variations between the national laws. As a result, the Distance Marketing of Financial Services Directive[113] became the first Directive to provide for a right of withdrawal on a maximum harmonisation basis. It was also the first where the withdrawal period was fixed at 14 calendar days.[114] The withdrawal period starts either when the contract is concluded or from the day when the consumer receives the written terms and conditions and other information if this happens later.[115]

The right of withdrawal is not available for contracts for financial services where the price depends on fluctuations in the financial markets which are outside the supplier's control, travel or baggage insurance policies of less than one month's

108 Periods expressed in working days exclude public holidays and weekend days: Art. 3, Regulation 1182/71.
109 Art. 6(3) of Directive 97/7/EC.
110 Art. 6(1), second part.
111 Arts. 6(1) and (2).
112 Art. 6(4).
113 Directive 2002/65/EC.
114 With the exception of contracts falling within the life insurance directive (Directive 2002/83/EC (2002) O.J. L345/1) and personal pension operations, for which the withdrawal period is 30 calendar days (Art. 6(1) of Directive 2002/65/EC).
115 Art. 6(1), second part.

duration, and contracts which have been fully performed before the consumer seeks to exercise his right of withdrawal.[116]

A consumer is entitled to exercise the right of withdrawal without penalty, and is not obliged to give any reasons for withdrawing.[117] A consumer seeking to withdraw has to do so in line with the 'practical instructions' provided before the contract was concluded, 'by means which can be proved in accordance with national law'.[118] Following withdrawal, a consumer is entitled to a refund of all prepayments.[119] In return, the consumer is required to return any sums or property received from the supplier. Both consumer and supplier must do so within 30 calendar days.

The shift from minimum to maximum harmonisation then began to be further felt when existing directives were reviewed and replaced. This is illustrated by the two Timeshare Directives. The earlier Directive[120] provided a right of withdrawal for a period of 10 calendar days from signing a timeshare contract. When the new Directive was adopted in 2008,[121] it changed from a minimum to a maximum harmonisation measure. As with other directives at the time, the complete provision of specific information (in this case in the contract) is a pre-condition before the withdrawal period starts. The right to withdraw from the contract without having to give a reason is available for a period of 14 calendar days from the conclusion of the contract or any binding preliminary contract,[122] or from the date the consumer receives the contract if this is later.[123] This Directive requires that a consumer is given a completed standard withdrawal form;[124] failure to do so extends the withdrawal period to one year and 14 calendar days.[125] Similarly, if the consumer does not receive a standard information form containing the required information, the withdrawal period only ends after three months and 14 calendar days. If the required information is given during these extended periods,

116 Art. 6(2). Moreover, Member States have the option to exclude from the right of withdrawal contracts for credit for the purpose of acquiring or retaining property rights in land or building, including for the purpose of renovating or improving a building; or credit secured either by a mortgage on immovable property or another right in immovable property (Arts.6 (3)(a) and (b). Paragraph (c) also excludes declarations by consumers using the services of an official).

117 Art. 6(1).

118 Art. 6(6).

119 A consumer can be required to pay for a service that has already been provided, subject to the requirements that the consumer must have been informed about the amount payable before the contract was concluded, and, if performance of the contract commenced before the expiry of the withdrawal period, that the consumer consented to the performance commencing (Art. 7).

120 Directive 94/47/EC.

121 Directive 2008/122/EC.

122 Art. 6(1) and (2)(a).

123 Art. 6(2)(b).

124 Art. 5(4).

125 Art. 6(3)(a).

the 14 day withdrawal period starts from that date. Following withdrawal, both parties are discharged from their obligation to perform the contract.[126] A consumer will not be liable to pay any costs, nor pay for any value of a service received before exercising his right to withdraw.[127] Furthermore, any ancillary contracts are also terminated automatically, at no costs to the consumer.[128] Finally, a consumer must not be required to make any advance payments before the end of the withdrawal period.[129]

The revised Consumer Credit Directive (2008/48/EC), which is of a maximum harmonisation standard, also allows a consumer to withdraw from a credit agreement within 14 calendar days. This is discussed more fully in Chapter 6.

The right of withdrawal in the Consumer Rights Directive

The development of the right of withdrawal in these directives provides a useful background for the enactment of a fully harmonised right of withdrawal in respect of distance and off-premises contract in the Consumer Rights Directive (2011/83/EU). There are eight articles in the CRD on the right of withdrawal, its exercise and consequences. There is, however, a surprisingly long list of contracts in respect of which there is also no right of withdrawal in Article 16, and these exclusions are mandatory for the Member States ('Member States *shall not* provide for the right of withdrawal'[130]). The full harmonisation nature of the CRD and the imperative wording of Art. 16 mean that Member States are precluded from extending the right of withdrawal to contracts listed in that Article.

A standard withdrawal period of 14 days for all distance and off-premises contracts[131] is provided for in Art. 9(1) CRD. As with previous directives, the point at which the withdrawal period commences varies for contracts for goods and services. For services, it starts on the day the contract is concluded,[132] but in the case of goods, it starts on the day the consumer receives the goods.[133] The CRD further deals with contracts for more than one item, or goods consisting of multiple pieces, which are not all delivered at the same time. In both instances, the withdrawal period starts when the last item has been delivered.[134] Moreover, in respect of a contract for the regular delivery of goods, the period starts once the first delivery has been made.[135]

126 Art. 8(1).
127 Art. 8(2).
128 Art. 11.
129 Art. 9.
130 Emphasis added.
131 With the exception of those contracts excluded from the scope of the CRD by Art. 3.
132 Art. 9(2)(a).
133 Art. 9(2)(b).
134 Art. 9(2)(b)(i) and (ii).
135 Art. 9(2)(b)(iii).

A consumer has to be given information about the right of withdrawal.[136] Where this does not happen, then the withdrawal period is extended by up to 12 months.[137] If the information is provided during this extension, then the 14-day withdrawal period starts from the day on which the information is given.[138] Although this rule may seem familiar from the earlier directives, there is one significant difference: the extension of the withdrawal period only happens where the trader has failed to inform the consumer about the existence of the right of withdrawal. Previously, this extension could happen for failing to comply with any of the pre-contractual information duties. In view of the very detailed information duties imposed by the CRD,[139] this seems to provide a fairer approach. Otherwise, a trader could be exposed to an extended withdrawal period for failing to provide an item of information even though the consumer has been fully informed about the right of withdrawal.

There are additional requirements with regard to the right of withdrawal where digital content or services are supplied before the period for exercising the right of withdrawal has expired. Where digital content is supplied other than on a tangible medium, and the consumer has consented expressly to performance of the contract commencing, then the right of withdrawal which would be available is lost at that point.[140] Therefore, the additional formal requirement is that the copy of the contract or contract confirmation must also include confirmation of the consumer's consent that performance is to begin before the end of the withdrawal period as well as the consumer's acknowledgement that the right of withdrawal is lost once performance commences.

As for services, if performance is to commence during the withdrawal period, the trader must ask the consumer to request this expressly and on a durable medium. There are no specific consequences provided in the Directive where this requirement is not complied with – presumably, a trader should not commence performance unless a request made in the required manner has been received. If the trader commences regardless of this, then one might assume that the withdrawal period is not curtailed as a result.

The modalities for exercising the right of withdrawal are provided for in Article 11 CRD. A consumer has to inform the trader of the decision to withdraw. This can be done either by using the model withdrawal form (Annex 1(B) to the Directive) or by an unequivocal statement of his decision to withdraw.[141] Also, a trader may provide an electronic version of the withdrawal form (or equivalent) on his website which the consumer can complete online. Where a consumer chooses to withdraw online, the trader has to acknowledge this on a durable

136 Art. 6(1)(h).
137 Art. 10(1).
138 Art. 10(2).
139 See discussion above.
140 Art. 16(m)
141 Art. 11(1).

medium and without delay.[142] As long as the consumer has sent his communication of withdrawal before the expiry of the withdrawal period,[143] the right has been exercised in time. This is so even if it could not arrive within the period as it had been posted minutes before the deadline. The consumer bears the burden of proving that the communication was despatched in time.[144]

The consequence of an effective exercise of the right of withdrawal is that the parties' respective obligations under the contract are terminated.[145] The Directive then goes on to specify a number of post-withdrawal obligations for both the trader and the consumer. The trader has to reimburse all payments received from the consumer without undue delay and no later than 14 days from the date of being informed of the consumer's decision to withdraw. The trader will be permitted to delay the reimbursement until he has received back the goods, or at least evidence from the consumer that the goods have been sent back to the trader, except where the trader has offered to collect the goods himself.[146]

The reimbursement has to include the costs of delivery, where applicable;[147] however, if the consumer selected a method of delivery other than the standard method offered by the trader, then the trader is not required to reimburse the difference in cost between those two methods.[148]

As far as the consumer's obligations are concerned, he is required to return the goods to the trader within 14 days of communicating his decision to withdraw from the contract, unless the trader has offered to collect the goods.[149] At the very least, the consumer has to send back the goods before the expiry of this 14 day period. The consumer will have to bear the direct costs of returning the goods to the trader,[150] but there are two exceptions to this obligation: first, where the trader has agreed to bear this cost (which, in practice, might be done by arranging for collection of the goods); and second, where the trader has failed to inform the consumer that the consumer would have to bear this cost.[151] Also, in the case of off-premises

142 Art. 11(3).
143 Art. 11(2).
144 Art. 11(4).
145 Art. 12.
146 Art. 13(3).
147 Art. 13(1), which reflects the CJEU in C-511/08 *Handelsgesellschaft Heinrich Heine GmbH v Verbraucherzentrale Nordrhein-Westfalen eV* [2010] ECR I-3047 that Art. 6 of the Distance-selling Directive precluded national legislation which allowed the trader to still charge the consumer for the cost of postage where the consumer had exercised the right of withdrawal.
148 Art. 13(2).
149 Art. 14(1).
150 It has been argued that the rule providing for the possibility that a consumer is required to bear these costs is not appropriate in all circumstances. It requires a consumer to weigh up the likelihood of wanting to exercise the right of withdrawal and the risk of incurring costs in deciding whether to enter into the contract: see E Hall, G Howells and J Watson, 'The Consumer Rights Directive – An assessment of its contribution to the development of European consumer contract law' (2012) 8 *European Review of Contract Law* p.139.
151 As required under Art. 6(1)(i).

contracts where the goods were delivered to the consumer's home at the time of concluding the contract, and where by their nature, the goods cannot be returned by post, the trader is required to collect the goods at his own expense.[152]

The full harmonisation nature of the CRD has seemingly made it necessary to introduce provisions which deal with quite specific issues. Thus, in addition to the direct cost of returning the goods, a consumer may also be liable for any diminution in the value of the goods if this has been caused by handling the goods beyond what is necessary to 'establish the nature, characteristics and functioning of the goods'.[153] In one sense, this provision is stating the obvious: a consumer should only make sure the goods are suitable and then decide whether to keep or return them. On the other hand, such a rule might create a loophole which would allow a trader to argue that goods have been used beyond what was necessary and that a reduction should be made from the refund. Overall, however, the rule ensures an adequate balance between the interests of consumers and traders.[154] It should be noted that the consumer will not be liable for any reduction in refund if the trader has failed to provide information about the right of withdrawal as required by Art. 6(1)(h).[155]

Another provision on an issue of detail exists in respect of contracts for a service. If performance has begun during the withdrawal period at the consumer's request, and then the consumer exercises his right of withdrawal, he will be required to pay for the proportion of the contract services received up to the point of withdrawal.[156] However, this does not apply if information about the right of withdrawal has not been given, or if the consumer has not given his consent to performance commencing;[157] a similar rule applies to digital content not supplied on a tangible medium.[158] There is no other liability on a consumer as a consequence of exercising the right of withdrawal.[159]

Finally, exercising the right of withdrawal in respect of an off-premises or distance contract also has the effect of terminating any ancillary contract automatically (Art. 15(1)), although the detailed provisions on this have to be determined

152 Art. 14(1).

153 Art. 14(2).

154 For an economic justification for this rule, see O Ben-Shahar and EA Posner, 'The right to withdraw in contract law' (2011) 40 *Journal of Legal Studies* p.115

155 In C-489/07 *Pia Messner v Firma Stefan Krüger* [2009] ECR I-7315, a case decided under the Distance-selling Directive, the CJEU had held that that Directive precluded a national rule which allowed the seller to claim compensation for the value of using the goods before the right of withdrawal was exercised. As a second issue, the CJEU left open the application of principles of national doctrines such as unjust enrichment or good faith in this regard, however, provided that the efficiency and effectiveness of the right of withdrawal are not undermined This second issue would seem to remain of relevance to Art. 14 CRD.

156 Art. 14(3).

157 Art. 14(4)(a). This proviso also applies to contracts for the supply of water, gas or electricity (unless sold in set quantity/limited volume) and district heating.

158 Art. 14(4)(b).

159 Art. 14(5).

at Member State level (Art. 15(2)). As already noted above, if the ancillary contract is a consumer credit contract, Art. 15 of the Consumer Credit Directive on the termination of credit agreements will apply (see above).

This account of the evolution of the right of withdrawal is a clear example of how the harmonisation approach to EU consumer law has evolved over the decades. From a quite general minimum requirement which gave considerable leeway to the Member States with regard to the design of the national laws giving effect to a right of withdrawal, there has been a creeping standardisation not only of the core features of the right of withdrawal, but also related provisions. The high-water mark of this development is the CRD, which has provided the most detailed set of rules yet. Such detailed regulation of so many aspects of the right of withdrawal invariably heightens concerns about the fact that some questions are not resolved in the CRD, e.g. what should happen if the consumer, having exercised his right of withdrawal, returns the goods back to the trader, but they are lost in transit? Solutions for such questions can, of course, be found in domestic law, but the detailed regulation and the maximum harmonisation standard of the CRD seem to put the burden on the EU, rather than national law, to deal with.

One final observation can be made about the CRD and its detailed rules on the right of withdrawal. The CRD is the result of the *Acquis Review*, one objective of which was to ensure greater coherence of the *acquis*.[160] It is therefore surprising that other directives which provide for a right of withdrawal were not amended so as to have one single consistent set of rules on the right of withdrawal.

As with pre-contractual information duties, the work on the DCFR included a strong focus on the right of withdrawal (again, primarily based on the work of the *Acquis* Group).[161] Book II, Chapter five, Section one of the DCFR contains a number of articles[162] which deal with the right of withdrawal. In substance, these provisions are similar to those in the CRD. However, they are presented in a more succinct format which avoids the reader getting lost in too much technical detail. In that respect, the DCFR provides a better set of rules than the CRD.

Right of withdrawal: Evaluation

The right of withdrawal is an essential feature of EU consumer law. In one sense, the right of withdrawal is an adjunct to the information-based focus of EU consumer law. It seeks to compensate for the fact that a consumer might not have

160 M Loos, 'Rights of withdrawal' in G Howells and R Schulze (eds), *Modernising and Harmonising Consumer Contract Law* (Sellier, 2009).

161 See E Terryn, 'The right of withdrawal, the Acquis Principles, the Draft Common Frame of Reference, and the proposal for a Consumer Rights Directive' in R Schulze (ed), *CFR and Existing EC Contract Law*, 2nd ed (Sellier, 2009).

162 Arts. II.-5:101- II.-5:106, with further details for contracts negotiated away from business premises and timeshare contracts in Arts. II.-5:201 and II.-5:202, respectively.

had sufficient information to evaluate fully a particular contract at the time it was concluded. The withdrawal period provides a consumer with an opportunity to reflect on whether the decision to conclude the contract really was the right one.

Furthermore, it illustrates how the harmonisation of consumer law has become increasingly detailed and technical whilst reducing and ultimately largely eliminating the scope for national variations beyond a minimum standard set at the EU level. With the adoption of the Consumer Rights Directive, there is a now in place a comprehensive, if not fully complete, set of legal rules governing the existence and exercise of the right of withdrawal, as well as its consequences for both trader and consumer. On the one hand, it seems that this is a welcome development, because the right of withdrawal had become somewhat infamous as an example of inconsistent EU legislation.[163] On the other hand, the standardisation and maximum harmonisation of the right of withdrawal which had been one of the objectives of the *Acquis Review* has only been achieved in part – whilst there is now a standard withdrawal period of 14 days across the various directives which make available a right of withdrawal, each of these directives continues to have its own set of legal rules, rather than simply relying on one fully standardised set of rules. One might have expected this to be achieved by the Consumer Rights Directive. If the EU continues with its current trajectory of harmonisation in the field of consumer law, then we might expect to see further developments with regard to the right of withdrawal in the future.

There is a wider question to be asked, however: to what extent is the right of withdrawal an effective means of consumer protection? To answer this, one needs to see whether consumers utilise their right, and also gain an understanding as to why consumers decide to exercise this right or not. Comprehensive empirical evidence on this has yet to be provided. In the absence of such evidence, Luzak offers an assessment of the right of withdrawal from a behavioural economics perspective.[164] Although she finds some support in that literature for the introduction of a right of withdrawal, she also identifies a number of significant factors which might discourage consumers from exercising that right. One of these is an aversion of consumers to loss, which might prevent a consumer from withdrawing from a contract because of the costs potentially associated with this.[165] Another factor is the endowment effect, according to which consumers might overvalue goods in their possession over the gain they would make by returning them.[166] Moreover, consumers might be more concerned about loss arising from taking action (exercising the right of withdrawal) than inaction (keeping the

163 See further P Rott, 'Harmonising different rights of withdrawal'. *German Law Journal* 7 (2006), pp.1109–1146.

164 JA Luzak, 'To withdraw or not to withdraw? Evaluation of the mandatory right of withdrawal in consumer distance selling contracts taking into account its behavioural effects on consumers' (2013) 37 *Journal of Consumer Policy* pp.91–111.

165 Ibid., p.100.

166 Ibid., p.101

goods).[167] These, and the other factors discussed by Luzak, all suggest that there are significant behavioural barriers to consumers making effective use of the right of withdrawal.

It has also been noted that the standardisation of the withdrawal period to 14 days was primarily driven by a desire for consistency in the legal rules.[168] However, this particular period might suffer from being too long for some transactions and not long enough for others.[169] A short period might suffice in respect of contracts concluded in the consumer's home, where the consumer will probably want to change his mind quickly. Indeed, a shorter period might encourage consumers to exercise their right because of the need to act swiftly. That said, even in this context, the full implications of the contract might not be realised immediately and more time might be needed. In contrast, for more complex transactions, a longer period might be better.

Indeed, the lack of a sound basis for withdrawal rights has been criticised, not least because withdrawal rights are effectively a derogation from the *pacta sunt servanda* principle.[170] As such, withdrawal rights should be used only where the benefits exceed their cost, because the costs involved for a trader to comply with the rules regarding rights of withdrawal will be shared among all consumers.[171] This suggests that a broadly available, but rarely utilised, right of withdrawal would impose costs for very little benefit. It has therefore been suggested that in many contexts, consumers might benefit from having an optional withdrawal right, rather than the mandatory right currently provided for.[172] An 'optional' withdrawal right would present consumers with a choice when concluding a contract whether they wish to benefit from the option of a right of withdrawal. If they do, they may pay a slightly higher fee. Clearly, such an approach would not work in circumstances where the right of withdrawal is provided because of the risk of pressure-selling. However, in other contexts, such as online shopping, it could work – and already does, in some instances.[173]

Conclusions

In this chapter, we have explored the development of the two of the most frequently deployed tools of consumer protection: the provision of pre-contractual

167 Ibid., p.102–103.

168 Ibid., p.95; also M Loos, 'Rights of withdrawal' in G Howells and R Schulze, *Modernising and Harmonising Consumer Contract Law* (Sellier, 2009), p.242.

169 P Reikati and R van den Berg, 'Cooling-off periods in the consumer laws of the EC Member States' (2000) 23 *Journal of Consumer Policy* p.371.

170 H Eidenmüller, 'Why withdrawal rights?' (2011) 7(1) *European Review of Contract Law*.

171 Ibid.

172 O Ben-Shahar and EA Posner, 'The right to withdraw in contract law'. *Journal of Legal Studies* 40 (2011), p.115; cf. JA Luzak, 'To withdraw or not to withdraw? Evaluation of the mandatory right of withdrawal in consumer distance selling contracts taking into account its behavioural effects on consumers' (2013) 37 *Journal of Consumer Policy* pp.91, 106–8.

173 For example, hotel rooms or travel tickets are often available at different pricing levels, with higher levels generally allowing for cancellation of the room or ticket.

information and the right of withdrawal. Both can be used together and seek to overcome perceived informational imbalances between a trader and consumer by making available as much information as possible to a consumer, giving a consumer the opportunity to acquire information about alternative products, and allowing a consumer to escape from a contract if, on reflection, he no longer regards that contract as suitable.

For the development of EU consumer law, we can see how there has been a gradual increase in the technical detail of both tools as a result of a shift towards maximum harmonisation. This provides us with one useful lesson: if maximum harmonisation is to be effective as a policy goal, then the legal rules in EU consumer legislation have to be both sufficiently detailed and comprehensive to minimise the scope for significant national variations. In the Consumer Rights Directive, this is evident both with regard to pre-contractual information duties and the right of withdrawal. It seems to have been possible to reach agreement on these detailed provisions, although they are not complete – even here, aspects still need to be resolved at national level. This makes it far from certain that maximum harmonisation would translate into other areas. Indeed, there are some rather obvious problems with the particular brand of maximum harmonisation pursued here. As seen, the rules on both the provision of pre-contractual information and the right of withdrawal have become very detailed and quite technical. One drawback is that the level of precision in these rules invariably invites exploration of the remaining loopholes. However, the case for such filigree-style regulation is not obvious. Moreover, it will raise questions about the adaptability of these rules as business models develop and new ways of supplying goods to consumers and traders emerge, particularly in the context of the digital revolution.[174]

Appendix I: Information required by Art. 5 CRD

a the main characteristics of the goods or services, to the extent appropriate to the medium and to the goods or services;

b the identity of the trader, such as his trading name, the geographical address at which he is established and his telephone number;

c the total price of the goods or services inclusive of taxes, or where the nature of the goods or services is such that the price cannot reasonably be calculated in advance, the manner in which the price is to be calculated, as well as, where applicable, all additional freight, delivery or postal charges or, where those charges cannot reasonably be calculated in advance, the fact that such additional charges may be payable;

d where applicable, the arrangements for payment, delivery, performance, the time by which the trader undertakes to deliver the goods or to perform the service, and the trader's complaint handling policy;

174 Cf. the papers in A De Franceschi (ed), *European Contract Law and the Digital Single Market* (Intersentia, 2016).

e in addition to a reminder of the existence of a legal guarantee of conformity for goods, the existence and the conditions of after-sales services and commercial guarantees, where applicable;
f the duration of the contract, where applicable, or, if the contract is of indeterminate duration or is to be extended automatically, the conditions for terminating the contract;
g where applicable, the functionality, including applicable technical protection measures, of digital content;
h where applicable, any relevant interoperability of digital content with hardware and software that the trader is aware of or can reasonably be expected to have been aware of.

Appendix II: Information required by Art. 6 CRD

a the main characteristics of the goods or services, to the extent appropriate to the medium and to the goods or services;
b the identity of the trader, such as his trading name;
c the geographical address at which the trader is established and the trader's telephone number, fax number and e-mail address, where available, to enable the consumer to contact the trader quickly and communicate with him efficiently and, where applicable, the geographical address and identity of the trader on whose behalf he is acting;
d if different from the address provided in accordance with point (c), the geographical address of the place of business of the trader, and, where applicable, that of the trader on whose behalf he is acting, where the consumer can address any complaints;
e the total price of the goods or services inclusive of taxes, or where the nature of the goods or services is such that the price cannot reasonably be calculated in advance, the manner in which the price is to be calculated, as well as, where applicable, all additional freight, delivery or postal charges and any other costs or, where those charges cannot reasonably be calculated in advance, the fact that such additional charges may be payable. In the case of a contract of indeterminate duration or a contract containing a subscription, the total price shall include the total costs per billing period. Where such contracts are charged at a fixed rate, the total price shall also mean the total monthly costs. Where the total costs cannot be reasonably calculated in advance, the manner in which the price is to be calculated shall be provided;
f the cost of using the means of distance communication for the conclusion of the contract where that cost is calculated other than at the basic rate;
g the arrangements for payment, delivery, performance, the time by which the trader undertakes to deliver the goods or to perform the services and, where applicable, the trader's complaint handling policy;
h where a right of withdrawal exists, the conditions, time limit and procedures for exercising that right in accordance with Article 11(1), as well as the model withdrawal form set out in Annex I(B);

- i where applicable, that the consumer will have to bear the cost of returning the goods in case of withdrawal and, for distance contracts, if the goods, by their nature, cannot normally be returned by post, the cost of returning the goods;
- j that, if the consumer exercises the right of withdrawal after having made a request in accordance with Article 7(3) or Article 8(8), the consumer shall be liable to pay the trader reasonable costs in accordance with Article 14(3);
- k where a right of withdrawal is not provided for in accordance with Article 16, the information that the consumer will not benefit from a right of withdrawal or, where applicable, the circumstances under which the consumer loses his right of withdrawal;
- l a reminder of the existence of a legal guarantee of conformity for goods;
- m where applicable, the existence and the conditions of after sale customer assistance, after-sales services and commercial guarantees;
- n the existence of relevant codes of conduct, as defined in point (f) of Article 2 of Directive 2005/29/EC, and how copies of them can be obtained, where applicable;
- o the duration of the contract, where applicable, or, if the contract is of indeterminate duration or is to be extended automatically, the conditions for terminating the contract;
- p where applicable, the minimum duration of the consumer's obligations under the contract;
- q where applicable, the existence and the conditions of deposits or other financial guarantees to be paid or provided by the consumer at the request of the trader;
- r where applicable, the functionality, including applicable technical protection measures, of digital content;
- s where applicable, any relevant interoperability of digital content with hardware and software that the trader is aware of or can reasonably be expected to have been aware of;
- t where applicable, the possibility of having recourse to an out-of-court complaint and redress mechanism, to which the trader is subject, and the methods for having access to it.

4 Unfair contract terms

Introduction

Unfair contract terms regulation as a key indicator of EU policy

In 1993, European contract and consumer law was pushed towards new frontiers through the adoption of the Unfair Contract Terms Directive.[1] This was the first step by the European lawmaker into the heartland of contract law. After this Directive traditional national private lawyers could no longer ignore the development of European rules. From a private lawyer's perspective, the adoption of the Unfair Contract Terms Directive was one of the most important among the first wave of European consumer law measures. In the beginning, Europeanisation in many jurisdictions appeared as mainly symbolical, as the Directive did not produce much European case law. In others, like the UK, the implementation of the Directive started major changes in practice. However, the CJEU's law on unfair terms has started to expand rapidly after the turn of the millennium.

The early focus of the European lawmaker on the issue of unfair contract terms is understandable, as unfairness regulation can be seen as a key indicator of the basic approach of the private law system. The differences between the Member States in approaching this issue were probably wider in principle than in day-to-day practice. The Directive is therefore one further step towards building a common European approach to fairness, but is blended with national approaches.

As the starting point of the private law system is the recognition of the binding force of contracts, the system is disturbed by the question of how law should react to the use of unfair contract terms. The way of dealing with unfair contract terms regulation directly reflects the basic understandings of contract and contract law in the jurisdiction. Therefore, the Unfair Contract Terms Directive forces the EU consumer law discourse to focus on basic contract law issues. Basic principles of contract law have been brought on the European table in the discussions concerning the drafting and the application of the Directive.

1 Council Directive 93/13/EEC of 5 April 1993 on unfair terms in consumer contracts.

Chapter themes

The discussions and practice around the Directive connect with the deeper layers of the contract law discourse. Moreover, they also illustrate the tendencies in European consumer policy outlined in Chapter 1. As will be noted below, the Directive both reflects and resists these tendencies. Looked at from the perspective of these tendencies, the Unfair Contract Terms Directive offers a complex – one could even say contradictory – picture. From this perspective it is also an illustrative expression of the deeper levels of European discourse.

Harmonisation and the need for national regimes

The Unfair Contract Terms Directive offers an enduring example of the tension between attempts to enhance further market integration through maximum harmonisation and the need for national regimes based on the culture and expectations of the actors in the local marketplace. As the issue has been on the agenda during various stages of drafting, implementation and amendment, the fate of the Directive illustrates the changes in the discourse during the relevant period. In fact, the variations in the focus of the practice of the CJEU also adds its own perspective to this picture.

When the Directive was first drafted, the starting point was fairly clear. The Directive should be a minimum harmonisation directive. This was due to several reasons – in addition to the fact that minimum harmonisation in consumer law was the prevailing model in most cases at the time. The fact that unfair contracts regulation, as noted above, is connected to deep cleavages between the Member States in their conception of the role of contract law would have made it difficult to pursue maximum harmonisation, which would have brought with it a need for further harmonisation of contract law as well. For example, the huge variety of national mandatory rules on various issues and contract types would have had to be scrutinised in order to check that their protection level did not rise higher than the Directive would allow. Therefore, the Directive appears as a minimum compromise between the very differing starting points in Europe (see 'The Unfair Contract Terms Directive as a European compromise').

The later attempts in the original proposal for a Consumer Rights Directive[2] to turn the Directive into a maximum one did not succeed because of opposition from several Member States, among them the Nordic states fearing it would prevent them from reviewing the core terms of contracts. This is an example showing that the tendencies outlined in Chapter 1 of the book are occasionally successfully resisted, in this case even in relation to an important matter.

Adopted as a minimum harmonisation measure, the Directive has been integrated into the national regimes. With the different starting points in national

2 COM (2008) 614 final; see e.g. G Howells and R Schulze (eds), *Modernising and Harmonizing Consumer Contract Law* (Sellier, 2009).

laws, this has been the natural solution, but it also means that the law is not fully harmonised in this area, and even in practice appears only marginally harmonised as the CJEU has left many of the concrete issues to the national courts. The internal market link has not been able to remove national systems and their objectives. Despite the suggested task of promoting European standard forms, no such forms have been developed on the basis of the Directive. Instead, the development of case law has reinforced the basic differences between the Member States and the need to connect the assessment to national legal surroundings – and so also to national consumer expectations (see 'Back to national culture').

However, even though the CJEU has recognised the important role of national law and national assessment of unfairness, the law has other dimensions as well. One can identify a willingness in more recent cases from the CJEU to move towards seeing the Directive as a more free-standing European consumer protection measure which offers the Court the means for gradually developing a European doctrine of fairness. As these cases usually have not questioned the minimum role of the Directive, but rather have discussed how far the protection offered by the Directive would reach both substantially (see 'Steps towards a free-standing consumer protection measure') and procedurally (see 'The next step: A procedural Jack-in-the-box'), they are difficult to criticise from a consumer protection angle. Harmonisation is in these cases pushed both by internal market reasons and by consumer protection arguments.

One may argue that more far-reaching harmonisation might seem needed with regard to e-commerce. Then, however, not only unfair contract terms regulation, but the whole area of contract and sales law (see Chapter 5), as well as access to justice (Chapter 8), is affected.

Information and distribution of risk

Contract terms have a price. The function of the Directive could therefore be seen as an obligatory insurance against unfair terms, administered by the business. In addition one should mention the transaction cost argument in this context: with regard to transaction costs (time used) it would seem preferable that one authority uses a few hours to check a standard form than having thousands of consumers using half an hour each to read the conditions (without even understanding them).

There are, however, few explicit indications of such insurance or transaction cost-thinking in the materials around the Directive. Despite this the Directive offers a good example of an insurance-like, welfarist approach to consumer protection – even though it stops halfway because of important limitations of scope of the Directive. As the Directive in practice develops towards becoming a more free-standing consumer protection measure, there is a need to discuss to what extent this does and can imply a move towards a more insurance-motivated welfarist substantive approach. At least the CJEU has adopted a level of protection in applying the Directive that is relatively high, as compared to case law regarding other directives (see 'Steps towards a free-standing consumer protection measure').

The Court seems to recognise that standard terms are often not understood by consumers, irrespective of their degree of vulnerability. The real issue is in other words often an issue of whether the substance is fair in general rather than an issue of what a particular person might understand. The familiar concept of legitimate expectations would rather seem like a good yardstick for the assessment (see 'Conclusions and ways forward').

Focus on enforcement

The general enforcement rules in the Directive are the same as in other directives (adequate and effective means). Demands for better enforcement apply to this Directive as well. In fact, the CJEU seems to have been exceptionally preoccupied with the issue of enforcement when applying this Directive. Case law regarding the Directive has to a considerable degree dealt with issues concerning procedural enforcement.

CJEU case law has brought the application of the Directive far into the heartland of procedural law – even so much that one could speak about a Jack-in-the-Box effect (see 'The next step: A procedural Jack-in-the-box'). The practice of the CJEU regarding these issues could be understood as an indication of a more serious engagement of the Court in ensuring effective enforcement of consumer law. The Court has been pushed in this direction by a recurring need to grapple with grave social problems due to the European recession.

Towards a European brand?

Being at the core of private law policy, the Unfair Contract Terms Directive has met interest also outside of the EU. Perhaps it is not legally as 'branding' as the Products Liability Directive, but it has been looked at as one of the models for coping with contractual unfairness, competing with traditional unconscionability standards. The model function of the Directive is enhanced by the fact that it has been at least partially incorporated in general proposals for codification of European contract law, such as the Principles of European Contract Law and the Draft Common Frame of Reference for European Private Law. This issue is discussed further in the last section of this chapter on 'Conclusions and ways forward'.

More generally, it would certainly be a brand advantage for European businesses, if it could convey the message that European businesses are not using 'deceptive' fine print to limit liability and shift fair balance of rights and obligations.

Being in such a central position, the Directive has inspired legal theory. Some have described unfair contract terms regulation as a legal irritant,[3] whilst others may use the metaphor of Jack-in-the-Box.[4] The Directive also offers good

3 G Teubner, 'Legal irritants: Good faith in British law or how unifying law ends up in new divergences' (1998) 61 *Modern Law Review* pp.11–32.

building blocks for the construction of a more general principle of fairness for European contract law.[5] The 'brand' of European contract theory is undoubtedly affected by the Directive.

The Unfair Contract Terms Directive as a European compromise

The process of drafting the Directive was not an easy one. The starting points of the Member States were very different. Both within the EU, as well as in a more broad international perspective one can distinguish four different approaches to unfair contract terms regulation.[6]

The *first* approach is the one that traditionally was adopted by the UK. This model *lacks a general rule on unfairness* of contracts, as the law should recognise what the parties have agreed on, without fraud or force, as a just solution. Only for particular situations or issues might the law direct the courts to disregard the terms of the agreement. Even the UK Unfair Contract Terms Act 1977 fits into this model, as it does not, despite its name, contain a general rule on unfairness, but is only applicable to exemption clauses. And for standard contract terms only some specific rules exist, such as the 'red-hand rule' requiring a party who uses an onerous standard clause to draw the other party's attention to it.[7] Only with the introduction of the Unfair Terms in Consumer Contracts Regulations 1994,[8] based on the EU Unfair Contract Terms Directive, did UK contract law take a step towards the other approaches.[9]

The *second* approach is particularly focused on the fairness problems related to the use of *standard form contracts*. The philosophy behind this approach could be described as an attempt to take the justifications for the binding force of contracts seriously. The binding force of contracts is based on the consent or will of the parties; when a party uses standard conditions, there is no real consent

4 On this metaphor, see T Wilhelmsson, 'Jack-in-the-Box theory on European Community law' in L Krämer, H-W. Micklitz & K Tonner (eds), *Law and Diffuse Interests in the European Legal Order* (Nomos, 1997).

5 See e.g. B Lurger, "The 'social' side of contract law and the new principle of regard and fairness" in A Hartkamp et al. (eds), *Towards a European Civil Code* 4th ed (Kluwer Law International, 2011).

6 This part of the chapter is based on T Wilhelmsson and C Willett, 'Unfair terms and standard form contracts' in G Howells, I Ramsay, T Wilhelmsson and D Kraft (eds), *Handbook of Research on International Consumer Law* (Edward Elgar, 2010), pp.158–191, at 165–169.

7 *Interfoto Picture Library v Stiletto Visual Productions Ltd* [1989] QB 433 (CA).

8 Replaced by the Unfair Terms in Consumer Contracts Regulations 1999 and later by the Consumer Rights Act 2015.

9 See Department of Trade and Industry, *Implementation of the EC Directive on Unfair Terms in Consumer Contracts (93/13/EEC), A Consultation Document* (London, 1993) 1: 'The main effect of the Directive will be to introduce for the first time a general concept of fairness into the UK law of contract'.

from the other party and therefore the law has to intervene. The internationally paradigmatic example of this kind of approach was the German Act on General Conditions from 1976,[10] which was later included as a part of the German Civil Code.[11] This legislation is based on the recognition that there is a risk of a partial market failure when standard form contracts are used. The market failure has to be remedied with the help of rules allowing interference against unfair contract terms in standard forms. As market failure relates to the use of standard forms and not to the particular role of the parties to the contract, the unfairness regulation in this approach usually covers both consumer contracts and commercial contracts.

The *third* approach takes its starting point in the protection that certain groups of parties to a contract – or parties in a particular role – are perceived to need. The main reason for rules concerning unfairness of contracts is *consumer protection* and protection of other types of weak parties. The application of the rules is in this case usually delimited to business-to-consumer relations (and perhaps to other similar relations between strong and weak groups of parties), and does not apply to business-to-business relations. On the other hand, as the need for protection of consumers is not necessarily limited to the situations in which standard contract forms are used, the fairness control may be extended to individually negotiated clauses in consumer contracts as well. French law has usually been mentioned as an illustrative example of such a consumer protection-based approach.[12] Later, the Consumer Rights Act moved UK law in this direction.

Finally, the *fourth* approach looks at unfairness of contracts in the most comprehensive way, including the perspectives of both the standard form contract and consumer protection models and extending them in principle to cover the whole area of contract law. One might call this a *general fairness* approach. Nordic law – that is Finnish, Swedish, Norwegian, Danish and Icelandic law – probably contains one of the best examples of this approach. The Nordic Contracts Acts include in Section 36 an internationally rather well-known provision, according to which a court may set aside or adjust a contract term, if its application leads to unfair results.[13] This provision is applicable both to consumer contracts and to business-to-business relationships, and it covers both standard form contracts and individually negotiated terms, including the price. The hurdle for making use of the clause is considerably lower when dealing with standardised consumer contracts. This kind of approach is based on the recognition that contracting can

10 Gesetz zur Regelung des Rechts der Allgemeinen Geschäftsbedingungen, BGBl 76 I 3317.

11 Gesetz zur Modernisierung des Schuldrechts, Bürgerliches Gesetzbuch Art. 305–310. Rules on general conditions (algemene voorwarden) have been included in the modern Dutch Civil Code as well, in Art. 6:231–247.

12 Loi Scrivener 1978 and now Code de la Consommation, Art. L212-1.

13 In Sweden Lag om avtal och andra rättshandlingar på förmögenhetsrättens område (1915:218), the general clause added by Act 1976:185, in Finland Laki varallisuusoikeudellisista oikeustoimista (228/1929), the general clause added by Act 956/82, in Norway Avtaleloven (1918/4), the general clause added by Act 1983/160, and in Denmark Lov om aftaler og andra retshandler på formuerettens område (1986/600).

lead to unfair results in all kinds of relationships and with regard to all kinds of terms, and on the understanding that the court system of a just state should not be used to enforce substantive unfairness.

As there were at least four different approaches adopted in Europe with regard to the regulation of contractual unfairness, the drafting of the European Unfair Contract Terms Directive was a challenge. How could these differences be reconciled in a way that was acceptable to all Member States?

The task was made somewhat easier by the fact that the practical consequences of the different approaches were not as different as one could expect. In all approaches – even the general fairness approach – there is in the overwhelming majority of cases of disagreement between contractual parties no reason for applying the unfairness provisions. And in that margin where unfairness does occur, very many of the cases concern consumer contracts based on standard forms – covered by all approaches. So the cases in which the differences between the approaches would gain relevance are perhaps not so many as one might expect. But certainly there are such cases.

In the Unfair Contract Terms Directive the problem of harmonizing such different approaches was solved through two aspects that made the Directive acceptable and easy to implement for the Member States, with provisions based on the second, third and fourth approaches. The Directive is focused on the most important group of cases, that is consumer contracts based on standard forms (a kind of combination of the second and third models), and other situations have been left outside its scope. However, in order to accommodate the remaining parts of the second and third models as well as the fourth model, the Directive was made a minimum harmonisation directive that allowed Member States to have more stringent rules than the Directive prescribed. In national law, it was still possible to protect consumers against individualised terms, as well as to have unfairness rules for business-to-business contracts which are outside the scope of the Directive.

The amendments of national laws because of the Directive therefore were often of minor importance. Only for countries like the UK, representing the first approach with little general regulation of unfairness, the Directive required thorough changes. First implemented by the UK in Unfair Terms in Consumer Contracts Regulation 1994, in 2015 the provisions on unfair contracts terms in consumer contracts were included in the Consumer Rights Act, Part 2.

The Directive in this way pushed a new standard into English contract law, the principle of fairness and good faith which might in a longer perspective have even broader implications. In a well-known paper, the German legal theorist Gunther Teubner therefore has called the good faith principle of the Directive a 'legal irritant' in English law, in many unforeseen ways affecting the English legal landscape, perhaps for example by triggering 'deep, long-term changes from highly formal rule-focused decision-making in contract law toward a more discretionary principle-based judicial reasoning.'[14]

14 Teubner, op. cit. at 21 (where Teubner also notes that this process would occur in a very different way than it would in Germany, because of the very different legal culture).

The main content and goals of the Directive

The drafting of the Unfair Contract Terms Directive started as early as the 1970s.[15] The goal was ambitious. In the first proposals of the Commission the Directive had a wide sphere of application, covering both individually negotiated and standard form contracts.[16] Later the scope was limited to a term 'which has not been individually negotiated' (Art. 3).

The limitation of the scope reflected criticism, in particular in German legal literature, according to which the fairness control of individually negotiated contracts was in conflict with private autonomy and the functioning of the market economy.[17] This reflected the German standard form contract approach to unfairness. Autonomy and real consent should be the guiding principles of unfairness regulation. In this perspective it is understandable that the Directive has been said to represent 'a victory for the consumer choice perspective'.[18]

In the preamble of the Directive the consumer protection goal is addressed in the language of abuse of power: 'acquirers of goods and services should be protected against the abuse of power by the seller or supplier, in particular against one-sided standard contracts and the unfair exclusion of essential rights in contracts' (Recital 9). At the same time the internal market aspect is underlined as well. It is noted that varying rules on unfair contracts may lead to distortions of competition and also deter active internal market consumers from making purchases in other Member States (Recitals 2 and 5). The idea of the confident cross-border shopping consumer, which has been referred to as a reason for much European regulation,[19] has already appeared in the context of this Directive.

Considering the Directive is primarily concerned with standard form contracts and is based on the internal market perspective, one could claim that the Directive was aimed at promoting a reasonable standardisation of consumer contract forms to improve the operation of the single market. The free movement of standard contract forms could at least impliedly be seen as a basic goal of the Directive.

The compromise nature of the Directive, relating it to several of the European models mentioned above, is reflected in its sphere of application.[20]

15 Preliminary programme for consumer protection and information policy, OJ 1975 C 92/1, at 18, 19, 24, 25.

16 OJ 1990 C 243/2 and OJ 1992 C 73/7.

17 HE Brandner and P Ulmer, 'The Community Directive on unfair terms in consumer contracts: Some critical remarks on the proposal submitted by the EC Commission'. *CMLR* 28 (1991), p.647, at 652 *et seq.*

18 H Collins, 'Good faith in European contract law'. *OJLS* 14 (1994), p.229, at 239.

19 For a criticism, see T Wilhelmsson, "The abuse of the 'confident consumer' as a justification for EC consumer law" (2004) 27 *Journal of Consumer Policy* p.317 and C Twigg-Flesner 'The importance of law and harmonisation for the EU's confident consumer' in D Leczykiewicz and S Weatherill (eds), *The Images of the Consumer in EU Law* (Hart, 2015).

20 In addition to the issues mentioned below there are a couple of cases stating that the Directive is not applicable to cases in the Member States who joined in (or after) 2004 which arose before accession: C-302/04 *Ynos kft v János Varga* [2006] ECR I-371,

First, it covers only consumer contracts. The definitions of 'consumer', as 'any natural person who … is acting for purposes which are outside his trade, business or profession', as well as of 'seller and supplier', as 'any natural or legal person who … is acting for purposes relating to his trade, business or profession, whether publicly owned or privately owned' are in line with similar definitions in other pieces of European consumer legislation and are analysed elsewhere in this volume.[21] The CJEU has for example ruled that tenancy agreements,[22] contracts for legal services,[23] and certain securities given by a consumer[24] are within the scope of the Directive.

Second, as mentioned above, the Directive only covers terms which have not been individually negotiated. Taken at face value, this seems to refer to standard contract terms, which obviously are at the core of the Directive. However, due to its compromise nature, the scope of the Directive is wider than just covering standard terms proper. It also covers 'pre-formulated individual terms', if they were not individually negotiated. A term is considered as not individually negotiated if it is drafted in advance and the consumer has therefore not been able to influence its substance (Art. 3(2)). The burden of proof that a term has been individually negotiated lies on the seller or supplier who makes that claim (Art. 3(2)). It does not matter how the not-individually negotiated terms are included in the contract. According to the preamble of the Directive oral agreements are also covered by the Directive (Recital 11).

The focus on terms that have not been individually negotiated is reinforced by the particular delimitation concerning the definition of the main subject matter of the contract and the adequacy of the price and remuneration, mentioned in Art. 4(2) of the Directive. According to the Directive, terms relating to these issues are outside the scope of the unfairness clause. However, the terms are not completely outside the scope of the Directive, as they are covered by the requirement that they should be expressed in plain intelligible language. As will be shown later,[25] this has been used to narrow the scope of the delimitation, as the transparency criteria have been set relatively high.

C-153/13 *Pohotovosť, s.r.o. v Ján Soroka* [2014], C-92/14 *Liliana Tudoran, Florin Iulian Tudoran, Ilie Tudoran v SC Suport Colect SRL* [2014].

21 See Chapter 1, p.25. On the Unfair Contract Terms Directive, see e.g. joined cases C-541-542/99 *Cape Snc v Idealservice Srl et Idealservice MN RE Sas v OMAI Srl* (2001) ECR I-9049 (only natural persons) and C-110/14 *Horaţiu Ovidiu Costea v SC Volksbank România SA* ECLI:EU:C:2015:538 (a lawyer concluding a credit agreement not linked to his profession may be regarded as consumer).

22 C-488/11 *Dirk Frederik Asbeek Brusse, Katarina de Man Garabito v Jahani BV* ECLI:EU:C:2013:341.

23 C-537/13 *Birutė Šiba v Arūnas Devėnas* ECLI:EU:C:2015:14.

24 C-74/15 *Dumitru Tarcău, Ileana Tarcău v Banca Comercială Intesa Sanpaolo România SA and Others* ECLI:EU:C:2015:772.

25 Section entitled 'Steps towards a free-standing consumer protection measure', see in particular C-26/13 *Árpád Kásler, Hajnalka Káslerné Rábai v OTP Jelzálogbank Zrt*

Third, contractual terms which reflect mandatory statutory or regulatory provisions and provisions or principles of international conventions are not subject to the Directive (Art. 1(2)).[26] More generally, statutory and regulatory provisions are excluded, when there is no contractual term altering the effect or ambit of those provisions.[27] But the limitation does not preclude applying the Directive to contract terms that reproduce a rule of national law to another category of contracts.[28]

The substantive rules of the Directive may also be divided into three groups.

First and foremost, the Directive attempts to formulate a European concept of unfairness. The basic rule of the Directive is a general clause, in Art. 3(1):

> A contractual term which has not been individually negotiated shall be regarded as unfair if, contrary to the requirement of good faith, it causes a significant imbalance in the parties' rights and obligations arising under the contract, to the detriment of the consumer.

In addition, in Art. 4(1) the Directive contains some guidelines for the application of the unfairness clause:

> Without prejudice to Article 7, the unfairness of a contractual term shall be assessed, taking into account the nature of the goods or services for which the contract was concluded and by referring, at the time of conclusion of the contract, to all the circumstances attending the conclusion of the contract and to all the other terms of the contract or of another contract on which it is dependent.

These general clauses are supplemented by a fairly extensive list of examples on unfair contract terms (Annex). As the Annex is expressly described as being indicative and non-exhaustive (Art. 3(3)) – a so-called grey-list – the fairly detailed nature of the Annex does not narrow the rather broad scope of decision-making power given to the courts through the general clauses.[29]

In other words, the ways in which the courts apply Art. 3(1) and 4(1) are decisive with regard to the question of whether the Directive reaches the goal that has

ECLI:EU:C:2014:282 and C-96/14 *Jean-Claude Van Hove v CNP Assurances SA* ECLI:EU:C:2015:262.

26 See C-473/00 *Cofidis SA v Jean-Louis Fredout* [2002] ECR I-10875 and C-92/11 *RWE Vertrieb AG v Verbraucherzentrale Nordrhein-Westfalen eV* ECLI:EU:C:2013:180, C-488/11 *Dirk Frederik Asbeek Brusse, Katarina de Man Garabito v Jahani BV* ECLI:EU:C:2013:341 and C-34/13 *Monika Kušionová v SMART Capital a.s.* ECLI:EU:C:2014:2189. Compare, however, C-613/15 *Ibercaja Banco SAU v José Cortés González* ECLI:EU:C:2016:195.

27 C-280/13 *Barclays Bank SA v Sara Sánchez García, Alejandro Chacón Barrera* ECLI:EU:C:2014:279.

28 C-92/11 *RWE Vertrieb AG v Verbraucherzentrale Nordrhein-Westfalen eV* ECLI:EU:C:2013:180.

29 See below, 'Back to national culture'.

been set for it. This issue is very much at the core of the following analysis. As will be shown, one can find both a fairly strong respect for the various national legal cultures in the practice of the CJEU, but lately also some steps towards a more truly European concept of unfairness.

Secondly, the Directive contains a provision on interpretation. In Art. 5 the Directive emphasises the significance of plain, intelligible language.[30] As mentioned before, this requirement concerning plain intelligible language also covers terms relating to the definition of the main subject matter of the contract and to the adequacy of the price and remuneration, even though these terms are not subject to assessment based on the unfairness clause (Art. 4(2)).

As a consequence of breach of the requirement of plain intelligible language, the Directive confirms the principle of interpretation *in dubio contra stipulatorem*. The interpretation most favourable to the consumer shall prevail. The Directive also states the obvious, that this rule shall not apply in collective injunction proceedings. It can of course not be a defence in such proceedings that the most favourable interpretation of an unclear term is not to be considered unfair. An objective interpretation allows for more frequent prohibition of unintelligible or ambiguous terms.[31]

Third, the main remedies and legal consequences of unfairness are defined by the Directive. The sanctions are both individual contract law remedies, as well as collective preventive measures.

As to contract law proper, the Directive states that unfair terms shall not be binding on the consumer (Art. 6(1)). The preventive measures again are defined through a phrase well-known from other directives. The Member States shall ensure that adequate and effective means exist to prevent the continued use of unfair terms in consumer contracts (Art. 7(1)). The provision expressly requires the acceptance of organizational action (Art. 7(2)) and includes business associations that recommend the use of standard terms in the sphere of possible defendants (Art. 7(3)). The provisions on remedies will be described in somewhat more detail later (see 'The next step: A procedural Jack-in-the-box'), as the procedural law context has become a focal area for European courts and the CJEU in Europeanising the unfair contract terms agenda.

The section on remedies also contains a rule related to choice of law, to strengthen the mandatory, non-exclusion nature of the Directive. Member States are obliged to take necessary measures to ensure that the consumer does not lose the protection of the Directive by virtue of the choice of the law of a non-Member country, if the contract has a close connection with the territory of the Member States. This vague provision allows for various national interpretations.

30 This rule has to be expressly implemented, and it is not sufficient that it is established in court practice, see Case C-144/99 *Commission of the European Communities v Kingdom of the Netherlands* [2001] ECR I-3541.

31 C-70/03 *Commission of the European Communities v Kingdom of Spain* [2004] ECR I-7999.

However, the vagueness cannot be removed through more precise national rules. 'Close connection' may be concretised by means of presumptions only, not by a combination of predetermined criteria.[32] As case law is scarce, it is hard to assess the harmonisation effect and the consumer protection value of this provision, and it will not be dealt with further in this chapter.

The fact that the fairness assessment of the Directive cannot be applied to contract terms that have been individually negotiated, to terms that relate to the definition of the main subject matter of the contract and to terms relating to the adequacy of the price and remuneration does not preclude, because of the minimum nature of the Directive, national fairness rules that cover individual terms, the main subject matter of the contract as well as the price.[33]

The continuing existence of a large variety of solutions in Europe has troubled the Commission. A project for a turn into a more harmonised legal landscape was started. The plans for a Consumer Rights Directive were elaborated, consolidating both unfairness legislation, as well as other consumer contracts legislation, in one maximum harmonisation directive.[34] However, as to the issue of unfair contract terms, the basic starting points of the Member States were so different, based on deep ideological commitments, that no sufficient agreement could be reached. With regard to the very different approaches in the various Member States (above, see 'The Unfair Contract Terms Directive as a European compromise') and the fairly nationally geared practice based on the Directive (below, 'Back to national culture') this result is not surprising.

The only result of this exercise regarding unfair terms was a new information provision in the Directive on Consumer Rights.[35] Article 32 provides that a Member State that adopts more stringent provisions on unfair terms than prescribed by the Directive shall inform the EU Commission thereof. In particular such information should be given on provisions extending the unfairness assessment to individually negotiated contractual terms or to the adequacy of the price or remuneration or lists of contractual terms considered to be unfair. The Commission shall ensure that this information is accessible to consumers and traders, *inter alia*, on a dedicated website and shall inform the other Member States and the Parliament. The goal of this provision seems to be transparency.

32 C-70/03 *Commission of the European Communities v Kingdom of Spain* [2004] ECR I-7999.

33 In C-484/08 *Caja de Ahorros y Monte de Piedad de Madrid v Asociación de Usuarios de Servicios Bancarios (Ausbanc)* [2010] ECR I-4785 the CJEU has expressly confirmed that the Directive does not preclude such national legislation.

34 Commission, *Proposal for a Directive of the European Parliament and of the Council on Consumer Rights*, COM (2008) 614.

35 Directive 2011/83/EU of the European Parliament and of the Council of 25 October 2011 on consumer rights, amending Council Directive 93/13/EEC and Directive 1999/44/EC of the European Parliament and of the Council and repealing Council Directive 85/577/EEC and Directive 97/7/EC of the European Parliament and of the Council.

The businesses and consumers of the Union should be aware of the various possibilities legally to interfere against unfairness of core terms within the Member States. But the value is obviously reduced by the fact that it covers only new national provisions. Therefore, the main aim of the information requirement might be the creation of a light incentive against new provisions going further than the Directive. But this is, of course, far from the original maximum harmonisation goal of the project.

The failed attempt to reform the Directive, resulting only in a notification duty, shows that the turn towards full harmonisation noted as one theme of this book has exceptions. The Unfair Contract Terms Directive rather indicates a sensibility towards basic national legal convictions. As will be shown in next section, this is reflected in case law of the CJEU as well. In addition, one might even claim that recent case law concerning the Directive indicates a commitment of the Court towards the original consumer protection-driven thinking rather than the ethos of market integration, expressed in the development of the Directive towards a more actively used consumer protection measure (see sections 'Steps towards a free-standing consumer protection measure' and 'The next step: A procedural Jack-in-the-box').

Back to national culture

A basic tension in the case law concerning the Unfair Contract Terms Directive arises in the relationship between European provisions on unfairness and national contract law provisions concerning the rights and obligations of the parties under a contract. As the latter are not harmonised it is difficult to develop a detailed European practice on unfair terms, recognizing that one of the arguments to take into account in the assessment on unfairness is the extent to which the term to be evaluated differs from the non-mandatory default rules of national law to be applied to the contract. The assessment of whether a term increases the obligations of the consumer or limits the rights of the consumer in an unfair manner requires knowledge of what obligations or rights the consumer would have without the term, and that knowledge is normally found in national law. This point of departure is natural in the Continental context, where often detailed non-mandatory default rules are understood as an essential part of the rules of the contractual relationship, but also from a common law perspective it has been argued that 'default rules have a key role to play'.[36]

In many cases, the CJEU has been quite sensitive to this tension between the European and the national domains. References back to national law are numerous. The Court acknowledges the variety of European legal cultures in the application of the Directive. Not only does the minimum harmonisation character of the Directive allow various solutions for the Member States, but, according to

36 C Willett, *Fairness in Consumer Contracts* (Ashgate, 2007), p.229.

the practice of the CJEU, national variations are unavoidable also in the detailed application of the common rules.

This attitude can be seen in rulings concerning the delimitations of the scope of the Directive. For example, on the limitation of the scope not to cover contractual terms which reflect mandatory statutory or regulatory provisions (Art. 1(2)), the CJEU has repeatedly stated that it is for the national court to determine whether a term reflects the content of a mandatory statutory or regulatory provision.[37]

A similar approach is taken towards the delimitation of scope mentioned in Art. 4(2). In jurisdictions where the scope of the fairness rule is delimited in the way that the Directive foresees, it is to a great extent left to the national courts to evaluate whether a certain term relates to the main subject matter of the contract. In *Árpád Kásler*,[38] dealing with a term in a foreign currency loan agreement, according to which the currency selling rate was applied for the purpose of calculating the repayment instalments, the CJEU found, as to the question whether this term could be considered to relate to the main subject matter of the contract, that 'it is for the national court to ascertain having regard to the nature, general scheme and stipulations of the contract and its legal and factual context, that that term lays down an essential obligation of that agreement which, as such characterises it'.

The tension between European unfairness regulation and national contract law of course is most visible in the unfairness assessment itself, in the application of the general clause in Art. 3(1) and its concretising general clause in Art. 4(1). Consequently, also in this core area of the Directive, much of the assessment of unfairness is left to the national courts.

The landmark case in which the role of national assessment is very clearly stated is *Freiburger Kommunalbauten*.[39] According to this decision, the national court had to decide whether a contractual term in a building contract requiring the whole of the price to be paid before the performance by the seller or supplier could be regarded as unfair. The CJEU here emphasised that in the assessment of unfairness the consequences of the term under applicable law had to be taken into account and that therefore consideration should be given to the national law. So even though the CJEU could interpret the general criteria defining the concept

37 C-488/11 *Dirk Frederik Asbeek Brusse, Katarina de Man Garabito v Jahani BV* ECLI:EU:C:2013:341, C-34/13 *Monika Kušionová v SMART Capital a.s.* ECLI:EU:C:2014:2189.

38 C-26/13 *Árpád Kásler, Hajnalka Káslerné Rábai v OTP Jelzálogbank Zrt* ECLI:EU:C:2014:282. See also C-96/14 *Jean-Claude Van Hove v CNP Assurances SA* ECLI:EU:C:2015:262 (certain insurance terms: national court finds that essential component and characterises it) and C-143/13 *Bogdan Matei, Ioana Ofelia Matei v SC Volksbank România SA* ECLI:EU:C:2015:127 (certain clauses in credit agreement not excluded from scope of Directive; but it is for the national court to verify that classification).

39 C-237/02 *Freiburger Kommunalbauten GmbH Baugesellschaft & Co. KG v Ludger Hofstetter and Ulrike Hofstetter* [2004] ECR I-3403.

of unfair terms, 'it should not rule on the application of these general criteria to a particular term, which must be considered in the light of the particular circumstances of the case in question.'[40] Therefore, it is for the national court to decide whether the term is to be regarded as unfair.

This line of reasoning is followed up in other cases.[41] Even in the landmark cases for developing a European doctrine of unfairness, for example *Mohamed Aziz*,[42] the Court starts its conclusion by noting that the concept of 'significant imbalance' has to be 'assessed in the light of an analysis of the rules of national law' in order to determine to what extent the consumer is placed in a less favourable position. In its reasoning the Court noted it as being 'clear' that the national court had to determine the fate of the contractual term under scrutiny, whilst the CJEU could only provide guidance.[43]

However, case law of the CJEU is not completely coherent in this respect. In the well-known *Océano* case,[44] the CJEU had declared a jurisdiction clause, according to which the court at the seller's place had jurisdiction in respect of all disputes arising from the contract, unfair, instead of leaving that assessment to the national court. This triggered an explanation by the court in the case *Freiburger Kommunalbauten*, in which the Court basically referred to the obvious character of the unfairness of the jurisdiction clause, being solely to the benefit of the seller and containing no benefit in return for the consumer, which made it unnecessary to assess it in relation to national law.[45] Later case law on similar jurisdiction clauses, however, seems ambivalent, bringing the assessment even of these clauses at least in principle under the main rule that the evaluation of unfairness of concrete terms should be made by the national court.[46] But the CJEU may give fairly detailed guidance on the assessment of such clauses, as well as other clauses in the Annex.

The eagerness to strike more or less directly at one-sided jurisdiction clauses may relate to the fact that the CJEU has been particularly active in safeguarding

40 *Freiburger Kommunalbauten*, para 22.
41 See e.g. C-76/10 *Pohotovosť s.r.o. v Iveta Korčkovská* [2010] ECR I-11557 (penalty clause in credit agreement) and C-472/10 *Nemzeti Fogyasztóvédelmi Hatóság v Invitel Távközlési Zrt.* ECLI:EU:C:2012:242 (term on unilateral amendment of fees for a service).
42 Case C-415/11 *Mohamed Aziz v Caixa d'Estalvis de Catalunya, Tarragona i Manresa (Catalunyacaixa)* ECLI:EU:C:2013:164, para 76. So also C-226/12 *Constructora Principado SA v José Ignacio Menéndez Álvarez* ECLI:EU:C:2014:10. See on both cases below in 'Steps towards a free-standing consumer protection measure'.
43 *Mohamed Aziz*, para 66.
44 Joined cases C-240/98 to C-244/98 *Océano Grupo Editorial SA v Rocío Murciano Quintero and Salvat Editores SA v José M. Sánchez Alcón Prades, José Luis Copano Badillo, Mohammed Berroane and Emilio Viñas Feliú* [2000] ECR I-4941.
45 *Freiburger Kommunalbauten*, para 23.
46 C-137/08 *VB Pénzügyi Lízing Zrt. v Ferenc Schneider* [2010] ECR I-10847 (jurisdiction clause must be regarded as unfair, in so far as it causes significant imbalance), C-243/08 *Pannon GSM Zrt v Erzsébet Sustikné Győrfi* [2009] ECR I-4713 (national court to determine).

the procedural rights of consumers when applying the Unfair Contract Terms Directive. A similar attitude seems to be prevailing in *Sebestyén*[47] in which the CJEU left the assessment of unfairness of an arbitration clause to the national court to determine, but at the same time gave very concrete criteria for the assessment of such an arbitration clause which most likely would lead to a finding of unfairness. The extensive use of the Directive to support the consumer procedurally is more closely described below (see 'The next step: A procedural Jack-in-the-box').

In any event, the general rule remains paramount. According to the practice of the CJEU, the assessment of the unfairness of a specific term shall be made by the national court, taking into account both all the circumstances of the case and the national legal context which the term is a part of. However, this acknowledgement of the national legal context has, during later years, been accompanied by a growing willingness of the CJEU to concretise the assessment, to establish more concrete criteria for the application of the general clauses, but – at least until now –[48] still respecting the national assessment of particular terms. This slow emergence of pieces of a European doctrine of unfairness is described in the next section of the chapter.

National courts have gladly made use of the leeway that the *Freiburger Kommunalbauten* doctrine offers them to make their own assessments of unfairness. In Europe, despite the Unfair Contract Terms Directive, fairness decisions are still to a large extent made at the national level. And with differing basic ideologies one can certainly not expect identical practical results. Courts from different jurisdictions naturally read the general clauses of the Directive in the light of their traditional national doctrines.[49] It will be interesting to see whether and how the gradual emergence of Europeanised principles, as analysed in the next section, will be received by European national courts, used to making concrete assessments of unfairness quite independently.

One good illustration, among others, of the difficulties to come is given by the much-cited English case *First National Bank*,[50] in fact decided before *Freiburger Kommunalbauten*. The decision and reasoning of the House of Lords indicate a preference for avoiding too much Europeanisation of the issue, even though the Court accepted the European starting point. Not only was the concrete

47 C-342/13 *Katalin Sebestyén v Zsolt Csaba Kővári, OTP Bank Nyrt., OTP Faktoring Követeléskezelő Zrt, Raiffeisen Bank Zrt* ECLI:EU:C:2014:1857. See also C-168/05 *Elisa María Mostaza Claro v Centro Móvil Milenium SL* [2006] ECR I-10421, according to which a national court in an action for annulment of an arbitration award must determine whether the arbitration clause is void.

48 It is probably too early to state that '*Freiburger Kommunalbauten* belongs to the past', as does H-W Micklitz in N Reich, H-W.Micklitz, P Rott and K Tonner, *European Consumer Law* (2nd ed, Intersentia 2014), at 152.

49 See eg P Nebbia, *Unfair Contract Terms in European Law. A Study in Comparative and EC Law* (Hart 2007).

50 *Director General of Fair Trading v First National Bank* [2001] UKHL 52.

assessment of the unfairness of a term kept at the national level (although arguably there should have been made a reference to the CJEU), but the assessment criteria were further elaborated nationally. In the words of Lord Bingham:

> If the meaning of the test were doubtful, or vulnerable to the possibility of differing interpretations in differing member states, it might be desirable or necessary to seek a ruling from the European Court of Justice on its interpretation. But the language used in expressing the test, so far as applicable in this case, is in my opinion clear and not reasonably capable of differing interpretations.... The requirement of good faith in this context is one of fair and open dealing. Openness requires that the terms should be expressed fully, clearly and legibly, containing no concealed pitfalls or traps. Appropriate prominence should be given to terms which might operate disadvantageously to the customer. Fair dealing requires that a supplier should not, whether deliberately or unconsciously, take advantage of the consumer's necessity, indigence, lack of experience, unfamiliarity with the subject matter of the contract, weak bargaining position or any other factor listed in or analogous to those listed in Schedule 2 of the regulations. Good faith in this context is not an artificial or technical concept; nor, since Lord Mansfield was its champion, is it a concept wholly unfamiliar to British lawyers. It looks to good standards of commercial morality and practice.

The ease with which Lord Bingham finds the general clause not allowing for differing interpretations in differing Member States is surprising. And so is the self-evident way in which the more concrete criteria for applying the fairness test are described. But the case shows very clearly the tensions between national context and Europeanised application of the Directive.[51] The possible striving towards a European doctrine on unfairness will certainly clash with national doctrines, so far acknowledged to have relatively much leeway by *Freiburger Kommunalbauten* and subsequent case law.

A part of the Directive that directly relates to the assessment of concrete terms is the Annex. It enumerates 17 cases of terms which may be regarded as unfair. However, as the Annex only contains an indicative and non-exhaustive list of potentially unfair terms (Art. 3(3)), it has not become a vehicle for developing a substantive European doctrine on unfairness. The CJEU has clearly stated that the indicativeness of the list implies that a term on the list does not necessarily have to be deemed unfair and, on the other hand, that the absence of a term from the list does not prevent it from being considered unfair.[52] Therefore it is up to

51 M Dean, 'Defining unfair terms in consumer contracts – crystal ball gazing? *Director General of Fair Trading v First National Bank plc*' (2002) 65 *Modern Law Review* p.773; also C Twigg-Flesner, *The Europeanisation of Contract Law*, ch.4, pp.141–145.

52 C-478/99 *Commission of the European Communities v Kingdom of Sweden* [2002] ECR I-4147.

the Member States how to implement the list, whether by legislation or, as in the Nordic countries, through a description of the list in the *travaux prèparatoires*, as long as the way of implementation offers a sufficient guarantee that the public can obtain knowledge of it.[53]

This does not mean that the list in the Annex lacks importance. It is certainly, at least in some jurisdictions, used in practice for example as a kind of a check list. The Annex also seems to have increasing relevance even in CJEU case law. Even though the CJEU tends to leave decisions on particular terms to national courts, it nevertheless, and to a growing extent, makes reference to particular terms in the Annex in its reasoning.[54] One may foresee the CJEU gradually generating a European understanding of the list.[55] It should be noted, however, that even in the case that has been referred to as a landmark in the move towards a more Europeanised doctrine of unfairness, *Mohamed Aziz*,[56] the CJEU expressly stated that the Directive must be interpreted as meaning that the Annex contains only an indicative and non-exhaustive list of terms which may be regarded as unfair.

The interventions of the CJEU are not the only judicial means for affecting the level of harmonisation of court practice related to the Unfair Contract Terms Directive. One might also foresee what could be called a 'free movement of legal ideas' directly across the national borders.[57] The various national courts could learn from each other. In order to facilitate such learning processes the Commission sponsored an extensive collection of cases – both cases from the time before the Directive and cases applying the legislation based on the Directive – which were published freely available on the web as CLAB Europe.[58] However, the relatively abstract and sometimes even unintelligible level of reporting in combination with the large amount of materials of varying quality that was received

53 *Commission v Sweden*, para 22.

54 See, e.g. joined cases C-240/98 to C-244/98 *Océano Grupo Editorial SA v Roció Murciano Quintero and Salvat Editores SA v José M. Sánchez Alcón Prades, José Luis Copano Badillo, Mohammed Berroane and Emilio Viñas Feliú* [2000] ECR I-4941, para 22, C-137/08 *VB Pénzügyi Lízing Zrt. v Ferenc Schneider* [2010] ECR I-10847, para 54, C-472/10 *Nemzeti Fogyasztóvédelmi Hatóság v Invitel Távközlési Zrt.* ECLI:EU:C:2012:242, paras 24–26, C-92/11 *RWE Vertrieb AG v Verbraucherzentrale Nordrhein-Westfalen eV* ECLI:EU:C:2013:180, paras 46, 49 and 52, C-415/11 *Mohamed Aziz v Caixa d'Estalvis de Catalunya, Tarragona i Manresa (Catalunyacaixa)* ECLI:EU:C:2013:164, para 75, and C-377/14 *Ernst Georg Radlinger and Helena Radlingerová v Finway a.s.* ECLI:EU:C:2016:283, interpreting the Annex point 1(e).

55 Micklitz in Reich et al., *European Consumer Law*, op. cit., at 159.

56 C-415/11 *Mohamed Aziz v Caixa d'Estalvis de Catalunya, Tarragona i Manresa (Catalunyacaixa)* ECLI:EU:C:2013:164.

57 See e.g. J Smits, *The Making of European Contract Law* (Antwerp, Intersentia, 2002), at 63, T Wilhelmsson, 'The design of an optional (re)statement of European contract law – real life instead of dead concepts' in S Grundmann and J Stuyck (eds), *An Academic Green Paper on European Contract Law* (Kluwer Law International, 2002) p.354.

58 See H-W Micklitz and M Radeideh, '*CLAB Europa* – the European database on unfair terms in consumer contracts' (2005) 28 *JCP* pp.325–360.

were probably the reasons why this material never seemed to have any impact. The project is now closed.[59] There still seems to be little horizontal movement of unfairness reasoning across the European borders. The Directive has so far not functioned as a catalyst for such an indirect harmonisation effect.

Summing up, it is easy to see that the Directive so far has not even in its heartland – in which the differences following from the minimum character of the Directive and its scope of application should be less prominent – been able to introduce a joint European approach to the issue of unfair contract terms. The idea of an area in which standard conditions could move freely across the borders, with similar legal consequences, has not materialised. Seen from the perspective of free movement of terms, the Directive is a failure. Still, if the Directive contributes to the removal of what one could call fairness-based hidden traps[60] for those doing cross-border trade, it has achieved something. And from a consumer protection point of view, the fairly strong emphasis on the national context is probably commendable, bearing in mind the variations in consumer culture and consumer expectations between the Member States.[61]

In fact, one may even assume that the Directive in one way works against the free movement of standard conditions. It has been argued that the requirement concerning intelligibility of terms implies that the consumer should receive them in an intelligible language, such as the mother tongue of the consumer.[62] If this is the case, terms would not be able to move freely across the borders without translation.

Steps towards a free-standing consumer protection measure

There is a certain emphasis on national law on the European unfair contract terms scene, following both from the minimum character of the Unfair Contract Terms Directive, and from the application of the Directive by the CJEU. However, there is another side of the coin as well. In much decision-making concerning the Directive, a focal issue is the balancing between the necessary relationship to national law and legal culture and the striving for a genuinely autonomous European understanding of unfairness. It seems that the European side of the balance has been given more weight in the more recent case law of the CJEU. The Court is said to have kissed awake the 'Sleeping Beauty'.[63] There is

59 H-W Micklitz, 'Reforming European unfair terms legislation in consumer contracts'. *ERCL* 6 (2010), pp.347–383, at 358.

60 On hidden traps, see H Beale, 'Finding the remaining traps instead of unifying contract law' in S Grundmann and J Stuyck (eds), *An Academic Green Paper on European Contract Law* (Kluwer Law International, 2002), p.67.

61 See, e.g. T Wilhelmsson, 'The average European consumer: A legal fiction?' in T Wilhelmsson, E Paunio and A Pohjolainen (eds), *Private Law and the Many Cultures of Europe* (Kluwer Law International, 2007) p.243.

62 H-W Micklitz in Reich et al., *European Consumer Law*, op. cit. at 143.

63 H-W Micklitz and N Reich, 'The Court and sleeping beauty: The revival of the Unfair Contract Terms Directive (UCTD)' (2014) 51 *CMLR* pp.771–808.

a growing number of signs of a turn towards the development of more common European standards.

It should, however, be emphasised that even such decisions that are attempting to develop genuinely European principles contain clear national references, both on substance and procedure. The question is not an either-or issue, it is a question of how to balance the national and the European assessment. Now the materials on the European side of the balance seem to be increasing. The CJEU has found it necessary to expressly recognise the European side of the balance:

> Article 267 TFEU must be interpreted as meaning that the jurisdiction of the Court of Justice of the European Union extends to the interpretation of the concept of 'unfair term' used in Article 3(1) of Council Directive 93/13/EEC of 5 April 1993 on unfair terms in consumer contracts and in the annex thereto, and to the criteria which the national court may or must apply when examining a contractual term in the light of the provisions of that Directive, bearing in mind that it is for that court to determine, in the light of those criteria, whether a particular contractual term is actually unfair in the circumstances of the case.[64]

An often-cited landmark case showing the readiness of the CJEU to start building a genuinely European unfairness test is *Mohamed Aziz*.[65] As mentioned before, however, even in this case the CJEU first noted the need for basing the significant imbalance test on an analysis of national law. But the Court then continued:

> in order to assess whether the imbalance arises 'contrary to the requirement of good faith', it must be determined whether the seller or supplier, dealing fairly and equitably with the consumer, could reasonably assume that the consumer would have agreed to the term concerned in individual contract negotiations.

Here the CJEU introduced a new, truly European, standard for assessing the fairness of a term, a hypothetical test concerning what the consumer might agree to. One could call the test, for example, a *possible agreement test*, reflecting what could be called a 'reasonable supplier standard'.[66] According to this test the standard of acceptable, fair terms should be defined with reference to what a consumer would have agreed to in individual contract negotiations. The test also includes an assessment of the behaviour of the seller or supplier. The decisive issue is what the business could reasonably assume about the readiness of the consumer to accept the term.

64 C-137/08 *VB Pénzügyi Lízing Zrt. v Ferenc Schneider* [2010] ECR I-10847.
65 C-415/11 *Mohamed Aziz v Caixa d'Estalvis de Catalunya, Tarragona i Manresa (Catalunyacaixa)* ECLI:EU:C:2013:164.
66 Micklitz and Reich, op. cit. at 790.

The possible agreement test introduced by the CJEU in a way overcomes the discussions on whether, in addition to substantive unfairness, the Directive requires procedural unfairness as well to trigger the sanctions of the Directive. In other word, is it sufficient that the content of a term is significantly imbalanced, or does the consumer have to show some breach of good faith in the procedures leading to the contract as well?[67] The possible agreement test, asking what the business could assume, at a first glance seems to imply a procedural approach to good faith. On a closer reading, however, it rather underscores the substantive approach, as it asks what the business 'could reasonably assume', underlining that there must be some substantive limits to what can be assumed. The focus is not on what the business actually assumed, but on what it had good reasons for assuming.

Other examples of more recent cases in which the CJEU has attempted to concretise European principles for the assessment of unfairness can be mentioned. Some statements are rather obvious, like the requirement that in the unfairness assessment, the court must take account of all the other terms of the contract.[68] Others contain clarifications that obviously deepen and delimit the understanding of the approach to unfairness established by the Directive. In *Constructora Principado*,[69] for example, the Court ruled that 'significant imbalance' according to the Directive does not require significant economic impact on the consumer, not even with regard to the value of the transaction. It suffices that the term leads to a serious impairment of the legal situation of the consumer, as compared to relevant national law.

These decisions do introduce elements of a free-standing European doctrine of unfairness. Still the development of more concrete guidelines for the assessment of unfairness does not as such run counter to the *Freiburger Kommunalbauten* doctrine, according to which the national courts should make the concrete assessment of the term under dispute against the backdrop of national law. In principle, the balance between the European and the national levels, as sketched in the previous section, is not undermined by these decisions.

However, in some recent cases the CJEU has added weight to the European side of the balance. Without directly proclaiming a particular term to be unfair, the Court has engaged in an extensive analysis of the criteria that have to be taken into account in the national decision concerning that term. The criteria are described in such detail that there is not very much left for national evaluation.

67 See e.g. Recital 16 of the Preamble to the Directive, describing such procedural factors.

68 See e.g. C-472/11 *Banif Plus Bank Zrt. v Csaba Csipai and Viktória Csipai* ECLI:EU:C:2013:88 and C-226/12 *Constructora Principado SA v José Ignacio Menéndez Álvarez* ECLI:EU:C:2014:10, as well as C-92/11 *RWE Vertrieb AG v Verbraucherzentrale Nordrhein-Westfalen eV* ECLI:EU:C:2013:180 and C-472/10 *Nemzeti Fogyasztóvédelmi Hatóság v Invitel Távközlési Zrt.* ECLI:EU:C:2012:242.

69 Case C-226/12 *Constructora Principado SA v José Ignacio Menéndez Álvarez* ECLI:EU:C:2014:10.

A good example is the case *Banco Popular Español*,[70] in which the CJEU underlined which arguments it considered to be of decisive importance, even though it left the final assessment to the national court:

> Article 3(1) and (3) of Directive 93/13 and Points 1(e) and (g) and 2(a) of the annex thereto must be interpreted as meaning that, in order to assess the unfairness of a contractual term accelerating the repayment of a mortgage, such as that at issue in the main proceedings, the following are of decisive importance:
>
> - whether the right of the seller or supplier to cancel the contract unilaterally is conditional upon the non-compliance by the consumer with an obligation which is of essential importance in the context of the contractual relationship in question,
> - whether that right is provided for in cases in which such non-compliance is sufficiently serious in the light of the contractual term and amount of the loan,
> - whether that right derogates from the rules applicable in the absence of agreement between the parties, so as to make it more difficult for the consumer, given the procedural means at his disposal, to take legal action and exercise rights of the defence, and
> - whether national law provides for adequate and effective means enabling the consumer subject to such a contractual term to remedy the effects of the unilateral cancellation of the loan agreement.
>
> It is for the national court to make such an assessment on the basis of the specific circumstances of the case before it.

Also in some other recent cases the CJEU has attempted to steer the decision-making of the national court in quite some detail.[71]

Some features of an emerging European doctrine of unfairness may indeed be visible in the practice of the CJEU, as described here. They improve and refine

70 Joined cases C-537/12 and C-116/13 *Banco Popular Español SA v Maria Teodolinda Rivas Quichimbo, Wilmar Edgar Cun Pérez and Banco de Valencia SA v Joaquín Valldeperas Tortosa, María Ángeles Miret Jaume* ECLI:EU:C:2013:759.

71 See e.g. C-472/10 *Nemzeti Fogyasztóvédelmi Hatóság v Invitel Távközlési Zrt.* ECLI:EU:C:2012:242 (term on unilateral amendment of fees: transparency, right to terminate), C-92/11 *RWE Vertrieb AG v Verbraucherzentrale Nordrhein-Westfalen eV* ECLI:EU:C:2013:180 (term on right for supplier to vary the charge for supply of gas: transparency, right of termination and whether it actually can be exercised), C-342/13 *Katalin Sebestyén v Zsolt Csaba Kővári, OTP Bank Nyrt., OTP Faktoring Követeléskezelő Zrt, Raiffeisen Bank Zrt* ECLI:EU:C:2014:1857 (arbitration clause: effect of clause as to consumer's rights, communication cannot alone rule out unfairness) and C-191/15 *Verein für Konsumenteninformation v Amazon EU Sàrl* ECLI:EU:C:2016:612 (choice of law clause that does not inform the consumer about the continuous protection of the mandatory provisions of applicable law unfair, as it leads the consumer into error).

the yardstick given to the national courts, when they make the final concrete assessment of the term in dispute. If this is the case, the following question is obvious: what kind of yardstick does the CJEU offer? What kind of consumers are protected by the Unfair Contract Terms Directive?

As described elsewhere in this volume,[72] the 'average consumer' protected by the Unfair Commercial Practices Directive is a person who is believed to be 'reasonably well-informed and reasonably observant and circumspect ... as interpreted by the Court of Justice'.[73] Is that the approach to be taken also when applying the Unfair Contract Terms Directive?

In *Pereničová*,[74] the CJEU expressly analysed the issue of the relationship between the Unfair Contract Terms Directive and the Unfair Commercial Practices Directive. In this case, the alleged unfair practice consisted of a misleading indication of the annual percentage rate of charge, whilst the issue concerning the unfairness of terms related to the cost of the loan. According to the Court the unfairness of the commercial practice is to be seen as one element among others on which the assessment of the unfairness of the terms can be based.[75] However, the unfairness of the commercial practice does not have a direct effect on the validity of the credit agreement. In other words, the relationship between the two Directives is not direct and automatic, but indirect, related to the general assessment of unfairness. If the commercial practice is unfair, this is just an additional argument, but not more, for considering a term related to the practice unfair.

This does not, of course, mean that the approach towards the fairness yardstick could not be similar in relation to both Directives. Also in the case law concerning the Unfair Contract Terms Directive, reference is made to 'the average consumer, who is reasonably well informed and reasonably observant and circumspect'.[76] However, when the CJEU then attempts to define what one may expect from such a consumer more precisely, it does not seem to be very demanding. Whilst in relation to commercial practices, a consumer is supposed to have at least given some thought, e.g. to the content of advertisements, and not just

72 Chapter 2, pp.67–69; also Chapter 1, pp.27–31

73 Unfair Commercial Practices Directive, Recital 18, referring to case law based on C-210/96 *Gut Springenheide GmbH and Rudolf Tusky v Oberkreisdirektor des Kreises Steinfurt - Amt für Lebensmittelüberwachung* [1998] ECR I-4657.

74 C-453/10 *Jana Pereničová, Vladislav Perenič v SOS financ, spol. s r. o.* ECLI:EU:C:2012:144. See also C-76/10 *Pohotovosť s.r.o. v Iveta Korčkovská* [2010] ECR I-11557, according to which a failure to mention the APR according to the Consumer Credit Directive may be a decisive factor in the assessment whether a term is written in plain intelligible language according to the Unfair Contract Terms Directive.

75 And in the other direction, the use of unfair terms may constitute an unfair commercial practice, S Orlando, 'The use of unfair contractual terms as an unfair commercial practice'. *ERCL* 7 (2011), pp.25–56.

76 C-26/13 *Árpád Kásler, Hajnalka Káslerné Rábai v OTP Jelzálogbank Zrt* ECLI:EU:C:2014:282, para 74.

looked at their headings, a consumer is not supposed to have thoroughly read and tried to understand the standardised terms under scrutiny. As the Court seems to presuppose, quite rightly, that the consumer in most cases has no choice as to the terms offered, the requirements related to what the consumer should understand seem downplayed in its case law concerning the Unfair Contract Terms Directive. The difference in approach may be explained by the fact that for example in the *Árpád Kásler* case the focus is on the meaning of 'plain intelligible language' rather than 'fairness' as such.

As a starting point, also in connection with this Directive, the CJEU takes consumer autonomy seriously. This is reflected in the possible agreement test, as defined in the case *Mohamed Aziz.*[77] The decisive test, according to this decision, is whether the business 'could reasonably assume that the consumer would have agreed to the term concerned in individual contract negotiations'. But the consumer is here a very hypothetical figure. The yardstick focuses on what a consumer reasonably would have agreed to, if the consumer would have had a chance to individually negotiate the term – a chance that in most cases the consumer does not have. So in fact, even though the possible agreement test pays tribute to the autonomous and active consumer, negotiating the terms, in fact it introduces a relatively objective and substantive test on the fairness of terms, the basic question being: how much deviation from background law to the detriment of the consumer is it reasonable to accept?

Even in cases in which the Unfair Contract Terms Directive clearly indicates a role for the active understanding of the consumer, by requiring terms to be drafted in plain, intelligible language (Art. 4(2) and Art. 5), the CJEU has shown considerable understanding for the weakness of the consumer in this respect. The hurdle for the transparency test to be fulfilled has been put relatively high.

In *Árpád Kásler*[78] and *Van Hove*,[79] Art. 4(2) of the Directive, according to which terms on the main subject matter and the price are outside the scope of the unfairness test if they are drafted in plain intelligible language, the transparency test was given an interpretation bringing it much further than covering a purely linguistic understanding of the terms. The terms and their real consequences should also be economically understandable to the consumer. The terms should not only be 'grammatically intelligible to the consumer', but the specific functioning of the term and the relationship to other terms of the contract should be set out transparently 'so that that consumer is in a position to evaluate, on the basis of clear [precise], intelligible criteria, the economic consequences for him which derive from it.'[80] The active consumer should have real tools to evaluate

77 C-415/11 *Mohamed Aziz v Caixa d'Estalvis de Catalunya, Tarragona i Manresa (Catalunyacaixa)* ECLI:EU:C:2013:164.

78 C-26/13 *Árpád Kásler, Hajnalka Káslerné Rábai v OTP Jelzálogbank Zrt* ECLI:EU:C:2014:282.

79 C-96/14 *Jean-Claude Van Hove v CNP Assurances SA* ECLI:EU:C:2015:262.

80 Citations from both cases identical in this respect, except for the one adjective: 'clear' (*Árpád Kásler*) or 'precise' (*Van Hove*).

the consequences of the terms. The consumer is not believed to be so circumspect that a pure grammatical intelligibility of the terms would be sufficient. To the extent possible, the information provided should neutralise information asymmetry between the parties.[81]

The CJEU has stated the requirement concerning enhanced intelligibility also in the assessment of procedural unfairness as an element of applying the general clause of the Directive. In *RWE*,[82] the Court said it to be of fundamental importance whether a contract in which an undertaking reserved the right to vary the charge for supply of gas 'sets out in transparent fashion the reason for and method of those charges, so that the consumer can foresee, on the basis of clear, intelligible criteria, the alterations that may be made'. The Court here seems to interpret the transparency requirement as a duty to disclose certain information, to support the active consumer.[83]

Looking at the case law from 2010 onwards, the CJEU is obviously striving to create at least some genuinely European principles concerning unfairness, to at least somewhat counterbalance the necessary national elements of the assessment. The content of the decisions also seems to indicate relatively ambitious goals as to the level of consumer protection. Both the 'possible agreement test' of *Mohamed Aziz*, introducing what is probably a relatively strict substantive requirement, and the cases turning the transparency requirement into a kind of duty of disclosure, probably going beyond what a circumspect consumer would expect, show a commitment from the Court to deliver real consumer protection in this area. The Unfair Contract Terms Directive is treated as a useful vehicle for improving the position of consumers. This tendency is strengthened by further CJEU activism in the area of remedies and procedure which is more closely looked at in the next section. The 'reasonably circumspect' consumer demands more transparency when the Unfair Contract Terms Directive applies, and there are good reasons for this line of reasoning.[84]

Even though the developed duty of disclosure is there to support the decision-making power of the active consumer, the relatively strict substantive approach in many of the principles indicates that the CJEU here has distanced itself from the strong information model predominant in other areas of European consumer law. The development could well be described as a gradual move towards a more insurance-like, welfarist approach to the issue of unfair contract terms. However, it is difficult to find explicit endorsement of such thinking in existing case law of the CJEU.

81 M Dellacasa, "Judicial review of 'core terms' in consumer contracts: defining the limits" (2015) 11 *European Review of Contract Law* p.152, at p.172.

82 C-92/11 *RWE Vertrieb AG v Verbraucherzentrale Nordrhein-Westfalen eV* ECLI:EU:C:2013:180.

83 Micklitz in Reich et al., *European Consumer Law*, op. cit. at 145.

84 C Willett, *Fairness in Consumer Contracts* (Ashgate, 2007), p.115.

The next step: A procedural Jack-in-the-box

As described in the previous section, the CJEU seems to have been eager to enforce consumer protection by developing relatively advanced principles for the assessment of unfairness and transparency. With regard to the number of cases, however, the scene is not dominated by these rulings concerning substantive issues. The ECJ has been even more active, and one may even say legally creative, in safeguarding and developing the remedies against unfairness and protecting the procedural position of the consumer trying to enforce his or her rights according to the Directive. The Court has taken the requirement concerning adequate and effective means (Art. 7) and the general European principle of effectiveness very seriously in this context.

This has meant two things. First, the CJEU has adopted a relatively forceful interpretation of the remedies included in the Directive (Art. 6 and 7), including for example a punitive element in the private law consequences of unfairness. Second, in order to safeguard the rights of the consumer under the Directive, the CJEU has moved into the heartland of civil procedure. It has turned the Directive into an instrument to fix new kinds of consumer protection issues, in particular in the area of procedural law. From the perspective of what one could expect on the basis of a contract law directive this turn can be regarded as so surprising that it could be called a very illustrative example of a – positive – Jack-in-the-Box effect.

As to the private law remedies, the Directive (Art. 6(1)) prescribes that unfair terms shall not be binding on the consumer and the contract shall continue to bind the parties, if it is capable of continuing without the unfair terms. This implies that the unfair term cannot be adjusted by the Court, but should be completely disregarded. In case the continuation of the contract without the unfair term would lead to unfairness against the business, this should not be remedied. In this sense the Directive contains a punitive element directed against the business. If the business uses unfair terms, it has to carry the risk that the contract becomes unfair against the business when these terms are eliminated. Such a punitive element is assumed to increase the preventive effect of the Directive.[85]

This understanding of the Directive was prevailing already after it was adopted.[86] The CJEU has several times emphasised this interpretation.[87] National legislation

85 See for example C-377/14 *Ernst Georg Radlinger and Helena Radlingerová v Finway a.s.* ECLI:EU:C:2016:283, para 98.

86 G Howells and T Wilhelmsson, *EC Consumer Law* (Ashgate, 1997), at 111.

87 See for example in addition to the cases mentioned in the text, joined cases C-482/13, C-484/13, C-485/13 and C-487/13 *Unicaja Banco, SA v José Hidalgo Rueda and Others, Caixabank SA v Manuel María Rueda Ledesma, Rosario Mesa Mesa, José Labella Crespo, Rosario Márquez Rodríguez, Rafael Gallardo Salvat, Manuela Márquez Rodríguez, Alberto Galán Luna, Domingo Galán Luna* ECLI:EU:C:2015:21 (national provisions on adjusting amounts under term not precluded, provided national court not prohibited from assessing fairness, and not prevented from removing the term, if found unfair), at 28.

that allows a court to revise the content of a term that it has found unfair is considered to be precluded by the Directive.[88] If a penalty clause, for example, is considered to be unfair, the court cannot reduce the amount of the penalty, but has to exclude the application of that clause in its entirety.[89] Moreover, if the cumulative effect of several terms is unfair, then all the terms found unfair should be excluded.[90] In case the contract cannot continue without any term on the issue, however, the national court may substitute the term with a supplementary provision of national law.[91]

In a recent case, the CJEU has also ruled out national case law that would limit the restitutory effects of a finding of unfairness to amounts overpaid after the court decision.[92] This decision can have huge economic consequences for businesses that might be facing considerable claims for repayment after a decision on unfairness.

In Art. 7 the Directive requires the Member States to ensure that adequate and effective means exist to prevent the continued use of unfair terms. Such means, according to the Directive, have to include provisions according to which 'persons or organisations, having a legitimate interest under national law in protecting consumers,' may take action before courts or administrative bodies to prevent the continued use of unfair terms. Such collective action may also be directed jointly against a number of businesses from the same economic sector or their associations which recommend the use of the terms.

It is not surprising that the CJEU has strived to safeguard the efficiency of the collective instrument of prevention as well.[93] The Court has, for example, accepted far-reaching legal effects of such collective proceedings. Even though one may assume that an injunction against further use of an unfair term would

88 C-618/10 *Banco Español de Crédito, S.A. v Joaquín Calderón Camino* ECLI:EU:C:2012:349.

89 C-488/11 *Dirk Frederik Asbeek Brusse, Katarina de Man Garabito v Jahani BV* ECLI:EU:C:2013:341.

90 C-377/14 *Ernst Georg Radlinger and Helena Radlingerová v Finway a.s.* ECLI:EU:C:2016:283.

91 C-26/13 *Árpád Kásler, Hajnalka Káslerné Rábai v OTP Jelzálogbank Zrt* ECLI:EU:C:2014:282. See also on the issue of continuing existence of the contract C-453/10 *Jana Pereničová, Vladislav Perenič v SOS financ, spol. s r. o.* ECLI:EU:C:2012:144 (annulment of contract based on unfair clause; according to the Directive, the national court cannot base its decision solely on the advantage for the consumer, but national law in this direction is acceptable, where that will ensure better consumer protection).

92 Joined cases C-154/15, C-307/15 and C-308/15 *Francisco Gutiérrez Naranjo v Cajasur Banco SAU, Ana María Palacios Martínez v Banco Bilbao Vizcaya Argentaria SA (BBVA), Banco Popular Español, SA v Emilio Irles López and Teresa Torres Andreu* ECLI:EU:C:2016:980

93 See also, above, C-70/03 *Commission of the European Communities v Kingdom of Spain* [2004] ECR I-7999 (*in dubio contra stipulatorem*-rule shall not apply in collective action, as this 'makes it possible to prohibit more frequently the use of an unintelligible or ambiguous term, which results in wider consumer protection').

be the natural remedy in this context, the Court has accepted that the term is declared invalid in an action for injunction and, furthermore, that this effect includes consumers who were not party to the injunction proceedings, if the decision is taken by a body that according to national legislation can produce effects with regard to all relevant consumers.[94] On the other hand, however, a collective action should not prevent consumers from bringing individual actions, if they want to dissociate themselves from the collective action.[95] The impact of collective actions may be extended to identical contract terms used by traders who were not subject to a collective action which held that the term was unfair and which have been included in a national public register of unfair terms. This is subject to the proviso that a trader not party to the collective action resulting in the inclusion on the register is able to challenge the conclusion that the terms used by that trader are equivalent to the term on the register.[96] 'Equivalent' here seems to mean the substantive effect of the term rather than literal correspondence.[97]

The CJEU has also insisted on having all parts of the provisions on collective enforcement of the Directive duly implemented. Italy was required by the Court to set up procedures that also could be directed against entities only recommending the use of unfair terms, without actually using them themselves.[98]

However, the emphasis on the effectiveness of collective proceedings has not hindered the CJEU from recognising national procedural rules concerning such proceedings.[99]

As noted above, the willingness of the CJEU to enhance the effect of the Unfair Contract Terms Directive has led to even more creative decisions in recent case law. It has brought the Court into areas of law when applying the Directive that one would not directly expect the Directive to have an impact on.

In its case law, the CJEU has not only emphasised the active role of the consumer as a contractual party. It has also made an effort to safeguard the procedural position of the consumer. Protection against unfairness in contract law is ineffective if the consumer does not have a reasonable possibility procedurally to plead that a term is unfair. So from the demand for fair contract terms there has been only a short step to a demand for fair procedure. This is a rather surprising effect of the Directive, as one could hardly foresee that a European directive dealing with unfair

94 C-472/10 *Nemzeti Fogyasztóvédelmi Hatóság v Invitel Távközlési Zrt* ECLI:EU:C:2012:242.

95 Joined cases C-381/14 and C-385/14 *Jorge Sales Sinués v Caixabank SA and Youssouf Drame Ba v Catalunya Caixa SA (Catalunya Banc SA)* ECLI:EU:C:2016:909.

96 C-119/15 *Biuro podróży 'Partner' Sp. z o.o, Sp. komandytowa w Dąbrowie Górniczej v Prezes Urzędu Ochrony Konkurencji i Konsumentów* ECLI:EU:C:2016:987.

97 Ibid., para [42].

98 C-372/99 *Commission of the European Communities v Italian Republic* [2002] ECR I-819.

99 See e.g. C-470/12 *Pohotovosť s.r.o. v Miroslav Vašuta* ECLI:EU:C:2014:101 and C-413/12 *Asociación de Consumidores Independientes de Castilla y León v Anuntis Segundamano España SL* ECLI:EU:C:2013:800.

contract terms suddenly might be used by the CJEU to reshape national procedural laws. But this is what the Court has done, and in quite a long line of cases.

The CJEU, for example, has used the Directive against certain aspects of national procedural law on enforcement proceedings. One of the most-discussed cases also in this respect is, again, *Mohamed Aziz*.[100] The case discusses Spanish procedural law, according to which the debtor could not object to the unfairness of a term of a loan agreement in mortgage enforcement proceedings. Such objections could be put forward only in separate declaratory proceedings. So what did the CJEU do, to protect the consumer against unfair terms? It declared that legislation to be in conflict with the Unfair Contract Terms Directive, as long as the court before which declaratory proceedings have been brought could not grant interim relief, in particular, the staying of the enforcement proceedings. In other words, the CJEU prescribed a new procedural remedy: it required a possibility of staying of the enforcement proceedings so that the possible unfairness could effectively be assessed. The basic message is that effectiveness requires that the decision-maker at some stage of the procedure should have a real opportunity to assess the fairness of the contract. The effectiveness of the Directive is undermined, if, for example, the consumer can face an enforcement order for payment without any fairness assessment during the proceedings.[101]

In particular the CJEU has attempted to downplay national requirements on procedural activity of the consumer. In order to make the Directive effective the Court has in several contexts demanded that the national court takes into account the possible unfairness of terms of its own motion. It is interesting to note that also in this context the CJEU seems to downplay standards of confident, active, and circumspect consumers, and admit that the consumer is likely to make omissions in the procedural setting as well. A functioning system of consumer protection should, therefore, allow courts to act on their own motion, at least in certain situations. In particular in common law countries, where judges less actively manage cases, this is startling, but the emphasis on courts acting on their own motion probably goes further than what has been the case in many continental jurisdictions as well.[102]

100 C-415/11 *Mohamed Aziz v Caixa d'Estalvis de Catalunya, Tarragona i Manresa (Catalunyacaixa)* ECLI:EU:C:2013:164. See also joined cases C-537/12 and C-116/13 *Banco Popular Español SA v Maria Teodolinda Rivas Quichimbo, Wilmar Edgar Cun Pérez and Banco de Valencia SA v Joaquín Valldeperas Tortosa, María Ángeles Miret Jaume* ECLI:EU:C:2013:759 and C-169/14 *Juan Carlos Sánchez Morcillo, María del Carmen Abril García v Banco Bilbao Vizcaya Argentaria, SA* ECLI:EU:C:2014:2099 (precluding a system of enforcement where proceedings may not be stayed; criticism against unbalanced procedure also based on Charter of Fundamental Rights).

101 C-49/14 *Finanmadrid EFC SA v Jesús Vicente Albán Zambrano, María Josefa García Zapata, Jorge Luis Albán Zambrano, Miriam Elisabeth Caicedo Merino* ECLI:EU:C:2016:98 (on *res judicata* in a payment enforcement procedure), in particular paras 45–46.

102 The obligation of the courts to act *ex officio* according to the Unfair Contract Terms Directive was (before *Pannon*!) not considered to be sufficiently clear in order to trigger Member State liability, C-168/15 *Milena Tomášová v Ministerstvo spravodlivosti SR, Pohotovosť s. r. o.* ECLI:EU:C:2016:602.

The classic case is *Cofidis*,[103] in which the CJEU ruled that a national time-limit for the court's power to set aside unfair terms of its own motion or following a plea by the consumer was precluded by the Directive. According to the Court, such a procedural rule would render the application of the protective rules in the Directive excessively difficult. This does not, of course, mean, however, that all procedural time-limits are forbidden by the Directive.[104]

The focus in *Cofidis* was predominantly on the issue concerning time limits. In other cases, there has been more emphasis on the power – and even duty[105] – of the court to react on its own motion.[106] This can early be seen in cases attempting to safeguard sufficient procedural options of the consumer. Already in *Océano*[107] the CJEU ruled that a national court should be able to determine of its own motion whether a jurisdiction clause was to be regarded as unfair. Similarly, according to *Asturcom*,[108] a national court in an action for enforcement of an arbitration award made in the absence of the consumer is required to assess of its own motion the fairness of the arbitration clause – but only if the court under national law can make such an assessment in similar actions of a domestic nature. The readiness of the CJEU to assist the consumer, when questioning an arbitration clause, can be seen also in *Mostaza Claro*,[109] according to which it should be possible for a national court to assess whether an arbitration clause was void and annul the arbitration award, even though the consumer had not pleaded invalidity in the arbitration proceedings.

Such emphasis on the active role of the court is not, however, limited to issues of jurisdiction only. The CJEU has clearly in general terms underlined that the protection by the Directive should cover cases in which a consumer fails to raise

103 C-473/00 *Cofidis SA v Jean-Louis Fredout* [2002] ECR I-10875.

104 See e.g. the reasoning in C-8/14 *BBVA SA, formerly Unnim Banc SA v Pedro Peñalva López, Clara López Durán, Diego Fernández Gabarro* ECLI:EU:C:2015:731, in which a transitional short time-limit was found to be precluded by the Directive, but after a thorough analysis of the situation.

105 S Weatherill, *EU Consumer Law and* Policy, 2nd ed, (Edward Elgar, 2013), pp.157–158.

106 Own motion of the court is mentioned also in joined cases C-537/12 and C-116/13 *Banco Popular Español SA v Maria Teodolinda Rivas Quichimbo, Wilmar Edgar Cun Pérez and Banco de Valencia SA v Joaquín Valldeperas Tortosa, María Ángeles Miret Jaume* ECLI:EU:C:2013:759 and C-49/14 *Finanmadrid EFC SA v Jesús Vicente Albán Zambrano, María Josefa García Zapata, Jorge Luis Albán Zambrano, Miriam Elisabeth Caicedo Merino* ECLI:EU:C:2016:98.

107 Joined cases C-240/98 to C-244/98 *Océano Grupo Editorial SA v Roció Murciano Quintero and Salvat Editores SA v José M. Sánchez Alcón Prades, José Luis Copano Badillo, Mohammed Berroane and Emilio Viñas Feliú* [2000] ECR I-4941. Similarly C-137/08 *VB Pénzügyi Lízing Zrt. v Ferenc Schneider* [2010] ECR I-10847 and C-243/08 *Pannon GSM Zrt v Erzsébet Sustikné Győrfi* [2009] ECR I-4713.

108 C-40/08 *Asturcom Telecomunicaciones SL v Cristina Rodríguez Nogueira* [2009] ECR I-9579.

109 C-168/05 *Elisa María Mostaza Claro v Centro Móvil Milenium SL* [2006] ECR I-10421, following up the competition law case on annulment of an arbitration award C-126/97 *Eco Swiss China Time Ltd v Benetton International NV* [1999] ECR I-3055.

the unfairness of the term, for example because of unawareness or fear of costs. Therefore '[t]he national court is required to examine, of its own motion, the unfairness of a contractual term where it has available to it the legal and factual elements necessary for that task. Where it considers such a term to be unfair, it must not apply it, except if the consumer opposes that non-application.'[110] The fairness for example of a penalty clause[111] and a clause on interest on late payments[112] should therefore be assessed by the court of its own motion. The court that has found a term unfair should also, without waiting for any application of the consumer, draw all the consequences of the finding and assess whether the contract can continue without the term.[113] However, the requirement that the legal system should support the consumer more or less on its own motion is of course not unlimited. The CJEU has emphasised that 'the principle of effectiveness cannot be stretched so far as to make up fully for the total inertia on the part of the consumer concerned'.[114]

The assistance of the court may be required during various stages of the procedure. According to the CJEU, the court must be able to assess the fairness of the term of its own motion at any stage of the proceedings.[115] In an appeal concerning the validity of terms, the court should have the power to examine grounds for invalidity, if clearly apparent from what was submitted at first instance, and assess of its own motion the unfairness of the terms.[116]

In the light of this case law, the CJEU seems, to a certain extent, to underline the active role of national courts, requiring the courts to take unfairness into account of their own motion, as an important part of a European unfairness doctrine supposed to effectively protect the consumer. However, this does not mean that the Court has disregarded national procedural law. At least in principle, the Court has subjected the active role of the courts to an understanding of what national law might accept. The Court has expressly recognised the principle of procedural autonomy of the Member States, but by noting that the procedural rules must not be less favourable for the consumer than those governing similar domestic actions (the principle of equivalence), it has been able to carry through a relativized demand for national courts to move of their own motion. If the court under internal procedural rules has the power to examine of its own motion whether a term is contrary to national rules of public policy, it must assess of its own motion the unfairness of

110 C-243/08 *Pannon GSM Zrt v Erzsébet Sustikné Győrfi* [2009] ECR I-4713 (in fact dealing with clause on jurisdiction). See also C-472/11 *Banif Plus Bank Zrt. v Csaba Csipai and Viktória Csipai* [2013] ECLI:EU:2013:88. The procedural consequences of the rider allowing the consumer to oppose non-application, at odds with the rationale of the *ex officio* approach, are unclear.
111 C-76/10 *Pohotovosť s.r.o. v Iveta Korčkovská* [2010] ECR I-11557.
112 C-618/10 *Banco Español de Crédito, S.A. v Joaquín Calderón Camino* ECLI:EU:C:2012:349.
113 C-397/11 *Erika Jőrös v Aegon Magyarország Hitel Zrt.* ECLI:EU:C:2013:340.
114 C-32/14 *ERSTE Bank Hungary Zrt v Attila Sugár* ECLI:EU:C:2015:637.
115 C-618/10 *Banco Español de Crédito, S.A. v Joaquín Calderón Camino* ECLI:EU:C:2012:349.
116 C-397/11 *Erika Jőrös v Aegon Magyarország Hitel Zrt.* ECLI:EU:C:2013:340.

terms according to the Directive. In the reference to internal procedural opportunities the Court has equalled the protection based on the Unfair Contract Terms Directive with public policy[117] which limits the restrictions on courts acting on their own motion that might follow from national law. In addition, it is said to follow from the principle of effectiveness that national rules are acceptable only if they do not render impossible in practice or excessively difficult the exercise of rights conferred by the Community legal order (the principle of effectiveness).[118]

The CJEU has also respected national arbitration law: with regard to an action concerning the enforcement of an arbitration award (issued without the participation of the consumer), it has prescribed that the court can set aside of its own motion an unfair arbitration clause or assess the unfairness of a penalty clause applied in the award – in fact set aside the arbitration award – only if it can carry out such an assessment in similar actions of a domestic nature, according to national procedural rules.[119] And the power of an appeal court to examine of its own motion the fairness of terms is to be used 'under its internal procedural rules'.[120] These bows towards national procedural law are easy to understand and do not contravene the general approach.[121]

There are also other decisions on national procedural rules in which such rules have been accepted, provided that they do not make the exercise of the rights of consumers excessively difficult. Whether this is the case has to be assessed by the national court.[122]

117 See e.g. C-168/05 *Elisa María Mostaza Claro v Centro Móvil Milenium SL* [2006] ECR I-10421, paras 35–38 and C-488/11 *Dirk Frederik Asbeek Brusse, Katarina de Man Garabito v Jahani BV* ECLI:EU:C:2013:341, para 44.

118 Similar references to procedural autonomy, the principle of equivalence and the principle of effectiveness are given, e.g. in C-168/05 *Elisa María Mostaza Claro v Centro Móvil Milenium SL* [2006] ECR I-10421, para 24, C-618/10 *Banco Español de Crédito, S.A. v Joaquín Calderón Camino* ECLI:EU:C:2012:349, para 46, C-415/11 *Mohamed Aziz v Caixa d'Estalvis de Catalunya, Tarragona i Manresa (Catalunyacaixa)* ECLI:EU:C:2013:164, para 50, C-488/11 *Dirk Frederik Asbeek Brusse, Katarina de Man Garabito v Jahani BV* ECLI:EU:C:2013:341, para 42, C-8/14 *BBVA SA, formerly Unnim Banc SA v Pedro Peñalva López, Clara López Durán, Diego Fernández Gabarro* ECLI:EU:C:2015:731, para 24 and C-49/14 *Finanmadrid EFC SA v Jesús Vicente Albán Zambrano, María Josefa García Zapata, Jorge Luis Albán Zambrano, Miriam Elisabeth Caicedo Merino* ECLI:EU:C:2016:98, para 40.

119 C-40/08 *Asturcom Telecomunicaciones SL v Cristina Rodríguez Nogueira* [2009] ECR I-9579 and C-76/10 *Pohotovosť s.r.o. v Iveta Korčkovská* [2010] ECR I-11557. Still the decisions have important repercussions on consumer arbitration law, see M Ebers, 'From Océano to Asturcom: Mandatory consumer law, ex officio application of European Union law and res judicata'. *European Review of Private Law* 18 (2010), p.823.

120 C-397/11 *Erika Jőrös v Aegon Magyarország Hitel Zrt.* ECLI:EU:C:2013:340.

121 See also C-32/14 *ERSTE Bank Hungary Zrt v Attila Sugár* ECLI:EU:C:2015:637, accepting the national role of a notary issuing an enforcement clause without review of unfairness.

122 C-567/13 *Nóra Baczó, János István Vizsnyiczai v Raiffeisen Bank Zrt* ECLI:EU:C:2015:88. See also C-34/13 *Monika Kušionová v SMART Capital a.s.* ECLI:EU:C:2014:2189.

In this long line of cases the CJEU has performed an interesting balancing act, formally endorsing the procedural autonomy of the Member States, but at the same time developing European procedural principles aimed at strengthening the procedural position of the consumer in cases related to unfair contract terms. Such an active developing of European procedural principles, in particular concerning the ability of the national court to act of its own motion, has almost by necessity forced the Court to move further into the heartland of procedure and describe in more detail how the court should proceed when taking up the unfairness issue of its own motion. In *Banif*[123] the CJEU, after having ascertained the right of the national court to declare a term invalid of its own motion, found it necessary in the operative part of the judgment to refer to the principle of *audi alteram partem* and therefore require the national court to inform the parties that it of its own motion had found a term unfair and invite the parties to set out views on that matter before the decision on validity was taken. This is a quite interesting case of detailed steering of national procedures, in view of the procedural autonomy of the Member States.

The activity of the CJEU in the area described in this section of the paper, on issues of procedure, underscores how the Unfair Contract Terms Directive has become an important vehicle for the Court in an endeavour to build a Europeanised, but nationally anchored legal consumer protection policy. It is not surprising that many of these cases have dealt with issues related to credit and mortgage that have become acute because of the financial crisis. Some have therefore interpreted case law in this area as a judicial answer to the problems that the crisis has led to for European citizens: 'Mr Mohamed Aziz and the thousands of Spanish homeowners who stand behind the *Aziz*-case highlight the macro-economic dimension of household debt in our economies.'[124] Looking at the cases, it is easy to agree that the consumer problems related to the financial crisis have strongly contributed to the recent development of a case law in which the effectiveness of the Unfair Contract Terms Directive is taken seriously. In *Mohamed Aziz* the Court expressly underlined that the mortgaged property was the family home of the consumer and that he faced definitive and irreversible loss of his dwelling.[125] The problems related to foreign currency mortgages in some of the Member States of Central and Eastern Europe have in a similar way promoted enforcement-related unfair terms litigation from those countries. The economic and financial crisis has led the CJEU to play a particularly important

123 C-472/11 *Banif Plus Bank Zrt. v Csaba Csipai and Viktória Csipai* ECLI:EU:C:2013:88. So also C-488/11 *Dirk Frederik Asbeek Brusse, Katarina de Man Garabito v Jahani BV* ECLI:EU:C:2013:341.

124 H-W Micklitz, 'Conclusions: Consumer over-indebtedness and consumer insolvency – from micro to macro' in H-W.Micklitz and I Domurath (eds), *Consumer Debt and Social Exclusion in Europe* (Ashgate, 2015), p.233.

125 C-415/11 *Mohamed Aziz v Caixa d'Estalvis de Catalunya, Tarragona i Manresa (Catalunyacaixa)* ECLI:EU:C:2013:164, para 61.

role in developing unfair contract terms law.[126] In addition to the numerous cases mentioned here, there is a considerable number of similar cases pending at the CJEU.

The line adopted by the CJEU, by scrutinising the procedural situation of the consumer, has forced European law to think of fairness more broadly than probably was anticipated. Fairness according to the Unfair Contract Terms Directive is not just about a fair balance of rights and obligations of the consumer under the contract, but also about how the legal order can safeguard the procedures for the consumer to obtain such a fair balance.

Conclusions and ways forward

The history of the Unfair Contract Terms Directive and the case law evolved around it offer a good illustration of the tension between national needs, internal market needs and consumer protection goals. This Directive shows that the European turn towards further integration based on maximum harmonisation at the expense of high consumer protection standards that recognise local needs is not a coherent process that would be adopted without exceptions. In fact, the narrative told in this chapter rather demonstrates the opposite: in this area there is a continuing sensitivity towards national standards as well as an aspiration to reach effective consumer protection on a relatively high level.

Like many of the consumer protection directives from the time when the EU started building a European consumer law, the Unfair Contract Terms Directive is a minimum harmonisation directive. This situation has not been uncontested. The general drive towards maximum harmonisation included a plan to adopt a general maximum directive on consumer rights, in which the unfair contract terms rules would be included. However, because of resistance from several Member States this plan did not succeed. Only a small remnant of the debate was included in the Consumer Rights Directive Art. 32, in the form of a Member State obligation to inform about such new legislation that makes use of the minimum character of the Unfair Contract Terms Directive (see 'The main content and goals of the Directive' in fine). With regard to unfair contract terms the move towards maximum harmonisation has not been successful.

This is not, however, the only way in which national needs are recognised. Also in the case law of the CJEU, much decision-making power has been left to the national courts, which explicitly should take into account the national legal setting in making their assessments. Even though the CJEU has set some general criteria to define unfairness, it has usually left the assessment of the particular term at stake to the national court. This is reasonable, and perhaps even inevitable. As long as background contract law is not harmonised one cannot introduce a completely harmonised fairness doctrine.

126 V Trstenjak, 'From the Ovid's Golden Age to modern European curia: The prominent role of the C.J.E.U. in shaping European consumer law' (2015) *EJCL* pp.3–6, at 4.

In recent case law, however, there are indications of a certain shift towards increasing Europeanisation of the issue. The CJEU has started to build a collection of European tests for determining unfairness. The 'possible agreement test' in *Mohamed Aziz*, directing the court to look at what the business could reasonably assume the consumer to agree to, is probably the best example. The CJEU has also in other respects concretised its guidance to the national courts to be used in their fairness assessment. However, even in such cases that clearly introduce at least elements of a genuinely European doctrine of unfairness, the final assessment of the particular term at hand is left to the national court. In the cases the necessity to make the concrete fairness assessment on the background of national law is still recognised, at least in principle.

Looking ahead one should not, however, understand the national and European assessments only as opposites where the increasing weight of one decreases the importance of the other. Rather one should see them both as vital parts of a European discourse on unfairness. Even with the necessary national perspective included and retained, the explicit European protection against unfairness increases the transparency of legal reasoning in the European system. Even though Europe does not have a joint fairness doctrine, European contract law can have a shared fairness discourse. Such a discourse, at least in the long run, could make the whole system more transparent. It would facilitate the free movement of legal ideas, increasing the learning potential of European consumer law. It would bring to the fore the various forms of fairness reasoning behind traditional contract law doctrines and thereby both make the system more efficient, focusing of open rather than covert tools of fairness control, and increase legal foreseeability at the European level. For businesses and consumers it would – at least somewhat – increase the possibilities to know and understand the working of contract law in different Member States.

Also, with regard to the level of consumer protection the emerging elements of a free-standing European unfairness doctrine in the case law of the CJEU seem to differ from the general tendency of EU consumer law. The Court does not seem to make as high demands on the consumer's circumspectness in comparison to some other areas of consumer law (see 'Steps towards a free-standing consumer protection measure'). The interpretation of the transparency test in the Unfair Contract Terms Directive has been relatively consumer-friendly, focusing on what is economically understandable for the consumer rather than just on grammatical intelligibility. And more importantly, the possible agreement test in *Mohamed Aziz* is much more substantive, as it asks what one reasonably could assume that a purely hypothetical individually negotiating consumer would accept.

Summing up, it seems that the locally sensitive consumer protection focus of the Unfair Contract Terms Directive has been maintained, and even developed further in case law of the CJEU. This chapter does not confirm one of the main theses of our book, on the tendency towards increased maximum harmonisation. It rather illustrates the exception to the rule. It shows that there is still room also for a consumer-oriented, culturally sensitive European consumer policy.

This impression of a consumer protection-sensitive CJEU is enhanced when looking at the rather abundant case law related to enforcement and procedural issues (see 'The next step: A procedural Jack-in-the-box'). The Court has been actively engaged in protecting the procedural position of the consumer in order to strengthen the effects of the Directive. It has proceeded far into the heartland of procedural law, much further than one at the outset would expect the Directive to reach. The case law concerning the Directive illustrates very well the drive towards improving the enforcement of European consumer law. In particular it shows the willingness of the Court to use the Unfair Contract Terms Directive as an instrument to mitigate the harsh consequences for the consumers of the European financial crisis, in their relationships to the banks and other creditors. However, at least formally, this intrusion into procedural law is usually done together with a rider referring to what is possible according to national law.

The relatively positive assessment of the present state of law does not rule out further improvements of the situation from the point of view of consumer protection. The goals could be made clearer, underlining insurance-like welfarist thinking and also consumer transaction cost arguments. One of the key issues in discussing the understanding of the fairness test is the relationship between substantive and procedural fairness, that is between the fairness of the substantive content of the contract and the fairness of the contracting procedure. In an insurance-like approach the emphasis would be on substantive fairness. In *Mohamed Aziz*, the CJEU – through the 'possible agreements' test – indeed seems to favour a relatively substantive assessment, but admittedly the case is open to more procedural interpretation as well. The substantive test could be made even clearer. One might, for example, explore the possibilities of building further on the principle of legitimate expectations, traditionally regarded as one of the guiding principles of EU private law[127] and performing well in the insurance-covered area of products liability. In fact, already in the preparation stage of the Directive the proposal was made that a term should be considered unfair if it 'causes the performance of the contract to be significantly different from what the consumer could legitimately expect'.[128] In fact the 'possible agreement test' offered by the CJEU seems to be quite close to the legitimate expectations test, but it focuses more clearly on the contracting situation, as the present wording of the Directive requires. If given a clearly substantive interpretation this test might therefore appear more focused than the relatively vague legitimate expectation test.

As the reasoning and ruling should be more geared towards the substantive content rather than the contracting procedure, one might also question the

127 See already H-W Micklitz, 'Principles of justice in private law within the European Union' in E Paasivirta and K Rissanen (eds), *Principles of Justice and the Law of the European Union* (Helsinki University Institute of International Economic Law, 1995), p.284, and G Howells and T Wilhelmsson, *EC Consumer Law* (Ashgate, 1997), p.320.

128 Re-examined Proposal for a Council Directive on unfair terms in consumer contracts, COM (93) 11, at 6, alternative text of Art. 3.

limitations of scope of the Directive. The limitation to terms which have not been individually negotiated has been criticised not only from a consumer protection point of view, but also with regard to the difficulties of drawing the exact borders of the exclusion and the possibilities for traders to exploit the situation.[129] The same kinds of criticism can be directed towards the exclusion of the main subject matter of the contract (and perhaps to some extent towards the exclusion of the price as well). From this point of view the attempt of the CJEU to narrow the effect of the limitation through a rather demanding understanding of the concept 'plain, intelligible language' in *Árpád Kásler* and *Van Hove* can be seen as a small step in the right direction.

Even when the substantive fairness is emphasised, the present Directive retains important elements of a procedural approach, as the assessment of unfairness is expressly directed to look at the situation when the contract was made. In Art. 4(1), the court is asked to look at all the circumstances attending the conclusion of the contract, 'at the time of conclusion of the contract'. Situations in which the application of the contract may become unfair because of subsequently arising circumstances are not covered. For coping with such situations the court has to look at other doctrines like the German doctrine of *Geschäftsgrundlage* and the English doctrine of frustration (even though it is not directed at unfairness). However, in principle it would be possible to bring such situations under the fairness regime as well. This is the case in Nordic law, in which the focus is on assessing the fairness of the consequences of applying a term, irrespective of whether the unfair consequences are related to the circumstances prevailing when the contract was made or to later changes.[130] In particular in a contractual landscape in which long-term relationships play an important role, this would be a way to legally recognise the particular needs relating to such relationships.[131] In a long-term relationship it can easily seem very impractical to direct the assessment of unfairness to be based on a combination of circumstances prevailing maybe years back, when the relationship may have developed and changed in many ways after the time of conclusion. For consumers, the fairness of such long-term relationships, e.g. regarding credit, tenancy and basic services may be of decisive importance both for their economy and well-being.

The suggested improvements of the European unfair contract terms regime are of minor importance. Even as it stands the Unfair Contract Terms Directive has proven to be a useful tool for developing European consumer protection. It has certainly been noted internationally among lawyers and law drafters modernising

129 C Willett, *Fairness in Consumer Contracts* (Ashgate, 2007), p.170.

130 See the legislation mentioned above, in footnote 13.

131 The need for better legal recognition of such relationships is forcefully defended by the EuSoCo group, see L Nogler and U Reifner (eds), *Life Time Contracts. Social Long-term Contracts in Labour, Tenancy and Consumer Credit Law* (Eleven International Publishing, 2014).

their contract law.[132] To some extent this may contribute to the emergence of a European brand that enhances trust in European businesses as actors that do not use unbalanced and unintelligible small print to advance their position in an unfair manner.

In the creation of the European fairness brand the more general path-breaking function of the Directive has been important as well. Through the Directive mechanisms for dealing with unfair contract terms have been introduced as themes for the general contract law discourse in Europe. Having been accepted by the European legislator, unfair contract terms rules based on the Directive have been included in the Principles of European Contract Law (the so called Lando Principles)[133] as well as in the Draft Common Frame of Reference,[134] and in both collections they have been extended to cover business-to-business relationships as well. These collections, again, have had and have an influence on the development of national contract law in various corners of Europe. In this way the principle of fairness has already become quite broadly recognised in European contract law, contributing to the general European fairness brand.

From a pure consumer protection point of view one might see a danger in extending protection against unfairness to business-to-business relationships as well, as this could imply a dilution of the protection of consumers. However, experience from Nordic law, with a broad general fairness approach, does not support such fears. A well-functioning fairness regime allows the court to take into account the status of the various parties as one factor to include in the assessment of unfairness. The acceptance of a more general fairness approach might even lower the hurdle for fairness-based decisions in consumer contract law.

132 As an example see the Australian Consumer Law 2011. See also L Mason, 'Inadequacy and Ineffectuality: Hong Kong's consumer protection regime against unfair terms in standard form contracts'. *HKLJ* 44 (2014), p.86, arguing for importing the UK Unfair Terms in Consumer Contracts Regulations to Hong Kong.

133 O Lando and H Beale (eds), *Principles of European Contract Law, Parts I and II* (Kluwer Law International, 2000), Art. 4:110.

134 Book II. – 9:401-9:410.

5 Consumer sales

Introduction

No book about consumer law would be complete without a discussion about the way the law regulates contracts for the sale of goods to consumers – after all, sales contracts are the paradigm contract type. EU legislation dealing with central aspects of consumer sales contracts has been in place since 1999, when the Consumer Sales Directive (99/44/EC) ('CSD') was adopted. Although the Directive itself has remained in force in (almost entirely[1]) unamended form since then, there have been several attempts to develop further the law on consumer sales contracts. This is why this area of law is an interesting case study not only of the EU's approach to regulating the substance of a particular type of consumer contract, but also the EU's varying approaches to legislation, and the limits to this: repeated attempts to change the level of regulation contained in the Consumer Sales Directive with a view to encouraging greater cross-border contracting on the part of consumers and traders alike have clashed with national-level interests. This was largely caused by a desire to shift from minimum to maximum harmonisation. The Consumer Sales Directive goes to the heart of private law, which might explain the reluctance of the Member States to accept more extensive regulation at the EU level.

Intriguingly, the number of references to the CJEU for preliminary rulings on the interpretation of the Consumer Sales Directive has been surprisingly low; there have been no more than a handful of such requests. This is in sharp contrast to the Unfair Contract Terms Directive, where there have been numerous references.[2]

This chapter will therefore examine the area of consumer sales contracts from a number of perspectives. To begin, there will be an initial overview of the Directive, covering (i) its scope, (ii) the requirement that goods must be in conformity with

1 A minor amendment was made by the Consumer Rights Directive (2011/83/EU) which inserted a new Article 33 which requires Member States to notify the Commission about the adoption of new and more stringent provisions, i.e. new national law rules which exceed the minimum standard laid down in the Consumer Sales Directive.

2 See Chapter 4.

the contract, (iii) remedies for non-conformities and (iv) guarantees. The relevant provisions which supplement those of the CSD and the Consumer Rights Directive (2011/83/EU) will also be discussed.

The discussion of the CSD will trace a number of the themes. In particular, this chapter will concentrate on the following aspects:

Single market vs consumer protection

As will be seen, the Consumer Sales Directive is a minimum harmonisation directive which introduced a general conformity requirement and several remedies.[3] The underlying intention was a common baseline to promote consumer confidence.[4] Generally speaking, the CSD's minimum harmonisation status means that Member States are permitted to adopt or maintain more protective rules, although the extent to which this provides *carte blanche* to depart from the provisions of the CSD is not without controversy. For example, Rott has argued Member States should not use minimum harmonisation as a justification for sidestepping provisions from a directive which had been carefully negotiated during the legislative procedure (such as the remedial hierarchy in Art. 3 of the Directive). This is because this would effectively undermine the agreement reached through the EU's legislative process.[5] Although interesting, it seems that minimum harmonisation has generally been regarded as allowing Member States rather more freedom than Rott's position would suggest.

In the proposal for the Consumer Rights Directive, an attempt was made to make the rules on consumer sales subject to a maximum harmonisation standard, with some modifications. However, this was criticised by the majority of legal scholars[6] and failed to gain political acceptance. It seemed that maximum harmonisation of consumer sales law would be going too far for both consumer lawyers and national governments. A particular stumbling block was the nature of the remedial scheme, which would have excluded the ability of a consumer to terminate a contract immediately even where the seriousness of a non-conformity might have justified this.

At the same time as work on the Consumer Rights Directive was in progress, the European Commission had sponsored work on a far more ambitious project:

3 Art. 8(2) CSD.

4 Recital 5.

5 P Rott, 'Minimum harmonisation for the completion of the internal market? The example of consumer sales law' (2003) 40 *Common Market Law Review* p.1107.

6 See e.g. M Faure, 'Towards maximum harmonization of consumer contract law?!?' *Maastricht Journal* 15 (2008), p.433; P Rott, and E Terryn, 'The proposal for a directive on consumer rights: No single set of rules'. *Zeitschrift für Europäisches Privatrecht* 17 (2009), p.456; and H Micklitz and N Reich "Crónica de una muerte annunciada: The Commission proposal for a 'directive on consumer rights'" (2009) 46 *Common Market Law Review* p.471. For a more positive view, see E Hondius, 'The proposal for a European directive on consumer rights: A step forward' (2010) 18 *European Review of Private Law* p.103.

an initiative in the field of European Contract Law. When it became clear that the rules on consumer sales contracts would not be changed by the Consumer Rights Directive, the focus shifted, and the development of new rules on consumer sales contracts became the first concrete legislative step for introducing a more extensive set of Contract Law rules at the European level. This was the proposal for a Common European Sales Law (CESL).[7] There were some obvious differences of approach when compared to the existing Consumer Sales Directive: (i) there was a wider range of topics and more rules, which were also more detailed; (ii) CESL would have been optional rather than automatically applicable; (iii) it focused on cross-border transactions, rather than establishing a single set of rules applicable to all consumer sales contracts; and (iv) the chosen legislative instrument was a regulation rather than a directive. This alternative approach also did not succeed, and the proposal for CESL was eventually withdrawn in December 2014. A third attempt to extend the regulation of consumer sales contracts was made in December 2015, with a new directive proposed to cover the distance and online selling of tangible goods,[8] and a separate proposal on the supply of digital content.[9] These proposals revert to the use of directives, and also seek to pursue a maximum harmonisation standard. At the time of writing, neither proposal had become law yet.

The EU brand of consumer protection

One critique which can be made of both the Consumer Sales Directive and the initiatives to enhance or replace it (especially CESL and the December 2015 distance sales proposal) is that the starting point seems to have been focused on what legal rules might be palatable from a national perspective so as to adopt an EU-level set of rules. For example, the Consumer Sales Directive was inspired by provisions of the UN Convention on the International Sale of Goods 1980 (CISG),[10] which had been ratified by most Member States (although not the UK and Ireland). This seemed to smooth the path towards adopting the Consumer Sales Directive because its fundamental approach was already familiar to (most) national legal systems. The proposal for CESL drew on the DCFR, which was the product of a detailed comparative law exercise to derive a best solution based

7 COM (2011) 635 final, 11 October 2011.

8 *Proposal for a Directive of the European Parliament and of the Council on Certain Aspects Concerning Contracts for the Online and Other Distance Sales Of Goods* COM (2015) 635 final, 9 December 2015.

9 *Proposal for a Directive of the European Parliament and of the Council on Certain Aspects Concerning Contracts for the Supply of Digital Content* COM (2015) 634 final, 9 December 2015.

10 Generally, S Grundmann, 'Consumer law, commercial law, private law: How can the Sales Directive and the Sales Convention be so similar?' (2003) 14 *European Business Law Review* p.237. For a discussion of potential clashes, see B Sandvik, 'The battle for the consumer: On the relation between the UN Convention for the International Sale of Goods and the EU Directive on Consumer Sales' (2012) 20 *European Review of Private Law* p.1097.

on the various rules found in the national laws of the EU Member States. And the December 2015 proposals largely harvest their rules from the ruins of CESL. A problem with this approach is that the main concern was to have a common set of rules, but insufficient care was taken to develop rules which would be suitable for consumer sales contracts in the Single Market. It seems that there has been little appetite at the EU level to consider whether this approach is the best way of providing rules that will encourage consumers and traders to take greater advantage of the potential offered by the Single Market, or whether an alternative approach, perhaps one which is much more principles-based and steps away from very detailed, technical rules,[11] would be more successful and could in turn create a legal framework that would be a positive feature of the EU's consumer protection brand.

EU approach to consumer protection at risk of being insufficiently protective

One of our key arguments is that the EU's approach to consumer protection risks under-protecting consumers because of its overarching purpose to create a level playing field to promote the use of the Single Market. A key problem with several areas of EU consumer law, including the area of consumer sales contracts, is that the objective of EU legislation frequently appears to overemphasise the desire to have common rules irrespective of their substantive content, which often means that EU legislation might fall short of providing proper solutions to the challenges consumers face in the Single Market. This is clearly apparent from Recital 5 of the Consumer Sales Directive, which states that 'the creation of a common set of minimum rules of consumer law, valid no matter where goods are purchased within the Community, will strengthen consumer confidence and enable consumers to make the most of the internal market'. The focus seems to be on having a common set of rules, but not necessarily one that tackles specific issues affecting cross-border contracts.

At times, a stronger problem-focused approach might be advisable, and legal rules could be better designed to reflect the specific issues that might arise when it comes to shopping in the Single Market. It often seems that one reason for the current approach is to ensure that EU rules work best within the national legal systems of the majority of Member States, but it does not follow from this that the EU rules are the *best* rules for the Single Market. For example, one aspect which the EU has repeatedly chosen not to pursue is the introduction of direct producer liability, i.e. making a manufacturer of goods liable for non-conformity of those goods.[12] This is in contrast to the imposition of liability for injuries or

11 For a general discussion of these approaches, see L Kaplow, 'Rules versus standards: An economic analysis' (1992) 42 *Duke Law Journal* p.557.

12 The Commission declined to put forward proposals on this issue when it last reported on the Directive: see on *Communication on the Implementation of Directive 1999/44/EC*

property damage caused by defective goods under the Product Liability Directive (85/374/EEC).[13]

The challenge of parallel regimes

The EU has toyed with the idea of parallel regimes as an alternative to the one-size-fits-all approach of harmonisation used thus far. CESL would have introduced different regimes for domestic and cross-border sales. Following the withdrawal of CESL, the focus appears to have shifted to online/distance as against in-store sales. The notion of parallel regimes should be approached with a high degree of caution due to the risk of confusion this might create.[14] Any arguments in favour of this approach need to be strong and clear, and the rules adopted need to be clearly suited for their respective contexts. There may be instances where specific rules for cross-border problems are needed, in which case there should be no hesitation to introduce these. However, for most aspects of consumer sales contracts, the same rules will be appropriate for both domestic and cross-border sales. For instance, the standard of quality mandated by the legal rules should be the same. Indeed, in line with our idea of an 'EU consumer law brand', it would be desirable to have a clear objective quality requirement applicable to all types of consumer sales contracts.

The Consumer Sales Directive

In this section, we will examine the rules from the Consumer Sales Directive and the additional rules relevant to consumer sales contracts provided by the more recent Consumer Rights Directive.

Scope and definitions

Sale

According to Article 1(1), the Directive's objective is 'the approximation of the laws, regulations and administrative provisions of the Member States on certain aspects of the sale of consumer goods and associated guarantees in order to ensure a uniform minimum level of consumer protection in the context of the internal market.' Its focus is therefore on contracts for the *sale* of consumer goods, and does not extend to other types of supply transactions which are also commonly encountered in the consumer context, such as hire-purchase contracts

Including Analysis of the Case for Introducing Direct Producers' Liability COM (2007) 210 final, p.12. For the arguments in favour, see R Bradgate and C Twigg-Flesner, 'Expanding the boundaries of liability for quality defects' (2002) 25 *Journal of Consumer Policy* pp.342–377; and also the contributions to M Ebers, A Janssen and O Meyer (eds), *European Perspectives on Producer Liability* (Sellier, 2009).

13 See Chapter 7.

14 See Chapter 1, pp.9–10.

or contracts of exchange (barter). Bearing in mind that the CSD primarily focuses on the legal requirements as to the quality of goods ('conformity with the contract'[15]) and associated remedies, this narrow focus on certain categories of contracts under which goods are supplied to consumers seems unduly restrictive. As the CSD is a minimum harmonisation directive, Member States are free to extend its provisions to other types of supply contracts.

Indeed, there is no definition of 'sale' in the Consumer Sales Directive, which leaves its scope somewhat imprecise. A definition of 'sales contract' can be found in the Consumer Rights Directive, which provides that "'sales contract' means any contract under which the trader transfers or undertakes to transfer the ownership of goods to the consumer and the consumer pays or undertakes to pay the price thereof, including any contract having as its object both goods and services".[16] However, the definition from the Consumer Rights Directive does not apply to the provisions of the Consumer Sales Directive – despite the intentions of the *Acquis Review* to standardise definitions across the various consumer law directives. The CRD definition would not cover contracts of hire or hire-purchase, or barter.

However, the Consumer Sales Directive includes a provision to the effect that certain contracts involving the supply of goods should be included within the notion of a contract for the sale of consumer goods. They are 'contracts for the supply of consumer goods to be manufactured or produced',[17] and contracts for the supply and installation of goods 'if installation forms part of the contract of sale … and the goods were installed by the seller or under his responsibility'.[18]

The inclusion of contracts for the supply of consumer goods to be manufactured or produced in the notion of sale essentially means that a contract is one of sale whenever a finished product is supplied to a consumer. As a result, a contract for a supplier to produce and supply a finished product are regarded as a sale of the finished product. This broad notion of 'sale' in Art. 1(4) will clearly cover a situation where a supplier provides both labour and materials to produce a finished item to be supplied to a consumer. Moreover, on the basis of Article 2(3) (discussed below), it must also cover a situation where at least some of the materials used by the supplier to make the finished product are provided by the consumer.

The more difficult situation is where all of the materials are provided by the consumer and the supplier merely produces the finished product. Intuitively, one might think that this type of contract would be for a service, i.e. producing the finished item from the materials supplied by the consumer.[19] However, it is equally possible to regard this contract as one for 'the supply of consumer goods

15 See below, p.179.
16 Art. 2(5) CRD.
17 Art.1(4) CSD.
18 Art.2(5) CSD.
19 Note the equivalent provision in Art. 3 CISG, which states in Art. 3(2) that 'This Convention does not apply to contracts in which the preponderant part of the obligations of the party who furnishes the goods consists in the supply of labour or other services.'

to be manufactured or produced'. This would mean that the supplier making the finished product would be liable for any non-conformities in the finished product in the same way as a seller of goods. This would be subject to the restriction that there would be no liability for any lack of conformity which originates in the materials supplied by the consumer: Article 2(3) states that 'there shall be deemed not to be a lack of conformity for the purposes of [the Directive] if ... the lack of conformity has its origin in materials supplied by the consumer', which clearly covers circumstances where some or all of the materials used by the supplier to make the finished product – whether based on a standard design or custom-made to the consumer's requirement – are supplied by the consumer. The situation becomes yet more complicated when the consumer also supplies the design which the supplier is to use for making the finished product. Intuitively, one might think that the supplier should not be liable in such a situation (although there may be a duty to warn the consumer about a defective design in tort law). Nevertheless, Art. 1(4) seems sufficiently broad to cover a situation where the consumer supplies the design for the finished product. It is possible that the supplier's liability for non-conformity might similarly be restricted by Art. 2(3) as it would where the consumer supplied the materials from which the finished product is to be made, but this would require a broad interpretation of the word 'materials' in Art. 2(3).

Recent technological advances have made this a topical issue: consumers are now able to design products using computer-aided design (CAD) software and to have these designs converted into physical items by utilising 3D-printing technology, often provided by a professional printing service. At present, the extent to which a 3D-printing service business might be liable for non-conforming goods is unclear, and there is at least a plausible argument that the Consumer Sales Directive would apply (by virtue of Art. 1(4)), but with some uncertainty whether liability under that Directive would be restricted through the application of Art. 2(3). It seems that clarification of this point and possible adjustments to the Directive might be needed. It is suggested that Art. 2(3) could be clarified to include designs supplied by a consumer, which would then, in turn, ensure an appropriate balance between the interests of consumers and sellers when it comes to goods 3D-printed to the consumer's design.[20]

Consumer

A consumer is 'any natural person who, in the contracts covered by [the] Directive is acting for purposes which are not related to his trade, business or profession' (Art. 1(2)(a)). This is a slightly narrower definition of consumer than the definitions found in other directives. In particular, the Consumer Rights Directive defines a consumer as a person who 'is acting for purposes which are outside his

20 See C Twigg-Flesner, 'Conformity of 3D prints – can current sales law cope?' in R Schulze and D Staudenmeyer (eds), *Digital Revolution – Challenges for Contract Law* (Nomos/Hart, 2016).

trade, business, craft or profession' (Art. 2(1) CRD). This is a more generous definition than that under the CSD. Under the CSD, the fact that goods are bought for a purpose which has some connection to the buyer's professional activity will mean that the buyer is not treated as a consumer.[21] The CRD did not amend the definitions of key terms such as 'consumer' in earlier directives such as the CSD. In practical terms, however, Member States can apply the slightly wider definition from the CRD to these national rules implementing earlier directives to ensure consistency.

Seller

In a similar vein, the definition of 'seller' is also narrower in the CSD than corresponding definitions elsewhere. Thus, the CSD defines 'seller' as 'any natural or legal person who, under a contract, sells consumer goods in the course of his trade, business or profession' (Art. 1(2)(c)).[22] By way of contrast, in the Consumer Rights Directive, a trader (which is now the preferred terminology) is defined as 'any natural person or any legal person, irrespective of whether privately or publicly owned, who is acting, including through any other person acting in his name or on his behalf, for purposes relating to his trade, business, craft or profession'.[23] The definition in the CSD requires a closer connection between the seller's professional activities and the particular contract than the Consumer Rights Directive.

In *Wathelet*,[24] the CJEU has held that the definition of 'seller' also includes a trader acting as an intermediary seller on behalf of a private individual where the trader has not informed the consumer that he is acting on behalf of a private individual. The consumer in *Wathelet* had bought a second-hand car from a garage which it sold on behalf of a private individual, but it had not told the consumer that this was the case. The consumer consequently assumed that the garage was the actual seller and selling the car in the course of its trade. The CJEU held that a seller has to disclose the fact when it is acting as an intermediary on behalf of

21 This discrepancy is not unique to the English version of the Directive. For example, in the German text, the CSD definition is 'jede natürliche Person, die im Rahmen der unter diese Richtlinie fallenden Verträge zu einem Zweck handelt, der nicht ihrer beruflichen oder gewerblichen Tätigkeit zugerechnet werden kann' whereas the CRD definition is 'jede natürliche Person, die bei von dieser Richtlinie erfassten Verträgen zu Zwecken handelt, die außerhalb ihrer gewerblichen, geschäftlichen, handwerklichen oder beruflichen Tätigkeit liegen. '

22 In German: 'jede natürliche oder juristische Person, die aufgrund eines Vertrags im Rahmen ihrer beruflichen oder gewerblichen Tätigkeit Verbrauchsgüter verkauft'.

23 In German: 'jede natürliche oder juristische Person, unabhängig davon, ob letztere öffentlicher oder privater Natur ist, die bei von dieser Richtlinie erfassten Verträgen selbst oder durch eine andere Person, die in ihrem Namen oder Auftrag handelt, zu Zwecken tätig wird, die ihrer gewerblichen, geschäftlichen, handwerklichen oder beruflichen Tä tigkeit zugerechnet werden können'.

24 C-149/15 *Sabrina Wathelet v Garage Bietheres & Fils SPRL* ECLI:EU:C:2016:840.

a private individual, because the consumer would otherwise not know whether he or she is protected by the rules on consumer sales law. This decision provides an important clarification on an issue which had not been addressed expressly in the definition of 'seller'. Its implications could stretch beyond the context of the CSD; increasingly, goods are sold via online platforms,[25] which are used by both private and professional sellers. Many platforms make it clear that they are acting as an intermediary only, but should they omit to do so, then *Wathelet* indicates that the platform could be liable as a seller under the CSD.

Taken together, the effect of the definitions of 'consumer' and 'seller' results in a narrower scope of the CSD compared to other directives. As already noted, it is unfortunate that the definitions in the CSD were not aligned to those found in the CRD (something on which agreement might have been possible because it would only have involved standardising essential definitions), but Member States can easily correct this by applying the wider definitions from the CRD.

Ex officio *application*

We need to note at this stage the significance of the ruling in *Faber v Autobedrijf Hazet Ochten*.[26] The facts of this case will be discussed below, but the case is important for a more general point. The CJEU was asked whether a national court should of its own motion consider whether the rules implementing the CSD should be applied to a particular case where one party is a consumer and the other a seller/trader even if the consumer has not sought to rely on their consumer rights. The CJEU gave an affirmative answer, holding that a national court which either already has the information necessary to determine whether consumer law applies, or could obtain this by asking for clarification, should determine whether a buyer under a contract of sale qualifies as a consumer. This ruling follows in the vein of decisions under other directives, particularly the Unfair Contract Terms Directive,[27] which seek to ensure that consumers can benefit from the protection of consumer law even if they are unaware of this.[28] It is a further indication that the *ex officio* doctrine should now be regarded as an integral element of EU consumer law.[29]

Consumer goods

Next, the Directive defines 'consumer goods' as 'any tangible movable item' with the exception of (i) goods sold by execution or otherwise by authority of law,

25 Famous names include eBay or etsy. See Chapter 9, p.336.
26 C-497/13 *Froukje Faber v Autobedrijf Hazet Ochten BV* ECLI:EU:C:2015:357.
27 See Chapter 4, pp.154–162.
28 See the discussion by P Rott, 'Improving consumers' enforcement of their rights under EU consumer sales law' (2016) 53 *Common Market Law Review* p.509
29 See Chapter 1, p.44.

(ii) water and gas when not 'put up for sale' in a limited volume or quantity, and (iii) electricity (Art. 1(2)(b)). Any type of goods can be 'consumer goods', but electricity is not goods, nor is gas or water supplied through the utility network. However, water or gas sold in a fixed quantity in a separate container will be within the definition of 'consumer goods'. Moreover, goods must be tangible and movable, which excludes sales of immovables such as land and houses from the scope of the Directive. The Directive does not consider the position of digital content, despite the fact that the status of computer software/digital content as goods (or otherwise) had been much debated when the Directive was being adopted.[30] It is only recently that the EU has moved towards adopting legislation which would cover contracts for the supply of digital content in a way that corresponds with the regulation of contracts for the supply of goods.[31]

Article 1(3) of the Directive gives Member States the option of excluding second-hand goods sold at public auction where consumers have the opportunity of attending the sale in person from the scope of the definition of 'consumer goods.' Many, but by no means all, Member States have utilised this provision. This restriction only applies to auctions which a consumer can attend in person, and auctions conducted purely over the internet are not within the scope of this exclusion. Conversely, this exclusion will apply as long as individuals have the opportunity of attending in person, irrespective of whether they actually attend.

Conformity with the contract requirement

The central obligation of the CSD is that the seller must deliver goods which are in conformity with the contract of sale. According to the Directive's recitals, 'the principle of conformity with the contract may be considered as common to the different national legal traditions'[32] of the EU Member States. The CSD itself was influenced by the provisions of the CISG, which was regarded as offering a common starting point for most Member States as many of them had ratified the Convention at the time when the CSD was proposed – although the UK and Ireland both had not ratified the CISG. The conformity with the contract in Art. 2 CSD is clearly inspired by Art. 35 CISG.[33]

30 See S Grundmann, 'Article 2: Conformity with the contract' in MC Bianca and S Grundmann (eds), *EU Sales Directive* (Intersentia, 2002), especially Chapter 2.

31 European Commission, *Proposal for a Directive of the European Parliament and of the Council on Certain Aspects Concerning Contracts for the Supply of Digital Content*, COM (2015) 634 final, 9 December 2015. Cf. A de Franceschi (ed), *European Contract Law and the Digital Single Market* (Intersentia, 2016).

32 Recital 7.

33 Cf. RF Henschel, 'Creation of rules in national and international business law: A non-national, analytical-synthetic comparative method' in CB Andersen and UG Schroeter (eds), *Sharing International Commercial Law across National Boundaries: Festschrift for Albert H. Kritzer on the Occasion of his Eightieth Birthday* (Wildy, Simmonds & Hill Publishing, 2008), esp. pp.198–193.

It is worth noting that in its *Green Paper on Guarantees for Consumer Goods and After-Sales Services*,[34] the Commission had proposed that goods should be required to conform to the consumer's 'legitimate expectations', described as 'a dynamic concept to be assessed taking all of the circumstances into account and, notably, the provisions of the contract, the presentation of the product, the price, the brand, the advertising or any information provided on the product, the nature of the product, its purpose, the laws and regulations concerning the product, and other features'.[35] A test along these lines would have focused more explicitly on the expectations of a consumer, and might therefore have been more suitable for the specific objectives pursued by the CSD. It would also have been similar to the test for 'defectiveness' found in the Product Liability Directive which is based on consumer expectations.[36] However, it seems that a safer way of reaching agreement on the text of the CSD was to build on familiar concepts, and so the 'conformity with the contract' requirement familiar both to most national legal systems and CISG-contracting states was chosen.

Article 2(1) therefore imposes a duty on the seller to deliver goods which are in conformity with the contract, and, as will be seen below, Art. 3 provides a range of remedies for circumstances when the seller has delivered goods which are not in conformity.

Time for assessing conformity: Delivery and risk

Delivery

The seller's duty under Art. 2(1) is to deliver the goods, and to deliver goods which are in conformity with the contract. However, the CSD is silent on two important issues: (i) there is no definition of 'delivery', leaving it unclear what the seller has to do to have delivered the goods; and (ii) no remedies are provided for circumstances when the seller does not deliver at all. This gap in the CSD was subsequently filled by the Consumer Rights Directive. According to Art. 18 (1) CRD, delivery requires that a trader transfers 'the physical possession or control of the goods to the consumer'. Article 18 further specifies that, unless otherwise agreed, delivery has to occur no later than 30 days from the date of conclusion of the contract. If the trader fails to deliver on time, the consumer can set a new deadline for delivery, and failure to comply with this new deadline would entitle the consumer to terminate the contract (Art. 18(2)). However, if the original date was essential, or if the trader has refused to deliver, then the consumer is entitled to terminate the contract immediately. Following termination, the trader has to reimburse any sums already paid 'without undue delay' (Art. 18(3)). This addition provides some clarity as to the meaning of delivery, and is quite

34 COM (1993) 509 final.
35 Ibid., p.86.
36 See Chapter 7, p.272.

consumer-friendly in that the moment of delivery is shifted to the point where the consumer acquires physical possession of the goods. However, the possibility that delivery may occur when a trader 'transfers … control of the goods' to the consumer creates some difficulty where the goods are given to a third-party carrier. At that point, the carrier could be regarded as having physical possession of the goods subject to the consumer's control. If that were so, then a trader could not be held responsible for any delays or delivery problems caused by the carrier, as the trader had already fulfilled his obligation to transfer control of the goods. However, according to Recital 51, a 'consumer should be considered to have control of the goods where he or a third party *indicated by the consumer* has access to the goods to use them as an owner, or the ability to resell the goods'.[37] This suggests that handing goods over to a carrier would not amount to delivery even if the consumer might be regarded as being in control under otherwise applicable domestic law, because the carrier would not be a third party 'indicated by the consumer'. This view also seems supported by the way the rules on the passing of risk treat the fact that goods are handed over to a carrier (see below). So overall, the provisions on delivery are consumer-friendly, but this could have been set out in a more straightforward manner.

Passing of risk

The Consumer Rights Directive also deals with the passing of risk – an issue which had been left untouched by the CSD.[38] According to Art. 20 CRD, the risk of loss or damage to the goods will pass from trader to consumer in one of two ways:

1 The consumer (or a third party indicated by the consumer) has acquired the physical possession of the goods; or
2 On delivery to a carrier if that carrier had been chosen by the consumer and the chosen carrier was not one offered by the trader.[39]

As with the provisions on delivery, this is quite a consumer-friendly rule. Generally, risk will transfer to the consumer with physical possession of the goods. The one exception is where a consumer rather than the trader has chosen a carrier – which would treat such a carrier in the same way as any other 'third party' indicated by the consumer. However, in the case of most online sales, the carrier options will

37 Our emphasis.
38 Recital 14 to the CSD merely states that 'references to the time of delivery do not imply that Member States have to change their rules on the passing of risk', although in practice, it was necessary to make some adjustments to ensure that the CSD would be implemented properly.
39 In this case, the consumer may have rights in national law against the carrier if the goods are lost or damaged in transit.

be offered by the trader, and so risk will not pass to the consumer until transfer of physical possession. As noted above, the notion of delivery should be analysed in the same way, with the effect that risk and delivery go together and take place once physical possession is transferred to the consumer. This is therefore a rule which is consumer-friendly and particularly helpful for goods ordered online – including from a trader in another Member State. In that sense, this is a small but noteworthy rule which is helpful for cross-border sales contracts.

Elements of conformity

The over-arching requirement in Art. 2(1) is that goods must be in conformity with the contract, which means that the terms of the contract themselves stipulate what the quality and fitness for purpose of the goods should be. The starting point in the CSD is therefore in line with party autonomy and the freedom of the contracting parties to agree on the particular requirements regarding those goods. In short, Art. 2 prioritises the subjective agreement of the parties, instead of laying down a fixed quality expectation which all goods must meet. The 'reasonable expectations' test suggested in the *Green Paper* would have been closer to a more objective test. The choice of a subjective test might have been made because this seemed familiar to most of the Member States, and those that preferred a more objective standard (such as the UK) could retain this based on the minimum harmonisation standard of the Directive. It does raise the question of what the function of a 'conformity' requirement should be, however: should this be simply a way of reinforcing the contractual agreement reached by the parties, or should it be an objective quality standard which all goods must meet? A purely subjective test based on agreement between the parties might fit party autonomy and freedom of contract best, but it does not reflect the realities of modern-day consumer contracts. So it would have been preferable to adopt a more objective quality standard,[40] which would also have supported the development of a European brand of consumer protection. Indeed, the EU could have been bold here and set an objective standard that goods have to be of 'reasonable quality', or 'satisfactory quality'.[41]

Admittedly, to a large extent, the CSD deals with the fact that in the case of most consumer sales contracts, there will be limited, if any, discussion between seller and consumer about specific conformity requirements. Article 2(2) CSD

40 See similar points made by J Smits, *The New EU Proposal for Harmonised Rules for the Online Sales of Tangible Goods: Conformity, Lack of Conformity and Remedies*, Study for the JURI Committee of the European Parliament (February 2016), p.9; and C Twigg-Flesner, 'Disruptive technology – disrupted law? How the digital revolution affects (contract) law' in A. De Franceschi (ed), *European Contract Law and the Digital Single Market* (Intersentia, 2016), p.45, in assessing the Commission's proposal for a directive on digital content.

41 The latter is the quality standard used in the UK in s.9 of the Consumer Rights Act 2015, and before then in s.14(2) of the Sale of Goods Act 1979. Other common law jurisdictions take a similar approach: see e.g. s.6 of the Consumer Guarantees Act 1993 (New Zealand) – goods to be of 'acceptable quality', with criteria similar to those in UK law.

establishes a rebuttable presumption that the goods are in conformity with the contract if the requirements listed in paragraphs (a)–(d) are satisfied. However, Art. 2(2) does not require that the goods must comply with all the requirements in Article 2(2). The presumption of conformity created by Article 2(2) is rebuttable, which means that goods which satisfy Article 2(2) could nevertheless be found not to be in conformity with the contract. Thus, Recital 8 states that 'in order to facilitate the application of the principle of conformity with the contact, it is useful to introduce a rebuttable presumption of conformity with the contract covering the most common situations' and 'that presumption does not restrict the principle of freedom of contract', before emphasising that 'in the absence of specific contractual terms ... the elements mentioned in this presumption may be used to determine the lack of conformity of the goods with the contract'. This suggests that the terms of the contract can both supplement and indeed displace the criteria in Art. 2(2). Furthermore, goods can still be regarded as being in conformity with the contract despite the fact that not all of the criteria in Art. 2(2) have been met. This is confirmed in Recital 8, which states that 'the elements mentioned in the presumption are cumulative; ... if the circumstances render any particular element manifestly inappropriate, the remaining elements of the presumption will nevertheless apply', which suggests that there will be instances when not all four elements of the presumption should be considered.

There are four elements to Article 2(2), which will now be considered in turn.

Compliance with description and sample:

The first element of the presumption in Article 2(2)(a) is that the goods 'comply with the description given by the seller and possess the qualities of the goods which the seller has held out to the consumer as a sample or a model'. There are two separate aspects to this element: first, compliance with the description given by the seller; and second, possessing the qualities of a sample or a model shown to the consumer.

There are a number of uncertainties about the first aspect (description). It is not clear which descriptive words would be taken into account, and then to which degree the goods must correspond with that description. One might assume that description will cover descriptive words that relate specifically to the goods. These could be words identifying the nature of the goods and their central features, as well as descriptive words on technical features of the goods which are mentioned in the contract. However, descriptive words which do not directly identify the features of the goods would not be relevant.[42]

In addition, Art. 2(2)(a) talks of descriptions 'given by the seller'. However, in the consumer context, goods sold are generally packaged by the manufacturer, and any descriptive words are more likely to have been given by the manufacturer. However, it can be assumed that the seller is effectively deemed to adopt

42 E.g. words along the lines of 'This lipstick is used by Madonna' would not describe any features of the lipstick itself.

the description given by the manufacturer as his description, and so any relevant descriptive words on the packaging can be said to have been 'given by the seller'. If there is an error in the description on the packaging, a seller can rely on Art. 2(3) to evade liability in this regard by making the consumer aware of the error and by providing a correct description.

The reference to goods possessing the qualities which the seller has held out as a sample or model is also important, because it can cover instances where a consumer has bought goods having seen a display model in-store. The model is on display in a shop but the consumer buys a packaged version of those goods. It also covers situations where a consumer is given a sample (e.g. a swatch for a carpet) to demonstrate what the goods look like.

Fitness for buyer's particular purpose

The second element of the presumption is that the goods must be 'fit for any particular purpose for which the consumer requires them and which he made known to the seller at the time of conclusion of the contract and which the seller has accepted'.

It seems that this is quite a strict requirement in that for the presumption to arise, the goods must be fit for the consumer's purpose, rather than merely that they must be reasonably fit for that purpose. There are two conditions relevant to this element: first, the consumer must have made the particular purpose known to the seller 'at the time of the conclusion of the contract', and second, the seller must have 'accepted' the consumer's purpose. The first condition should be easy to satisfy by the consumer simply stating to the seller – which in practice would be a shop-assistant – the purpose for which the goods are required.[43] The second condition is more problematic, because it requires that the seller must 'accept' the purpose made known by the consumer. In particular, it is not clear if this requires that the seller expressly assents, or if proceeding with the sale having been made aware of the consumer's purpose would suffice. So the difficult situation might be where the seller does not expressly respond to the consumer who has stated that the goods are required for a particular purpose, especially in the case of a shop-assistant who does not have relevant expertise. This second condition could therefore operate in a way that might disadvantage a consumer, unless a pragmatic reading of this condition prevails and proceeding with a transaction after the consumer has stated his particular purpose suffices to constitute 'acceptance'. This would certainly be the appropriate approach when the seller has the relevant expertise. Furthermore, one needs to bear in mind that it would be for the consumer to show that the purpose was made known to the seller and that the latter accepted this, which could pose practical difficulties.

43 One might question how this criterion could operate in the context of online or distance sales, where there is usually no direct opportunity for a consumer to communicate with the seller about the particular purpose for which goods might be required.

Goods are fit for the purposes for which goods of the same type are normally used

The third element is that goods must be fit for normal purposes. Once again, there is some uncertainty whether this requires absolute fitness, or if reasonable fitness ('it's good enough') will suffice. The yardstick for establishing fitness is in respect of purposes for which goods of the same type are 'normally used', which seems to focus on the manner in which consumers use goods, even if they were not *commonly supplied* for such a purpose. A common example is a screwdriver, which is supplied for screwing screws into wood, but are also frequently used to open tins of paint. If a seller wishes to exclude such uses (which are normal but perhaps not among the purposes for which the goods are supplied), then a clear warning or statement to that effect should achieve this.

Quality and performance

The fourth element in Article 2(2)(d) is that the goods must show the quality and performance which are normal in goods of the same type and which the consumer can reasonably expect, given the nature of the goods and taking into account any public statements on the specific characteristics of the goods made by the seller, the producer or his representative, particularly in advertising or labelling. This element is the only one which explicitly alludes to the consumer's reasonable expectations, and there are two factors by which such expectations are shaped: the nature of the goods, and public statements made by the seller or producer, including in advertising.

The phrase 'the nature of the goods' is somewhat vague. Recital 8 includes the statement that 'the quality and performance which consumers can reasonably expect will depend *inter alia* on whether the goods are new or second-hand', and so the nature of the goods as being 'second-hand' or 'ex-display' will have a bearing on establishing what consumers might reasonably be entitled to expect. However, one should assume that obvious quality features flowing from the nature of the goods are clearly within the consumer's reasonable expectations: foodstuffs should be suitable for consumption (but need to be stored properly and consumed in a timely manner), books should be readable and a hammer should withstand being used for driving a nail into wood.

A more significant inclusion is the reference to advertising and similar public statements. Advertising by its very nature is designed to influence consumers into buying particular goods and/or particular brands, and any expectation of quality shaped through such advertising should be taken into consideration in assessing whether goods are in conformity with the contract.[44] However, liability for non-conformity falls on the seller, and so there is some recognition that

44 See also Chapter 2 on how the Unfair Commercial Practices Directive regulates advertising and other marketing activities.

the seller should not be liable for expectations created by all the public statements made by someone other than that seller. Article 2(4) therefore allows the seller to escape liability for public statements about the goods if he can show that (a) he was not, and could not reasonably have been aware of the statement; or (b) at the time of conclusion of the contract the statement had been corrected; or (c) the consumer's decision to buy the goods could not have been influenced by the statement. The first two of these reasons focus on the seller's position: liability is avoided where the seller could not have been aware of the public statement, or where the seller can show that the statement had been corrected when the contract was entered into. The latter reason does not require that the seller corrects the statement himself, nor does it require that the seller shows that the consumer was aware of the correction. The third reason will turn on the context of the particular contract of sale and whether the statement was influential in the consumer's decision to purchase. Such influence may be absent where the consumer was not aware of the public statement before concluding the contract, or where the statement was clearly so exaggerated that it could not have been intended to shape the consumer's expectations as to quality and performance.

Finally, a number of factors which might be important for a consumer are not included explicitly in Art. 2. These include factors such as durability and freedom from cosmetic or minor defects.[45] However, these are likely to be matters which would be covered by the consumer's reasonable expectations as to quality under Art. 2(2)(d), and so they are covered implicitly. A more difficult issue is the treatment of consumer expectations regarding the manufacturing process for goods.[46] This includes whether goods were made in an environmentally sustainable manner, as well as the absence of forced labour or child labour in the manufacturing process. A seller with a public commitment to selling only ethically-sourced goods might be held responsible for a non-conformity if goods have been manufactured in conditions of forced labour. However, it might be questioned whether this is an issue for a general conformity standard – it might be more appropriate to deal with issues such as this in separate measures.

Limitations on the conformity requirement

Article 2(3) provides for two instances when the seller can escape liability for a non-conformity even though the goods otherwise fail to be in conformity with the contract. The first is that there is deemed to be no lack of conformity if, at the time the contract was concluded, the consumer was aware of the non-conformity

45 Cf. the list of factors in s.9(3) of the UK's Consumer Rights Act 2015, which were introduced into UK law in light of reform proposals made by the Law Commissions to make sales law more suitable for consumer sales: see Law Commissions, *Sale and Supply of Goods* (HMSO, 1987).

46 Cf P Rott and C Glinski, 'Umweltfreundliches und ethisches Konsumverhalten im harmonisierten Kaufrecht' (2003) *Europäische Zeitschrift für Wirtschaftsrecht* p.649.

or could not reasonably have been unaware of it. The obvious way in which a seller can avoid liability for any lack of conformity or defect is by pointing this out to the consumer. It should also cover instances where a non-conformity is obvious from looking at the goods. However, this limitation is phrased in unnecessarily vague terms. Asking whether a consumer was 'aware' invites unnecessary discussion as to what is required for such awareness, and in particular, whether anything short of pointing-out a specific matter or something obvious on an examination carried out by the consumer would suffice. Reasonable awareness of a non-conformity seems a looser notion than having a non-conformity pointed out by the seller or a matter obvious by looking at the goods. This particular provision seems more favourable towards the seller than the consumer, but in any event, its vagueness is not appropriate in the context of a consumer transaction, where clearer and more straightforward rules are preferable.

A second limitation arises in respect of a contract for the supply of goods to be manufactured or produced by the seller. As noted, under such a contract, the conformity requirement applies to the finished goods supplied under the contract. However, Article 2(3) provides that there is deemed not to be a lack of conformity where such lack 'has its origin' in materials supplied by the consumer. This was considered earlier.[47]

Installation of goods and conformity

One provision of the Directive which introduced a consumer-friendly provision is Article 2(5), which deals with the installation of goods and applies in two circumstances; the first is where the contract includes a requirement that the goods supplied are to be installed by the seller or 'under his responsibility'. Here, any lack of conformity resulting from incorrect installation 'shall be deemed to be equivalent to lack of conformity of the goods'. In effect, it would not be sufficient for the seller to argue that he acted with due care and skill in installing the goods if the installation was nevertheless not sufficient to ensure that the goods meet the contractual requirement of conformity.

Second, where goods are installed by the consumer and a lack of conformity results from incorrect installation which is due to 'a shortcoming in the installation instructions', then this will also be a non-conformity for which the seller is liable. There is a lack of clarity about the ambit of the word 'installation', because its natural English meaning does not extend to goods which have to be assembled.[48] The word used in the German language version of the Directive is 'Montage' which has a broader meaning and covers assembly. So the word 'installation' should be interpreted broadly to include both installation in its main meaning (e.g. connecting a washing-machine to the plumbing system in

47 See above for a discussion of 'materials' and possible reform.

48 This is significant insofar as Art. 2(5) has been referred to as the 'IKEA clause', which alludes to challenges sometimes encountered with the assembly of flat-pack furniture.

the consumer's home) and the assembly of goods from their components. In both cases, the installation instructions must be such as to enable the consumer to install the goods correctly. The question arises by which standard it should be determined whether there are 'shortcomings' in the instructions. Although not spelled out in the Directive, it would seem that if an average consumer could not follow the instructions and install the goods correctly, then this should mean that there are shortcomings in the instructions.

The burden of proof

It is not entirely clear from the Directive as to who has the burden of proof in respect of a question of non-conformity – does the consumer have to establish that there was a non-conformity, or is the onus on the seller to show that the goods are conforming? This question arises because Article 2 presents the conformity requirement in terms of a rebuttable presumption, which suggests that once a consumer has alleged that the goods are not in conformity, it would be for the seller to show that the criteria of conformity are met. If the seller succeeds in doing so, the burden then falls on the consumer to rebut the presumption of conformity, e.g. by showing that the goods fail to comply with some other express requirement of the particular contract. In *Faber*, the CJEU observed that 'the onus is, in principle, on the consumer to furnish the evidence that a lack of conformity exists and that that lack of conformity existed at the time when the goods were delivered.'[49] This would suggest that the initial onus is on the consumer, but leaves open whether the consumer has to establish a non-conformity as against the criteria in Art. 2(2).

Reversed burden of proof

The point at which the conformity of the goods with the contract is assessed is the point of delivery, but any lack of conformity will not become apparent for some time thereafter. As explained above, it would be for the consumer to prove that a lack of conformity existed at the relevant time. However, Art. 5(3) reverses that burden during the first six months after the date of delivery, and introduces a presumption that any lack of conformity which appears within six months is deemed to have existed at the time of delivery. It would then be for the seller to rebut this presumption by showing that the lack of conformity raised by the consumer did not exist at the time of delivery. Art. 5(3) states that this will be also the case where this presumption would be incompatible with the nature of the goods, or the nature of the lack of conformity. The former might be relevant, e.g. in respect of perishable goods which are expected to last for less than six months.

49 Para [52].

The operation of the burden of proof rule was explored in the *Faber* ruling.[50] Ms Faber bought a second-hand car from Hazet in May 2008. In September of the same year, the car caught fire whilst being driven by Ms Faber, and was severely damaged. The wreckage of the car was taken to a scrapyard, where it was kept until the following May. It was then scrapped. A few days later, Ms Faber brought an action against Hazet for compensation. As part of that claim, she tried to have an expert report into the cause of the fire prepared, but the experts were unable to do so as the car had been scrapped. One of the questions referred by the national court concerned the matters a consumer had to establish in order to invoke the reversed burden of proof. The CJEU held that a consumer had to show (i) that a lack of conformity existed, and (ii) that the lack of conformity materialised within 6 months.[51] Once the consumer has established these points, it will not be necessary for the consumer to prove that the non-conformity was present at the time of delivery (when the seller's obligation arises).[52] Moreover, a consumer is not required to show what caused the lack of conformity, nor does he have to prove that the non-conformity can be attributed to the seller.[53] This is significant in that the CJEU effectively makes it clear that establishing liability for a non-conformity does not involve any fault-based element. The seller then has to prove that the lack of conformity was not present at the time of delivery, but rather arose as a result of something that happened after the goods had been delivered to the consumer.

Remedies for non-conformity

Article 3 provides for four remedies if the goods are not in conformity with the contract. Here, the Directive reflects the influence of the Continental legal tradition of trying to keep a contract alive when there has been a breach.[54] The primary focus of the remedies is therefore to ensure that the contract is performed, with termination ('rescission') a remedy of last resort only.

The relationship between the various remedies is a complex one. There is a two-stage hierarchy of remedies in Article 3: at the first stage, the consumer is entitled to require the seller to repair or replace the goods. The second stage is engaged if neither of these remedies is available, or if the seller fails to complete the requested remedy within a reasonable period of time or without significant inconvenience to the consumer. The intention behind the remedial scheme therefore is to ensure performance of the seller's contractual obligations. However, because of the minimum harmonisation character of the CSD, it has been possible for Member States to retain other remedies such as the possibility of

50 C-497/13 *Froukje Faber v Autobedrijf Hazet Ochten BV* ECLI:EU:C:2015:357.
51 Para [70].
52 Para [72].
53 Para [70].
54 See also H Sivesand, *The Buyer's Remedies for Non-Conforming Goods* (Sellier, 2005).

permitting a consumer to terminate the contract immediately rather than having to give the seller an opportunity to repair or replace the goods first.[55] Moreover, the CSD does not contain any provisions dealing with the relationship of the remedies in Art. 3 with any potential claim for damages – which might be relevant for dealing with consequential losses caused by non-conforming goods. This has the potential to cause difficulties in practical terms, because often, consumers will have suffered direct and quantifiable losses arising from and in addition to the non-conformity of the goods, but whether these are recoverable depends on national law.

Stage 1: Repair or replacement

Initially, the consumer's choice is between repair and replacement. 'Repair' is defined as 'in the event of lack of conformity, bringing consumer goods into conformity with the contract of sale' (Article 1(2)(f)). It has been argued that

> [o]bviously, this does not mean that they have to be in a brand-new state. The definition requires repair, which is so effective that the goods compared to the requirements of the contract would have been acceptable originally.[56]

Presumably, what is meant is that repair must cure the lack of conformity which existed in the goods when they were delivered. A problem with the definition of repair is that goods might have several latent causes of lack of conformity, which do not manifest at the same time. Assume one of these manifests and it is successfully repaired by the seller, but then a second non-conformity appears. On a strict application of the definition of repair, the seller's repair has not been successful because of the further lack of conformity which arose subsequently. This is potentially problematic because a failure to repair the goods could entitle the consumer to move to the second-stage remedies, although this would not seem appropriate where a new problem arises. It is therefore suggested that the definition of 'repair' should be interpreted as requiring the seller to resolve the particular lack of conformity the consumer has complained about, and when a second non-conformity manifests, then this should not mean that the consumer can immediately proceed to the second-stage remedy. One omission from the CSD to note here is that there is no indication as to how many separate non-conformities a consumer should have to put up with.

There is no definition of 'replacement', but presumably this means substituting the non-conforming item with an identical, but conforming item (e.g. a

55 The UK has defended this right and retained it – in a more consumer-friendly form – in the recent Consumer Rights Act 2015: see ss.20–22 of the Act.

56 D Staudenmeyer, 'The Directive on the Sale of Consumer Goods and Associated Guarantees – a milestone in the European consumer and private law' (2004) 4 *European Review of Private Law* p.555.

camera with a damaged lens can be replaced with a camera with an undamaged lens). This remedy might therefore not be available where the goods in question are unique.

Either remedy must be provided free of charge, which refers to 'the necessary costs incurred to bring the goods into conformity, particularly the cost of postage, labour and materials'.[57]

The consumer has the right to choose between repair and replacement, but this is subject to two restrictions: first, a consumer cannot require the seller to repair or replace the non-conforming goods if the chosen remedy is impossible or disproportionate.[58] So when a consumer choses one of repair or replacement, it is first necessary to consider whether it is possible to provide that remedy, and then whether it is proportionate in comparison to the other remedy, assuming that the other remedy would also be possible. Importantly, it is only permissible to compare repair with replacement and *vice versa*, but not to compare repair with, e.g. price reduction.[59] This is in line with the focus of Art. 3 on prioritising the performance of the contract. However, it might be seen as creating a risk for unfairness, because both repair and replacement might be significantly more expensive to the trader than price reduction, which might be a more appropriate remedy.[60]

Impossibility

A consumer's chosen remedy will not be available if it is impossible to provide this. Repair may be impossible for several reasons. First, the lack of conformity might be so severe that repair could not bring the goods into conformity. Second, repair might also be impossible if spare parts required are not available. A seller might also argue that repair is not possible because it would be uneconomical to try and repair the goods, e.g. because of the costs of labour or a lack qualified staff able to repair the goods. However, this should not be regarded as a question of impossibility; rather, such economic considerations might be relevant in considering whether repair would be disproportionate when compared to replacement (see below – note that disproportionality of repair can only be considered relative to the alternative remedy of replacement).[61] A further difficulty arises where the goods have had to be installed and then a non-conformity arises, either in the goods themselves or as a result of the installation (including where the incorrect installation was by the consumer and resulted from a shortcoming in the installation instructions). In order to repair the goods, the seller would have

57 Art. 3(4) CSD.

58 Article 3(3), final part.

59 This point was confirmed at para [68] in C-65/09 *Weber v Wittmer* and C-87/09 *Putz v Medianess Electronics* ECLI:EU:C:2011:396: '[I]t is clear from the wording and purpose of Article 3(3) of the Directive that it refers to two remedies provided for in the first place, namely the repair or replacement of the goods not in conformity.'

60 Cf. the discussion below concerning disproportionality and installation.

61 C-65/09 *Weber v Wittmer* and C-87/09 *Putz v Medianess Electronics* ECLI:EU:C:2011:396.

to uninstall and subsequently re-install the goods, which could be problematic if the consumer bought goods for self-installation. However, of itself, this should not mean that repair is impossible.

The instances when replacement will be impossible are also likely to be rare. It should not be regarded as impossible simply because the item in question is no longer in the seller's stock, as long as a replacement could be obtained by the seller from another supplier. If this would be too costly, then the seller would have to show that replacement would be disproportionate as compared to repair. On the other hand, it seems that replacement will generally be impossible in the case of second-hand goods. Recital 16 states that 'the specific nature of second hand goods makes it generally impossible to replace them', although this does not necessarily mean that replacement would always be impossible when it comes to second-hand goods. As there is no definition of 'replacement' in the Directive, it is unclear whether a replacement item has to be identical. If it is necessary that the goods have to be replaced with an identical item, then replacement would only be possible where an identical substitute is available, and with second-hand goods, this will usually not be so.[62]

It seems that there will be few circumstances where either remedy will be 'impossible', which reflects the underlying objective to ensure that the seller performs his contractual obligations. However, even though a remedy is possible, it might still be unavailable if it is 'disproportionate'.

Disproportionality

Assuming that both repair and replacement are possible, the seller may yet wish to resist the consumer's request for one of these by arguing that providing this remedy would be disproportionate. Article 3(3) provides that a remedy is deemed to be disproportionate 'if it imposes costs on the seller which, in comparison with the alternative remedy, are unreasonable'. In applying this test, three factors are to be taken into account:

1 the value the goods would have had if they had been in conformity with the contract,
2 the significance of the lack of conformity and
3 whether the alternative remedy could be completed without significant inconvenience to the consumer.

According to Recital 11, this is an objective test. However, it is important to note that the costs of a particular remedy are not considered in isolation in order to assess whether it would be disproportionate, but have to be compared with

62 Note that it is always possible for consumer and seller to agree on any remedy, so the seller could offer to replace non-conforming goods with a near-identical substitute, and the consumer could accept this.

the costs of the alternative remedy. It is clear from the location of the disproportionality test in Article 3(3) that the comparator remedy will always be repair or replacement. In *Weber and Putz*,[63] the CJEU was asked whether the disproportionality test was one of 'relative' or 'absolute' disproportionality, i.e. could repair only be regarded as disproportionate when compared to replacement (and *vice versa*), or could repair/replacement be disproportionate without comparison to the alternative remedy. The Court held that 'Article 3(3) defines the term "disproportionate" exclusively in relation to the other remedy, thus limiting it to cases of relative lack of proportionality.'[64]

In applying the disproportionality criterion, it needs to be considered which of repair or replacement is going to be less costly for the seller to provide. However, as there will inevitably be some difference in cost between repair and replacement, the fact that one is cheaper than the other will not make the more expensive remedy disproportionate. The threshold in the CSD is that the costs of the more expensive remedy must be *significantly* higher.[65]

In addition, the costs to the seller have to be balanced against the other factors. The second is the value the goods would have had if there was no lack of conformity. In the case of low-value goods, the cost of repair would probably significantly exceed the market value of the goods (not least because of the cost of labour and parts required), and so repair would probably be disproportionate when compared to replacement. Conversely, with high-value goods, even an expensive repair might not be disproportionate when compared to replacement. The significance of the lack of conformity is also relevant. For example, if the lack of conformity renders the goods essentially useless but easily repairable, then even an expensive repair will be justified where the goods are of high value, whereas replacement would be more appropriate for low-value goods. Also, if a lack of conformity is so severe that repair would be very cumbersome, then replacement might be better.

The final factor is the degree of inconvenience caused to the consumer by the particular remedy. This allows for the interests of the consumer to be balanced against the costs for the seller of providing a remedy. A classic example is a washing machine that has broken down. Usually, the cost of repair will be cheaper than replacing the machine, and the respective costs would mean that replacement would be considered disproportionate. However, if it will take a long time to effect a repair (e.g. because of the difficulties of sourcing spare parts), then the inconvenience to the consumer would be significant, and this could shift the balance in favour of replacement.[66]

63 C-65/09 *Weber v Wittmer* and C-87/09 *Putz v Medianess Electronics*, para [68]. ECLI:EU:C:2011:396.

64 Ibid., para [68].

65 As confirmed by Recital 11: 'In order to determine whether the costs are unreasonable, the costs of one remedy should be significantly higher than the costs of the other.'

66 The position might be different if the supplier were in a position to take away the defective machine for repair and provide the consumer with a substitute in the interim.

Disproportionality and installation

The difficulties that might arise where goods have been installed and then a non-conformity is discovered have already been noted. What happens when a consumer has bought goods and installed these correctly himself, or a third party did so, but a lack of conformity is subsequently discovered in those goods and they need to be replaced? Two questions arise: (i) who has to bear the cost of replacement; and (ii) if the cost falls on the seller, do the additional costs of replacing non-conforming goods render replacement disproportionate? This was the issue in *Weber and Putz*.[67] In *Putz*, the consumer had bought a dishwasher online, and had paid a third party to install this, but discovered afterwards that the dishwasher was faulty and had to be replaced. The facts in *Weber* were perhaps more unusual; the consumer had bought floor tiles from a builders' merchant and laid these himself before discovering cracks in the glaze which meant that the tiles had to be replaced.

The CJEU had to consider whether the seller had to uninstall the non-conforming goods installed and install the replacement or bear the cost of removal and reinstallation, despite the fact that seller had not been required to install the goods under the sales contract. The Court reasoned that precluding the consumer from recovering the cost of uninstalling the faulty goods and installing the replacement would mean that an additional financial burden would fall on the consumer which would not have arisen had the goods been in conformity when delivered. In the Court's view, this would mean that replacement would not be 'free of charge', contrary to Article 3(4). Also, it would be a significant inconvenience for the consumer if the goods were not removed and reinstalled. However, in both cases, the sellers argued that they should not be compelled to replace the goods because of the significant additional cost of uninstalling the non-conforming goods, and then installing conforming goods. In *Weber*, the tiles had cost approximately €1,380, but the full cost of replacing them would amount to €5,830. As mentioned above, the Court held the sellers could only invoke disproportionality of replacement when compared to repair (but repair was not in issue in these cases). The Court came up with a difficult solution to this issue; on the one hand, it held that a seller cannot refuse to replace goods because the cost of this is disproportionate in view of the value of the goods without a lack of conformity and the significance of the lack of conformity. On the other hand, the Court then develops an additional criterion for the seller's benefit in that the consumer's right to reimbursement of the cost of uninstalling non-conforming goods and installing the replacement could be limited to a proportionate amount. In justifying this, the CJEU observes that Article 3

> aims to establish a fair balance between the interests of the consumer and the seller, by guaranteeing the consumer, as the weak party to the contract,

67 C-65/09 *Weber v Wittmer* and C-87/09 *Putz v Medianess Electronics*, para [68]. ECLI:EU:C:2011:396.

> complete and effective protection from faulty performance by the seller of his contractual obligations, while enabling account to be taken of economic considerations advanced by the seller.[68]

However, there is then another proviso added by the Court in paragraph [76], where it states that any reduction to a proportionate amount should not 'result in the consumer's right to reimbursement of those costs being effectively rendered devoid of substance'.

This leaves the national courts with a complex balancing act between a range of different factors which takes into account the respective interests of consumers and traders. However, it also illustrates starkly the impact of harmonisation of only selected aspects of a particular area: the CSD covers most of the relevant remedies, but one important one has been omitted – damages. There is no indication what the relationship between damages and the CSD remedies should be. It seems that the complexity of the ruling in *Weber and Putz* is the result of two distinct issues not being kept separate: the right to free-of-charge replacement, and the right to claim damages for consequential losses. A less complicated solution which the CJEU could have adopted would have been to say that the additional costs incurred for uninstalling and reinstalling the goods should be recoverable as damages in national law.[69] This could be subject to a clarification that the principle of effectiveness (*effect utile*) requires national law not to preclude damages on this basis outright, but could apply criteria of foreseeability and remoteness to ensure that the seller would not incur disproportionate costs.[70] In *Weber and Putz*, this would have provided a better solution, and it would have avoided the complex interpretation adopted by the CJEU to get to the same result. As the CSD is a minimum harmonisation measure, it remains possible for the Member States to clarify their national laws to reflect this ruling whilst adopting clearer rules on this point – had the CSD been a maximum harmonisation measure, then there would have been no means of clarifying the legal position in national law.

Provision of remedy within reasonable time and without inconvenience

Once the consumer has chosen between repair and replacement, Article 3(3) requires that this is provided within a reasonable time and without any significant inconvenience to the consumer. If the seller fails to do so, the consumer can move to the second-stage remedies of rescission of the contract or reduction of the price (Article 3(5)). However, it is not clear if, assuming both repair and replacement were available, whether the consumer could ask for a replacement

68 Para [75].
69 Cf. B Kresse, 'Anmerkung' (2012) 20 *European Review of Private Law* pp.255–262.
70 See also the discussion by A Johnston and H Unberath, 'Joined cases C-65/09 *Weber v Wittmer* and C-87/09 *Putz v Medianess Electronics*' (2012) 29 *Common Market Law Review* pp.793–808.

if repair has not been satisfactorily effected, or vice versa, before proceeding to the second-stage remedies.[71] It is suggested that this should be possible, not least because that would be in accordance with the performance-focused approach to remedies in the CSD.

It is also not clear whether the consumer can request a stage two remedy in anticipation of the seller's failure to provide repair or replacement within a reasonable period of time or without significant inconvenience. The wording of Article 3(5) suggests that the consumer has to wait, because it is phrased in terms of the seller not having 'completed' the requested remedy. However, if there is no doubt that the seller will not comply, the consumer should not have to wait until a reasonable time has expired, but should be able to move immediately to a 'second stage' remedy sooner.

Relevant factors for establishing whether repair or replacement were provided within a reasonable period and without significant inconvenience are the nature of the goods and the purposes for which the consumer required them. For example, it would probably be a significant inconvenience if it took two months for a washing machine to be repaired/replaced.

Payment for using goods before replacement

A question which arose in the *Quelle* case[72] was whether a consumer who returns a non-conforming item to be replaced under Article 3 can be required to pay to the seller a sum of money as compensation to reflect the fact that the consumer might have had use of the goods for a period of time before their replacement. The rationale for this would be that the consumer will have used the goods for a while and therefore have had some benefit, and then receives a new item as replacement. In this case, the consumer had bought a cooker which she had used for 18 months or so before it broke down. She asked for a replacement, which was provided, but the seller requested that the consumer pay a sum of money for using of the appliance prior to its return. German law provided for this, but the compatibility of the German rule was challenged before the CJEU. As discussed below, a consumer who returns goods after rescinding the contract is entitled to a refund, but this can be subject to a deduction to reflect the period of time during which the consumer used the goods. It was argued that this should also be the case when goods are returned to be replaced, but the CJEU rejected this, holding that a consumer could not be required to pay compensation of this kind when non-conforming goods are replaced. As a result, consumers are entitled to receive a conforming item by way of replacement without having to pay any additional charges.[73]

71 MC Bianca, 'Article 3: Rights of the consumer', in MC Biana and S Grundmann (eds), *EU Sales Directive* (Intersentia, 2002), paragraphs 73–74.

72 C-404/06 *Quelle AG v Bundesverband der Verbraucherzentralen und Verbraucherverbände* [2008] ECR I-2685.

73 Cf P Rott, 'The *Quelle* case and the potential of and limitations to interpretation in the light of the relevant directive' (2008) 12 *European Review of Private Law* pp.1119–1130.

Stage two: Price reduction or rescission

If neither repair nor replacement cure the lack of conformity, or neither is available, the consumer can instead request a partial or full refund of the price paid by asking for price reduction or rescission. According to Art. 3(5), this is possible where

a the consumer is entitled to neither repair nor replacement;
b repair or replacement is available but the seller has not completed the repair or replacement within a reasonable time;
c repair or replacement is available but the seller has not completed the repair or replacement without significant inconvenience to the consumer.

It can be seen that 'significant inconvenience to the consumer' is a criterion relevant both to Article 3(3) in assessing whether repair or replacement is 'disproportionate', and here in considering the availability of rescission and price reduction. For the purposes of Article 3(3), this criterion has to be applied with a degree of speculation, as this is done before repair or replacement are attempted. In contrast, the same criterion in Article 3(5) applies with the knowledge of whether an attempt to repair or replace was effected without significant inconvenience. It could be questioned whether rescission would be an appropriate remedy if repair or replacement has successfully cured the lack of conformity, albeit by causing significant inconvenience. This situation might be better dealt with by awarding damages for the inconvenience caused, but as the CSD does not deal with damages, this alternative is not available.

Price reduction

One of the stage-two remedies is price reduction. The Directive does not provide any guidance on how the amount of any price reduction should be calculated. This could be either a flat-rate deduction based on the difference between (i) the value the goods would have had had they conformed to the contract and (ii) the value of the goods as delivered; or a proportionate reduction of the purchase price, in the same ratio as the value of the goods as delivered bears to the value they would have had, had they conformed to the contract. As these remedies are based on the CISG, it would seem that the proportionate reduction approach should be applicable here, too.[74] The following examples illustrate this:[75]

Example 1: A buys a smartphone for £100. Had it been in conformity with the contract, it would have been worth £100, but as delivered, it is defective

74 See e.g. MC Bianca, 'Article 3: Rights of the consumer', in MC Bianca and S Grundmann (eds), *EU Sales Directive* (Intersentia, 2002), para 39 and R Bradgate and C Twigg-Flesner, *Blackstone's Guide to Consumer Guarantees* (Oxford University Press, 2003), pp.100–102.
75 These examples are based on Bradgate and Twigg-Flesner (above), p.101.

and worth only £80. A proportionate price reduction would mean that the consumer would have to pay 80/100 of the contract price, i.e. the price reduction would be £20.

Example 2: Assume the same facts as in Example 1, but now a smartphone in conformity with the contract would, in fact, have been worth £120 (so the consumer paid less for the phone than its value). The proportionate reduction approach would require the consumer to pay 80/120, which is £66.66, and so the price reduction would be £33.34.

Example 3: Finally, assume that a smartphone in conformity with the contract would have been worth only £90, but the consumer paid £100 for it. The proportionate reduction approach would require the consumer to pay 80/90, i.e. £88.89, and so the price reduction would be £11.11.

Rescission

A remedy of final resort is rescission, although this is not available where the lack of conformity is minor (Article 3(6)). There is no guidance on when a lack of conformity will be minor. This could cause practical difficulties if a consumer would like to rescind a contract, e.g. for cosmetic defects. There would then be scope for disagreement as to when a non-conformity is minor. However, a consumer would only be able to seek rescission if repair and replacement are not available or once they have been attempted and failed. Many minor lacks of conformity can be cured by repair (or sometimes replacement), so if rescission is considered, it will be because the seller has failed to repair or replace the non-conforming item within a reasonable time or without a significant inconvenience. If the non-conformity is minor, the consumer would then only receive a price reduction but that would seem an appropriate outcome.

However, the question of whether a lack of conformity is minor could create difficulties for a consumer who brings a claim only for rescission and that claim fails because the lack of conformity is minor. In *Hueros*,[76] the CJEU held that in such circumstances, a court should be able to substitute price reduction as an appropriate remedy even though the consumer had not pleaded this as an alternative.

Generally, a consumer who rescinds the contract is entitled to a refund of the purchase price, but as already alluded to above, Recital 15 states that Member States may provide that account may be taken of the use the consumer has had of the product, i.e. there might be a deduction-of-use allowance and a consumer may not get back the full purchase price. There are two reasons for such a rule: (i) the consumer may have had the goods for a considerable period of time before the lack of conformity manifested; and (ii) the value of goods returned after some time will have depreciated significantly. However, such a rule also adds to the complexity of the remedial scheme, because it will necessitate consideration of (a)

76 C-32/12 *Soledad Duarte Hueros v Autociba SA, Automóviles Citroën España SA* ECLI:EU:C:2013:637.

whether the seller should make a deduction at all and (b) if so, what the amount of the deduction should be.

Also, whilst the CSD is silent on this, it is likely that a pre-condition to exercising rescission is that the consumer is able to return the non-conforming product, unless this is not possible because of the lack of conformity. Until there is a CJEU ruling on this point, this matter is left uncertain.

Consequential losses/damages

The discussion on *Weber and Putz* highlighted the fact that the CSD does not address the relationship of the remedies in Article 3 with the national rules regarding damages. However, damages will be important because often, consumers will not only seek a remedy to deal with the non-conformity of goods itself, but also seek compensation for consequential losses beyond the immediate non-conformity. The circumstances in which it is possible to award damages for consequential losses (and also for the direct loss instead of one of the other remedies) are left to national law. Here, one can also identify quite significant variations in the way the Member States deal with the availability of damages as a remedy. In the common law countries, damages are available for all breaches of contract, and are preferred to other remedies such as specific performance. Other jurisdictions will not award damages solely because there was a breach of contract, but will also require that it is demonstrated that the seller was somehow at fault in bringing about the breach of contract.[77]

Other key provisions

Two-year time limit for liability

Under the CSD, the liability of the seller is limited to any lack of conformity which becomes apparent within a period of two years from the date the goods were delivered (Art. 5(1)). The consumer will have to prove that any lack of conformity which arises during this period was present at the time of delivery (subject to the presumption discussed below). This period is different from a limitation period which sets the time-limit for commencing legal action, but Art. 5(1) postulates that such a limitation period must not be shorter than two years. This means that there is a minimum period of two years in respect of both the seller's liability and the right to take legal action, although the latter can be longer – i.e. the limitation period could be three years or even longer.[78] In addition, because of the minimum harmonisation character of the CSD, Member States could also extend the two-year period required by Art. 5(1). Moreover, Member States are

77 Cf. K Zweigert and H Kötz, *An Introduction to Comparative Law*, 3rd ed (Oxford University Press, 1998), Chapter 36.

78 In the UK, for example, the limitation period is six years from the date of the breach (i.e. the time of delivery in the case of a consumer sales contract): Limitation Act 1980, s.5.

given the option to allow the parties to agree on a shorter period of liability for second-hand goods (although this cannot be less than one year).[79]

Optional notification period

Member States are given the option of introducing a requirement that a consumer must notify the seller within a period of two months, starting on the date when he discovered the lack of conformity. This option was initially utilised by just over half of the Member States.[80] It is debatable whether a provision such as this should be included in a consumer law measure.[81] On the one hand, such a rule encourages swift action by a consumer who has discovered a lack of conformity and ensures that a remedy can be provided without delay. On the other hand, it could have the effect of depriving a consumer of his ability to obtain a remedy at all because a rule such as this could create scope for arguments between sellers and consumer as to whether a consumer delayed notifying the seller whenever a non-conformity arose more than two months after delivery. Whilst a consumer can benefit from the reversed burden-of-proof for six months, it creates an additional hurdle for the consumer to establish that notification was made on time.

In *Faber*, the CJEU provided additional guidance as to the amount of detail a consumer should be expected to provide if he is required to give notice of a non-conformity. The Court first held that the essence of this obligation is merely to notify the seller that a lack of conformity has been discovered. However, the consumer cannot be required to identify the cause of the lack of conformity, because of 'his weak position *vis-à-vis* the seller as regards the information relating to the qualities of those goods and to the state in which they were sold'.[82] The approach taken by the CJEU here reflects the classic assumption that rules on non-conformity are fundamentally designed to deal with the informational asymmetries between seller and consumer with regard to the goods. However, this seemingly clear guidance is somewhat undermined by the CJEU when it goes on to state that

> in order for the notification to be of use to the seller, it must include a certain number of particulars — the degree of precision of which will necessarily vary depending on the specific circumstances of each case — relating to the nature of the goods in question, the wording of the contract of sale in respect of those goods and the way in which the alleged lack of conformity became apparent.[83]

79 Art. 7(1) CSD.

80 See H Schulte-Nölke, C Twigg-Flesner and M Ebers (eds), *EC Consumer Law Compendium* (Sellier, 2008), p.432.

81 See C Jeloschek, *Examination and Notification Duties in Consumer Sales Law* (Sellier, 2006).

82 C-497/13 *Froukje Faber v Autobedrijf Hazet Ochten BV* ECLI:EU:C:2015:357, para [63].

83 Ibid.

Whilst the last point – the way in which the non-conformity materialised – is uncontroversial, it may prove more difficult for a consumer to refer to the relevant elements of the contract of sale. It would surely be sufficient for the consumer to state what the goods are, when they were bought, and what the lack of conformity forming the basis of the complaint is. Any other requirements for the notification would make it unnecessarily difficult for a consumer as it would allow a trader to claim that inadequate notice of the non-conformity had been given (as, indeed, was the situation in *Faber*).

Guarantees

In addition to the conformity requirement and associated remedies, the CSD also contains a number of rules regarding 'guarantees', i.e. voluntary undertakings given by a retailer or manufacturer in respect of the goods.[84] EU terminology has been inconsistent in this regard, as the phrase 'commercial guarantee' is sometimes used to refer to these guarantees, and contrasted with the notion of a 'legal guarantee' which is in fact the conformity requirement. Indeed, this was the case in the *Green Paper*, which contained a number of proposals for the regulation of guarantees. Primarily, these focused on disclosure of clear information about the scope of any guarantee offered. It was also proposed that where the required information was not given, a 'default' guarantee would have applied. There was also a suggestion for a European Guarantee which would have provided identical cover in all the Member States of the European Union, and that where goods were sold through a defined distribution network, all the members of the network would have had to honour relevant guarantees. Finally, guarantees should have provided consumers with benefits above the protection consumers have through their legal rights. Few of these ideas made it into the final version of the CSD.[85]

In the CSD, 'guarantee' is defined as

> any undertaking by a seller or producer to the consumer, given without extra charge, to reimburse the price paid or to replace, repair or handle consumer goods in any way if they do not meet the specifications set out in the guarantee statement or in the relevant advertising.

The CSD is therefore only concerned with guarantees given free-of-charge, and its rules do not apply to guarantees which consumers are asked to pay for. It applies to guarantees given by both the seller and the 'producer' of the goods. 'Producer' has an extended meaning for the purposes of the CSD and includes the manufacturer, importer into the Union or own-brander of the goods who by

84 C Twigg-Flesner, *Consumer Product Guarantees* (Ashgate, 2003).

85 A Wiewiórowska-Domagalska, *Consumer Sales Guarantees in the European Union* (Sellier, 2013).

placing his name, brand, etc. on the goods purports to be their producer (Article 1(2)(d)).

Moreover, the definition covers not only guarantees provided on a document enclosed with the goods, but also those mentioned in advertising. This makes it clear that statements in advertising are potentially relevant to the overall scope of any guarantee offered and, any undertakings given in general advertising could be treated as a guarantee. Of course, not all advertising statements will be regarded as being part of a guarantee, because a guarantee must be an 'undertaking' by the seller or manufacturer in respect of the goods.

Article 6 then introduces a number of rules on guarantees. A crucial provision is Article 6(1) which states that:

> A guarantee shall be legally binding on the offerer under the conditions laid down in the guarantee statement and the associated advertising.

This confirms unequivocally that guarantees are to be legally binding, and whilst the Directive is silent on the legal nature of their enforceability, it is assumed that the intention was for this to be contractual. This means that the provisions of the Unfair Terms Directive apply to the terms and conditions on which guarantees are provided.

Several further points can be made: first, only the person giving the guarantee (known as 'the offerer') is bound by it, and a consumer can only enforce the guarantee against the offerer. This could create difficulties where the guarantee envisages that a retailer will handle claims under the guarantee on behalf of the manufacturer (which is a common arrangement for certain categories of goods). It might be that in such circumstances, the retailer is treated as an agent acting on the manufacturer's behalf, although from a consumer's perspective, this could be confusing. Second, it is unclear from Article 6(1) as to who can enforce the guarantee against the offerer. Art. 6(1) does not restrict the benefit of a guarantee to the initial purchaser, but it also does not expressly mention that it is transferable to subsequent owners of the goods.

The offerer is bound by the guarantee 'under the conditions laid down in the guarantee statement and the associated advertising'. A difficulty arises where a guarantee is mentioned in advertising, but the guarantee statement enclosed with the goods fails to include aspects of the guarantee referred to in advertising. By virtue of Article 6, any such additional aspects would also be binding on the offerer, but there is no indication how conflicts between the guarantee statement and the associated advertising should be resolved. The most appropriate solution would be to adopt a *contra proferentem* approach and let the combination of aspects most favourable to the consumer prevail.

Guarantees will only bind the offerer under the conditions set out in the guarantee and the relevant advertising. There are two potential interpretations of 'conditions' in this context: first, it may cover the steps a consumer has to take before he is entitled to benefit from the guarantee, e.g. registering the purchase or guarantee with the offerer. Provided such requirements are clear and not too onerous, then the guarantee will only be binding once they have been fulfilled. Second, 'conditions' can also be the terms and conditions on which the guarantee is provided. This includes terms setting out the length of the guarantee period, how to claim under the guarantee, charges for parts and labour, matters relating to the goods not covered by the guarantee (e.g. consumables), or maintenance requirements. All of these conditions are set by the offerer, subject to the application of the Unfair Contract Terms Directive.

The only clear restriction applies via Article 7, which provides that the rights of consumers under sales law cannot be restricted or excluded in any way, which means that it would not be permissible to use a guarantee to exclude the operation of Articles 2 and 3 of the CSD. Moreover, Article 6(2) requires that a guarantee states 'that the consumer has legal rights under applicable national legislation governing the sale of consumer goods and make clear that those rights are not affected by the guarantee', which entails that guarantees cannot have the effect of restricting consumer rights under sales law.

Article 6(2) further requires that the guarantee document

> set[s] out in plain intelligible language the contents of the guarantee and the essential particulars necessary for making claims under the guarantee, notably the duration and territorial scope of the guarantee as well as the name and address of the guarantor.

The requirement that the guarantee set out the consumer's rights in 'plain, intelligible language' is familiar from the Unfair Terms Directive, but it is unclear whether the same extended meaning developed in CJEU case law in that context would apply here, too.[86] Consistency of approach would suggest that this should be so. Also, Art. 6(4) gives Member States the option to require that guarantees are drafted in one or more of the official languages of the European Union.

Generally, Article 6(2) is rather vague. It is not clear what might be the 'contents' of the guarantee other than those items mentioned in Art. 6(2) (duration, geographical scope, and the name and address of the guarantor). Presumably, it extends at least to details of what is covered as well as any restrictions or conditions. Similarly, it is not clear what the 'essential particulars' for making a claim under the guarantee are.

Article 6(3) then provides that

> On request by the consumer, the guarantee shall be made available in writing or feature in another durable medium available and accessible to him.

The purpose behind this provision is not obvious, although it seems to be a specific instantiation of the information-based approach popular in many areas of EU

86 See Chapter 4, p.152.

consumer law. Allowing consumers to read guarantees arguably gives them the opportunity to compare guarantees given on products made by different manufacturers and take this into account as part of their decision-making process. This is reflected in Recital 21, in which it is claimed that guarantees are one aspect on which manufacturers (and sellers) may compete, and in order to promote such competition, consumers are encouraged to compare guarantees given with similar goods before deciding on a purchase. Also, Article 6(3) is not limited to the pre-purchase context – so it could also be helpful if a consumer has misplaced the guarantee document but needs it to bring a claim.

Finally, Article 6(5) states that a failure to comply with the requirements in Article 6 does not affect the validity of a guarantee and consumers can still rely on it. A guarantee document which does not include the details required by Article 6(2), will therefore nevertheless be legally binding – but as it will potentially be difficult to figure out what the terms and conditions of the guarantee are, this might not be that helpful a provision. There are no other sanctions envisaged in the directive other than the possibility of enforcement using the Injunctions Directive (cf. Art.10 CSD).[87]

Towards a more coherent sales law … or not?

The CSD was adopted in 1999 and had a far-reaching impact on some national legal systems. Although its basis in the CISG has made it perhaps less difficult to manage for those jurisdictions which have ratified the convention, there were still significant challenges. In Germany, for example, the need to implement the CSD was the trigger for a much more detailed review of the civil code.[88] In the UK, the creaking and heavily-patched Sale of Goods Act was further amended to introduce the new remedies of repair and replacement into the Act for consumer sales contracts, but the initial implementation was far from successful,[89] not least because the focus on ensuring performance of the contract through the primacy accorded to the remedies of repair and replacement sat rather uneasily with the common law's general reluctance to consider specific performance as a remedy for breach of contract. The minimum harmonisation standard afforded some leeway to the Member States to integrate the provisions of the CSD with their existing rules on sales contracts. However, an inevitable consequence of this was that even after the implementation of the CSD in all the Member States, there remained significant variations between the national laws in respect of

87 The DCFR contained more extensive provisions on guarantees: see C Twigg-Flesner, "Consumer goods guarantees in the DCFR – 'best solution' or grasping the wrong nettle?" (2009) 17 *European Review of Private Law* p.641.

88 The 'Schuldrechtsmodernisierung' of 2002. See e.g. H-W Micklitz, 'The new German Sales Law: Changing patterns in the regulation of product quality' (2002) 25 *Journal of Consumer Policy* p.379.

89 A matter singled out for criticism in the Davidson Review, *Implementation of EU Legislation – Final Report* 2006, paras 3.10–3.23.

the matters harmonised by the CSD.[90] With the European Commission keen to pursue maximum harmonisation, there have been a number of attempts to reform the CSD.

Reforming the CSD: Attempt 1

At the European level, the *Acquis Review* which was launched in 2005 sought to identify whether the CSD had achieved its goal of harmonising consumer sales law, and the extent to which its minimum harmonisation standard meant that there continued to be variations. A study for the European Commission found that there were noticeable variations between the Member States after the implementation of the CSD, many of which were the result of both the regulatory options included in the directive and the fact that its minimum harmonisation standard left room for Member States to retain more protective rules. The Commission deduced from this that continuing variations between domestic consumer sales law required reform which would convert the CSD and other directives to a maximum harmonisation standard.[91] Its thinking was set out in the *Green Paper on the Review of the Consumer Acquis*, published in February 2007.[92] In this, a range of issues were proposed for reforming the existing rules on consumer sales contracts, both with regard to scope and points of detail.[93] One controversial matter raised for discussion was whether there should be direct liability of a producer for non-conforming goods. This was discussed in the report on the implementation of the Consumer Sales Directive, which ruled out any action in this regard.[94]

The proposal for a directive on consumer rights[95] contained a separate chapter dealing with sales contracts,[96] including some provisions familiar from the CSD, but also some significant modifications. Some of these were very technical and were probably a result of the intention to move towards a maximum harmonisation directive. Thus, the chapter on sales would not have applied to any spare parts replaced by a trader to repair non-conforming goods, and as for

90 See H Schulte-Nölke, C Twigg-Flesner and M Ebers (eds) *EC Consumer Law Compendium* (Sellier, 2008), pp.407–451.

91 European Commission, *Consumer Policy Strategy 2007–2013* COM (2007) 99 final, p.7.

92 COM (2006) 744 final.

93 See C Twigg-Flesner, 'No sense of purpose or direction? The modernisation of European consumer law' (2007) 3 *European Review of Contract Law* p.198.

94 *Green Paper*, page 30 and *Communication on the Implementation of Directive 1999/44/EC Including Analysis of the Case for Introducing Direct Producers' Liability* COM (2007) 210 final, p.12.

95 COM (2008) 614 final. See C Twigg-Flesner and D Metcalfe, 'The proposed Consumer Rights Directive – less haste, more thought?' (2009) 6 *European Review of Contract Law* p.368.

96 C Twigg-Flesner 'Fit for purpose? The proposals on sales' in G Howells and R Schulze (eds) *Modernising and Harmonising Consumer Contract Law* (Sellier, 2009); J Stuyck, 'The provisions on consumer sales' in H Schulte-Nölke and L Tichy (eds), *Perspectives for European Consumer Law* (Sellier, 2010).

mixed-purpose contracts involving both goods and services, it would only have applied to the goods elements. Also, new provisions on delivery and passing of risk were proposed, and, as already discussed above, these are the only provisions from the proposal which survived in the final version of the CRD.

The rules on conformity with the contract remained virtually unchanged from the CSD. However, whilst the remedies from the CSD were retained, it was proposed that the *trader* should have the choice between repair and replacement, not the consumer. Perhaps by way of balance, it was also suggested (in proposed Article 26(4)) that the "consumer may resort to any [available] remedy [if]: (a) the trader has implicitly or explicitly refused to remedy the lack of conformity [implicit] meaning that 'the trader does not respond or ignores the consumer's request' (Recital 42); (b) the trader has failed to remedy the lack of conformity within a reasonable time; (c) the trader has tried to remedy the lack of conformity, causing significant inconvenience to the consumer; (d) the same defect has reappeared more than once within a short period of time".

The shift to maximum harmonisation also entailed additional rules on the operation of the existing two-year liability period. Thus, it was proposed that if the trader had previously replaced the goods, the two-year period would start from the time of replacement (Article 28(2)). In addition, the previously optional requirement that the consumer must notify the trader of the lack of conformity within two months would have been turned into a firm rule.

There is no need to go into any more detail here, because almost all the provisions on sales contracts (except for those on delivery and passing of risks) were eventually deleted from the Directive during its legislative stages, not least because it turned out to be impossible to find a consensus between the Member States on these provisions. In addition, there had been other developments which meant that any changes to the rules on consumer sales had moved to an altogether different level: the proposal for a Common European Sales Law.

The Common European Sales Law

In 2001, the European Commission issued a *Communication on European Contract Law*,[97] in which it invited views on whether EU legislation on contract law should be considered. In light of the responses received to this initial Communication, the Commission refined its views in follow-up documents in 2003 (*A More Coherent European Contract Law – an Action Plan*)[98] and 2004 (*European Contract Law and the Revision of the Acquis: The Way Forward*).[99] At the core of this process was a huge academic project to create what has become

97 COM (2001) 398 final, 11 July 2001. See also 'On the way to a European contract code?' (editorial comments) (2002) 39 *Common Market Law Review* pp.219–255.

98 COM (2003) 68 final.

99 COM (2004) 651 final, 11 October 2004. See D Staudenmeyer, 'The way forward in European contract law' (2005) *European Review of Private Law* pp.95–104.

known as the 'Draft Common Frame of Reference on European Contract Law',[100] or DCFR for short. The idea for the DCFR was that it would be a toolbox providing principles and rules of contract law, which might then in turn be the basis for more detailed legislation on European Contract Law.[101] Following the publication of the DCFR, the Commission issued a further *Green Paper*,[102] and established an expert group to produce a more focused common frame of reference on contract law from the DCFR.[103] The expert group's output was not a common frame of reference, but instead a so-called 'feasibility study' for an optional instrument. This, in turn, became the proposal for a Common European Sales Law (CESL).[104]

There were several interesting aspects of the proposal for CESL.[105] It would have been introduced by means of a regulation rather than a directive, thereby obviating the need for Member States to adopt legislation to transpose it into domestic law. Instead, the effect of CESL would have been to introduce a parallel set of legal rules for sales contracts into the laws of the Members States, with the intention that parties would have had a choice between the existing rules of the applicable domestic law or the rules from the CESL. The proposal covered contracts for the sale of goods as well as for the supply of digital content, and would have applied in respect of contracts where one party was a business and the other either a consumer or a small or medium-sized enterprise (SME). Moreover, CESL would have been limited to cross-border contracts only.[106] It was designed as a so-called 'optional instrument', i.e. consumers and traders would have been given the choice between CESL and the national law which would be applicable in accordance with the provisions of the Rome-I Regulation.[107] Although

100 Study Group on a European Civil Code/Research Group on the Existing EC Private Law (Acquis Group) (eds) *Principles, Definitions and Model Rules on European Private Law – Draft Common Frame of Reference* (OUP, 2010).

101 Generally, see e.g. L Miller, *The Emergence of EU Contract Law – Exploring Europeanization* (Oxford University Press, 2011) or C Twigg-Flesner, *The Europeanisation of Contract Law*, 2nd ed (Routledge, 2013).

102 *Green Paper on Policy Options for Progress towards a European Contract Law for Consumers and Businesses* COM (2010) 348 final.

103 Commission Decision setting up the Expert Group on a Common Frame of Reference in the area of European Contract Law (2010) O.J. L105/109.

104 COM (2011) 635 final, 11 October 2011. See e.g. M Schmidt-Kessel (ed), *Ein einheitliches europäisches Kaufrecht?* (Sellier, 2012); H Schulte-Nölke, F Zoll, N Jansen and R Schulze (eds), *Der Entwurf für ein optionales europäisches Kaufrecht* (Sellier, 2012).

105 G Dannemann and S Vogenauer, *The Common European Sales Law in Context* (Oxford University Press, 2013).

106 See C Twigg-Flesner, 'CESL, Cross-border transactions and domestic law – why a dual approach could work (although CESL might not)' (2015) 23 *European Review of Private Law* pp.231–249; also C. Twigg-Flesner, *A Cross-Border-Only Regulation for Consumer Transactions in the EU – A New Approach to EU Consumer Law* (New York: Springer, 2012).

107 Regulation 593/2008 on the law applicable to contractual obligations (2008) O.J. L 177/6. See also see P Cachia, 'Consumer Contracts in European private international law: The sphere of operation of the consumer contract rules in the Brussels I and Rome I Regulations' (2009) 34 *European Law Review* p.476.

presented as an option for both consumer and trader, in reality, the only person making that choice would have been the trader, so optionality would have been limited.[108] However, the idea of the optional instrument is interesting in terms of the creation of a European Brand of Consumer Protection.[109] The choice in favour of applying the optional instrument would have been made by clicking on a so-called 'blue button'[110] on the trader's website. The notion of the 'blue button' soon took hold in the discussions surrounding CESL, although this was not enough to secure the adoption of CESL.

In terms of coverage, CESL would have been much more comprehensive than any directives adopted by the EU thus far. Its objective was to provide a much more comprehensive sales law to cover the making of a contract, the respective obligations of seller and buyer and corresponding remedies, and related matters such as unfair terms and prescription periods. There were a total of 186 substantive Articles in 18 chapters, and a separate chapeau regulation provided the rules detailing the envisaged scope of application.

However, CESL received a somewhat lukewarm reception, with some Member States arguing that the proposal was not compatible with the principle of subsidiarity.[111] The European Parliament suggested many amendments as well as a restriction of scope to cross-border consumer contracts concluded at a distance.[112] In December 2014, the European Commission withdrew the proposal for CESL, but also indicated that it had not been abandoned completely.[113] In its *Digital Single Market Strategy*,[114] the European Commission announced plans to modernise consumer protection rules for online and digital purchases, indicating that there would be two initiatives, one on harmonised EU rules for online purchases of digital content, and a second on 'a focused set of key mandatory EU contractual rights for domestic and cross-border online sales of tangible goods.'[115] At that stage, it remained unclear how this would be achieved; one

108 Cf. M Hesselink, 'How to opt into the Common European Sales Law? Brief comments on the Commission's proposal for a regulation' (2012) 20 *European Review of Private Law* p.195

109 See Chapter 1, p.5.

110 An idea promoted especially by Hans Schulte-Nölke. See e.g. H Schulte-Nölke, "EC law on the formation of contract – from the Common Frame of Reference to the 'Blue Button'" (2007) *European Review of Contract Law* p.332.

111 E.g. the UK's House of Commons European Scrutiny Committee, *Reasoned Opinion on Common European Sales Law*, 23 November 2011. Reasoned opinions were also made by the German Bundestag, the Austrian Bundesrat and the Belgian Parliament.

112 See C Twigg-Flesner, 'CESL, Cross-border transactions and domestic law – why a dual approach could work (although CESL might not)' (2015) 23 *European Review of Private Law* p.231.

113 European Commsision, *Work Programme 2015 – A New Start* COM (2014) 910 final, Annex II, p.12.

114 European Commission, *Communication on a Digital Single Market Strategy for Europe* COM (2015) 192 final, available at http://ec.europa.eu/priorities/digital-single-market/docs/dsm-communication_en.pdf.

115 *Single Market Strategy*, p.5

option might have been to amend the proposal for CESL but restrict its scope to online contracts. However, in the end, the Commission decided that the way forward would be to revert to harmonisation by directives.

Reforming the CSD: Attempt two

In December 2015, the European Commission issued proposals for two new directives,[116] one in respect of online sales of tangible goods,[117] and a second for the supply of digital content.[118] If adopted, these directives would be of a maximum harmonisation standard. This is somewhat surprising, because the fate of the sales proposals in the Consumer Rights Directive suggests that there is little appetite on the part of the Member States for the full harmonisation of aspects of substantive private law, and the lack of support for CESL indicates that this position is unlikely to have shifted significantly. At the very least, this puts a big question mark over the chances of the proposal for the online sales of goods proposal, not least because it seems to overlap with the existing directives on consumer sales and consumer rights.

Alongside these proposals, the European Commission also launched a so-called 'fitness check' of EU consumer law measures (REFIT).[119] This is, in effect, another review of the consumer *acquis*, which might result in proposals for reform of the existing directives. It is not due to report until the second half of 2017, so at the time of writing, it is unclear whether there will be major changes to the current rules on consumer sales.

Influence beyond sales law

The Consumer Sales Directive introduced a set of remedies which prioritise the performance of the trader's contractual obligations by requiring the seller to repair or replace goods which are not in conformity with the contract in the first instance. This performance-oriented approach to remedies has since found its way into other areas, notably the revised Package Travel Directive (2015/2302/EU) ('PTD'). This Directive deals with a range of issues regarding package travel contracts. A package is a combination of at least two different travel services (defined as including accommodation, carriage of passengers,

116 See papers in A. De Franceschi (ed), *European Contract Law and the Digital Single Market* (Intersentia, 2016).

117 *Proposal for a Directive of the European Parliament and of the Council on Certain Aspects Concerning Contracts for the Online and Other Distance Sales Of Goods* COM (2015) 635 final, 9 December 2015.

118 *Proposal for a Directive of the European Parliament and of the Council on Certain Aspects Concerning Contracts for the Supply of Digital Content* COM (2015) 634 final, 9 December 2015.

119 See http://ec.europa.eu/consumers/consumer_rights/review/index_en.htm [accessed 5 December 2016]

vehicle hire and other tourist services[120]).[121] Under Art. 13 PTD, the organiser (defined as a trader who combines and sells/offers for sale packages either directly or through another trader[122]) is responsible for the performance of package. A traveller[123] is required to notify the organiser of the package without undue delay of 'any lack of conformity which he perceives during the performance of a travel service'.[124] The use of the phrase 'lack of conformity' is interesting, because it mirrors the language used in the CSD; however, it does not seem to sound right in the context of a package travel contract. It has been given a separate definition as 'a failure to perform or improper performance of the travel services included in a package'.[125] It would have been clearer to use the phrase 'non-performance' or 'improper performance' rather than 'lack of conformity'. The parallels with the CSD are more apparent still when one considers the specific remedies. Thus, Art. 13(3) PTD obliges the organiser to 'remedy the lack of conformity', unless this (a) is impossible; or (b) would entails disproportionate cost, taking into account (i) the extent of the lack of conformity and (ii) the value of the travel services affected. Where either of these provisos applies, Art. 14(1) PTD provides for an 'appropriate price reduction' for the period of travel during which there was a lack of conformity, unless this lack was attributable to the traveller. The parallels with the criteria found in Art. 3 CSD are easily seen.

In some instances, the organiser may be required to provide what could broadly be described as 'substitute performance', or 'replacement' in CSD language: Art. 13(5) PTD stipulates that if a significant proportion of the travel services cannot be provided as agreed, the organiser has to offer suitable alternative arrangements of equivalent or higher quality to ensure the continuation of the package. If it is of lower quality, then the organiser has to provide an appropriate price reduction. The traveller can reject this alternative only if is not comparable to what was originally agreed, or if the price reduction is inadequate.[126]

However, there are also improvements to the remedial scheme in the PTD when compared to that in the CSD. Thus, Art. 13(4) PTD states that if the organiser does not remedy the lack of conformity within'a reasonable period set by the traveller', the traveller may do so himself and request reimbursement of any necessary expenses from the organiser. This provision therefore clearly establishes the right of the traveller to take action themselves and subsequently seek

120 Art. 3(1) PTD.
121 Art. 3(2) PTD.
122 Art. 3(8) PTD.
123 Defined as 'any person who is seeking to conclude a contract, or is entitled to travel on the basis of a contract concluded, within the scope of this Directive' (Art. 3(6) PTD). This is a broader definition than the usual 'consumer' definition, and it also extends to persons covered by a contract who are not necessarily contracting parties.
124 Art. 13(2) PTD.
125 Art. 3(13) PTD.
126 Art. 13(5) PTD.

reimbursement from the organiser – a matter not provided for in Art. 3 CSD. Moreover, the traveller does not have to set a time limit if the organiser refuses to provide a remedy or an immediate remedy is required.[127]

The PTD also provides for a right of termination, but only in circumstances where the lack of conformity 'substantially' affects performance of the package, and the organiser has failed to remedy this within reasonable period set by traveller. Where this is the case, the traveller may terminate the contract and request a price reduction or compensation, as appropriate.[128] This is akin to the right to rescind the contract under the CSD, which is subject to the proviso that the lack of conformity is not 'minor'.[129] If package includes carriage of the traveller, the organiser has to repatriate travellers with equivalent transport without undue delay and at no extra cost to traveller.[130]

The remedies in the PTD offer a further improvement in comparison to the CSD by including an entitlement to compensation: Article 14(2) grants the traveller an entitlement to 'appropriate compensation ... for any damage which the traveller sustains as a result of any lack of conformity'. Such compensation also extends to 'non-material damage, such as compensation for loss of enjoyment'.[131] Although this does not provide a comprehensive rule on damages claims (questions such as remoteness are not addressed directly and may require clarification by the CJEU), it is significant because it is an express recognition of the place of damages/compensation in a performance-oriented remedial regime.

Taken as a whole, the remedial regime in the Package Travel Directive has all the elements of the performance-oriented approach of the CSD – there are elements of correcting performance (repair), substitute performance (replacement), price reduction and termination. It is an improvement because of the explicit inclusion of an entitlement to compensation for damages. Although the extent to which compensation may be recoverable is not fully spelled out, Art. 14 PTD contains a number of limitations on the right to compensation. The PTD's more comprehensive system of remedies could be a template for any changes that might be made to the CSD as part of the REFIT exercise.

Conclusions

This chapter illustrates a number of the more problematic features of EU consumer law. First, it was suggested that the focus has, thus far, been on the introduction of rules on consumer sales for the sake of having common rules, rather than with a sufficiently clear focus on the specific issues that arise in the context

127 Art. 13(4) PTD.
128 Art. 13(6) PTD.
129 Art. 3(6) CSD.
130 Art. 13(6), 3rd para PTD.
131 Recital 34 PTD. This reflects the ruling in C-168/00 *Simone Leitner v TUI Deutschland* (2002) ECR I-2631 under the old Package Travel Directive (90/314/EEC).

of consumer sales contracts within the Single Market. The CSD introduces rules on conformity and associated remedies, but they are rather more complex than one might like for consumer sales contracts, and one can question whether these rules really help to boost consumer confidence in the way intended.[132] The subsequent attempts to reform EU rules on consumer sales – first in the original proposal for the Consumer Rights Directive and then in the ill-fated proposal for a Common European Sales Law – demonstrate that there is a considerable degree of political resistance to further EU-level regulation of sales contracts. A possible explanation for this is that sales contracts remain the paradigm contract type and therefore at the heart of national contract law regimes. Some harmonisation has been achieved, but the complexity of these rules – especially Art. 3 on remedies – raises the question whether this directive has really helped to improve consumer protection. One is certainly tempted to point to the very small number of CJEU cases on the Directive over the last two decades (at the time of writing, there had only been five substantive cases, as well as some on non-transposition) and conclude that national courts are reluctant to provide the CJEU with too regular an opportunity for using its rulings as a vehicle for extending the reach of EU law into the depths of domestic contract law.

This raises the inevitable question of why the EU has struggled so much with adopting a coherent set of legal rules on consumer sales contracts which could facilitate cross-border shopping by consumers. One answer might be that the EU legislature has approached this challenge from the wrong angle: instead of pursuing any kind of harmonised set of rules to level the playing field,[133] it should have identified the specific problems for consumers posed by the cross-border shopping environment. This might have resulted in clearer rules on conformity and remedies, but even more so have encouraged the Commission to take more seriously the need to develop innovative solutions. The reluctance towards the introduction of direct producer liability – and perhaps even network liability– stands out as a major missed opportunity for providing EU-level rules that could support consumers seeking to participate in cross-border shopping.

At the time of writing, the EU is committed to reviewing all of the EU consumer *acquis* to check whether it is still fit for purpose.[134] Although the findings of this exercise and details of any potential follow-up action are not yet known, one

132 C Twigg-Flesner, 'The importance of law and harmonisation for the EU's confident consumer' in D Leczykiewicz and S Weatherill (eds), *The Images of the Consumer in EU Law* (Hart, 2015).

133 As is evident from Recitals 3 ('the laws of the Member States concerning the sale of consumer goods are somewhat disparate, with the result that national consumer goods markets differ from one another') and 5 ('the creation of a common set of minimum rules of consumer law, valid no matter where goods are purchased within the Community, will strengthen consumer confidence and enable consumers to make the most of the internal market') of the CSD.

134 See http://ec.europa.eu/consumers/consumer_rights/review/index_en.htm [accessed 5 December 2016].

would hope that this exercise might provide the opportunity to think carefully about what sort of aspects of cross-border shopping require EU action, and what might be appropriate solutions to address the problems consumers face. In this regard, it needs to be borne in mind that the way consumers buy goods is undergoing a major transformation through the digital revolution and the emergence of new business models.[135] This development could make it even more urgent to come up with rules on consumer sales which are fit for this new environment – and such rules need to be much more problem-focused then the rules in the current CSD. Hopefully, REFIT will be more than merely another attempt to shift from minimum to maximum harmonisation without at the same time fundamentally reforming the substance of the CSD.

135 C Twigg-Flesner, 'Disruptive technology - disrupted law? How the digital revolution affects (contract) law' in A. De Franceschi (ed), *European Contract Law and the Digital Single Market* (Intersentia, 2016).

6 Consumer and mortgage credit

Introduction

General introduction

Consumer credit has been regulated by the EU since 1986.[1] The first measure was rather modest, but a much more wide-ranging Directive was adopted in 2008.[2] A directive regulating mortgages was added in 2014.[3]

Chapter themes

Harmonisation

This is a good topic in which to explore the maximum harmonisation debate. A push to maximum harmonisation was a plank of the 2008 Consumer Credit Directive reforms. By contrast, in the mortgage area the maximum harmonisation ambitions were limited to the field of pre-contractual information and calculation of the Annual Percentage Rate of Charge (APRC). This more limited approach seems preferable. APRCs need to have the same meaning in all the Member States if consumers are meaningfully to compare deals across borders. Common documentation may make it easier for businesses to trade across borders, allow non-local consumers to compare with similar documents from their home state and reduce to some extent the impact of language barriers. However, more extensive harmonisation in this area seems unjustified. The impact of some rules will be marginal to the workings of the internal market. Credit is a complex area in which uniformity will be hard to achieve and is often linked to local traditions and cultures. Even in the field of information some local variations may be valuable.

The loss of local flexibility caused by adopting maximum harmonisation does not seem justified with a product like consumer credit, and even more so

1 Directive 87/102/EEC on consumer credit (1987) OJ L42/48.
2 Directive 2008/48/EC on credit agreements for consumers (2008) OJ L133/66.
3 Directive 2014/17/EU on credit agreements for consumers relating to residential immovable property (2014) OJ L60/34.

mortgages, as there are a lot of factors encouraging consumers to purchase in familiar national markets. Local factors such as traditions of use of credit and familiarity with established forms of protection push in favour of national regulation. Equally, the dynamism of the credit market may call for agile regulatory responses at the national level without the straightjacket of a European regime.

Even where maximum harmonisation has been adopted in the field of consumer credit, its assistance to the internal market is limited, because there are so many factors requiring creditors still to look to local regulation: issues regarding scope; exemptions; minimum harmonisation provisions; local discretion built into the directive; and, open-textured terms subject to interpretation according to local traditions and national implementation styles, particularly where the national rules go into more detail than the European rules. In practice, the need to have national legal advice is unlikely to be a major issue for creditors as their investment in products sold across borders will usually be substantial and legal costs will be built into their planning.

The market for cross-border credit is small and there have been no calls for a separate regime for cross-border credit sales. This is certainly not an area where the 'brand Europe' is used to export the product. Little European consumer credit will be sold outside the European borders. Equally we doubt these laws will have much impact on state laws beyond Europe as credit laws are usually detailed and based on national traditions. Positive aspects, such as moves towards responsible lending practices, may be seen as part of a trend underpinned by international standards.[4]

Information

Credit law is also a rich terrain for exploring the information model of consumer protection. The pattern adopted by the EU very much conforms to the traditional model that values quantity of information over quality. The insights of behavioural economics have not been embraced to gear information disclosure to the particular needs of different types of lending situations and borrowers. Personalised disclosure is not addressed and the use of warnings is limited and

4 OECD, *G20 High-level Principles on Financial Consumer Protection* (OECD, 2011), https://www.oecd.org/g20/topics/financial-sector-reform/48892010.pdf [accessed 22 March 2016]; The World Bank, *Good Practices for Financial Consumer Protection* (The World Bank, 2012), http://siteresources.worldbank.org/EXTFINANCIALSECTOR/Resources/282884-1339624653091/8703882-1339624678024/8703850-1340026711043/8710076-1340026729001/FinConsumerProtection_GoodPractices_FINAL.pdf [accessed 22 March 2016]; FinCoNet, *FInCoNet report on responsible lending* (FinCoNet, 2014), http://www.finconet.org/FinCoNet-Responsible-Lending-2014.pdf [accessed 22 March 2016]; Consumers International, *Responsible Lending: An International Landscape* http://www.consumersinternational.org/media/1412472/ciresponsiblelending_finalreport_06-11-13.pdf [accessed 7 July 2016]. Often these reports take a broader view of responsible lending than is taken in this work and include all aspects of the regulatory and supervisory regime.

perhaps lacking in sophistication and hence impact. The EU interventions on information disclosure and warnings, if linked to maximum harmonisation, potentially impede the freedom of national authorities to develop helpful information obligations and warnings based on local needs and customs. There are only a few nods in the direction of recognising the life-time nature of many credit and mortgage contracts may require ongoing communication.[5]

In brief the basic approach to information policy in EU credit law seems rather unimaginative. It also risks stifling national initiatives and experimentation that could then be shared between regulators. The underlying policy is very much one of promoting transparency and information to allow a free market to generate offerings from which informed consumers can select. There are only a few glimpses of a more imaginative policy that ensures consumers understand the information and that creditors take some responsibility to lend responsibly. These are fairly modest and ultimately in most market situations fail to challenge the freedom-of-contract model by introducing a more co-operative ethic that requires the creditor to take into account the interests of consumers.[6] For example, the duty to inform is enhanced by an obligation to provide adequate explanations, but this stops short of requiring the creditor to counsel against taking the credit even where that would be in the consumer's best interests. The major control derives from the credit-worthiness test, but this focuses on affordability and not on whether the loan is in the consumer's best interest. Only in the mortgage sector, when advisory services are offered, do the interests of consumers need to be to the fore in lending practices.

Risk sharing

Credit is about risk sharing. The cost of credit reflects in part the risk of default amongst the consumers of that particular product. Those who do not default subsidise those who do. Social institutions like credit unions specifically seek to provide for such cross-subsidisation.[7] Consumer protection rules that ensure creditors better assess consumers should lead to less cross-subsidisation if creditors are better able to assess the risk of particular consumers. This may ironically lead to less solidarity amongst consumers i.e. less risk sharing.

One way of sharing risk is to mandate core protections which apply to everyone so all benefit from the mandatory rules. There are, however, in EU credit law

5 L Nogler and U Reifner, *Life Time Contracts: Social Long-term Contracts in Labour, Tenancy and Consumer Credit Law* (Eleven International Publishing, 2014).

6 R Brownsword, "'Good faith in contracts' revisited". (1996) 49 *Current Legal Problems* p.111. Signs of a more co-operative ethic in this vein have begun to emerge in the CJEU's jurisprudence on unfair terms, Case C-415/11 *Mohamed Aziz v Caixa d'Estalvis de Catalunya, Tarragona i Manresa (Catalunyacaixa)* ECLI:EU:C:2013:164. See Chapter 4, p.148.

7 See for example, G Griffiths and G Howells, 'Britain's best kept secret – an analysis of credit unions as an alternative source of credit' (1991) 14 *Journal of Consumer Policy* p.443.

only a few restrictions on the form of the contractual agreement. Another means is to control what products can be offered so that the vulnerable cannot be left exposed to particularly risky products. Again, there are few examples of this at EU level. There is, for example, no EU usury law. The effects of such laws are debatable. They can exclude consumers from the market.[8] However, creditors may also still decide to lend to some consumers at lower rates than previously. Finally, risk can be shared by mitigating the impact of default, through mechanisms like the UK's time order[9] that allow debt rescheduling, or ultimately by debt forgiveness in bankruptcy. These have not been addressed legislatively at the EU level. The EU prefers to focus on perfecting the market and to rely on individual responsibility of consumers and traders. However, the nature of credit and the unpredictable incidents of normal social life require protection for consumers when things go wrong and the credit contract cannot be completed as planned.

Credit use in the EU

The level of consumer credit usage varies greatly across Europe depending on economic conditions and cultural attitudes to credit. The UK, Spain, Germany, France, Italy and Poland accounted for more than 80% of the total consumer credit outstanding in December 2008.[10] In Cyprus, outstanding consumer credit was 25% of the GDP, whereas in Latvia, Netherlands, Lithuania, Hungary, Estonia, Luxembourg and Slovakia it was less than 5%.[11] Between 2009 and 2011 consumer credit debt as a percentage of GDP dropped from 9.1% to 8.2%. Cyprus still leads the way with 19%, followed by Greece with 15% and then Hungary and the United Kingdom with 14%.[12]

In 2014, outstanding residential mortgage debt in the EU stood at €6,909,057m, equal to 49.6% of EU GDP. By far the highest amounts of debt were in the UK (€1,666,902m) and Germany (€1,237,410m); whilst, as a percentage of GDP, mortgage debt varied dramatically within the EU from 114.0%

8 D Cayne and M Trebilcock 'Market considerations in the formulation of consumer protection policy' (1973) 23 *Univ of Toronto LJ* p.396 and for a more recent review of arguments see I Ramsay "'To heap distress upon distress?' Comparative reflections on interest rate ceilings" (2010) 60 *The University of Toronto Law Journal* p.707.

9 Consumer Credit Act 1974, s. 129.

10 GHK, *Final Report – Establishment of a Benchmark on the Economic Impact of the Consumer Credit Directive on the Functioning of the Internal Market in this Sector and on the Level of Consumer Protection* (GHK, 2009), 22; http://ec.europa.eu/consumers/archive/rights/docs/ccd_benchmarking_study_en.pdf [accessed 12 March 2016]. See also W Kösters, S Paul and S Stein, *An Economic Analysis of the EU Commission's Proposal for a New Consumer Credit Directive* (Essen, 2004) which showed the UK had large growth in credit during 1990s bringing it up to the top of the consumer credit league along with Germany.

11 European Commission, *Report on the Implementation of Directive 2008/48/EC on Credit Agreements for Consumers* COM (2014) 259 final, 11; *Final Report – Establishment of a Benchmark on the Economic Impact of the Consumer Credit Directive on the Functioning of the Internal Market in this Sector and on the Level of Consumer Protection* (GHK, 2009).

12 COM (2014) 259 final, 11.

in Denmark to far lower levels in the new Member States, with Romania having lowest figure at 6.7%.[13]

The aim of the EU consumer policy in this field has not necessarily been to increase credit consumption; rather, it has sought to promote competition and ensure consumers have a transparent choice on fair conditions. However, easier access to credit may be a by-product of its liberal regulatory approach. It has opened markets up so that credit has become available in all Member States in more popular forms through firms skilled in advertising and marketing. The fact consumer credit use has dropped in recent times is probably due to external factors in the wake of the financial economic crisis rather than anything related to the Directives.

How much credit is good for a society is a much-debated topic.[14] There is a risk of over-consumption of credit as individuals find it hard to compare the value of immediate access to money against the long term cost of repayment of capital plus interest.[15] There is a general trend in many Member States towards credit being necessary to maintain expected standards of living. This process known as 'financialization'[16] can be productive[17] but can also increase risks.

Cross-border trade

There is relatively little cross-border selling of credit.[18] Instead businesses have moved to consumers by setting up subsidiaries or branches and often purchasing a local vehicle.[19] This practice makes one wonder whether maximum harmonisation

13 European Mortgage Federation, *Hypostat 2015* (European Mortgage Federation 2015); http://www.hypo.org/PortalDev/Objects/6/Files/Hypostat_2015.pdf [accessed 22 March 2016].

14 TA Durkin, G Elliehausen, ME Staten and TJ Zywicki, *Consumer Credit and the American Economy* (Oxford University Press, 2014); G Bertola, R Disney and C Grant (eds) *The Economics of Consumer Credit* (MIT Press, 2006). J Niemi et. al., "'Wannabe WAGS' and 'credit binges': The construction of overindebtedness in the UK" in J Niemi, I Ramsay and WC Whitford (eds), *Consumer Credit, Debt and Bankruptcy* (Hart, 2009).

15 D Laibson, A Repetto and J Tobacman, 'A Debt Puzzle', in P Aghion, R Frydman, J Stiglitz, and M Woodford (eds), Knowledge, Information and Expectations in Modern Economics: In Honor of Edmund S. Phelps (Princeton University Press, 2003).

16 C Poppe, *Financialisation of social welfare – the role of credit and financial counselling for social inclusion and exclusion* (SIFO 2011), 3; http://www.sifo.no/files/Project_Description.pdf [accessed 12 March 2016].

17 U Reifner, "'A call to arms' – for regulation of consumer lending", in J Niemi, I Ramsay and WC Whitford, *Consumer Credit, Debt and Bankruptcy* (Hart, 2009); I Ramsay, 'Consumer credit regulation after the fall: International dimensions' (2012) *J Eur Cons and Market Law* p.24 helpfully reviews some of the theories of consumer credit. These include viewing it as a form of lifecycle model of consumption, loans making up for gaps in wages or as the fuel for excessive consumerism.

18 *Final Report – Establishment of a Benchmark on the Economic Impact of the Consumer Credit Directive on the Functioning of the Internal Market in this Sector and on the Level of Consumer Protection* (GHK 2009), pp.40–41, which states that in 2008 67% of respondents to the GHK survey say they do not engage in cross-border lending.

19 Ibid.

is really needed in this sector. Although consumer credit regulatory rules are one barrier to cross border trade, others are often influential such as language and culture, consumer preference for local providers, local tax laws, national anti-money laundering regulation, debt recovery practices and insolvency laws.[20]

There are some potential consumer gains if credit markets can be made more competitive. For instance, the average APRC[21] in 2008 was 31% in Estonia and only 7% in nearby Finland.[22] However, there are also risks attached with liberalisation. Where consumers have experimented with credit in different currencies, typically the Swiss franc, strong fluctuations in currencies have brought their own problems for consumers.[23] Foreign-currency loans can be for domestic transactions. The risk of currency fluctuation exists in any cross-border consumer credit agreement where the consumer contracts in a currency other than their own. Their complexity can also be problematic for consumers to understand.[24] This risk is of course eliminated within the Eurozone for loans in euro.

Despite the limited cross-border trade in consumer credit, there has been a lot of rhetoric about opening up the consumer credit markets. This was even encouraged by some consumer groups, particularly in the new Member States, where competition was weak. Maximum harmonisation was seen as a tool to achieve greater cross-border trade. But, it is unlikely to be very effective, given the other factors pulling consumers towards local creditors.

The mortgage market is even more distinctly national in character than the general consumer credit market and has a very limited internal market dimension. National traditions vary greatly as regards the financing of home ownership and natural human conservatism intensifies the propensity to prefer products from the national market. There are sound reasons why consumers should play safe with such important investments. Borrowers and lenders both seem more comfortable working within familiar frameworks. Lenders in particular fear the 'adverse selection' problem, whereby only borrowers who have struggled to find a loan in the local market will seek one from another state. Only if loans are being promoted in the consumer's state and the lending is subject to their state's laws do consumers

20 Ibid. Interestingly the implementation of the Consumer Credit Directive in France was part of a package of reforms also including insolvency law, S Charlton, *National Report on the Transposition of the Consumer Credit Directive in France* (European Legal Studies Institute, 2012).

21 See below.

22 *Final Report – Establishment of a Benchmark on the Economic Impact of the Consumer Credit Directive on the Functioning of the Internal Market in this Sector and on the Level of Consumer Protection* (GHK, 2009).

23 Such foreign-currency loans can be either from foreign or national creditors. See P Yeşin, 'Foreign Currency Loans and Systemic Risk in Europe' [2013] *Federal Reserve Bank of St. Louis Review* p.218 available at https://research.stlouisfed.org/publications/review/13/03/219-236Yesin.pdf [accessed 7 July 2016].

24 Such loans have been subject to litigation in the CJEU where the Court has used unfair terms law to require they be intelligible to the consumer: see Case C-26/13 *Árpád Kásler, Hajnalka Káslerné Rábai v OTP Jelzálogbank Zrt* ECLI:EU:C:2014:282 and Case C-96/14 *Jean-Claude Van Hove v CNP Assurances SA* ECLI:EU:C:2015:262.

seem interested in looking at new products.[25] In smaller Member States with limited market offerings there may be some advantages to looking across borders. The Commission concedes that the level of cross-border sales is less than 1%.[26] Even after citing a study it commissioned listing advantages that could be derived from integrating markets,[27] the Commission sagely noted:

> Limits to the potential for integration should however be acknowledged. The influence of factors such as language, distance, consumer preferences, or lender business strategies cannot be underestimated.[28]

Understandably, therefore some Member States were unenthusiastic about the need for a directive regulating mortgages.

History of EU regulation

The EEC ventured into the field of consumer credit at a fairly early stage in the development of the consumer *acquis*. Perhaps because it was adopted at this early stage[29] – combined with the inherently challenging task of regulating in this area – Council Directive 87/102/EEC when adopted in 1986 had limited ambitions.[30] Its minimum harmonisation character meant that the impact on Member States' laws with sophisticated consumer credit regimes was limited or non-existent, the latter being the case with the United Kingdom.

In 1995 and 1996 reports were published on the operation of the Directive with a summary of reactions to the 1995 paper being published in 1997.[31] As Recital

25 London Economics, *The Costs and Benefits of Integration of EU Mortgage Markets* (London Economics, 2005) pp.8–9 and chapter 5.

26 Commission, *Mortgage Credit in the EU* COM (2005) 327 final, para 11.

27 Suggested benefits were an increase in GDP by 0.7% and private consumption by 0.5% and lowering interest rates by up to 47 basis points i.e. reducing interest payable on 100,000 euro loan by 470 euro per year: *The Costs and Benefits of Integration of EU Mortgage Markets* (London Economics, 2005). Mercer, Oliver Wyman and the European Mortgage Federation put the benefits at 0.12–0.24 of EU GDP in Simon Low and others, *Study on the Financial Integration of European Mortgage Markets* (Mercer, Oliver Wyman and the European Mortgage Federation, 2013).

28 Commission, *White Paper on the Integration of EU Mortgage Credit Markets* COM (2007) 807 final, 2.

29 Other early directives such as that on doorstep-selling were similarly rudimentary, see Directive 85/577/EEC on contracts negotiated away from business premises (1985) L372/31.

30 Directive 87/102/EEC on consumer credit (1987) OJ L42/48.

31 Commission, *Report on the Operation of Directive 87/102/EEC for the Approximation of the Laws, Regulations and Administrative Provisions of the Member States Concerning Consumer Credit* COM (95) 117 final; Commission, *Report on the Operation of Directive 90/88 Amending Directives 87/102 (as amended by Directive 90/88) for the Approximation of the Laws, Regulations and Administrative Provisions of the Member States Concerning Consumer Credit* COM (96) 79 final; Commission, *Report on the Operation of Directive 87/102 for the Approximation of Laws, Regulations and Administrative Provisions of the Member States Concerning Consumer Credit* COM (97) 465 final.

3 of Directive 2008/48/EC[32] indicates, these revealed substantial differences in regulation between states, with Member States using consumer protection mechanisms outside the scope of the 1987 Directive based on their national legal and economic circumstances. Following the modern trend in favour of maximum harmonisation, the differing mandatory national provisions were cited as a reason to favour full harmonisation. They were said to 'restrict consumers' ability to make direct use of the gradually increasing availability of cross-border credit'.[33] The reform process was, however, protracted. A proposal was published in 2002,[34] which after a couple of modified drafts[35] finally emerged as the 2008 Directive. This is less radical than the 2002 draft, for example, with respect to responsible lending, the removal of a ban on door-to-door selling, the exclusion of equity release schemes and surety agreements, the narrowing of the definition of total costs of credit and the application of a light information regime to certain loans, such as overdrafts.[36] It was still far more extensive than the first Consumer Credit Directive.

The Commission started a process of looking at ways of removing barriers to the internal market for mortgages in 2003 and published a Green Paper in 2005[37] and White Paper in 2007.[38] These culminated in Directive 2014/17/EU on credit agreements for consumers relating to residential immovable property (hereafter Mortgage Credit Directive).[39] This is a classic example of the EU intervening for consumer protection in an area that is undoubtedly of great importance to consumers (as for most consumers home purchase is their most important decision) and where there is a need for good practice (and plenty examples of bad practice). However, the internal market justifications are less compelling.

As the Mortgage Credit Directive was being developed, Europe suffered the global financial crisis which in part was based on poor mortgage lending practices particularly in the subprime market and the subsequent toxic securitisation of the resulting debt.[40] This highlighted the need for good responsible lending standards and sensitive handling of default cases. Absent effective specific

32 Directive 2008/48/EC on credit agreements for consumers (2008) OJ L133/66.

33 Directive 87/102/EEC, Recital 4.

34 Commission, *Proposal for a Directive of the European Parliament and of the Council on the Harmonisation of the Laws, Regulations and Administrative Provisions of the Member States Concerning Credit for Consumers* COM (2002) 443.

35 Commission, *Amended Proposal for a Directive of the European Parliament and of the Council on the Harmonisation of the Laws, Regulations and Administrative Provisions of the Member States Concerning Credit for Consumers Repealing Directive 87/102/EC and Modifying Directive 93/13/EC* COM (2004) 747; Commission, *Modified Proposal for a Directive of the European Parliament and of the Council on Credit Agreements for Consumers Amending Council Directive 93/13/EC* COM (2005) 483.

36 S Franken, 'The political economy of the EC Consumer Credit Directive' in J Niemi, IRamsay and WC Whitford, *Consumer Credit, Debt and Bankruptcy* (Hart, 2009).

37 COM (2005) 327 final.

38 COM (2007) 807 final.

39 Directive 2014/17/EU.

40 C. Peterson, 'The political economy of consumer credit securitization: Comparing predatory lending in home finance in the US, UK, Germany and Japan' in in J Niemi, I Ramsay and WC Whitford, *Consumer Credit, Debt and Bankruptcy* (Hart, 2009).

regulations, the Unfair Contract Terms Directive has been called upon to provide remedies in mortgage cases.[41] There have also been soft law regulator-driven initiatives at the European and international level to address these concerns. At the international level the Financial Stability Board on 18 April 2012 passed its *Principles for Sound Residential Mortgage Underwriting Practices* and on 13 June 2013 the European Banking Authority adopted an Opinion on *Good Practices for Responsible Mortgage Lending* and *Good Practices for the Treatment of Borrowers in Mortgage Payment Difficulties.* These were taken into account when developing the Mortgage Credit Directive.[42]

Philosophy underpinning the Directives

The Directives formally seek to promote the internal market in consumer and mortgage credit.[43] The default rule underpinning the Directives' philosophy is freedom of contract. There are, for example, no bans on practices such as the sale of credit on the doorstep that existed in some Member States. Only limited controls exist on the substance of agreements and default procedures are only controlled in the mortgage context, and even then only in a limited manner.

Disclosure rules lie at the heart of the Directives – in advertising and at the pre-contractual and contractual stages. They seek to ensure that consumers can chose in an informed way from as wide a range of products as possible, whilst ensuring that lending is undertaken responsibly. However, even with access to so much mandatory information, it can be difficult for consumers to determine which offer best suits their needs or indeed whether taking out credit at all is in their best interest. Credit offers can involve a highly complex range of terms affecting the price and involves risks that many consumers find difficult to understand and compare. Consumers will frequently be over-optimistic about their use of credit and, for instance, discount penalties they hope not to pay and concentrate on low headline rates.[44] There are few requirements to use warnings to alert consumers to risks. A permissive approach to marketing gives businesses leeway to promote their products and the multiplication of offers makes the task of making an informed choice even more challenging.[45] The limited controls can be seen as

41 See Case C-415/11 *Mohamed Aziz v Caixa d'Estalvis de Catalunya, Tarragona i Manresa (Catalunyacaixa)* ECLI:EU:C:2013:164.

42 See the Mortgage Credit Directive, Recital 3.

43 Consumer Credit Directive, Recital 6; Mortgage Credit Directive, Recital 2.

44 O Bar-Gill, *Seduction by Contract: Law, Economics, and Psychology in Consumer Markets* (OUP, 2012), p.10.

45 These are some of the lessons from behavioural economics: see the special issue of Journal of Consumer Policy, 'Behavioural economics, consumer policy and consumer law'. *J Consum Policy* 34 (2001), pp.271–398; A Duggan and I Ramsay, 'Front end approaches to access to justice: The example of consumer credit' in M Trebilcock, A Duggan and L Sossin (eds), *Improving Access to Justice for the Middle Class* (University of Toronto Press, 2012); M Muynck, 'Credit cards, overdraft facilities and European consumer protection: A blank cheque for unfairness?' (2010) *European Review of Private Law* p.1187.

encouraging consumption of credit with the risk that it increases collective 'bads' such as over-indebtedness.

To balance this, some national regulators are adopting a 'treat your customer fairly' principle. There are a few provisions in that direction in the Directives, such as the duty to provide adequate explanations and to check creditworthiness – but these do not go so far as to require the creditor to have the debtor's interest to the fore. Only in the mortgage context, where advisory services are provided, do creditors, credit intermediaries or appointed representatives have to act in the best interest of their consumer.[46]

The Directives focus on regulating the transacting process with limited regulation of the substance of the agreement, no regulation of default procedures (save to a limited extent in the mortgage context) and few post-contractual obligations. Certain aspects of the agreement are regulated such as the right to early repayment and, in the consumer credit context, joint and several liability for goods supplied under linked agreements. For mortgages there are some controls on types of agreements that are high risk, such as foreign-currency loans or loans at variable rates, but these involve setting out ways of providing such contracts rather than proscribing them. Member States can give additional guidance or set limits on, for example, loan-to-value or loan-to-income ratios.[47] The Directives themselves have few controls on the substance of the agreement. There is no substantive control through usury laws or product regulation. Modern thinking based on behavioural economics whereby consumers would default to a 'vanilla product' unless they explicitly opt into more complex products was not part of the discussions.[48]

Scope

Consumer Credit Directive

The definition of 'credit agreement' in the Consumer Credit Directive is intended to be broad and functional so as to future-proof against product innovation[49] and covers a 'deferred payment, loan or similar financial accommodation'.[50] The recitals explain that the scope of harmonisation is determined by the Directive's definitions.[51] Significantly, the definition of consumer is limited by the traditional formula to a 'natural person who, in transactions covered by this Directive, is acting for purposes which are outside his trade, business or profession.'[52] Thus,

46 See below.
47 Recital 55 to the Mortgage Credit Directive.
48 A Duggan and I Ramsay, 'Front end approaches to access to justice: The example of consumer credit' in M Trebilcock, A Duggan and L Sossin (eds), *Improving Access to Justice for the Middle Class* (University of Toronto Press, 2012).
49 Consumer Credit Directive, Recital 7.
50 Ibid., Art. 3(c). There is an exception where goods or services of the same kind are always paid by instalment e.g. a newspaper account or gym membership.
51 Consumer Credit Directive, Recital 10.
52 Ibid., Art. 3(a).

regulation of all loans to businesses are left to national law. Surety agreements are also not covered, although they were included in the initial proposal.[53]

Art. 2 lists 12 exclusions from the scope of the Directive. These are quite broad, for instance agreements for less than 200 or more than 75,000 euro; mortgages; hire or leases; pledges; various categories of free or low-interest loans; and, credit agreements that are part of settlements reached in court or before statutory bodies. Member States can of course, as a matter of national law, extend the Directive's rules to transactions not within its scope.[54]

Mortgage Credit Directive

The Mortgage Credit Directive applies to credit agreements (a) secured by a mortgage or by another comparable security commonly used in a Member State on residential immovable property or secured by a right related to residential immovable property; and (b) credit agreements the purpose of which is to acquire or retain property rights in land or in an existing or projected building.[55] The latter type of lending where no security is provided is quite rare.[56] Most home purchase loans operate by way of mortgage, but in some countries, such as France and Belgium, home loans use personal guarantees.[57]

The definition is rather broad. The underlying policy issue is whether such lending should be under the general consumer credit laws or a specific mortgage regime. The Directive, for instance, requires that second-charge mortgages be treated in the same manner as first-charge mortgages. There is explicit recognition that the regime adopted has followed that of the Consumer Credit Directive in order to ensure a consistent framework.[58]

Certain types of lending are excluded from the Directive.[59] From a policy perspective, the most important exemption is for equity release schemes that are often

53 Commission, *Proposal for a Directive of the European Parliament and of the Council on the Harmonisation of the Laws, Regulations and Administrative Provisions of the Member States Concerning Credit for Consumers* COM [2002] 443 final. In C-208/98 *Berliner Kindl Brauerei AG v Andreas Siepert* (2000) ECR I-1741 it had been excluded from being classed as a credit agreement and in C-45/96 *Bayerische Hypotheken- und Wechselbank AG v Edgar Dietzinger* [1998] ECR I-1199 guarantees were not covered by the Doorstep-selling Directive unless linked to a credit contract that was within scope. Rott argues that there is an internal market justification for regulating in guarantees because bank consumers do not have property and so the third-party guarantee has become a common surety and it is sensible to introduce common rules for what are in effect integral parts of many credit transactions: P Rott, 'Consumer guarantees in the future Consumer Credit Directive; Mandatory ban on consumer protection' (2005) 13 *European Review of Private Law* p.383.

54 K Sein, 'Transposition of the new Consumer Credit Directive in Estonia' (2012) 20 *European Review of Private Law* p.435.

55 Mortgage Credit Directive, Art. 3(1).

56 Mortgage Credit Directive, Recital 18.

57 London Economics (n 26) 1, 12–13.

58 Consumer Credit Directive, Recital 20.

59 Ibid., Art. 3(2).

known as 'lifetime mortgages'. These are products where in return for a lump sum or periodic payment the creditor is repaid from a future sale of the property on the happening of a specific event e.g. death.[60] Similarly, home reversion schemes, where all or part of the property is sold to a reversion company in exchange for a lump sum or periodic payments, are excluded. These do not need many of the normal consumer credit protection measures; for instance, affordability is not an issue since there are no repayments and loss of a home on default is not at stake. However, such schemes do raise significant distinct consumer protection concerns, especially as they are often targeted at elderly potentially vulnerable consumers. Consumers need to consider if these complex products are the best option for them and their family and there is a risk they are placed in jeopardy should they breach any of the contractual rules. Protection in these instances has to be afforded at the national level. However, if any such schemes require the regular repayment of capital they will not be exempt from the Mortgage Credit Directive.

Other exemptions cover employer loans that are interest free or at lower than the prevailing APRC; interest-free loans; overdrafts repayable within one month; settlements from court or statutory bodies; and, free-of-charge deferments of existing debts.

Member States are given a discretion to exclude certain loans.[61] Bridging loans can be excluded. The same applies to loans by credit unions and loans under a statutory provision for a general-interest purpose at free or lower than the prevailing interest rate, so long as there are alternative arrangements concerning advertising and pre-contractual information. Where mortgage security is used, but not to acquire interests in the residential property, the rules on advertising and pre-contractual information can be replaced by the rules in the Consumer Credit Directive.

So-called buy-to-let mortgages can also be excluded. The rationale for this exclusion is that the debtor's home is not at risk on default (at least not by virtue of sale of the property) and they are often purchased for profit motives. Indeed many would have been excluded in any event as they are purchases for renting at a profit, and consumer is defined in the same way as under the Consumer Credit Directive in a manner which would exclude such small business operators. Only in situations where home-owners find themselves in circumstances requiring them to let out property, for instance if they could not sell their house or it was inherited would they be consumers within the scope of the Directive.

No avoidance of rules

As with most consumer protection rules, the rights granted to consumers by both Directives cannot waived by them.[62] The consumer credit rules cannot be

60 See U Reifner, S Clerc-Renaud, Elena Pérez-Carrillo, A Tiffe and M Knobloch, *Study on Equity Release Schemes in the EU* (Institüt für Finanzdienstleistungen e.V., 2009).

61 Mortgage Credit Directive, Art. 3(3).

62 Consumer Credit Directive, Art. 22(2); Mortgage Credit Directive, Art. 41(a).

avoided by choice of third-country law if the credit agreement has a close link to one or more Member States.[63] The drafters of the Directives were also astute to the craftiness of contract drafters and so provided that the consumer rights could also not excluded even if the agreement was integrated into one which because of its character or purpose would be outside the scope.[64]

Running and regulating credit businesses

Consumer credit

In many European states the Central Bank plays an important role in regulating creditors; whereas in others a public consumer protection authority has this role, such as the UK's Financial Conduct Authority (FCA). These authorities can have a significant impact on the actual conduct of business through the standards they set down. For instance, the license requirements in the United Kingdom permit practices to be condemned even though strictly legal and codes of conduct developed by such authorities can set high standards. The Consumer Credit Directive is not prescriptive as to the form, but simply requires supervision or regulation of creditors by a body or authority independent of financial institutions.[65] Unlike the first proposal, it contains no obligation to require registration and the duties of the regulatory body are not spelt out. The European Banking Authority also has responsibilities for promoting transparency, simplicity and fairness in the market for consumer financial products or services.[66]

There is a separate obligation to ensure there are adequate and effective out-of-court dispute resolution procedures.[67] There is also the typical rule about Member States needing to ensure compliance by having penalties which are 'effective, proportionate and dissuasive'.[68]

Mortgages

There can be several parties involved in supplying mortgages. Mortgage products are often sold through complex trading structures. Creditors will frequently use intermediaries or appointed representatives to supply them with customers.[69] Credit intermediaries are allowed by the Mortgage Credit Directive and made subject to regulatory requirements.[70] Member States can decide to allow them

63 Ibid., art 22(4); There is no similar provision in Mortgage Credit Directive.
64 Ibid., art 22(3); Mortgage Credit Directive, Art. 41(a).
65 Ibid.
66 Regulation 1093/2010/EU establishing a European Supervisory Authority (European Banking Authority) (2010) OJ L331/12, Art. 9.
67 Consumer Credit Directive, Art. 24.
68 Ibid., Art. 23.
69 Creditors are responsible for actions of their credit intermediaries and any appointed representative of themselves or a tied intermediary; credit intermediaries are responsible for the actions of their appointed representative: Mortgage Credit Directive, Arts. 29, 31.
70 See Mortgage Credit Directive, Arts. 30, 33, 34.

to have appointed representatives.[71] There is a passport provision to allow them, subject to certain constraints, to operate throughout the Union.[72]

The scope for advice may vary depending upon the relationship of the intermediary and creditors. A broker may be able to select the best market offering for the consumer; whereas some intermediaries may be tied to certain creditors or have incentives to provide products from certain business. Face-to-face sales will offer different opportunities for advice than sales through websites. Business have to state whether advisory services are being provided and whether the selection will be from their range of products or from across the market.[73] Where advisory services are offered, advisors need to act in the best interest of the consumer and obtain sufficient information, consider a sufficiently large number of products and recommend suitable credit agreements.[74] As the term 'advisor' might lead consumers to assume they will be offered impartial advice in their best interests, Member States retain the freedom to prohibit such terms.[75]

The Mortgage Credit Directive is more demanding in its controls of the mortgage industry than the Consumer Credit Directive. It specifically requires Member States to have a competent authority with sufficient investigative and enforcement powers and adequate resources.[76] They must also promote consumer financial education.[77] The competent authorities are under an obligation to co-operate with one another.[78]

Member States must ensure creditors, intermediaries or appointed representatives have appropriate levels of knowledge and competence.[79] Host states[80] must establish minimum requirements based on Annex III principles concerning the products, law, purchasing process, security valuation, land registers, market, business ethics, assessment of creditworthiness, financial and economic competence. States can rely on professional qualifications and experience and may have different requirements for levels and types of actor. Thus, it is recognised that a salesperson needs different requirements to the person who designs the products.

All these actors are subject to a requirement to act honestly, fairly, transparently and professionally and are required to take account of the rights and interests

71 Ibid., Art. 31.
72 Ibid., Art. 32.
73 Ibid., Arts. 22(1), (2).
74 Mortgage Credit Directive, Art. 22(3).
75 Ibid., Recital 63.
76 Ibid., Art. 5.
77 Ibid., Art. 6.
78 Ibid., Arts. 36–37.
79 Ibid., Art. 9(1).
80 Where creditors act in more than one state these standards are fixed by the home state, with the host state retaining the right to establish its own minimum standards in specific areas i.e. law, purchasing process, land register and local market: Ibid., Art. 9(3)(ii).
81 Ibid., Art. 7(1). Taking account of consumer interests is different from having to take their interests into account, which is only required when advisory services are offered: see Ibid., Article 22(3).

of the consumers.[81] In the past, criticism has centred around the way staff or intermediaries or appointed representatives are remunerated. The pressure to meet targets and commission scheme incentives was blamed for over-selling and the promotion of inappropriate products.[82] Principles are set out which seek to avoid conflicts of interest and to support sensible risk management.[83] Any information provided under Directive obligations must be supplied free of charge.[84]

As with the Consumer Credit Directive, Member States must provide sanctions that are 'effective, proportionate and dissuasive'[85] and ensure there are appropriate and effective complaints and redress mechanisms for out of court settlements of disputes.[86]

Harmonisation

Introduction

Competition in the European consumer credit markets is more likely to be increased by creditors establishing a presence in more Member States than by foreign firms selling credit products across borders. Nevertheless, the Consumer Credit Directive's recital emphasises the need for consumer to enjoy a 'high and equivalent level of protection … to create a genuine internal market'.[87] Maximum harmonisation is the order of the day in the field of consumer credit, but there are some significant exceptions to this.[88]

82 International Financial Consumer Protection Organisation (FinCoNet), *Report on Sales Incentives and Responsible Lending* (FinCoNet, 2016), http://www.finconet.org/Report_Sales_Incentives%20_Responsible_Lending.pdf [accessed on 2 March 2016]; BEUC, *Financial Supervision in the EU – a Consumer Perspective* (BEUC, 2011), http://www.beuc.eu/publications/2011-00396-01-e.pdf [accessed 2 March 2016]; BEUC, *Protecting Consumer Interests in the Retail Financial Services Area: Need for Independent and Efficient National Supervisors Everywhere in the EU* (BEUC, 2011), http://www.beuc.eu/publications/2011-09879-01-e.pdf [accessed 2 March 2016]; Consumers International, *Responsible Lending: An International Landscape* (Consumers International, 2013), http://www.consumersinternational.org/media/1412472/ciresponsiblelending_finalreport_06-11-13.pdf [accessed 2 March 2016]; Consumers International, *Risky Business: The Case for Reform of Sales Incentives Schemes in Banks* (Consumers International, 2014), http://www.consumersinternational.org/media/1529404/sales-incentivereport_riskybusiness_final2_151014.pdf [accessed 2 March 2016]; Which?, *Here to Help? Bank Staff Reveal the Truth about Working for Britain's Big Banks* (Which?, 2012), http://www.which.co.uk/documents/pdf/our-research-on-banking-staff-pdf- 305345.pdf [accessed 2 March 2016]; Which?, 'Is Your Bank Mis-selling?' *Which? Magazine* (September 2015), pp.52–54.

83 Mortgage Credit Directive, Arts. 7(2)–(4).

84 Ibid., Art. 8.

85 Ibid., Art.38

86 Ibid., Art. 39.

87 Ibid., Recital 9.

88 A useful discussion in line with our approach is given by O Cherednychenko, 'Full harmonisation of retail financial service contract law: A success or a failure?' in S Grundmann and Y Atamer (eds), *Financial Services, Financial Crisis and General European Contract Law* (Kluwer Law International, 2011).

Full harmonisation is limited by the scope of the Directive. Member States remain free to extend the provisions of the Directive to operations not covered by the Directive or indeed to maintain or introduce more protective measures outside its scope. Issues not covered by the Directive can continue to be regulated by national law, subject to the general Community law e.g. on the free movement of goods and services.[89] Within the scope of the Directives, Member States are in some areas expressly given the freedom to decide whether to apply selected provisions. Furthermore, there are several cases where Member States are expressly allowed to maintain or introduce more protective rules or are granted a discretion. There is also a risk of fragmentation resulting from the use of general terms that are interpreted according to national traditions and contexts. The Commission has even noted open wording was used to enable Member States to adjust the directive to their legal culture and market situation.[90] The more limited the scope and the greater the number of exceptions, the less difference there is between minimum and maximum harmonisation.[91] The presence of so many factors means that businesses will need to have local advice and so maximum harmonisation in this form cannot remove all barriers to trade. Our argument is that convergence is useful as it makes trading environments familiar, but there should not be a pretence that the rules can be treated as identical and applied without reference to local conditions. Moreover, some flexibility may be desirable to meet local conditions and to allow for regulatory experimentation.

Factors limiting maximum harmonisation under the Consumer Credit Directive

Measures outside the Directive's scope

The scope of the Consumer Credit Directive has already been analysed.[92] Any credit supplied outside the scope remains subject to national law. Equally any legal rules not covered remain subject to national law. Thus national usury or fairness controls or rules on procedures on default would continue to apply. In the United Kingdom for instance, the rules on default notices, time orders allowing debt to be rescheduled, protection for goods from being repossessed under hire-purchase agreements where a third of total price has been paid, the extensive recently introduced post-contractual information duties and rules governing unfair relationships will be unaffected. Similarly, Member States' usury laws remain in place. The Directive also has some specific rules on what is inside and outside its scope.

89 C-602/10 *SC Volksbank România SA v Autoritatea Naional pentru Protecia Consumatorilor - Comisariatul Judeean pentru Protecia Consumatorilor Clrai* [2012] 3 CMLR 45.

90 COM (2014) 259 final (n 14), 8.

91 B Gsell and HM Schellhase, 'Vollharmonisiertes Verbraucherkreditrecht – Ein Vorbild für die weitere europäische Angleichung des Verbrauchervertragsrechts?' [2009] *Juristenzeitung* p.20.

92 See above, pp.220–221.

Recital 18 states: 'Member States should remain free to regulate information requirements in their national law regarding advertising which does not contain information on the cost of the credit.' The UK has retained certain rules on the basis that since they do not relate to the cost of credit they are outside the scope of the Directive.[93] This applies to the rule requiring in many instances disclosure of a postal address.[94] The UK also continues to place controls on how certain restricted statements can be used e.g. 'overdraft', 'interest free', 'no deposit', 'loan guaranteed' or 'pre-approved', or 'gift', 'present' or any similar expressions.[95] The UK has interpreted the Directive as giving the right to regulate aspects other than the cost and denies it simply provides the power to extend Art. 4 regulation (that sets out the standard information in advertisements) to advertisements that do not give the interest rate or any figures relating to costs.[96] On a literal reading, this interpretation seems strained, but the recital is ambiguous. It does not make a clear distinction between *which* advertisements can be regulated and *what aspects* of the advertisements should be regulated.

Recital 9 specifically mentions the limited scope of measures covered as a reason why Member States are able to maintain or introduce national provisions on matters of joint and several liability of creditor and seller or service provider;[97] rules regulating the cancellation of goods or services contracts if the consumer exercises his right to withdraw from a credit contract and return of goods;[98] and, minimum periods before reimbursement can be required after being demanded under open-ended credit agreements.[99] In some cases there is a specific reference back to national law to flesh out the provisions. One example is as regards the proof needed for notification of withdrawal from a contract.[100]

Partial exemption

Member States may decide not to apply some of the Directive's provisions to certain agreements. For instance, agreements entered into by various social lenders such as credit unions or where the agreement is rescheduled because a consumer is in default.[101] Concerning overdrafts, there are options as regards the inclusion of the APR in the standard information to be included in advertising,

93 Department for Business Enterprise and Regulatory Reform, *Consultation on Proposals for Implementing the Consumer Credit Directive* (Department for Business Enterprise and Regulatory Reform, 2009), para 2.8; http://www.berr.gov.uk/files/file50962.pdf [accessed 22 March 2016].

94 Consumer Credit (Advertising) Regulations 2010, S.I. 2010/1970, Reg 4(1)(b). and 10.

95 Ibid., Reg 9.

96 Department for Business Enterprise and Regulatory Reform, *Consultation on Proposals for Implementing the Consumer Credit Directive* (Department for Business Enterprise and Regulatory Reform, 2009), para 2.36; http://www.berr.gov.uk/files/file50962.pdf [accessed 22 March 2016].

97 Consumer Credit Directive, Art. 15(3).

98 Ibid., Recital 35.

99 Ibid., Recital 9.

100 Ibid., Art. 14(3)(a).

101 Ibid., Arts. 2(5), (6).

pre-contractual information and contract agreements.[102] Member States may provide that the right of withdrawal can be disapplied to contracts concluded by notary.[103] The rules on early repayment can be made subject to a national threshold of not more than 10,000 euro in any 12 month period [104] and the amount of compensation increased if creditors can prove losses were higher than set by the formula.[105]

Minimum harmonisation provisions

Express licence is given to Member States with respect to specific rules to maintain or introduce national provisions. In some cases, this is contingent upon there having been pre-existing national rules.[106] Examples include

- national rules requiring APRC to be shown in advertising which does not indicate an interest rate or figures relating to any cost of credit to the consumer can be maintained without triggering the standard disclosure requirements;[107]
- national rules regarding the validity of the conclusion of credit agreements;[108]
- rules modifying withdrawal periods in those states that already had a rule that funds could not be made available until a specified period had expired;[109]
- rules on creditor's compensation under the right of early repayment.[110]

Besides these, there are also certain other rules that give Members States a discretion to depart from the Directive. Thus, whilst Art. 3(n)(i) limits 'linked credit agreements' to credit exclusively financing the supply of specific goods, Recital 10 allows the Directive's provisions to be applied to credit where the financing of such purchases is only the partial reason for the credit. Also Member States can maintain or introduce prohibitions on creditors requiring a debtor in connection with the credit agreement to open a bank account or take out another ancillary service or to pay the costs associated therewith.[111] Any national requirement

102 Ibid., Arts. 4(2)(c), 6(2), 10(5)(f). The favoured status of creditors providing overdrafts is criticised in M Muynck, 'Credit cards, overdraft facilities and European Consumer Protection: A blank cheque for unfairness?' (2010) *European Review of Private Law* p.1187 as they are a seductive way for creditors to accumulate debt and in his opinion overdrafts are increasingly 'disguised' instalment credit.

103 Consumer Credit Directive, Art. 14(6).

104 Ibid., Art. 16(4)(a).

105 Ibid., Art. 16(4)(b).

106 Ibid., Arts. 8(1) and 14(2).

107 Ibid., Art. 4(1).

108 Ibid., Art. 10(1).

109 Ibid., Art. 14(2).

110 Ibid., Art. 16(4).

111 Ibid., Recital 22. Where such combined offers are possible the consumers should be informed of their compulsory nature and where possible the costs included in the total cost of the credit.

to consult databases when assessing creditworthiness can be maintained.[112] The Directive is also without prejudice to national laws providing for joint and several liability between seller/supplier and creditor.[113] National law can also establish a period within the withdrawal period during which the performance of the contract cannot begin.[114]

Member States must make use of the Standard European Consumer Credit Information (SECCI) form in Annex II to comply with the pre-contractual information requirements in Art. 5.[115] However, for overdrafts and certain other specific credits suppliers have the freedom to choose whether to make use of the European Consumer Credit Information (ECCI) form in Annex III. Ten states have made the ECCI mandatory for these agreements, although there does not seem to be any specific legal base permitting this in the Directive.[116] The rules seem to leave it to the supplier to decide whether to use the ECCI for overdrafts.

Member States' discretion

Members States have a discretion as to how to implement certain provisions. Thus Member States can determine the extent and the conditions under which remedies should be available against creditors where the seller or supplier has not properly redressed any non-conformity.[117] The potentially binding character of pre-contractual information and the period during which the creditor is to be bound to it is also left to the Member States.[118]

Open-textured wording

The Directive also uses open-textured wording to allow discretion. Examples of this are:

- the concept of 'insignificant charges' with regard to credit agreements under which credit has to be repaid within three months;[119]
- 'in good time' with regard to the provision of pre-contractual information;[120]
- 'adequate explanations' that the creditor and credit intermediaries are under a duty to provide;[121]

112 Ibid., Art. 8(1).
113 Ibid., Recital 38.
114 Ibid., Art. 14(7).
115 See pp.273–276.
116 COM (2014) 259 final (n 14) 9.
117 Consumer Credit Directive, Art. 15(2).
118 Ibid., Recital 25.
119 Ibid., Art. 2(f).
120 Ibid., Arts. 5(1) and 6(1).
121 Ibid., Art. 5(6).

- 'sufficient information' with regard to the obligation to assess the creditworthiness of the consumer;[122]
- 'sufficient increase' in total amount of credit with regard to the obligation to re-assess the creditworthiness of the consumer;[123]
- 'significant overrunning' of a current account;[124]
- 'fair and objectively justified compensation' for early repayment.[125]

These terms range from quite technical matters, such as what amounts to 'insignificant charges' through to concepts that really determine the level of protection, such what is understood by 'adequate explanations' or 'sufficient information' to assess creditworthiness. Cherednychenko claims these implicit discretions pose a serious risk to full harmonisation.[126] Where rules are not tightly drawn and instead merely set down a general approach using open-textured terms, there is a risk differences emerge by stealth. Cherednychenko also suggests that the impact of the rules might vary depending upon whether they are implemented into financial supervision legislation or into the Civil Code.[127]

Conclusions on consumer credit harmonisation

Many creditors will have a mixed portfolio of products, some of which fall exclusively within the scope of the Directive and others outside. To the extent that the objective is to give creditors the confidence to sell across borders, the existence of dual regimes is likely to be problematic. It will be for national authorities to decide the extent to which products outside the Directive are brought under the same rules.

Within the scope of the Directive, there are significant areas where Member States have lost the freedom to provide any greater protection that that provided by the Directive: these concern aspects such as information duties, calculation of the APRC, right of withdrawal and conditions for early repayment (subject to allowed variances). However, there are many exemptions, references back to national law, discretions and use of broad discretionary concepts. It will be hard for any creditor to have faith that they can act in another Member States much more easily after the Directive without risk of falling foul of some national rule or national interpretation of an EU-inspired rule. Indeed even beyond the examples of potentially different national approaches listed above, it seems clear that the implementation of many of the rules will require detailed national regulations

122 Ibid., Art. 8(1).
123 Ibid., Art. 8(2).
124 Ibid., Art. 18(2).
125 Ibid., Art. 16(2).
126 O Cherednychenko, 'Full harmonisation of retail financial service contract law: A success or a failure?' in S Grundmann and Y Atamer (eds), *Financial Services, Financial Crisis and General European Contract Law* (Kluwer Law, International 2011), p.240.
127 Ibid., p.242. Whilst common law countries do not have civil codes the distinction between general law and specialist financial services law is known.

that will afford plenty of scope for different interpretations to emerge. There are likely to be differences emerging from legislative styles. The United Kingdom, for instance, will continue to use a very detailed form of implementing regulations covering more aspects than might be the case in other Member States.

A Commission report found that it was hard to assess the impact on the internal market of the choices made by the Member States where they had made regulatory choices to diverge from the Directive. One suspects this is because the differences were marginal and indeed cross-border credit is itself a marginal activity. This underlines that this is one area where maximum harmonisation is perhaps not appropriate or at least not a high priority. Moreover, it removes a lot of the scope for Member States to react to local issues or test out solutions that best suit local needs. Warnings are a prime example. Their messages are best geared to local conditions. However, use of warnings may be restricted unless they can be said to lie outside the scope of the Directive.

Minimum harmonisation (mainly) of mortgages

The Mortgage Credit Directive is more circumspect than the Consumer Credit Directive as regards interference with national rules. The basic rule is minimum harmonization.[128] Maximum harmonisation is limited to pre-contractual information duties and the use of European Standardised Information Sheet (ESIS, the equivalent of the SECCI) and the calculation of the APRC.[129] This limited approach to maximum harmonisation is justified due to the different national markets, products and procedures for granting mortgage credit.[130]

Information is the main consumer protection paradigm

Introduction

Information is a key element of the consumer protection strategy in the Consumer Credit and Mortgage Credit Directives.[131] There was a deliberate policy to apply similar approaches to both consumer credit and mortgage credit in order to promote a consistent consumer protection framework.[132] The duties are found in the advertising, pre-contractual, contract and to a limited extent post-contractual stages.

The provision of information in advertising and during the pre-contractual stage allows the consumer to make a more informed choice. The limited power of information to turn the consumer into a rational *homo economicus* are well known

128 Mortgage Credit Directive, Art. 2(1).

129 Ibid., Art. 2(2).

130 Ibid., Recital 7.

131 An emphasis on information rights had already been present in the first Directive: see S Grundmann 'European contract law(s) – of what colour?' (2005) 1 *European Review of Contract Law* pp.198–201.

132 Mortgage Credit Directive, Recital 20.

from the behavioural economic literature[133] and apply with particular force in this area.[134] At one level the very decision to take out credit is affected by the human preference for (and hence over-valuation of) immediate gratification and the downplaying of the long-term costs of repayment.[135] Moreover, credit is a complex product that few consumers understand well. Their judgement may be affected by matters such as ease of dealing with a particular creditor or the repayment schedule, rather than being based on the real cost of borrowing.[136] They may be over-optimistic about their ability to repay and so either face default charges they had not expected or have to take out roll-over loans. They might have anticipated being able to repay earlier and then fail to do so and thus pay more interest than anticipated.

These factors are hard to correct through disclosure alone. Nevertheless, there may still be some value to such disclosures. They at least afford consumers the opportunity to make comparisons if they want to. Also the disclosures can be checked by authorities and consumer groups for compliance with legal rules. The contractual document rules provide the consumer with a record of what has been agreed. The post-contractual rules can help the consumer keep track of their affairs.

Describing the costs of credit

Although complaint data about consumer credit across the EU is limited, it seems one of the main concerns is transparency of interest rate rises, fees and other charges.[137] Unsurprisingly price figures prominently in the information obligations. The Consumer Credit Directive refers to three key terms: the borrowing rate, total cost of credit and the annual percentage rate of charge ('APRC').[138] The Mortgage Credit Directive cross-references to the borrowing rate and total cost of credit and has its own annex calculating the APRC.[139]

133 Cf. Chapter 1.

134 See C Garcia and W Van Boom, *Information disclosure in the EU Consumer Credit Directive: Opportunities and limitations* (Rotterdam institute of Private Law Working Paper, 8 December 2009), http://ssrn.com/abstract=1538111 [accessed on 12 March 2016]; O Bar-Gill, *Seduction by Contract: Law, Economics, and Psychology in Consumer Markets* (OUP, 2012), p.10.

135 This is known as hyperbolic discounting and involves valuing proximate utilities more than distant ones: see Durkin et al., (n. 14) pp.152–155.

136 I Crow, G Howells and M Moroney, 'Credit and debt: Choices for poorer consumers' in G Howells, I Crow and M Moroney (eds), *Aspects of Credit and Debt* (Sweet & Maxwell, 1993), pp.11–51.

137 GHK, *Final Report – Establishment of a Benchmark on the Economic Impact of the Consumer Credit Directive on the Functioning of the Internal Market in this Sector and on the Level of Consumer Protection* (GHK 2009), vi.

138 There is a tension between giving the consumer information on as many dimensions of the credit offer as possible without confusing him with too many terms: the first proposal had unhelpfully also included the 'total lending rate' meaning the sums levied by the creditor expressed as an annual percentage of the total amount of credit.

139 Mortgage Credit Directive, Arts. 4(13), (15), (16) and Annex I.

The Consumer Credit Directive definitions will be used. The borrowing rate refers to the 'rate of interest expressed as a fixed or variable percentage applied on an annual basis to the amount of credit drawn down.'[140] However, this may not reflect the true cost of interest if other charges are added on and it may depend upon the intervals at which the money is repaid. This is why it is important to also have the APRC which is the 'total cost of credit' (TCC) expressed as an annual percentage rate.[141] The 'total cost of credit' is defined as 'all the costs including interest, commissions, taxes and any other kind of fees which the consumer is required to pay in connection with the credit agreement and which are known to the creditor except for notarial costs; costs in respect of ancillary services relating to the credit agreement, in particular insurance premiums, are also included if, in addition, the conclusion of a service contract is compulsory in order to obtain it on the terms and conditions marketed.'[142]

This is a fairly inclusive definition, which makes it less susceptible to manipulation than the US equivalent.[143] However, firms may prefer to raise revenue through default charges than interest, because charges for non-compliance are not included in the TCC. Given the tendency of consumers to be over-optimistic about repayment, creditors can rely on recovering some additional money by means of such default charges. The function of price disclosure is to allow consumers to make comparisons and hence promote competition, though a secondary effect may be to alert consumers to the cost of borrowing which may cause them to show restraint.[144]

The 1987 Directive had left most decisions about the total charge for credit and method of calculating the APR to Member States. Obviously, it is important in a cross-border context to have this figure calculated in a consistent manner so valid comparisons can be made between prices. Thus, steps were taken to harmonise the calculations, even before the latest revision of the Directive. Directive 90/88/EEC[145] had sought greater harmonisation, but had allowed Member States a transition period to retain their existing formula. A common formula was introduced by Directive 98/7/EC[146], but this still did not tackle the problem of a substantial amount of the costs facing consumers (estimated to be around 30%) not being figured into the APR.[147] Insurance premiums were

140 Ibid., Art. 3(j).

141 Ibid., Arts. 3(i), 19 and Annex I as amended.

142 Ibid., Art. 3(1)(g).

143 Bar-Gill, *Seduction by Contract* (n. 43).

144 A Duggan and I Ramsay, 'Front end approaches to access to justice: The example of consumer credit' in M Trebilcock, A Duggan and L Sossin (eds), *Improving Access to Justice for the Middle Class* (University of Toronto Press, 2012), p.114.

145 Directive 90/88/EEC (1990) OJ L61/14.

146 Directive 98/7/EC (1998) OJ L101/17.

147 U Reifner and others, *Harmonisation of Cost Elements of the Annual Percentage Rate of Charge* (DG SANCO contract No. AO-2600/97/000169, Hamburg, 17 March 1998), http://iff-finanzierungsratgeber.de/index.php?id=1129 [accessed 12 March 2016].

the most problematic. The definition in the 2008 Directive is more inclusive and the position is now much improved.[148] It includes all costs which the consumer is obliged to pay. Though issues surrounding, for example, payment protection insurance demonstrate there may in practice continue to be lack of clarity by consumers as to the voluntary nature of any insurance or other charges.

The complex nature of the APRC is illustrated by the fact a further amendment had to be made subsequent to the 2008 Directive.[149] It is not uncommon for it to be alleged that the APRC has been incorrectly calculated. The CJEU has confirmed this can amount to an unfair commercial practice, but this will only be one factor to be taken into account in assessing whether it is an unfair term.[150]

Advertising

Consumer credit

Article 4 of the Consumer Credit Directive sets out the information obligations in relation to advertising. Unlike the Mortgage Credit Directive it does not contain its own general rule that advertising and marketing should be fair, clear and not misleading, but rather is content to cross-reference to the Unfair Commercial Practices Directive.[151] Its provisions focus on the standard information that in certain situations needs to be provided.

These information requirements are more extensive than under the 1986 Directive, which had merely required the APR be disclosed. More information about the credit has to be given along with details of any compulsory ancillary service, such as insurance. However, these obligations only arise where there is an indication of an interest rate or other figure relating to the costs of credit.[152] It is common practice for many payday lenders to avoid mentioning price and focus on the friendliness and flexibility of the service. There are, for instance, no controls on the use of cartoons, comedy, upbeat feelings or trivialisation of taking out loans in credit advertisements. These are common features of sub-prime advertising that merit control. Equally controls might be useful on advertising that focuses on speed and ease of application process. There are no particular rules requiring qualification criteria to be spelt out or that certain terms such

148 G Soto, *Study on the Calculation of the Annual Percentage Rate of Charge for Consumer Credit Agreements* (European Commission Directorate-General Health and Consumer Protection, 2009) http://ec.europa.eu/consumers/rights/docs/study_APR_en.pdf [accessed 12 March 2016].

149 Directive 2011/90/EU providing additional assumptions for the calculation of the annual percentage rate of charge (2011) OJ L296/35.

150 Case C-453/10 *Pereniová and Pereni v SOS financ spol. s r. o.* [2012] 1 CMLR 28.

151 See Directive 2005/29/EC, Recital 18. See Chapter 2.

152 Some Member States require the inclusion of the APRC in advertisements. Art. 4(1) para 2 makes it clear that the obligations in Art. 4 do not automatically arise just because such national rules require disclosure of APRC in advertising if there is no mention of an interest rate or any figures relating to the cost of the credit. This is understandable so as not to impose the full obligations as a consequence of a more limited national rule.

as 'pre-approved', 'interest free' or 'bad credit no problem' be prohibited.[153] Given the limited scope of the Directive on this topic, a lot of advertising regulation remains subject to the general EU rules on unfair commercial practices or national laws.

There are some national rules, often in Codes of Conduct, on these aspects. The extent to which they withstand review will depend on whether these comply with the requirements of the Unfair Commercial Practices Directive,[154] which is a maximum harmonisation standard.

The Directive does not require the advertised rates reflect the rate actually charged. In practice, screening of applicants may lead to different rates being offered. One condition is that the example given must be a representative example. Differences may emerge as Member States implement this rule in different ways. The United Kingdom Regulations[155] stipulates a 51% rule to determine the representative APR. i.e. the advertiser must expect 51% of concluded agreements to be at the advertised rate. This produces a class of representative agreements out of which the advertiser must determine, based on reasonable expectations, which of the agreements in that class is representative.[156]

Given the variety of advertising media, it may be challenging to comply with these rules in contexts as varied as text messages, phone calls, radio, TV and websites. Unlike the position for pre-contractual information, there are no special rules for voice-telephony and means of communication at a distance that do not enable compliance with general rules.[157] States may leave this to the suppliers to work out or set in place guidance, as has happened in the United Kingdom.[158] This is another area in which one can see national practices might diverge.

Mortgage credit

Advertising plays less of a role for mortgage credit than for general consumer credit. Nevertheless, there is a general principle that advertising and marketing should be fair, clear and not misleading and should not create false expectations regarding the cost or availability of credit.[159] There is also an obligation to provide standard information in similar circumstances as there is for consumer credit.

153 C Garcia and W Van Boom, *Information Disclosure in the EU Consumer Credit Directive: Opportunities and Limitations* (Rotterdam Institute of Private Law Working Paper, 8 December 2009), p.26.

154 See Chapter 2.

155 Consumer Credit (Advertisements) Regulations 2010 (CCAR 2010), Regs 1(3), 5. Previously it had a 66% requirement.

156 See, Department for Business Innovation and Skills (BIS), *Guidance on the Regulations Implementing the Consumer Credit Directive* (August 2010), 22; https://www.gov.uk/government/uploads/system/uploads/attachment_data/file/422707/bis-10-1053-consumer-credit-directive-guidance.pdf [accessed 12 March 2016].

157 Arts. 5(2)(3) and 6(4) Consumer Credit (Advertisements) Regulations 2010, S.I. 2010/1970.

158 BIS Guidance on the regulations implementing the Consumer Credit Directive (August 2010), p.26.

159 Mortgage Credit Directive, Art. 10.

Detailed advertising rules often place obligations of disclosure in relation to specific products, but for mortgages there is also an obligation to provide more general information about the full range of available products.[160] An obligation to provide this general information is imposed on creditors, tied intermediaries or their appointed representative. Member States can extend this obligation to non-tied credit intermediaries.[161] This information, in addition to detailed information on the creditor and product, must include a general warning about the consequences of non-compliance with the commitment linked to the credit agreement. Member States can also require other types of warning, though any such rules should be notified to the Commission without delay.[162]

Pre-contractual

Consumer credit

Pre-contractual information duties owed by creditors or, where applicable, credit intermediaries are set out in Art. 5 of the Consumer Credit Directive.[163] Their express rationale is to enable consumers to compare offers.[164] Therefore, it is sensibly required that the information must be provided in good time before the consumer is bound. However, it is difficult to see how this can be a strong requirement necessarily providing a period of reflection as often credit contracts for practical reasons are entered into quickly and it is hard to see how 'good time' can be given any more stringent meaning than simply prior to the contract becoming binding. Indeed some implementing laws merely refer to the information being given before the consumer is bound.[165] The burden of proving the information rules have been complied with is a matter for national law, but the CJEU has made it clear that the burden cannot be placed on the consumer nor can the burden effectively be reversed by including in a standard form contract a clause by which the consumer confirms they have been provided with the information.[166]

Up to 19 substantive pieces of information are required including those covering aspects of the cost of credit (with the APRC and total amount payable being illustrated by means of representative example), various warnings and information on consumer rights. An attempt has been made to ease compliance for creditors and to make the information available to consumers in an accessible and consistent manner by mandating (Art. 5) or encouraging (Art. 6) the use of Standard European Consumer Credit Information (SECCI) in the form provided in Annexes II and III.[167] The information must be provided on paper or on

160 Ibid., Recital 38.
161 Ibid., Art. 13.
162 Ibid., Art. 13(2).
163 Specific rules are set out for overdrafts and certain specific credit agreements in Art. 6.
164 Mortgage Credit Directive, Recital 19.
165 COM (2014) 259 final (n 14) 8.
166 C-449/13 *CA Consumer Finance SA v Ingrid Bakkaus and Others* ECLI:EU:C:2014:2464.
167 Consumer Credit Directive, Art. 5(1) says the information 'shall be provided by means of the SECCI'. Cf. Art. 6(2) where it provides that it may be provided by means of SECCI. A reduced set of information is required where voice telephony communication is used: Art. 5(2).

another durable medium. If the means of distance communication used does not make this practical then the SECCI form should be given immediately after the conclusion of the contract.

The SECCI provides a safe harbour against claims of non-compliance with the information duties, but has been criticised from both a trade and consumer perspective. Criticism of the SECCI is that it is too long and detailed to allow consumers easily to compare costs.[168] There have also been criticisms about the lack of clarity concerning the difference between the borrowing rate and APR, the information on the costs in case of late payment and the procedure for early repayment.[169] Also, the warnings about what might happen in 'worst-case scenarios' are still relatively weak; for instance, the risk factors for default like divorce or unemployment might have been flagged-up.[170] The argument of some creditors that the SECCI unduly increases creditor costs is not very persuasive as creditors can relatively easily accommodate information obligations. More concerning is the fear that the form's complexity will impact on consumers, who will find it hard to understand.[171]

Using information to improve consumer choices depends not only on the content of the information required, but also upon the form and timing of its provision.[172] Even with requirements that the information be provided in good time prior to the contract there is a risk that the consumer is psychologically committed to the deal before being provided with the information so that it has only a limited impact. The amount of information that has been included in the SECCI and the staid manner in which it has been presented leaves the measure open to criticism that the lessons of behavioural economics have not been taken on board. As a record of the agreement, having plenty of detail is fine and indeed desirable, but if the intention is to affect consumer decision-making there could be a better focus on key terms being presented in a more digestible format. There are risks to this focussed approach and there may well be disagreements about which elements are essential. This is one of the difficulties of operationalising the insights of behavioural economics. The position would be mitigated if Member States could experiment with approaches, but this is prevented by the maximum harmonisation approach.

168 Directorate-General for Internal Policies, *Implementation of the Consumer Credit Directive* (European Parliament, 2012), pp.31–32.

169 C Garcia and W Van Boom, *Information Disclosure in the EU Consumer Credit Directive: Opportunities and Limitations* (Rotterdam institute of Private Law Working Paper, 8 December 2009), p.13 citing OPTEM; *Qualitative Study through the 27 EU Member States on Pre-Contractual Information for Financial Services* (European Commission, 2008).

170 S Grundmann and C Hofmann, 'EC financial services and contract law – developments 2007–2010' (2010) *European Review of Contract Law* pp.467, 479.

171 M Muynck, 'Credit cards, overdraft facilities and European consumer protection: A blank cheque for unfairness?' (2010) *European Review of Private Law* pp.1227–8.

172 C Garcia and W Van Boom, *Information Disclosure in the EU Consumer Credit Directive: Opportunities and Limitations* (Rotterdam institute of Private Law Working Paper, 8 December 2009).

Mortgage credit

Prior to the Mortgage Credit Directive, there had been a Code of Conduct agreed between the European Consumers Association and the European Credit Sector Association, which was supported by an EU Recommendation on pre-contractual information.[173] The standard information rules for mortgages in the Directive parallel those for consumer credit, but are adapted to mortgage credit. There are some additional rules based on the nature of mortgage credit. For instance, it must be stated that the credit will be secured by mortgage or comparable security. There is an obligation to mention the identity of the creditor, or where applicable the credit intermediary or appointed representative.

For mortgages, all types of businesses dealing with consumers must provide personalised information on paper or another durable medium through the ESIS (the equivalent of SECCI).[174] This must be provided without undue delay after the consumer has provided necessary information on his needs, financial situation and preferences and in good time before the consumer is bound by any credit agreement or offer. There have also been criticisms of the wording of ESIS and the UK government has amended some wording e.g replacing ‘exit charge’ with ‘early repayment charge’. The Government felt unable to do more and even this change might be questionable.[175]

In some countries, mortgage offers can be binding on the creditor: in such cases an ESIS must be provided with the binding offer if one has not been provided previously or the characteristics of the offer have changed. Member States can require the ESIS be provided prior to a binding offer in which case a second ESIS will only be required if the terms change.[176] This would not seem to capture indicative offers or ‘decisions in principle’, but could include binding offers subject to conditions so long as a blanket right to re-underwrite the loan was not reserved.[177]

Credit intermediaries and appointed representatives must also provide information about themselves, including most significantly whether they are tied, offer advisory services and details of fees payable by consumers or any commission.[178]

Contractual document

The contractual document itself serves the purpose of providing a record of what was agreed. Surprisingly, there are no rules on this in the Mortgage Credit

173 Commission Recommendation on pre-contractual information to be given to consumers by lenders offering home loans (2001) OJ L69/25.

174 Special rules apply for voice telephony communications: Mortgage Credit Directive, Art. 14(10).

175 Financial Conduct Authority, *Implementation of the Mortgage Credit Directive and the New Regime for Second Charge Mortgages, Feedback to CP14/20 and Final Rules* (PS15/9, Financial Conduct Authority March 2015) 13.

176 Mortgage Credit Directive, Art. 14(4).

177 Financial Conduct Authority (n 183) 13.

178 Mortgage Credit Directive, Art. 15.

Directive. One can only assume this is because this might interfere with national conveyancing practices.

Consumer credit agreements must be drawn up on paper or another durable medium.[179] There is again an extensive list of up to 22 information obligations. The Directive states that all contracting parties should receive a copy, but it might have been better to have made it clear that a duty is imposed on the creditor to provide the consumer and any surety with a copy of the agreement – that was surely what was intended. The documents need not be a single document, but if reference is made to any other document such as general terms and conditions this should also be given to the consumer before the contract is entered into and be on paper or another durable medium.[180] Surprisingly there is no general indication as to when the contracts should be provided to the consumer, but the Austrian implementing law requires this to be without undue delay, which seems a sensible rule.[181] But it does seem like an obligation undertaken at the time of contracting or immediately after the contract has been concluded. There is no requirement the document be signed but the CJEU has confirmed national law can require this.[182] The CJEU has held that failure by a lender to include in the credit agreement all the required information may be penalised by Member States by forfeiture of entitlement to interest and charges where the failure to provide such information may compromise the ability of a consumer to assess the extent of his liability.[183] There is no obligation to provide subsequently a duplicate agreement on request, though national laws on this point would seem to be outside the scope of the Directive and therefore unaffected by any maximum harmonisation effect. The United Kingdom also continues to have the form requirement that the consumer sign the agreement and this will usually be in a signature box. These rules of course undermine the objective of allowing the same form and procedures to be used across Europe.

The European Court has held that to promote consumer protection the *ex officio* doctrine applies to the information obligations. The national court must check of its own motion they have been complied with and establish the consequences under national law. These must be effective, proportionate and dissuasive.[184]

Post-contractual

The continuing information duties take account of the fact that credit is a long-term social contract.[185] Debtors need to be kept informed of the progress of the

179 Consumer Credit Directive, Art. 10(1).
180 C-42/15, *Home Credit Slovakia as v Biroova* ECLI:EU:C:2016:842.
181 Directorate-General for Internal Policies, *Implementation of the Consumer Credit Directive* (European Parliament, 2012), p.34.
182 C-42/15, *Home Credit Slovakia as v Biroova* ECLI:EU:C:2016:842.
183 C-42/15, *Home Credit Slovakia as v Biroova* ECLI:EU:C:2016:842.
184 C-377/14, *Radlinger and another v Finway AS*, [2016] 3 C.M.L.R. 28.
185 L Nogler and U Reifner, *Life Time Contracts: Social Long-term Contracts in Labour, Tenancy and Consumer Credit Law* (Eleven International Publishing, 2014).

relationship. There is a lot that could be done to influence consumers' post-contractual behaviour through information. Such information because of its more personalised nature might be expected to have an impact on individuals. For instance, information could be provided on interest paid annually on credit cards or default fees paid on loans.

The Consumer Credit Directive has not been demanding as regards post-contractual information obligations. It only imposes very specific and limited post-contractual information obligations.[186] It includes an ongoing obligation in consumer credit contracts to provide an amortisation table where there is a capital amortisation of a credit agreement of fixed duration.[187] There is also an ongoing duty to inform on paper or durable medium about changes in the borrowing rate before the change enters into force. However, parties can agree to do this by notice being provided periodically where the change is caused by a change in a reference rate.[188] There is a similar duty to inform about changes in borrowing rate in relation to overdrafts as well as an overarching duty to provide information on the state of the account.[189] Where current accounts can overrun, information on the borrowing rate and applicable charges should be provided in the initial agreement and on a regular basis.[190] Where there is a significant overrunning for more than a month, the creditor should inform the consumer of the amounts, applicable borrowing rate and any penalties, charges or interest.[191]

There is scope to use technology to enhance consumer knowledge of how they are using products. In the context of overdrafts, for instance, technology could be used to warn consumers when they would be using an overdraft facility and the costs associated with it. This would allow them to decide in an informed manner whether to proceed. There is a lot of scope for innovation in information duties taking account of the lessons of behavioural economics, but the Directive is rather traditional in its approach.

The Mortgage Credit Directive contains post-contractual obligations only in relation to foreign-currency loans.[192] It suggests the need for a review of rights and obligations at the post-contractual stage should be part of any future review.[193]

Credit intermediaries

Credit intermediaries need to indicate whether they work exclusively for one or more creditors or are independent.[194] Any fees payable to the intermediary

186 Directorate-General for Internal Policies, *Implementation of the Consumer Credit Directive* (European Parliament, 2012), p.8.
187 Consumer Credit Directive, Art. 10(3).
188 Ibid., Art. 11.
189 Ibid., Art. 12.
190 Ibid., Art. 18(1).
191 Ibid., Art. 19.
192 Mortgage Credit Directive, Art. 23.
193 Ibid., Recital 81.
194 Consumer Credit Directive, Art. 21(a).

must be disclosed on paper or another durable medium before the agreement is concluded[195] and any fee communicated to the creditor to calculate the APRC.[196]

Moving beyond information – adequate explanations and creditworthiness

Adequate explanations

Providing consumers with information is a pre-requisite to informed consumer decision-making. The Directive sets out detailed obligations. These are over and above the Unfair Commercial Practices Directive's obligation not to omit material information the average borrower needs to make an informed decision. Such passive provision of information may still not be enough for consumers to gain a proper understanding of a complex product like credit. Consumers may need advice to understand the information and possibly how it relates to their particular circumstances. For most credit products consumers will not actively seek advice, beyond perhaps consulting a comparison website.[197] They are more likely to seek advice (and that advice is more likely to be independent) in the case of investment services[198] and mortgage credit. With credit, any advice is likely to come from the creditor, though possibly an intermediary might be involved. Third-party (independent) advice is more common in the mortgage market.

The Consumer Credit Directive places on creditors[199] a duty to provide adequate explanations so the consumer can assess whether the proposed agreement meets their needs.[200] Where appropriate, this should involve explaining the pre-contractual information, the essential characteristics of the proposed agreement and the special effects they may have on the consumer including the consequences of default in payment. Member States are given wide scope to adapt the assistance given and who gives it depending on the circumstances in which the agreement is offered, who it is offered to and the type of credit. For instance, the United Kingdom has embraced within this an obligation to explain the right of withdrawal.[201] Often these explanations will be given in writing and the obligation

195 Ibid., Art. 21(b).

196 Ibid., Art. 21(c).

197 European Banking Authority, *Financial Innovation and Consumer Protection – An Overview of the Objectives and Work of the EBA's Standing Committee on Financial Innovation (SCFI) in 2011–2012* (European Banking Authority, 2012), pp. 17–18 https://www.eba.europa.eu/documents/10180/15962/EBA-BS-2012-003-Financial-Innovation-and-Consumer-Protection--Overview-of-EBA-work-in-2011-2012.pdf [accessed 22 March 2016]. This found that consumers welcomed comparison sites but were concerned about their independence, whether they collected enough information to give tailored advice and whether quality factors as well as price could be factored into the equation.

198 Directive 2004/39/EC on markets in financial instruments (2004) OJ L145/1.

199 Credit intermediaries might play a role in this but creditors should ultimately be responsible for ensuring the explanations and advice are given: BIS (n 162) 30.

200 Consumer Credit Directive, Art. 5(6).

201 BIS, Guidance on the regulations implementing the Consumer Credit Directive (August 2010), p.32.

may not go far beyond the provision of the required information in the documentation, but in appropriate circumstances it may be necessary to give an oral explanation. The CJEU has acknowledged the explanations can be given orally, but seems to view this with some caution stating 'the possibility cannot be ruled out that those explanations may be given orally by the creditor to the consumer in the course of an interview'.[202] In appropriate cases personal counselling should not be viewed as second best and can be effective if done with consumer welfare in mind. In the United Kingdom this requirement has been interpreted as requiring the consumer to be told to consult disclosed information.

However, the thrust of this provision is still for the most part about making the information transparent. It stops short of requiring creditors in appropriate cases to counsel a consumer against taking out the loan. It merely requires advice on the use of credit in particular circumstances that are reasonably foreseeable or specifically made known. For instance, it might require an explanation that a particular loan was not suitable for long-term borrowing.[203] It seeks to enhance, but does not challenge, the autonomy of the consumer. If the consumer is to be dissuaded by the creditor from entering a contract deemed not to be in his best interest it will have to be on the basis of national laws giving the responsible lending provisions a substantive content.[204]

There is also a duty to provide adequate explanations under the Mortgage Directive[205] This extends to explaining, if products are bundled, whether they can be terminated separately and the implications of doing so.[206]

In the next section we consider the creditor's duty to assess the borrower's creditworthiness. The provision of adequate information can be given before that assessment is carried out so that the consumer can decide if that is the right type of loan. However, the assessment may reveal the need to adapt the explanations that had been given.[207]

Creditworthiness assessment

Consumer credit

Article 8 requires that creditors need to assess creditworthiness, both when making the initial loan and when significantly increasing the total amount of credit, on the basis of sufficient information, which may where appropriate be obtained

202 C-449/13 *CA Consumer Finance SA v Ingrid Bakkaus and Others* ECLI:EU:C:2014:2464.
203 BIS Guidance on the regulations implementing the Consumer Credit Directive (August 2010), p.30.
204 T Jørgensen, 'Credit advice' (2012) 4 *European Review of Private Law* p.961. Cf. Commission, *Proposal for a Directive of the European Parliament and of the Council on Credit Agreements relating to Residential Property* COM (2011) 142 final.
205 Mortgage Credit Directive, Art. 16.
206 Ibid., Art. 16(1)(d).
207 C-449/13 *CA Consumer Finance SA v Ingrid Bakkaus and Others* ECLI:EU:C:2014:2464.

from the consumer. Credit reference agencies are in practice very important.[208] However, there is no formal requirement in the Directive to consult them. Creditors can in appropriate cases rely solely on information provided by the debtor, though the courts will hopefully be vigilant when assessing whether that alone is sufficient information.[209]

Member States whose legislation requires consultation of relevant databases can retain any such existing requirement. There is an ancillary provision requiring Member States to allow non-discriminatory access by creditors in other Member States to databases for assessing creditworthiness. However, the nature and extent of databases varies across the Union with some, for example, only including negative credit history, whereas others include positive so-called 'white-data'. Practices will continue to vary. There are no supervision arrangements for credit registers, but the Mortgage Credit Directive does raise the prospect of examining the need for such.[210] If a database consultation leads to the rejection of the application the consumers should be informed immediately and without charge of the result and the particulars of the database consulted.[211]

The Directive's creditworthiness test is creditor-focused, as it concentrates on the ability to repay. A more ambitious responsible lending test might be broad enough to cover consideration of whether taking on the borrowing is in the consumer's interest.[212] It might be thought that the interest of creditor and borrower coincide as creditors do not want loans to be unpaid, but creditors can engage in a cycle of extending credit and generating profit from consumers placed in a 'sweatbox' where they pay interest and penalty charges at a sufficient level to make the loan profitable regardless of whether it is eventually repaid.[213] This can impact severely on consumers. As the European Coalition for Responsible Credit and Debt on our Doorstep explains:

> If someone is likely to repay but cannot afford it, then we can only assume that this means that the borrower will either default on other financial commitments (for example, rent or Council Tax, or on other credit commitments that they have) or else will have to reduce their regular expenditures to a degree which would be harmful to themselves or other members of their household (for example, by living in cold homes or cutting back or reducing expenditure on food).[214]

208 F Ferretti, *The Law and Consumer Credit Information in the European Community: The Regulation of Credit Information Systems* (Routledge-Cavendish, 2008).

209 C-449/13 *CA Consumer Finance SA v Ingrid Bakkaus and Others* ECLI:EU:C:2014:2464.

210 Mortgage Credit Directive, Art. 45.

211 Ibid., Art. 9(2).

212 K Fairweather, 'The development of responsible lending in the UK' in J Devenney and M Kenny (eds), *Consumer Credit, Debt and Investment in Europe* (CUP, 2012).

213 R Mann, 'Bankruptcy reform and the 'sweatbox' of credit card debt". *University of Illinois Law Review* (2007), p.384.

214 European Coalition for Responsible Credit and Debt on our Doorstep, *Implementing the Consumer Credit Directive – Response to Consultation* (ECRC, June 2009), http://www.responsible-credit.net/index.php?id=1980&viewid=43056 [accessed 13 March 2016].

Mortgages

Member States are also under an obligation in relation to mortgages to ensure creditors assess creditworthiness and only extend credit when the obligations are likely to be met.[215] The provisions are rather brief in the body of the Directive, focusing mainly on procedure. One aspect that is specifically mentioned is that the assessment should not predominantly rest on the value of property exceeding the credit.[216] The value of the property is of course crucial in such lending decisions and provision is made for national standards to be set down for property valuation by Member States to ensure impartial and objective valuations.[217] The recitals expand on this duty to assess.[218] For instance, future rental income might be taken into account when offering buy-to-let mortgages, but the availability of a guarantor should not lead the lender to ignore a credit-worthiness assessment that a consumer is not likely to be able to repay. Member States are allowed to set limits on loan-to-value ratios or loan-to-income ratios and are encouraged to implement the FSB's Sound Residential Mortgage Underwriting Practices.

In assessing creditworthiness, access to databases is important. Member States should ensure this is on a non-discriminatory basis.[219] Consumers should be advised in advance that a database is to be consulted.[220] Creditors should specify the information and independently verifiable evidence the consumer needs to provide.[221] Provision of incomplete information should not be a ground for terminating the agreement[222] unless the consumer knowingly withheld or falsified information.[223]

If an application is rejected the consumer should be informed without delay, and where applicable told that it was based on automatic processing of data. If it resulted from consulting a database the creditor should inform him of the result of that consultation and the particulars of the database consulted.[224] The Data Protection Regulation allows subjects to object to decisions being based solely on automatic decision-making including profiling.[225]

The obligations are more consumer protection-centred where, in relation to mortgages, creditors, credit intermediaries or appointed representatives offer advisory services.[226] They must then act in the best interests of consumers and this

215 Mortgage Credit Directive, Art. 18. This also applies to any significant increase in credit not included in original assessment: Art. 18(6).
216 Ibid., Art. 18(3).
217 Ibid., Art. 19
218 Ibid., Recitals 55-62.
219 Ibid., Art. 21.
220 Ibid., Art. 18(5)(b).
221 Ibid., Art. 20.
222 Ibid., Art. 20(3) and Recital 58.
223 Ibid., Art. 20(4).
224 Ibid., Art. 18(5)(c).
225 Regulation EU 2016/679: OJ L119/1, Art. 22(1). Credit consumers are specifically mentioned in Recital 21.
226 Ibid., Art. 22.

includes obligations to obtain necessary information regarding the consumer's personal and financial situation, his preferences and objectives so as to enable the recommendation of suitable credit agreements and must involve surveying a sufficiently large number of their products or, if they are not tied, those products that are on the market.

Moving beyond explanations towards responsible lending?

The Directive's approach to responsible lending is typical of EU consumer contract law which focuses on procedure rather than controlling the substantive content of the contract. One of the novel features of the original proposal to amend the Consumer Credit Directive in 2002 was the inclusion of a provision on responsible lending.[227] This concept was at that time only known in the legal orders of Netherlands and Belgium[228] though France had fairly extensive rules going in the same direction.[229]

The first proposal had been far stronger in this respect than the final directive. For instance, the advice function had extended to establishing which of their products offered 'the most appropriate type and total amount of credit taking into account the financial situation of the consumer, the advantages and disadvantages associated with the product proposed, and the purpose of the credit.'[230] There had been no proposal that the creditor should be obliged to advise that other suppliers may be more appropriate; it would have been merely a duty to select the best product from amongst their range. At one level that seems reasonable; who would want to give business away? But this is a segmented market and one policy objective is to encourage consumers to find cheaper sources of credit. It does not seem unreasonable to require those traders working in the niche sectors of high-risk lending to alert consumers that they might not need to turn to their high-cost sector. If they are offering expensive credit to inappropriate consumers that is a sign that the market is not working effectively. It may, however,

227 COM(2002) 443 (n 36), Art. 9.

228 I Ramsay, 'Consumer credit regulation after the fall: International dimensions' (2012) *J Eur Cons and Market Law* p.33 notes there are also international models such as in Australia (Australian National Consumer Credit Protection Act 2009, s 129) and South Africa (South Africa National Credit Act 2005, s 80).

229 Consumers had to fill in a '*fiche de dialogue*' setting out their financial situation, creditor's staff had to be trained in how to help complete this form and give adequate explanations and there were case-law developed duties to warn (*devoir de mise en garde*) and a prohibition on excessive loans (*interdiction d'octroi de prêts excessifs*): see Charlton (n 22).

230 COM (2002) 443 (n 36), Art. 6(3). Grundmann and Hoffmann went so far as to say that such a rule would have 'abolished the very principles of European contract law' as the national remedy would have, in their opinion, relieved the debtor of any obligation to repay a credit he should not have taken out: S Grundmann and C Hofmann, 'EC financial services and contract law – developments 2007–2010' (2010) *European Review of Contract Law* p.480. However, it is not clear that such a stark consequence is required. The sanction could have been a regulatory one or merely to pay only the costs of the more appropriate loan or to cancel the interest but require some of the capital to be repaid.

be complicated to find criteria to trigger individual alerts that products are inappropriate and so it may be necessary for this to be a general warning. That of course runs the risk of it becoming ritualised. There is also a risk that if consumers seek to shop around for cheaper credit and are turned down, those refusals might in themselves be a reason why their credit rating is adversely affected.

The earlier proposal had also required assessment of whether the consumer could reasonably be expected to discharge their obligations under the agreement.[231] This would have addressed the issue of whether the creditworthiness assessment was creditor or debtor-focused, and required such an assessment to be made in a more consumer-centred manner.

There is no longer any provision in the directive headed 'responsible lending'. This phrase has been moved to Recital 26 which talks of 'member states taking appropriate measures to promote responsible practices during all phases of the credit relationship' and about it being important 'that creditors should not engage in irresponsible lending or give out credit without prior assessment of creditworthiness.' There is no longer a duty to lend responsibly. It is the obligation to assess creditworthiness which remains.

Can Member States go beyond this creditworthiness concept and retain (in the case of Netherlands and Belgium) or introduce affordability into the responsible lending concept? In 2006, the United Kingdom had, in advance of the Directive, included within the criteria for assessing the grant of a credit license conduct which appeared to the then-Office of Fair Trading to involve irresponsible lending.[232] The OFT (now FCA) guidance[233] seemed to have tried to avoid the maximum harmonisation argument by separating out assessments of credit-worthiness and assessments of affordability and having only direct legal consequences flow from breach of the former under s. 55B Consumer Credit Act 1974. However, as guidance impacts on licensing obligations it is unclear if this argument is watertight. The UK government's consultation on implementation had argued that some element of assessment of affordability was implicit in Art. 8 save for all but the smallest loans.[234] Recital 26 of the Consumer Credit Directive, which calls on Member States to promote responsible lending practices, might be used to flesh out Art. 8 and support such national practices, but it would have been better if the right of Member States to have responsible lending/affordability rules had been made more explicit. There is at least an argument that given the decision to adopt a creditworthiness approach this pre-empts any more stringent national standards. Hopefully, such a restricted reading would not prevail, but the lack of any express mention of the freedom to go beyond its provisions may be read as restricting the freedom of Member States.

231 COM (2002) 443 (n 36), Art. 9.

232 Consumer Credit Act 2006, s 25(2B).

233 Office of Fair Trading, *Irresponsible Lending – OFT Guidance for Creditors* (Office of Fair Trading, 2009).

234 Department for Business Enterprise and Regulatory Reform *Consultation on Proposals for Implementing the Consumer Credit Directive* (Department for Business Enterprise and Regulatory Reform, 2009), para 5.7.

Consequences

A strong responsible lending regime would have three stages: (i) information collection, (ii) assessment and (iii) consequences for taking action inconsistent with the assessment. The Directives deal with only (i) and (ii). It is unclear whether breach of the Directives gives rise to any private law claim such as for damages or avoidance of the contract.[235] It is generally assumed that any additional sanction for the assessment not being properly undertaken or complied with should be a matter for national law. These national rules must, however, be effective. French rules which replaced the contractual rate with a statutory rate that was increased by 5%, if debts were not repaid within two months, were not deemed sufficient by the CJEU. On the facts of the case referred, they imposed only a minimal sanction on the creditor and on other facts could even make him better-off.[236]

What should happen if a creditor concludes it is not in the best interest of the consumer to enter into the agreement? One would hope the creditor would refuse to enter into the agreement and supervisory authorities would sanction creditors who failed to do so. However, in Norway, which has one of the most advanced regimes of responsible lending, there is only a duty to advise against a particular course of action, Failure to give an adequate notice permits the courts to mitigate the obligation to a limited extent; but in practice this has been conservatively applied with claims normally only being reduced by half.[237] Grundmann and Hoffmann argue that in fact the Directive's conception of the obligation is simply a requirement the consumer be advised and leaves it to the consumer to decide whether or not to enter into the agreement.[238]

Conclusion

In many respects the Directives' provisions fall short of a responsible lending regime. The focus is still on informed choice with limited obligations on creditors to consider the interests of consumers. Only in the mortgage context where advisory services are offered is there a duty to act in the best interests of consumers.[239] The Mortgage Credit Directive requires a report by March 2019 assessing the wider challenges of private over-indebtedness directly linked to credit activity.[240] Although stated to be comprehensive review and, where appropriate, leading to legislative proposals, it is unclear how broad the scope will be. It will, however, include discussion of the need for supervision of credit registers and the possibility for the development of more flexible and reliable markets.

235 K Sein, 'Transposition of the new Consumer Credit Directive in Estonia' (2012) 20 *European Review of Private Law* p.440.

236 Case C-565/12 *LCL Le Credit Lyonnais SA v Kalhan* ECLI:EU:C:2014:190.

237 T Jørgensen, 'Credit advice' (2012) 4 *European Review of Private Law* pp.980–982.

238 S Grundmann and C Hofmann, 'EC financial services and contract law – developments 2007–2010' (2010) 467 *European Review of Contract Law* p.481.

239 Mortgage Credit Directive, Art. 22(3)(d).

240 Ibid., Art. 45.

The right of withdrawal – completing the information protection paradigm

Consumer credit

The right of withdrawal is not the invention of the EU, but has become a pillar of its policy.[241] Its extension to consumer credit contracts marks an important confirmation of the importance of this right from the EU legislator's perspective. Art. 14 gives the consumer 14 days to withdraw[242] from the credit agreement from the conclusion of the contract or, if later, the day when the consumer receives the correct contractual documentation.[243] Where existing national law relating to linked credit agreements provides that funds could not be made available for a period of time, Member States can provide that the withdrawal period can be reduced to this period at the explicit request of the consumer.[244] As the right of withdrawal is linked to the provision of contractual documentation, this gives the consumer a long-term right of withdrawal where there has been non-compliance with information duties. This is contrary to the Consumer Rights Directive, which puts an outer limit of one year on the right to reject.[245] This right of withdrawal does not apply where there is an existing right to withdraw under the Distance Marketing of Financial Services Directive or the Doorstep-selling Directive.[246] Member States can also provide for contracts concluded through the services of notaries to be exempted, subject to certain conditions.

To exercise the right of withdrawal, the consumer must notify the creditor within the withdrawal period.[247] The question of proof of notification is left to national law, but any notification on paper or other durable medium that is available and accessible to the creditor is treated favourably as being within the deadline if dispatched before it expired. This means that, for example, putting a letter in the post within the period is sufficient, even though it may have no chance of being received within the withdrawal period. Obviously in such circumstances

241 See Chapter 3, pp.115–125.

242 The German implementing law has been criticised for giving an alternative remedy of allowing the goods to be returned instead of revoking the contract. This can be too limited a remedy as the credit contract may stay in place or be too generous – and thus breach maximum harmonisation principle – as goods contracts are not always cancelled: See European Parliament (IMCO), *Implementation of the Consumer Credit Directive* (2012), p.36.

243 Consumer Credit Directive, Art. 14(1). The French implementing law may be problematic in this respect as it provides the period runs from the consumer's declaration to be bound by contract, but the lender has seven days to give notice that he will lend the money, see Charlton (n 22).

244 Consumer Credit Directive, Art. 14(3).

245 See Chapter 3.

246 Consumer Credit Directive, Art. 14(5). The Doorstep-selling Directive is repealed by the Consumer Rights Directive which excludes financial services, including credit from its scope: see Peter Rott, 'Renationalisation of direct selling – the impact of the new Consumer Rights Directive on Financial Services' (2012) *ERA Forum* p.35.

247 Consumer Credit Directive, Art. 14(3)(a).

the notification cannot be available and accessible to the creditor until received. However, this must be the correct interpretation otherwise the reference to dispatch would be meaningless.

Funds can be paid to the consumer straightaway, though Member States are entitled to keep in place some existing restrictions.[248] Also national law may continue to set a period during which performance of the contract may not begin.[249] A consumer who withdraws from a credit contract has to pay back the capital and interest within 30 days.[250] The interest is at the borrowing rate. Sometimes, on payday loans for instance, the interest can be very high and have already increased the sum to a figure consumers cannot pay back. Nevertheless, this provision seeks to strike a balance between consumers who regret the decision they have made and creditors who have loaned money expecting a certain return. At least it restricts the impact of high-interest loans to a limited period and allows 30 days for alternative funds to be secured.

It is a moot point whether the right to withdraw is lost if the money is not repaid within 30 days.[251] The Directive simply proceeds on the assumption that the money will be repaid. It might be argued that if the condition of returning the money is not fulfilled, the consumer has failed properly to exercise the right and it is lost. However, there is a risk that it is vulnerable consumers, who take out extortionate loans they cannot afford to repay, that are left with onerous and unsuitable contracts. The better view is to see the repayment as a consequence of the exercise of the right of withdrawal – that accords with the wording of Art. 14(3), which talks about what needs to be done after exercising the right.[252] The consumer is also no longer bound to any ancillary service relating to the credit agreement, such as insurance, if it was provided by the creditor or by a third party on the basis of an agreement with creditor.[253]

In the context of the mis-selling of credit on the doorstep, German experience had shown that the cancellation of the credit element under doorstep-selling law may not assist if the underlying contract remained in force.[254] Strangely, the

248 This exception applies to where the member states had prohibited the advancing of funds under a linked credit agreement. If this option is taken the member state can also reduce the withdrawal period to the period in their law.

249 Consumer Credit Directive, Art. 14(7). In France for example the consumer cannot make the funds available until 7 days after the consumer accepts the contract on pain of a 30,000 euro fine: Code de la consommation, Art. L. 311-14 and L. 311-50.

250 Consumer Credit Directive, Art. 14(3)(b).

251 K Sein, 'Transposition of the new Consumer Credit Directive in Estonia' (2012) 20 *European Review of Private Law* 435 p.442 and C Wendehorst, 'Die neue Verbraucherkreditrichtlinie: Rücktritt, Kündigung , vorzeitige Rückzahlungen' (2009) *Österreichisches BankArchiv* p.34 both suggest this question needs to be referred to the European Court of Justice.

252 BIS, *Guidance on the Regulations Implementing the Consumer Credit Directive* (August, 2010), p.51.

253 Consumer Credit Directive, Art. 14(4). Ancillary service means a service offered to the consumer in conjunction with the credit agreement: Art. 4(4).

254 P Rott, 'Linked contracts and doorstep selling' in *The Yearbook of Consumer Law 2007*, (Ashgate, 2007)

Directive does not address this issue, but rather leaves this as a matter of national law along with associated questions such as those concerning the return of the goods, which might include whether there should be any compensation for the use of goods.[255] German law now provides in s. 358(2) of BGB that withdrawal from a credit agreement automatically cancels a linked agreement. However, Sein is correct to state this should be at the option of the consumer, though the conditions for exercising that option, such as how long the consumer has to exercise the option, need to be established.[256]

The Directive has rules on linked agreements, but only makes a link as regards the right of withdrawal where the purchase agreement is cancelled under Community law.[257] Then the consumer will no longer be bound to a credit agreement. This provision might have been better placed in the Directives granting those specific rights of withdrawal. It would have been fairer to consumers to have also provided that in linked agreements the purchase agreement is cancelled if the right of withdrawal for the credit agreement is exercised rather than leaving this to national law.

Mortgage credit

The equivalent provisions for mortgages are strangely not set out in a separate provision, but rather form part of the pre-contractual information duties. There must be a seven-day period during which the consumer can consider the offer.[258] Due to different traditions within the Member States, this can be either a reflection period before the formal conclusion of the contract or a withdrawal period. From a harmonisation perspective, it is unfortunate that a common approach was not possible as between reflection and withdrawal periods, but perhaps this is an indication of strong national traditions that are not yet ripe for full harmonisation.

If a reflection period is chosen, the offer shall be binding on the creditor during that period and the consumer can accept the offer at any time during that period. Member States are free to provide that the offer cannot be accepted for a period not exceeding the first ten days of any reflection period. This, however, is the exception and the general rule is to allow the consumer to proceed within the reflection period. Also, to promote legal certainty it can be provided that this period and any right of withdrawal shall cease where the consumer undertakes any action that results in the creation or transfer of property, makes use of the funds obtained or transfers the funds to a third party. It is peculiar that the Directive mentions these

255 Consumer Credit Directive, Recital 35.
256 K Sein, 'Transposition of the new Consumer Credit Directive in Estonia' (2012) 20 *European Review of Private Law* p. 442.
257 Consumer Credit Directive, Art 15(1). Recital 37 makes it clear this does not affect the position where a national right to withdraw is exercised or there has been breach of national rules requiring a signed contract before any commitment to supply or payment can be made.
258 Ibid., Art. 14(6).

detailed rules Member States can adopt only in Recital 23 and not within the main provision. There is also no provision, for instance, about the return of funds if they had been forwarded during the reflection or withdrawal period. Normal practice by mortgage lenders would presumably be to wait until the withdrawal period expired before releasing funds. Also, national rules may bring the period to an end if funds are used. The lack of detail on effects of withdrawal may not therefore be serious in practice but could helpfully have been addressed.

Restrictions on contractual freedom

Introduction

Freedom of contract is a highly-prized value. There are no general EU-wide controls on the types of credit product that can be supplied. There is a philosophical debate between those who argue any product control will stifle the creativity of the market to deliver products best-suited to consumer needs and those who see this heterogeneity as obfuscating the market and hindering transparency as well as allowing some products which are likely to harm consumers. Credit products may not be like some physically unsafe products, which are always likely to cause harm. Nevertheless, some credit products carry such risks that they can be deemed so unsafe they should be removed from the market. Others believe that even high-risk products should be available to informed and advised consumers. The EU is not unaware of these arguments, but has preferred to leave to Members States the power of decision on sensitive issues such whether to impose limits on loan-to-value or loan-to-income ratios.

The Directives also do not seek to impose any controls on interest rates. There is no European usury law. Such controls can be viewed as product bans to the extent they exclude certain lending. They also affect the socialisation of risk to the extent creditors lend to a pool of consumers at a lower rate when previously they were are prepared to pool lower and higher-risk consumers. One rare example of risk sharing considered below are the rules making creditors liable for the failures of suppliers under linked agreements.

Variable rates are allowed, and there is no control on the grounds for variation. Though the CJEU seems disposed to subject the terms allowing variation to assessment for fairness.[259] As regards mortgages, Member States must ensure that any indexes or reference rates used for variable rates are clear, accessible, objective and verifiable.[260] Historical records must be kept by the providers of indexes or creditors. There are also obligations to inform about any change in the borrowing rate.[261] A similar duty to inform applies for consumer credit.[262]

259 In the credit context see C-143/13 *Matei v SC Volksbank Romania SA* ECLI:EU:C:2015:127 building on C-472/10 *Nemzeti Fogyasztóvédelmi Hatóság v Invitel Távközlési Zr* ECLI:EU:C:2012:242.

260 Mortgage Credit Directive, Art. 24.

261 Ibid., Art. 27.

262 Consumer Credit Directive, Art. 11.

The Directives allow the market a wide degree of freedom, but at the margins some controls are imposed. Tying of products is not allowed, but bundling is.[263] Foreign currency loans are permitted, but subject to certain conditions to provide a measure of protection.[264]

Credit and particularly mortgage products are so complex that it can be hard for consumers to determine what they should bargain for. Moreover most credit products are offered on standard-form contracts. Consumers are therefore unlikely to appreciate what they should bargain over and in any event be unable to negotiate individual terms. Some rules exist therefore that, whilst not restricting the essential elements of the products available, seek to balance the rights on technical issues which the consumer would not think to consider or indeed be able to influence in the open market. Examples are the rules on early repayment,[265] termination of open-ended agreements[266] and assignment considered below.[267] In similar vein, Member States may also prohibit or impose restrictions on consumer payments prior to the conclusion of the agreement.[268]

Early repayment

Consumers often want to pay off a loan early either because their circumstances change or they have found a better deal. This is also seen as being important to increase competition in the market.[269] Both the Consumer Credit Directive[270] and Mortgage Credit Directive[271] enshrines their right to do so, either in full or partially. However, the Member States can require the mortgage consumer to have a legitimate interest in doing so during a fixed-rate period.[272]

However, creditors also have legitimate demands for compensation as they will receive less than anticipated. Art. 16(2) of the Consumer Credit Directive provides they should receive fair and objectively justified compensation. This right only applies where the early repayment is during a period when the rate is fixed.

The costs recovered must be directly linked to early repayment. Thus the United Kingdom considers closing administrative costs are not recoverable as they would have been payable in any event. Instead it cites as recoverable the loss if interest rates had dropped since the agreement was taken out so any relending would be less profitable.[273] One suspects there will be different national interpretations of 'fair and objectively justified compensation'. The amount should

263 See pp.255–256.
264 See p.255.
265 See p.252.
266 See p.254.
267 See pp.254–255.
268 Mortgage Credit Directive, Art. 7(5).
269 Mortgage Credit Directive, Recital 66.
270 Consumer Credit Directive, Art. 16(1). Some limited exceptions are set out in Art. 16(3).
271 Mortgage Credit Directive, Art. 25.
272 Ibid., Art. 25(5).
273 BIS, *Guidance on the Regulations Implementing the Consumer Credit Directive* (August, 2010), p. 62.

in any event not exceed 1% of amount repaid early if the agreement at time of repayment had more than one year to run or 0.5% if there was less than one year left. Moreover, it should not, in any event, exceed the interest that would have been paid.

Attitudes of Member States to this provision varied. Some were less open to providing compensation and so it is provided that Member States can remove the right below a threshold that cannot be more than 10,000 euro per year.[274] Others would be more generous to creditors and are therefore allowed to provide that creditors may exceptionally claim higher compensation than allowed for in the Directive if greater loss can be proven. This is a good example of the Directive trying to harmonise in the face of different national traditions. It certainly undermines the maximum harmonisation principle, but probably does not seriously affect the prospects of cross-border supply of credit.

The Mortgage Credit Directive likewise requires that any fair and objective compensation must be for costs directly linked to the early repayment.[275] There are no fixed limits for compensation under the Directive, but it must not exceed the financial loss to the creditor. Member States can provide levels it must not exceed or provide that it is not allowed for a certain period.

In the mortgage context, upon request the creditor should provide the information to allow the consumer to consider the early repayment option.[276] Member States may provide conditions for the exercise of the right, for instance, concerning the timing of the exercise of the right, differences depending on types of borrowing rate or the circumstances when it can be exercised.

Linked agreement

For there to be a linked credit agreement, the consumer credit must have financed the supply of specific goods or a specific service.[277] The supply and credit agreements must be a commercial unit either because they are provided by the same person; or, a creditor gets the supplier to conclude or prepare the agreement; or, the specific goods or specific service are specified in the credit agreement. Previous case law under the former Directive, which had a different structure, had held that a line of credit could form a linked agreement even if the goods or services had not been specified in advance.[278] This would also seem possible under the new rules as the line of credit can be identified with specific goods or services when the credit is called upon and specification of goods or services in the credit contract is just one means of establishing there was a commercial unit. Credit cards would normally fall outside the definition as though specific goods or services are bought with

274 Consumer Credit Directive, Art. 16(4)(a).
275 Mortgage Credit Directive, Art .25(3)
276 Ibid., Art. 25(4).
277 Consumer Credit Directive, Art. 3(n). The relationship between the creditor and supplier need not be exclusive: see decision on former directive, C-509/07 *Luigi Scarpelli v NEOS Banca SpA* [2009] ECR I-3311.
278 C-429/05 *Rampion and Godard v Franfinance SA* [2007] ECR I-8017.

the credit, they are neither specified in the credit contract nor does the supplier always conclude or prepare the credit agreement. However, where the suppliers do prepare the contract, as in case of store cards, then linked transactions could arise.

The definition of linked credit agreement is crucial to the rights when exercising a Community right of withdrawal.[279] Also in a linked agreement the consumer can pursue remedies for non-supply or lack of conformity against the creditor if he has failed to obtain satisfaction from the supplier.[280] It is left to Member States to determine the extent and conditions for invoking the remedies. The Recital makes it clear that this does not prevent consumers relying on more extensive joint and several liability rights under national laws, such as s. 75 of the UK's Consumer Credit Act 1974. That Act is also broader in covering any breach of contract and also under a separate provision misrepresentations.[281]

Termination of open-ended credit agreements

By their nature open-ended credit agreements, such as standing overdrafts or credit cards, do not have a set expiry date. Art. 13 provides consumers with the right to terminate such contracts free of charge at any time, unless a period of notice has been agreed which in any event should not be more than one month.[282]

A creditor's right to standard termination must have been provided for in the contract. Termination is possible on paper or other durable medium and there must be atleast two months' notice.[283] In addition, for objectively justified reasons creditors may (so long as it is provided for in the contract) terminate the consumer's right to draw down further on an open-ended credit agreement. The reasons for such termination should be provided on paper or other durable medium, where possible before termination or at least immediately afterwards. No reasons need be given if provision of such information is prohibited by Community legislation or is contrary to public policy or security: one can imagine this applies to money-laundering and suspected terrorist activities.[284] If the creditor fails to provide for such rights it seems he will be unable to terminate the agreement for any reason. This seems rather strict.

Assignment

If a creditor assigns his rights the consumer retains the right to plead against the assignee any right he had against the original creditor, including set-off.[285]

279 Consumer Credit Directive, Art. 15(1).
280 Ibid., Art. 15(2).
281 Consumer Credit Act 1974, s 56.
282 Consumer Credit Directive, Art. 13(1). The United Kingdom has introduced the possibility for the creditor to require this to be in writing: see Consumer Credit Act 1974, s 98A(1).
283 Ibid., Art. 13(1).
284 Ibid., Art. 13(2).
285 Ibid., Art. 17(1).

The consumer should be informed of any assignment unless the original creditor agrees to service the credit.[286]

Foreign currency mortgages

One of the riskiest products is a mortgage in foreign currency. These may look like dream deals if the currency offers a lower interest rate, but can turn into nightmares if currency fluctuates dramatically in the wrong direction. For the purposes of the Mortgage Credit Directive foreign currency loans are defined as credits in currency other than that of the Member State in which the consumer is resident. Loans in the currency of the consumer's state of residence will only be foreign currency loans if the consumer receives income or holds the assets from which the credit is to be repaid in another currency.[287] So a British Pensioner with a euro mortgage on a Spanish home being repaid out of a UK sterling pension would have a foreign currency loan. In practice many such loans were issued in Eastern Europe in Swiss francs and there has been considerable fallout from the consequences of the Swiss franc rising sharply in value. There are numerous examples of consumer detriment from such loans. These have led to national legislation and litigation which has also reached the CJEU. The CJEU has shown itself sympathetic to arguments that borrowers had not had the details of the arrangements fully explained to them.[288]

The Directive offers one palliative, namely the right for the consumer to convert the loan into an alternative currency that has some connection to the consumer through residence, income or assets.[289] This is essentially a tactic to stop things getting any worse. It is supported by obligations to warn the consumer if the amounts owed become more than 20% higher due to currency variations and to mention the right to convert to an alternative currency. Member States are given greater scope to regulate such loans.[290] These national rules might include caps on the increase due to fluctuations or the use of warnings. In any event the Directive requires, where there is no limit to the exchange-rate risk, that the ESIS should include an illustrative example of the impact of a 20% fluctuation.[291]

Tying and bundling

Given the range of products and services involved in mortgages it has become a frequent practice for suppliers to bundle them into one package. This gives the trader the advantage of selling more products and usually the consumer benefits from a lower overall price than if they had been bought separately. The Directive's approach is to allow bundling of this type, but not normally to allow

286 Ibid., Art. 17(2).
287 Ibid., Art. 28(4).
288 Case C-26/13 *Kásler v OTP Jelzálogbank Zrt.* ECLI:EU:C:2014:282.
289 Mortgage Credit Directive, Art. 23.
290 Ibid., Art. 23(5) and Recital. 30.
291 Ibid., Art. 23(6).

tying i.e. the products should be available to be purchased separately and their purchase should not be made the condition of offers.[292]

Tying is only allowed in specific circumstances where it is justified to provide means of payment, additional security or the pooling of resources.[293] Member States may permit creditors to require consumers to hold an insurance policy, but the creditor must accept a policy from a supplier other than his preferred supplier if it offers equivalent cover. Interestingly, in light of the above discussion on the general lack of product restrictions, Member States can standardize, wholly or in part, insurance policies to facilitate comparison.[294]

Arrears and foreclosure

The security offered by a mortgage is key to lending decisions and also a factor in reducing rates compared to unsecured lending. Member States must ensure security is enforceable.[295] Where consumers are in default Member States can allow creditors to charge default fees, but these must be either no more than required to compensate for the costs incurred or must be capped.[296] It is possible for the agreement to provide that return or transfer of the security or proceeds of sale is sufficient to repay debt. Where debtors are in trouble, creditors must be encouraged to exercise reasonable forbearance before initiating foreclosure proceedings.[297] Sales, where the amount recovered affects the consumer's debt, must be undertaken in a manner to enable the best-efforts price to be obtained.[298] After sale any further repayment required should be made under a scheme that protects consumers.

The EU therefore puts a protective framework in place, but if the consumer needs to move into bankruptcy this remains subject to national law. Despite undertaking studies which have prompted calls for EU intervention[299] the EU has resisted acting in the personal bankruptcy field.[300] However, it is now proposing to amend the Regulation on Insolvency proceedings to include personal insolvency.[301] Nevertheless it is disappointing that the EU has not issued

292 Ibid., Art. 12 and Recitals. 24–25.
293 Ibid., Art. 12(2).
294 Ibid., Recital. 25.
295 Ibid., Art. 26(1).
296 Ibid., Art. 28(3).
297 Ibid., Art. 28(4).
298 Ibid., Art. 28(5).
299 For an early example, see N Huls *Overindebtedness of Consumers in the EC Member States: Facts and Search for Solutions* (Story-Scientia, cop. 1994); G Betti, N Dourmashkin, MC Rossi, V Verma and Y Yin (2001). *Study of the Problem of Consumer Indebtedness: Statistical Aspects.* (Commision of European Union No. B5-1000/00/000197), http://www.iaclaw.org/Research_papers/iff_OverindebtednessandConsumerLaw.pdf [accessed 26 Oct 2012]; U Reifner, N Huls, J Niemi-Kiesiläinen, and H Springeneer, (2003), *Study on the Legislation Relating to Consumer Overintebtedness in all European Union Member States.*
300 There is a Council of Europe Committee of Ministers Recommendation (2007) 8E on Legal Solutions to Debt Problems and it is left to member states whether personal insolvency is within Insolvency Regulation 2000 OJ [2000] L160/1: J Niemi, 'Consumer insolvency in the European legal context' (2012) 35 *Journal of Consumer Policy* p.443.
301 COM (2012) 744 final.

a recommendation giving Member States encouragement to promote consumer protection through modern bankruptcy laws. This might have strengthened the trend that already exists in many States for more consumer-friendly bankruptcy procedures. The Commission is obliged to issue a comprehensive report on the wider challenges of private over-indebtedness directly linked to credit activity.[302]

Looking forward

Credit is likely to remain a local product. Even if maximum harmonization is needed in some areas of consumer protection to promote cross-border sales, this is not one of them. It is unlikely that the EU will step back from its current maximum harmonization approach to consumer credit, but it should at least resist taking further steps forward and in particular should refrain from extending that approach to mortgage credit.

There are certain key areas where flexibility needs to be built in to the legal systems. Warnings are one such aspect of regulation. They need to be geared to local conditions and cultures. To the extent Member States do not currently have freedom to develop their own warning regimes, they should be allowed to.

Credit is also a classic area calling out for the application of behavioural economics insights. Again warnings are one area to which these insights can be applied. Information duties are another. Both need to hit the mark if they are to be effective. Forms like the SECCI and ESIS need to be revised so their format gives impact and the information that is most relevant is selected out and made prominent. The need to tailor this to local needs might require more diversity being brought in even in this heartland of the maximum harmonization philosophy.

Information might also be provided in a more personalised manner showing, for example, how a consumer is likely to use or has used credit, e.g. showing on credit card statements interest and charges paid in last year.

Indeed there is much scope for the development of post-contractual rules. However, we do not want to fall into the trap of the EU mandating such rules. Those that are fundamental might be introduced as minimum harmonization requirements, but on the whole the Commission could use something akin to the open method of co-ordination to share experiences and promote best practice.

There are several areas of credit law which the EU does not touch. In particular it imposes relatively few controls on the substance of the agreement; where this is a debated topic often it leaves these questions for the Member States. This is not a bad policy. EU law might fix minimum standards where there is consensus and in other areas prompt Member States to engage with the issues in ways which make sense for the local context. Credit is not a product or service that needs the European brand for export, but the EU does need to protect its own citizens to help them gain the advantages of credit without suffering the effects of overdosing on a potentially dangerous product.

302 Mortgage Credit Directive, Art. 45.

7 Product liability and safety

Introduction

General introduction – distinguishing product liability and product safety

The right to safety is probably the most important consumer concern.[1] It is assured through a mixture of regulatory and private law rules. Product safety laws are upstream regulatory rules that seek to prevent dangerous products from being marketed or to remove them before they cause harm. Technical harmonisation and conformity assessment play a major role in developing standards in particular sectors, but the main focus in this chapter will be on the General Product Safety Directive.[2] This is the centrepiece of EU consumer safety law. It ensures broad and effective controls on all consumer products circulating in the market by covering all products not under sectoral directives[3] and making a range of regulatory powers available for all products. By contrast, product liability laws are downstream rules that compensate for harm caused by unsafe products. Although primarily intended to provide compensation for harm caused by unsafe products, the rules can also have a deterrent effect as the risk of paying compensation should promote safer product design, production and marketing. The EU has been less involved with service liability and safety.[4]

Chapter themes

A good example of European branding

Consumer safety has long been a primary concern of the EU.[5] Consumer safety has become a major concern in modern times as technology creates more

1 It was one of the four basic rights in Presidents Kennedy's famous 15 March 1962 speech to US Congress, subsequently known as the Consumer Bill of Rights: text available at http://www.presidency.ucsb.edu/ws/?pid=9108; [accessed 1 December 2016]. It has been consistently a part of EU consumer protection programmes and action plans.
2 General Product Safety Directive 2001/95/EC (2001) OJ L 11/4.
3 A well-known example is Directive 2009/48/EC on the safety of toys (2009) OJ L170/1.
4 See below, pp.266–267.
5 Europe has amassed many regulations governing food safety, which merit detailed consideration in their own right and are therefore not covered in this volume. For a

exciting consumer products, which, however, can also carry increased risk. Mass production also means the effects of unsafe products can be widespread. The modern regulatory state has seen itself as having a role in protecting its citizen from harmful products. This applies to everyday consumer products just as much as it does to high-risk products such as asbestos, pharmaceuticals, cosmetics, contraceptives, protective devices, airplanes or automobiles.

Some of the first European interventions concerning safety were indirect through the development of common technical standards, which helped assure minimum safety standards for key product sectors.[6] But the adoption of a General Product Safety Directive placed Europe at the forefront of modern safety laws. The CE marking is a visible symbol of EU standards being complied with. Consumers may not always be well informed about the CE marking. They may not understand its meaning or wrongly consider it to be a safety mark like the German GS mark. In fact, it merely indicates compliance with EU new approach directives. But in international trade it has become a strong symbol of the European regulatory regime.[7]

Equally, the European form of strict product liability introduced by the Product Liability Directive[8] has inspired reform in many regions of the world.[9] This is somewhat surprising as product liability in the US was the most developed and might have been expected to have been the model states looked to. However, the notoriety of US product liability law and its high profile negative impact on certain sectors caused many states to shy away from adopting its rules. In many respects the European substantive rules are stricter than the US rules, especially after reforms in the US Restatement (Third) of the Law of Torts: Product Liability.[10] Rather it was US procedural rules and damages law that in practice impacted heavily on American industry (class action, non-pecuniary damage levels, care costs and punitive damages). European product liability laws have, by contrast, caused relatively

review of early development see: EU Commission, *The General Principles of Food Law in the European Union*, 30 April 1997, COM (97) 176 final; See also A Alemanno ed, *Foundations of EU Food Law and Policy: Ten Years of the European Food Safety Authority*, (Routledge, 2014) and B van der Muelen (ed), *EU Food Law Handbook*, (Wageningen Academic Publishers, 2104).

6 A major push was made following the adoption of Council Resolution 85/C 136/01 of 7 May 1985 on a new approach to technical harmonisation and standards: OJ 1985 C 136/1: see G Howells, *Consumer Product Safety*, (Ashgate, 1998), Chapter 2.

7 D Hansom, *CE Marking, Product Standards and World Trade*, (Edward Elgar, 2005).

8 Council Directive 85/374/EEC on the approximation of the laws, regulations and administrative provisions of the Member States concerning liability for defective products: OJ 1985 L 210/29.

9 G Howells, *Comparative Product Liability* (Ashgate,1991); M Reiman, 'Product liability in a global context: The hollow victory of the European model'. European Review of Private Law 11 (2003), p.128; A McDougall and P Popat, *International Product Law Manual* (Wolters Kluwer, 2011); J Kellam, *Product Liability in the Asia-Pacific*, 3rd ed (Federation Press, 2009); L Nottage and S Thanitcul, *Asean Product Liability and Consumer Product Safety Law* (Winyuchon, 2015).

10 G Howells and M Mildred, 'Is European product liability more protective than the Restatement (Third) of Torts: Product Liability?' (1998) 65 *Tennessee Law Review* p.985; David Owen, *Product Liability Law*, 2nd ed (West, 2005).

few problems for trade. This has made them more palatable to governments and industry and facilitated their spread around the globe.[11]

Product liability and safety laws have been influential in branding Europe as a region producing reliable, quality products. These laws are the leading example of European success in exporting its consumer regime. Not only are the EU rules regarded as models for other legislators, but the generally high standards set underpin confidence in European products.

Strong emphasis on maximum harmonisation

This is an interesting topic to explore the maximum harmonisation theme. The rationale for technical harmonisation rules adopting maximum harmonisation is clear. These rules seek uniformity to remove barriers to free circulation. It is not so obvious that this should be applied to the more general obligations in the General Product Safety Directive as higher national levels of protection may not require specific modifications of products. Apparently even within the Commission opinions were divided on whether the first Directive[12] was maximum in character, but it now seems clear that the General Product Safety Directive is treated as being maximum. Importantly, the European rules leave room for legislators to take actions against products that pose a danger to consumers, even if they are formally complying with the law. This safeguard approach has not been applied to EU maximum harmonisation laws dealing with consumer economic interests.[13] This is something that might be regretted.

The CJEU has also confirmed that the Product Liability Directive is a maximum harmonisation measure.[14] That seems hard to justify from a policy perspective as differences in liability laws have only a marginal impact on decisions to market across borders. One only has to look to the USA for an example of a region with different state product liability laws that do not appear unduly to restrict trade. There are in any event exceptions to the maximum harmonisation principle on the face of the Directive. Significantly it does not affect the ability to rely on various liability regimes in place when the Directive was adopted.[15]

A balance between information and substantive socialisation of risk

Consumer information plays an important role in protecting consumers' safety. The instructions and warnings provided with products are factors to be taken into account when assessing safety. However, there is also a recognition that

11 M Reimann, 'Liability for defective products at the beginning of the twenty-first century: Emergence of a worldwide standard' (2003) 51 *American Journal of Comparative Law* p.751; J Kellan and L Nottage, 'Europeanisation of product liability in the Asia-Pacific region: A preliminary empirical benchmark' (2008) 31 *Journal of Consumer Policy* p.217; D. Campbell, *International Product Liability* (LLP Publishing, 1993).

12 Directive 92/59/EEC on general product safety.

13 See e.g. Chapter 2 on the Unfair Commercial Practices Directive.

14 See below.

15 See below.

there should be some limits on the extent to which producers can rely on such techniques. Modern society brings with it increased risks.[16] Producers need to take responsibility for their products and this may involve their redesign rather than mere warning. For unavoidable risks, there seems to be an acceptance that a degree of socialisation of risks is necessary. This is not always spelt out and possibly is too radical for many rule makers to follow through to its logical conclusion. This debate on socialisation of risk is most evident in the product liability field where the Directive's recital states:

> Whereas liability without fault on the part of the producer is the sole means of adequately solving the problem, peculiar to our age of increasing technicality, of a fair apportionment of the risks inherent in modern technological production.[17]

However, determining what is a fair apportionment of those risks is an open question that has not been fully explored, yet alone answered. Nevertheless, some degree of sharing of risks has been accepted. The policy behind the Directive also assumes that producers will be deterred from producing products where they would be liable to pay compensation that exceeded their profits. Thus some risks (products) should be excluded from the market. In product safety law, similar controls are exerted by the rule that any risk should the minimum compatible with the product's use.[18] These rules should impact on the range of products consumers can choose from compared to an unregulated market. Such controls do not mandate product design, but place limits on the designs that can be marketed. Some commentators note the potentially regressive impact on poorer consumers of laws that require safety features which make products more expensive.[19] Poorer consumers are therefore priced out of access to the products, or at least price rations their access to them in a way that affects them more than the affluent consumer. However, the standards only establish minimum levels of safety. Provided these are pitched as levels where fundamental safety issues are at stake, this should be seen as an important protective safeguard for the poor to prevent them being exposed to products that can pose a serious risk. If there was freedom to risk using products posing serious risk merely because the risk was warned against, the welfare of consumers might be lowered as they might not be able accurately to assess the risks involved.

Enforcement

Enforcement has been given priority in the safety field. From the first General Product Safety Directive there was the requirement on Member States to

16 U Beck, *Risk Society* (Sage, 1992).
17 Recital 2.
18 General Product Safety Directive Art. 2(b).
19 G Priest, 'The current insurance crisis and modern tort law' (1987) 96 *Yale Law Journal* pp.1585–1586.

have an enforcement authority for consumer safety.[20] Regulation (EC) No 765/2008[21] required Member States to entrust market surveillance authorities with the powers, resources and knowledge necessary for the proper performance of their tasks. A notable feature of the latest reform proposals[22] is the proposed requirement that Member States satisfy the Commission they have properly resourced their authorities and given them sufficient powers to survey the market. By contrast, product liability actions have depended upon national civil litigation cultures. The EU has resisted introducing measures requiring class actions. That would help promote product liability litigation. In part, the reluctance to mandate such reforms was because the Commission was scared away from replicating the US experience where class actions have been considered to fuel litigation.[23]

History

In 1976 the Council of Europe issued the Strasbourg Convention on Products Liability in regard to personal injury and death. In the same year the European Commission published its first proposal for a directive on product liability,[24] but it was not adopted until 1985.[25]

In the product safety field there had been early attempts to promote technical harmonisation, but these had been difficult to adopt due to the need to deal with particular products individually and to seek unanimity. As part of the push for the Single European Market the pace of adopting technical standards increased under the new approach directives.[26] These now cover categories of products and set down safety expectations as broad standards. Annexes contain essential safety requirements which are fleshed out in CEN[27] standards.

The *new legislative framework for the marketing of products* comprises:

a Regulation (EC) 764/2008[28] laying down procedures relating to the application of certain national technical rules to products lawfully marketed in another Member State. This seeks to ensure technical rules in non-harmonised areas do not unduly impede trade.

20 Directive 92/59/EEC (1992) OJ L 228/24, Art. 5.
21 (2008) OJ L 218/30.
22 See COM (2013) 78 final.
23 The then-Commissioner Kuneva made her position clear when she said 'there will not be any (class action). Not in Europe, not under my watch.' (Speech on 10 November 2007, Lisbon).
24 (1976) OJ C 241/9.
25 Council Directive 85/374/EEC on liability for defective products: (1985) OJ L 210/29.
26 Council resolution a new approach to technical harmonisation and standards (1985) OJ C 136/1.
27 CEN is European Committee for Standardisation.
28 (2008) OJ L 218/21.

b Regulation (EC) No 765/2008[29] setting out accreditation and market surveillance requirements relating to the marketing of products and in particular setting out the criteria for national accreditation bodies and general principles for the CE marking.
c Decision 768/2008/EC[30] setting a common framework for the marketing of products which sets out requirements for conformity assessment and rules on affixing the CE mark.[31]

In addition to sectoral measures, in 1992, the EU adopted the first General Product Safety Directive (92/59/EEC).[32] This was a horizontal directive intended to cover products outside the scope of vertical harmonisation measures. Even for products covered by specific vertical regulations, it sought to ensure a full range of measures was available. Many of the specific laws had, for instance, no provisions on matters such as notification of risks.

In 2001 consumer safety regulation was overhauled and a new General Product Safety Directive 2001/95/EC adopted.[33] The EU should be applauded for its work revising the General Product Safety Directive to clarify concepts, fill gaps that had been identified and to increase coherence. Currently there is a new reform package proposed that seeks to revise the General Product Safety Directive[34] and introduce a market surveillance package providing a common framework for enforcement.[35] It is unfortunate these measures have not (yet) been adopted, but the Commission has shown its desire to keep the law in this area modernised. It is understood that the major stumbling block with the current reform proposals is over a proposed requirement to show the country of origin. This is not directly a safety issue and it is unfortunate it is holding up valuable reforms.

The ongoing reform of product safety laws contrasts with the Product Liability Directive. It has had only one minor amendment[36] since it was adopted. This may be because the Product Liability Directive has been relatively uncontroversial in practice and no one wants to rock the boat by proposing reforms that might destablise the equilibrium. Equally, it could be because enforcement has been privatised and personal injury lawyers do not have sufficient incentives to lobby for reform of an area of practice that is niche and high risk. Perhaps it is because

29 (2008) OJ L 218/30.
30 (2008) OJ L 218/82.
31 One issue that often causes concern is whether the ability to forum-shop for conformity assessment services can lead to a race to the bottom.
32 (1992) OJ L 228/24.
33 (2001) OJ L 11/4.
34 See *Proposal for a Regulation on Consumer Product Safety* COM (2013) 78 final (hereafter 'CPS Regulation Proposal').
35 *Proposal for a Regulation on Market Surveillance of Products* COM (2013)75 final (hereafter 'Market Surveillance Regulation Proposal 2013').
36 Removing the discretion of Member States to exclude primary agricultural produce and game: see Directive 1999/34 amending Council Directive 85/374/EEC (1999) OJ L 141/20.

the Directive is the responsibility of the Internal Market Directorate-General, currently DG GROWTH – Internal Market, Industry, Entrepreneurship, and SMEs. The Commission was also strongly of the view that it was an internal market rather than primarily a consumer protection measure. This was needed to justify its legal base. Many measures in the consumer field share a common legal base linked to the establishment and functioning on the internal market. However, product liability perhaps has a weak justification for such a base as its impact on cross-border trade is at best indirect. Having its home in a Directorate with more pressing internal market issues may make its review less of a pressing priority for the relevant Commissioner. However, there has now recently been a move to consider reviewing the Directive, with the impetus being the need to make it relevant to the digital age and the Internet of Things.[37]

Maximum harmonisation

Technical harmonisation is one area in which maximum harmonisation seems justified as its objective is to promote the free circulation of goods by not allowing national divergences in standards to act as barriers to trade. However, the new approach directives achieve this in a very sophisticated way that both promotes diversity and safeguards consumer protection. Products have to meet a safety standard that is fleshed out through essential safety requirements. The surest means of compliance is to satisfy approved European (CEN) standards as translated into national standards. However, producers remain free to meet the essential safety requirement through alternative means. Importantly, even if a product is deemed to meet the required standard there is a safeguard clause allowing action to be taken against products that pose a threat to safety.

This is a model that might have inspired a broader more flexible approach to maximum harmonisation in other areas, such as unfair commercial practices. It might be classed as soft or flexible maximum harmonisation. It offers a safe harbour way of complying with obligations, but rather than imposing a specification standard that demands a certain production method is used (or not used), it favours a performance standard that gives producers the freedom to choose how to achieve the required level of safety. It nudges producers to use the preferred means of compliance through the inducement of legal protection if the standard approach is used. However, consumer protection is equally safeguarded by allowing action to be taken in situations where risks materialise despite compliance with rules.

The need for maximum harmonisation is less clear when applying a general safety standard, but after some initial doubts, even with differences within the Commission, it seems clear that the General Product Safety Directive is a maximum

37 See European Commission, *Evaluation of the Directive 85/374/EEC concerning liability for Defective Products* (2016), http://ec.europa.eu/smart-regulation/roadmaps/docs/2016_grow_027_evaluation_defective_products_en.pdf [accessed 24 October 2016].

harmonisation directive. Once again there is a safeguard clause to protect consumer safety in circumstances where a product complies with the criteria of the general safety requirements, but there is evidence that it is still dangerous.[38]

The Product Liability Directive provides for an additional parallel liability regime to those already existing at the time the Directive was adopted. Art. 13 provides:

> This Directive shall not affect any rights which an injured person may have according to the rules of the law of contractual or non-contractual liability or a special liability system existing at the moment when this Directive is notified.

The preservation of existing regimes, by Art. 13, has itself been used as an argument that the Directive is maximum in character. Otherwise it is suggested there would be no need for the express preservation of these rights. Also, as particular matters have been left to the option of Member States (i.e. the development risks defence,[39] ceiling on damages for personal injury[40] and originally the exclusion of primary agricultural produce and game[41]) or particular issues have been left expressly to national law[42], the assumption is that as regards other matters there is maximum harmonisation. The CJEU has confirmed that the Product Liability Directive should be viewed as a maximum harmonisation directive.[43] The Court was also influenced by the lack of a minimum harmonisation clause and Recital 1 which made out the economic internal market case for harmonisation. These CJEU decisions have concerned some important issues such as the refusal in *Commission v France*[44] to allow national law

38 Art. 3(4) of Directive 2001/95/EC.

39 Art. 7(e) and Art. 15(1)(b).

40 Art. 16(1).

41 This was removed by Directive 1999/34/EC (1999) OJ L 141/20.

42 Art. 5 prescribes joint and several liability and Art. 8 no reduction in producer liability even if the damage is also caused by the act or omission of a third party, but leaves it to national law to govern matters concerning the rights of contribution and recourse. The rules on damages in Art. 9 are without prejudice to national provisions relating to non-material damage. The limitation rules in Art. 10 do not affect Member States' rules on the suspension or interruption of the limitation period.

43 See C-52/00 *Commission v France* [2002] ECR I-3827, paras 17–20; C-154/00 *Commission v Greece* [2002] ECR I-3879, paras 13–16; C-183/00 *González Sanchez v Medicina Asturiana SA* [2002] ECR I-3901, paras 26–29.

44 C-52/00 *Commission v France* [2002] ECR I-3827. On this see also later decision of C-402/03 *Skov AEG v Bilka Lauprisvarenhus A/S* [2006] 2 CMLR 16. The Court was not influenced by Point 2 of the minutes of 1025th meeting of the Council of Ministers of 25 July 1985 which stated: 'With regard to the interpretation of Articles (3) and (13), the Council and the Commission are in agreement that there is nothing to prevent individual Member States from laying down in their national legislation rules regarding liability for intermediaries, since intermediary liability is not covered by the Directive. There is further agreement that under the Directive the Member States may determine rules on the

to impose similar liability to producer liability on suppliers. In the same case it was also held that whilst there was a freedom to remove the development risks defence, a halfway house imposing more conditions on the use of the defence was not allowed. But this maximum harmonisation approach has also extended to relatively minor rules such as the need to continue the €500 threshold on property damage.[45]

González Sanchez v Medicina Asturiana was more concerned with the interpretation of Art. 13. The CJEU refused to accept any national rules that could be seen as imposing a general strict product liability regime different to that laid down in the Directive. Member States can maintain their existing general rules and any specific regime in place. What they cannot do is develop competing regimes focused on strict product liability. Thus general rules of law like negligence and sale of goods law can be applied as well as specific regimes such as that established in Germany for drugs by the Pharmaceutical Act 1976. What cannot be maintained are systems that apply a distinct strict product liability regime that is not limited to a particular sector.

The maximum harmonisation effects of the Directive only extend as far as the scope of the Directive. Thus, in *Moteurs Leroy Somer v Dalkia France*,[46] national law could continue to apply where the damage was caused to property intended for professional use. Such damages were outside the scope of the Directive. Equally a national system requiring public healthcare establishments to pay compensation, even when they are not at fault, for damage sustained by a patient as a result of the failure of equipment or products used in the course of treatment was not incompatible with the maximum harmonisation scope. It had a different base of liability and did not affect liability of producers under the Directive.[47] It also does not impact on national regimes that enable information on the adverse effects of pharmaceutical products to be obtained, even if this impacts on product liability litigation practice.[48]

Scope of consumer safety laws

Definition of product

Relationship with service liability and safety regulation

As their names suggest, both the Product Liability Directive and General Product Safety Directive relate to products and not services. One of the

final mutual apportionment of liability among several liable producers (see Article 3) and intermediaries.'

45 C-52/00 *Commission v France* [2002] ECR I-3827 and C-154/00 *Commission v Greece* (2002) ECR I-3879.

46 C-285/08, *Moteurs Leroy Somer v Dalkia France* [2009] ECR I-4733.

47 C-495/10, *Centre Hospitalier Universitaire de Besançon v Thomas Dutrueux and Caisse Primaire d'Assurance Maladie du Jura* [2011] ECR I-14155.

48 C-310/13 *Novo Nordisk Pharma GmbH v S.* ECLI:EU:C:2014:2385.

weaknesses of EU consumer safety law is that it fails to address services in a systematic manner. There had been a proposal for a directive on service liability.[49] It would not have introduced strict liability, but merely have reversed the burden of proof for negligence liability. However, it was not adopted. Directive 2006/123/EC on services in the internal market[50] contains mechanisms requiring Member States to provide mutual assistance and to alert other Member States about risks[51] as well as a requirement that providers of services that present a direct and particular risk carry insurance.[52] The EU has only adopted the occasional soft law rules relating to service safety.[53] However, some Member States have when implementing the EU product safety directives extended them to cover to services.[54]

The line between service and product liability is particularly debated to the context of the General Product Safety Directive. The crucial issue is whether the products remain controlled by the service provider, and hence are part of a service, or are used by the consumer. Recital 9 makes it clear that the Directive extends to 'products that are supplied or made available to consumers in the context of service provision for use by them.' Thus a supermarket trolley or gym equipment would be included in the consumer safety regime, but a shampoo applied by a hairdresser would be excluded as it remained under the control of the professional. The Directive's Recital makes it clear that the safety of the equipment used by service providers and the equipment on which consumers ride or travel if operated by the service provider belong to service safety and are excluded from the scope of the Directive.

Products covered

The Product Liability Directive covers all moveable products even if incorporated into another moveable or an immoveable. Human body parts and blood would seem to be covered despite some religious objections.[55] The original option

49 *Proposal for a Council Directive on the Liability of Suppliers of Services*: (1991) OJ C 12/8. The Commission has since published *A Report on the Safety of Services for Consumers* COM (2003) 313 final, which concentrates on administrative and regulatory matters.

50 (2006) OJ L 376/36.

51 Arts. 29 and 32.

52 Art. 23.

53 See for example, Council Recommendation 1986/666 on fire safety in existing hotels: (1986) OJ L 384/60.

54 Finland, Norway and Sweden have included general service safety rules in product safety laws, whereas Spain and Portugal include them in consumer protection laws: see Commission Staff Working Paper, *Summary of Member States' Policies and Legislation on the Safety of Services*, SEC (2003) 625, pp.4–5.

55 Certainly contaminated blood has been subject to litigation under the Directive: A v National Blood Authority (2001) 3 All ER 289 and Scholten v The Foundation Sanquin of Blood Supply Rb Amsterdam 3 February 1999, NJ 1999, 621: reported on Product Liability Forum Database.

given to Member States to exclude primary agricultural produce and game was removed in 1999.[56]

The General Product Safety Directive applies to all products,[57] unless there is a specific Community provisions with the same objective.[58] Where an issue is properly addressed in a sectoral rule, then that specific rule takes priority. But the General Product Safety Directive acts as a safety net for risks not covered in specific regulations or to provide obligations like notification and reporting obligations if not found in the specific regulations. The complexity of the relationship between the GPSD and sectoral rules is evident in the forty page *Guidance Document on the Relationship Between the General Product Safety Directive and Certain Sector Directives with Provisions on General Safety*.[59] This Guidance concedes there is much scope for interpretation about what the Directive means when it refers to 'aspects and risks or categories of risks' not covered by the specific rules, as well as room for debate on whether the rules have the same objective.

The CPS Regulation Proposal 2013 tries to draw a clearer distinction. It is helped by the Market Surveillance Regulation Proposal 2013 applying to all products covered by Community legislation. The general provisions in Part One of CPS Regulation Proposal 2013 set out the general safety requirement which would apply even to products covered by other EU harmonised legislation. Such products are only exempted from the following chapters that implement the general provisions. However, there would be a presumption of safety as regards risks covered by Union-harmonised legislation designed to protect human health and safety so long as those requirements were conformed with.

Incorporeal products

The Product Liability Directive specifically covers electricity. This has led to debate as to whether other incorporeal products are excluded. The most important debate has been around software and digital products.[60] The only country to have addressed this issue directly in its implementing legislation is Belgium, which restricts the definition of product to tangible movables, thus excluding software.[61] Whether this is in line with the Directive is debateable. At one time, it was common to draw a distinction between software supplied on a durable medium, such as a compact disc, and programmes that were simply downloaded.

56 Directive 1999/34.

57 It does not apply to antiques or products supplied to be repaired or reconditioned so long as the supplier makes this purpose clear.

58 Art. 1(2).

59 Available at: http://europa.eu.int/comm/consumers/cons_safe/prod_safe/gpsd/guidance_gpsd_en.pdf [last visited 13 October 2005].

60 S Whittaker, 'European product liability and intellectual products'. 105 *Law Quarterly Review* (1989), p.125 and K Alheit, 'The applicability of the EU Product Liability Directive to software' (2001) 34 *Comparative and International Law Journal of Southern Africa* p.188.

61 Act of 25 February 1991 on defective product liability, Art. 2.

The physical nature of the disc encouraged some commentators and judges to treat the former as products. But as it has become more common to simply make software available for downloading the appeal of this distinction has faded. A more rational distinction turns on whether software is standardised or bespoke. There might be some value in equating off-the-peg software with a mass-produced product and viewing bespoke products as an individualised service. The same rationales for strict liability might then apply to the mass-produced standardised software. However, artisan goods are not treated any differently under the Directive as compared to standardised products. A more convincing distinction is between software which undertakes actions itself and software that produces information which is then acted upon by a person. The latter sort of information-producing software requires human intervention to use it and arguably is similar in quality to the information found in a book and so should not be subject to strict liability. However, if software directly has a material output, such as operating a heating system or cooker in your home or helping land a plane, then it seems valid to treat it as a product and subject it to strict liability. These are likely to be component parts for which the producer of the final product would be liable for in any event.

The debate on this issue has not been as strong in relation to the General Product Safety Directive, but similar issues might arise. In the sales context, a separate category of conformity rules is being created for digital goods.[62] Some similar clarification could usefully be provided in relation to safety and liability.

Limited to consumer products?

The General Product Safety Directive only covers products intended or likely under reasonably foreseeable conditions to be used by consumers. It had previously been unclear whether so-called migrating products (commercial products that came to be used by ordinary consumers) were included. Problematic cases had included surveyors' laser pens, large fireworks intended for commercial displays and heavy-duty DIY hire equipment. They are now clearly included as the Directive clarifies that products cover those 'intended for consumers or likely, under reasonably foreseeable conditions, to be used by consumer *even if not intended for them*.' By contrast, the Product Liability Directive applies to all products. The limitation of damages to property used for private use or consumption is discussed below.[63]

Damages recoverable

The Product Liability Directive provides that liability for damage caused by death and personal injuries and damage or destruction of property is covered. Damages

62 See Chapter 9, pp.334–347.
63 See p.270.

can sometimes be difficult to categorise. For instance, the CJEU left it to the national court to decide whether damage to a kidney about to be transplanted was personal injury or property damage.[64]

Property damage does not include damage or destruction of the defective product itself: that is seen as the province of sales law. Also there is a threshold of 500 ECU. Most Member States treat this like an insurance deductible, but the UK and Netherlands rules provide that once the threshold is exceeded the amount can be recovered in full.[65] This approach seems preferable given the policy rationale is to avoid disputes over small amounts.

The damaged property must also be of a type ordinarily intended for private use or consumption and actually used by the injured person mainly for those purposes. A commercial product is subject to the Directive and may create liability for personal injury or damage to a consumer product. However, any harm caused by any product to commercial products is excluded. If a product catches fire and damages a work computer and a PlayStation, only damages for the latter are recoverable. Damage to commercial products is outside the scope of the Directive and subject to national law.[66]

Parties liable

Product liability

The Product Liability Directive channels liability towards the producer. This contrasts with the US approach of making all those in the supply chain potentially liable. It has the advantage of economic efficiency, as there is no need for several parties to insure against the same risk. However, it risks leaving the consumer without a defendant if the producer is insolvent. The producer can be the manufacturer of a component or a finished product or the producer of any raw material.[67]

The choice of producer as the main focus of liability was probably due to the producer normally having most control over the product's safety and often being a wealthier defendant than many retailers. However, those assumptions are not always correct. In part this is recognised by the extension of the definition of producer to cover a person who by putting their name, trade mark or other distinguishing feature on the product presents themselves as its producer.[68] This might capture large stores who own-brand their products. Although, they may be able to escape liability by appropriate labelling making it clear they are not the producer. Celebrity endorsements would not normally make the personality liable as they would not be seen as presenting themselves as the producer.

64 *Veedfald v Århus Amtskommune*, Case C-203/99 [2003] 1 CMLR 41.
65 S190(1)(b) Dutch Civil Code and s. 5(4) UK Consumer Protection Act 1987.
66 C-285/08 *Moteurs Leroy Somer v Dalkia* [2009] ECR I-4733.
67 Art. 3 (1).
68 Art. 3 (1).

Importers into the Community will also be deemed to be producers.[69] Liability attaches to the first party to import into the Union, meaning there might still not be a target defendant in the consumer's home state. In fact, it is even possible that the importer into the EU is established outside the EU. The General Product Safety Directive is more concerned to find a responsible person in the consumer's home state.

Suppliers have a subsidiary liability under the Product Liability Directive.[70] The *Skov* case[71] makes it clear that Member States cannot increase their liability beyond the extent allowed for in the Directive by making the supplier liable for defects. Supplier liability will arise if the producer cannot identify the producer or the person who supplied him within a reasonable time. In the case of imported products, the importer must be identified even if the producer is indicated. Presumably this is because the producer will be outside the EU.

In *Aventis Pasteur SA v OB*,[72] the English distributor of a vaccine manufactured by its French parent company had been wrongly sued and the claimant wanted to substitute the proper defendant outside the ten-year-long stop period. The Directive has both a three-year limitation period and a ten-year-long stop from when the product was put into circulation.[73] One basis the CJEU found for making the subsidiary potentially liable was that it had not, of its own initiative and promptly, disclosed the name of the producer. This seems to be in conflict with the United Kingdom implementing law which requires there to have been an express request. It was in truth an attempt to prevent the companies benefitting from the corporate structures used by groups of companies. The CJEU would also exceptionally allow substitution if the producer had directed the supplier to supply the product.

General product safety

The GPSD distinguishes between producers, who bear the full force of the responsibilities under the Directive and distributors who have the lesser duty to act with care to help ensure compliance. Producer covers similar groups as under the Product Liability Directive. The producer[74] is the manufacturer, but only when established in the Community. This is because of the need to have a person within the EU to take enforcement action against; if the manufacturer is not established in the Community the producer is the manufacturer's representative or the importer. The producer can also be a person who presents himself as the manufacturer by affixing to the product his name, trade mark or other distinctive

69 Art. 3(2).
70 Art, 3(3).
71 Discussed below.
72 C-358/08 ECR [2009] I-11305. This litigation had already been to the CJEU on the same issue – see C-127/04 *O'Byrne v Sanofi Pasteur MSD* (2006) ECR I-1313.
73 Art. 10.
74 Art. 2(e).

mark. A reconditioner is also stated to be a producer. Other professionals can be producers in so far as their activities may affect the safety properties of a product. This might cover someone who stores products or assembles them. Distributors are professionals in the supply chain who do not affect the safety properties of the product.[75]

Enforcement action can be taken against producers, distributors and any other person where this is necessary to avoid risks arising from the product. The emphasis on local enforcement is seen in the particular mention of action being taken against the party responsible for the first stage of distribution on the national market.[76]

Substantive safety standards – protection by information and warnings vs socialisation of risk

General standards – consumer expectations vs risk: utility

The Product Liability Directive premises liability on the presence of a defect. A defect exists when the product does not provide 'the safety which a person is entitled to expect.'[77] All the circumstances should be taken into account, including:

a the presentation of the product;
b the use to which it could reasonably be expected that the product would be put;
c the time when the product was put into circulation.

However, an English judge, Burton J in *A v National Blood Authority*,[78] held that all the circumstances meant only all the *relevant* circumstances. This is perhaps self-evident but his conclusion as to what were relevant was quite radical. He held relevant circumstances did not include the avoidability of the harmful characteristic – i.e. impossibility or unavoidability in relation to precautionary measures; the impracticality, cost or difficulty of taking such measures and the benefit to society or utility of the product (except possibly where there has been full disclosure and the risk was, and ought to have been, accepted).[79] This approach was deemed necessary to prevent the discussion collapsing back into negligence-style analysis and requiring the claimant to spend a lot of resources on evidence. It was also justified by the presence of the development risks defence, which protected the producer against specific types of unavoidable harm due to the lack of scientific knowledge.

The Directive establishes a liability based on consumer expectations and Burton J in *A v National Blood Authority* favoured the approach set out by

75 Art. 2(f).
76 Art. 8(4).
77 Art. 6(1).
78 [2001] 3 All ER 289.
79 Para 68.

Dr Bartl under which the judge acts as the appointed representative of the public at large.[80] The consumer cannot expect products to be free of risk, but can expect to have his legitimate expectations met. These should be judged objectively. This objectivisation of the standard is intended to counter the criticism of the consumer expectation standard in the US, which is in some applications considered to be overly subjective. It also seems to rule out a strict application of a risk:benefit analysis, but in practice this may come back into the frame when analysing what are legitimate safety expectations; particularly for design defects.

The literature, and even some Member States laws,[81] distinguish between different types of defects. A basic distinction is between a manufacturing defect where the defective product differs from the intended design and design defects where the product is claimed intrinsically not to offer sufficient safety.[82] Manufacturing defects might arise because of a construction error or due to imperfect materials. Design defects might be further categorised according to whether the actual design is flawed or the problem lies with instructions for use or inadequate warnings. The US has revised its Restatement (Third) of Torts: Products Liability and now draws distinctions between these categories of defect on the face of its law and restricts true strict liability to manufacturing defects.[83] The EU Directive applies the same standard to all defects. However, in practice it is easier to find an improperly made product fails to meet expectations of safety than to challenge a design. Designs involve polycentric decisions balancing safety against performance, efficiency, aesthetics and cost. The safest product may simply not be acceptable for other reasons. There will often need to be trade-offs. In evaluating design choices risk and utility are likely to play some role. Stapleton and Newdick consider this goes so far as to mean strict liability collapses back into a form of negligence.[84] However, one does not have to be so pessimistic and yet still agree with the extra-judicial comments of a Law Lord that some kind of risk:utility balancing would have to be undertaken. [85]

80 Para 56, referring to H Bartl, *Produkthaftung nach Neuem EG-Recht* (Moderne Industrie, 1989).

81 Article 5(3) of the Italian Decree 224 of 24 May 1988 provides that a product shall be considered defective if it does not provide for the safety which is usually provided for by other models of the same type (translation in C Hodges *Product Liability* (Sweet & Maxwell, 1993) at p 442), see also Art. 3(2) of Spanish Law 22/94 of 6 July 1994 which provides that: 'In any case a product is defective if it does not offer the safety normally offered by models in the same line' (self-translation).

82 Burton J preferred a distinction between standard and non-standard products.

83 See § 2 Categories of Product Defect. G Howells and M Mildred, 'Is European product liability more protective than the Restatement (Third) of Torts: Products liability?' (1998) 65 *Tennessee Law Review* p.9.

84 J Stapleton, *Product Liability* (Butterworths, 1994); J Stapleton 'Products liability reform – real or illusory'. *Oxford Journal of Legal Studies* p.392 and C Newdick, 'The future of negligence in product liability' (1987) 104 *Law Quarterly Review* p.288.

85 Lord Griffith and V Dorner, 'Developments in English product liability law: A comparison with the American system' (1988) 62 *Tulane Law Review* p.353.

The General Product Safety Directive defines a safe product in order to set minimum levels for entry into the marketplace. Often failure to meet this standard will lead to some form of criminal or administrative sanction, but in some systems like the French it is merely an organising concept for remedial powers, such as those allowing dangerous products to be removed from the market.[86] In this regulatory field the standard of safety is not based on expectations, but rather on the seemingly more objective requirement that the product does not 'present any risk or only the minimum risks compatible with the product's use'.[87] However, just as expectations are made objective by the judges using the public at large as their yardstick when assessing what are reasonable expectations, so equally are risks measured against what is acceptable – so long as this is consistent with a high level of protection.[88] The product liability and product safety standards may in practice not be far apart.

Any product deemed unsafe under the General Product Safety Directive should be classed as defective in product liability law. The minimum standard should be that products meet the level required for lawful circulation in the marketplace. However, it is possible to imagine products that carry the minimum acceptable risks still being considered defective as they did not offer the expected level of safety. Drugs might, for example, still be justifiably marketed despite having side effects that affect some users. Product liability can be viewed as a mechanism to compensate the unfortunate victims whose injury comes at the expense of the majority, who benefit from the product without suffering the side effects. A classic example is aspirin; it has undoubted benefits and its withdrawal would be unjustified despite some random users suffering from internal bleeding. Sadly the theoretical rationale for the Product Liability Directive is unclear; without a clearer indication of policy it is doubtful whether in such cases the courts would impose liability. At best the court might be willing to find liability if the public had not been made sufficiently aware of the danger.

Compliance with standards

Compliance with standards is not a defence under product liability. There is a very narrow defence where mandatory public regulations have been complied with, but it only applies where the defect was due to compliance.[89] It will be rare for compliance to require a product to be made in a way that is defective. There have been calls for a pre-emption defence, but this has even been rejected for drugs in US.[90] A more subtle argument is that regulations, standards or approvals from regulatory bodies represent the expectations of safety of the community at large. Therefore a potential argument is that compliance can indirectly lead to a finding

86 G Howells, *Consumer Product Safety*, (Ashgate, 1998), Chapter 6.

87 Art. 2(b)

88 The general safety requirement also requires the reasonable consumer expectations concerning safety to be taken into account; Art. 3(3)(f).

89 Art. 7(d).

90 *Wyeth v. Levine*, 555 U.S. 555 (2009), but on modified devices, see Riegel v Medtronic 552 U.S. 312.

of lack of defect as these are indicators of what safety can be expected. However, such determinations are made for different reasons than civil liability. They may not have benefitted from full disclosure of risks and may become outdated.[91]

The General Product Safety Directive's general product safety requirement is deemed satisfied when there is compliance with national rules.[92] There is a presumption of compliance when it conforms to voluntary national standards transposing European standards.[93] Beyond that a range of other standards, recommendations and codes of good practice should be taken into account.[94] However, significantly, even if this deference to standards approach leads to a product being deemed safe, competent authorities are not barred from taking measures to restrict the product's marketing or requiring its withdrawal or recall where there is evidence it is dangerous.[95]

Socialisation of risk

The Product Liability Directive proudly asserts that 'liability without fault on the part of the producer is the sole means of adequately solving the problem, peculiar to our age of increasing technicality, of a fair apportionment of the risks inherent in modern technological production.'[96] However, it gives few clues as to what amounts to a fair apportionment. Strict liability is clearly not absolute liability. Several defences are allowed[97] and liability is premised on the defeating of reasonable expectations, thereby implying a limit to the circumstances where mere harm being caused by a product can lead to liability. Similarly, the General Product Safety Directive does not preclude all risk. It is merely concerned to keep risk within acceptable limits.

National courts when assessing defectiveness in product liability have adopted wide divergences in approach. In *A v National Blood Authority*[98] Burton J was keen to show that the Directive was indeed intended to strike a different approach from negligence. Other courts have slipped back into negligence analysis. Indeed, several academic commentators have argued this is inevitable given the formulation of defectiveness in the Directive.[99] This would be regrettable. Clearly

91 M Mildred, 'Pharmaceutical products: The relationship between regulatory approval and the existence of a defect' (2007) 18 *European Business Law Review* p.1267.

92 Art. 3(2) para 1.

93 Art. 3(2)para. 2.

94 Art. 3(3).

95 Art. 3(4).

96 Recital 2.

97 Art. 7 provides defences for not having put product into circulation; defect not existing when put into circulation; product not sold or supplied for economic purpose nor manufactured or distributed in course of business; defect being due to compliance with mandatory regulations; development risks defence and a defence for component part manufacturers where defect due to design of final product or instructions given by its manufacturer. The burden of proving the defence is on defendant.

98 (200s1) 3 All ER 289. A more conservative approach has been adopted in the recent English case Wilkes v De Ley International [2016] EWHC 3096.

99 See n 84.

something different from negligence was intended when the Directive was adopted. However, even the Commission has been guilty of slipping back into this traditional negligence style thinking. Its Third Report on the Directive talked about situations where Member States have redressed the claimant's difficulties in proving fault.[100] Claimants under the Directive certainly do not need to prove fault. Some courts have even gone so far as to find defect from the mere fact that a product behaved in an unexpected manner. French courts have, for instance, relied on a tyre exploding to presume it was defective without being concerned to identify the precise cause or have imposed liability where a glass window exploded in circumstances where the precise cause was unknown.[101]

At one extreme the view could be taken that if harm is caused by a product behaving in an unexplained way that in itself is a defect, because the product does not offer the safety a consumer was entitled to expect. This would reflect a desire to socialise risk. At the other end of the spectrum are cases where the courts have required the cause of the defect to be proven. This risks slipping back into fault-style analysis.[102] In between there are positions which accept that defeating consumer expectations may be in itself amount to defectiveness without the need for the product to be shown to be physically flawed, but still require more than mere harm having been caused by a product. Instead of a physical defect, defectiveness can be based on the producer having unduly raised of expectations of safety.[103] The problem arises when the product behaves in an unexplained manner; often the reason for the harm will be impossible or disproportionately expensive to discover. Sometimes the courts may use circumstantial evidence to establish defect. Lenze argues this was the correct approach of the Austrian Supreme Court in a case involving an exploding firework.[104] This can be assisted by a rule like Art. 217.6 of the Spanish Law of Civil Procedure which states that the court should bear in mind, when distributing the burden of proof, the availability of and ease of access to the evidence for each party.[105]

The CJEU has recently, in *Boston Scientific*,[106] given a strong lead that the Directive was intended to socialise risks by holding that a defect can exist because products belonging to the same group or forming part of the same production

100 COM(2006) 496 final.

101 Decision of the Court of Appeal of Toulouse of 7 November 2000 and Decision of Tribunal de Grande Instance in Aix-en-Provence of 7 November 2000 see S. Whittaker, *Liability for Products* (2005), p.75.

102 *Foster v Biosil* [2001] 59 BMLR 185.

103 G Howells, 'Defect in English law – lessons for the harmonisation of European product liability' in D Fairgrieve (ed) *Product Liability in Comparative Perspective* (CUP, 2005).

104 S Lenze, 'German product liability law: Between European directives, American restatements and common sense' in D Fairgrieve (ed) *Product Liability in Comparative Perspective* (CUP, 2005).

105 J Huerta and B Muñiz, 'Feature – an overview of product liability in Spain' (2005) 18/5 *European Product Liability Review*.

106 Joined cases C503/13 and C504/*13 Boston Scientific Medizintechnik GmbH v AOK Sachsen-Anhalt – Die Gesundheitskasse and Betriebskrankenkasse RWE* ECLI:EU:C:2015:148.

series have a potential defect. It is unclear if this is limited to high-risk products, like pacemakers and implantable cardioverter defibrillators, which were involved in the cases heard. Where such products are at potential risk of failure the question often arises as to whether any remedial action should be treated as damage. In the case of such medical products, this might require an operation. The CJEU held that if an operation was needed to remedy the defect that should be considered as damage caused by death or personal injury.

A lack of clarity about the ultimate objectives of product liability, nevertheless, makes it hard to determine how much it is concerned with the socialisation of risk. To test this, five aspects will be analysed: the extent to which vulnerable groups are taken into account; responsibility for inappropriate use by the product user; liability for inherent risks; the ability of instructions and warnings to exculpate defendants; and, the development risks defence. This discussion will mostly be about product liability, but the General Product Safety Directive is also relevant as it concerns what products are allowed on to the market. Liability socialises risk though compensation. Regulatory law restricts choices for the common good.

Vulnerable groups

Certain groups of consumers are often considered to be particularly vulnerable. For example, young and old consumers may have particular needs or face particular risks. The same might apply to groups with disabilities or those with particular allergies. Being unable to speak the local language or badly educated can also expose consumers to risks. Of course not all members of these groups will be equally vulnerable. Some elderly consumers are, for instance, very alert and able to protect their own interests. But there are vulnerable features which affect many in the class.

The greater the socialisation of risk the more these vulnerabilities will be taken into account. The General Product Safety Directive requires account to be taken of the categories of consumers at risk when using the product, in particular children and the elderly.[107] Often the answer will be to include a warning or finesse instructions for use, but sometimes an adaptation may be necessary. Only rarely will a risk be so serious and unavoidable that a product of value to society generally will be banned due to risk to individuals. Similar steps will be required by the Product Liability Directive as the general public will require reasonable account to be taken of the safety needs of vulnerable groups. The expected steps will depend on the seriousness of the risk and the numbers affected. The regulatory and liability regimes might for policy reasons come to different solutions, with a product being legally marketed despite an unavoidable risk to particular consumers justifying compensation. Sadly the rationale for product liability is not spelt out with sufficient clarity to be certain such losses are covered. However, the

107 Art. 2(b)(iv).

vulnerability of consumers may be taken into account when assessing the use to which it reasonably be expected the product will be put. In particular, products aimed at children will be judged by high standards and producers of such products should be expected to take account of the propensity for children to act in an 'irrational' way judged by adult standards.

Responsibility for inappropriate use

The General Product Safety Directive judges products under 'under normal or reasonably foreseeable conditions of use'. This implies that some reasonably foreseeable conditions of use may not be normal.[108] The Product Liability Directive assesses defectiveness in the product in the light of 'the use to which it could reasonably be expected that the product would be put.' This again requires that it is not merely the intended or prescribed purposes, but also inappropriate but foreseeable uses that should be considered. For example, several products are geared to the professional market. They may carry risks for the general public, but are safe in the hands of professionals. Examples might include large display-standard fireworks that are known to be used by the general public and chemical compounds popular with hobby craft artists. Producers might be able to avoid liability by making it clear that their products are for professional use only, but otherwise the safety will be judged as if supplied to the general public. Liability might arise from inappropriate instructions or warnings.

A problematic issue can arise where a secondary market in product accessories is created, e.g. for motor vehicles. It may be inappropriate to use them with the main product, but producers might still be under a duty to monitor the secondary market and warn against using certain products that are unsafe in combination with their product.[109]

Many consumers will in fact use products in ways that are inappropriate and the producer has to make their products safe in so far as these uses are foreseeable. A simple example concerns a pair of glasses. It is clearly not intended that consumer chew their glass frames; yet this is a common practice. Therefore producers need to ensure they do not contain allergenic or otherwise harmful substances.[110]

Vulnerable groups, especially children, can be expected to use products in inappropriate ways. This is expressly factored into the assessment under the General Product Safety Directive, but would also be relevant for product liability defectiveness assessment. Of course the more extreme the misuse or the more unique the behaviour is, the less likely it will render the product unsafe or defective.

108 Art. 2(b).

109 In a German case, decided on negligence basis, a manufacturer of a motorcycle was found liable in negligence for failing to supervise the accessories market when parts made by another producer, but aimed at his products, rendered them dangerous: (1986) NJW 1009.

110 K Taschner and E Frietsch, *Produkthaftungsgesetz und EG Produkthaftungsrichtlinie* (Beck, 1990) p. 299.

Inherent risks

Products will always contain some risks. Even the most innocent product can be involved in accidents and for some products risk is inherent in the product's functionality: that is why the General Product Safety Directive talks about 'the minimum risks compatible with the product's use'.[111] Knives need to be sharp to cut; cars need to move at speed and, perhaps more controversially, alcohol, tobacco and foods with high salt or sugar content carry inherent risks to health. This is what Børge Dahl described as 'system damage'.[112] Typically product liability regimes do not provide liability for such risks so long as such risks are socially acceptable. Controlled drugs have unacceptable risks, whereas society accepts those in fast food, tobacco and alcohol.

Liability issues often turn on whether such inherent risks were sufficiently well known. In *Brinkmann v Masterfood*[113] the Higher Regional Court of Düsseldorf held that consumers could not complain about the sugar in chocolate bars as they were taken to know that excessive consumption of sugary products could lead to severe health problems, such as obesity. The court contrasted the facts in the instant case with the toddler tea case, where liability had been imposed in negligence for failure to warn of the risk of tooth decay if sweetened tea was given in bottles left with babies.[114] That risk needed to be warned against as parents might understandably not be aware of it.

The lack of liability for inherent risks results from the expectations consumers are entitled to expect. If a risk is necessary and immoveable then a consumer may not be entitled to expect that it would be removed. So long as the product is socially useful, the most consumers might expect is that they are sufficiently warned about the inherent risk. Even this might not be necessary for very widely understood risks e.g. sharp knife blades.

There have been calls for liability regimes to be based solely on causation, particularly in the field of tobacco liability.[115] This would logically impose liability for inherent risks. Indeed that is the policy motive behind the proposed tobacco regimes. This makes sense if the desire is to internalise risk. There will still be

111 Art. 2(b).

112 B Dahl, 'Product liability in Scandinavian law'. *Scandinavian Studies in Law* 19 (1975), p.84

113 Oberlandsgericht Dűsseldorf, 20 December 2002, 14 U 99/02: M Hannes, 'Stressing consumers' responsibility, Higher Regional Court of Dűsseldorf dismisses appeal claim for damages against Masterfood' (2003) 10/31 *European Product Liability Review.*

114 See (1992) NJW 560.

115 D Garner, 'Cigarettes and welfare reform' (1977) 26 *Emory L.J.* p.269; R Ausness, 'Compensation for smoking-related injuries: An alternative to strict liability in tort'. *Wayne L. Rev.* 36 (1990), p.1085; P LeBel, 'Beginning the endgame: The search for an injury compensation system alternative to tort liability for tobacco-related harms' (1997) 24 *N. Ky. L. Rev.* p.457; J Hanson and D Kysar, 'Taking behaviouralism seriously: The problem of market manipulation'. (1999) 74 *N.Y.U. L. Rev.* p.632; 'Taking behaviouralism seriously: Some evidence of market manipulation' (1999) 112 *Harv. Law Rev.* p.1420; 'Taking

a need to show how the product contributed to the damage; otherwise many products could actually be implicated in accidents which were in no way related to their characteristics.[116] It might, for instance, be argued that all smoking-related deaths based on specific diseases should be attributed to tobacco use on policy grounds even if there cannot be a proven link in all cases. But it would seem excessive to make a knife manufacturer liable for an attack carried out with it.

Instructions and warnings

Instructions for use and warnings should be taken into account both in determining whether a product is safe under the General Product Safety Directive[117] and defective under the Product Liability Directive.[118] The General Product Safety Directive refers to 'the presentation of the product, the labelling, any warnings and instructions for its use and disposal and any other indication or information regarding the product.'[119] The Product Liability Directive simply refers to presentation, but this has been taken to include instructions and warnings. Indeed, presentation is just one particular factor, but the standard makes it clear all, or at least all relevant[120], circumstances should be taken into account.

Instructions tell consumers how to use or not use the product. Products that carry a risk can be rendered safe by appropriate instructions. For example, a risk might be addressed by the instructions to use safety equipment or the advice only to use a product in certain situations. Incorrect instructions can also render a product defective; for example, the instructions may specify an unsafe manner of use. Thus, a particular fire extinguisher may be useful in many situations, but may not be safe when used on electrical appliances. It will be unsafe/defective if this limitation is not explained in the instructions.

Instructions can include warnings about using the products in certain ways. Some warnings apply however the product is used as they refer to irremovable or unavoidable risks. These may affect certain types of consumers or be warnings about random effects. Their validity depends upon the extent to which that risk is socially accepted. The less easily risks are deemed social acceptable the greater the socialisation of the sharing of risk. Warnings should not be used to escape liability if the risk can be removed by a reasonable adjustment in the design.[121]

In assessing warnings the insights of behavioural economics should be used to determine whether they have been given in the appropriate manner so as to

behaviouralism seriously: A response to market manipulation'. *Roger Williams University Law Rev.* 6 (2000), p.259. This is understandable in the context of tobacco as by all normal standards this product would be defective, but for social custom.

116 Australian Law Reform Commission, *Product Liability*, Report No 51 (1989).

117 Art. 2(b).

118 Art. 6 refers to presentations.

119 Art. 2(b)(iii).

120 Following *A v National Blood Authority* (2001) 3 All ER 289.

121 Schmidt-Salzer, *Produkthaftung* (Recht und Wirtschaft, 1990), p.655.

have the optimum impact. One such insight is into the problem of consumer information overload.[122] The impact of warnings can be reduced if there are too many of them. Yet if there are many risks to be warned against it is likely that there will be a long list of warnings – see the length of side effects listed for many pharmaceuticals. Courts may find it difficult to condemn a producer for giving too many warnings, especially if the risk warned against has materialised. Good practice, however, might suggest that prominence be given to the most obvious and dangerous risks. Failure to do so or the use of poorly worded warnings may be the basis of liability.

In *A v National Blood Authority*[123] Burton J raised the question of whether a warning is in fact an exclusion clause, which is not permitted under the Product Liability Directive.[124] If warnings can too easily immunise producers from liability then it would drastically reduce the degree of socialisation of risk. The best approach is probably to distinguish between specific warnings and too-general warnings that are really there just to seek to avoid liability. [125] Consumers can use specific warnings to assess whether they should expose themselves to an inherent risk that cannot be avoided if the product is to maintain its functionality or other desirable characteristics

Development risks

The timeframe for assessing the product's safety is perhaps the best test of how far the regime socialises risk and involves a different assessment from one based on fault.[126] This is best understood by distinguishing the state-of-the-art from the development risks defence. Although these terms are often used interchangeably, they should be distinguished.

'State-of-the-art' will be used to refer to the safety expected given the current state of known risks at the time of supply. Thus a product with a known risk that was socially accepted at the time of marketing would not be considered unsafe just because standards moved on. Hence cars without seatbelts in the rear were once common. As standards developed rear seatbelts became required. This did not render the earlier-supplied cars without rear seatbelts unsafe, for they continue to be judged by the prevailing standards at the time of supply.

By contrast, development risks refer to risks that were not known about at the time of supply, but if they had been known about would have caused the product to be considered unsafe, even by the then-prevailing expectations of safety. The

122 BRE/NCC, Better Regulation Executive and National Consumer Council (2007), 'Warning: Too much information can harm', London - www.bis.gov.uk/files/file44367.pdf.

123 (2001) 3 All ER 289.

124 Art. 12.

125 G Howells, 'Information obligations and product liability – a game of Russian roulette?' in G Howells, A Janssen and R Schulze (eds) *Information Rights and Obligations – a Challenge for Party Autonomy and transactional fairness* (Ashgate, 2002)

126 N Terry, 'State of the art evidence: From logical construct to judicial retrenchment' (1991) 20 *Anglo-American Law Review* p.285.

most obvious example is the thalidomide drug whose teratogenic effect on the unborn foetus was not known about. If it had been, the product would not have been considered safe to use on pregnant mothers. This tragedy prompted the reform movement that led to the Product Liability Directive, but ironically liability might still not be available for similar unknown risks in those Member States adopting the development risks defence.

The General Product Safety Directive provides that in assessing the general safety requirement the state of art and technology should be taken into account.[127] Arguably this encompasses both the state-of-the-art and development risks criteria. In any event, development risks might be captured by the additional relevant factor of taking account of the reasonable expectations concerning safety.[128] In any event, in the safety context even if the general safety requirement is not breached and so, for instance, no criminal or administrative sanction can be imposed it is always of course possible to take remedial action to remove dangerous products.

Most discussion of this issue has centred on product liability, where the distinctions are crucial for liability. State-of-the-art considerations are inherent in the definition of safety itself. This specifically mentions the time when a product is put into circulation as a relevant circumstance.[129] It goes on to provide that a product shall not be considered defective for the sole reason that a better product is subsequently put into circulation.

There is a specific development risks defence, which places the burden of proof on the defendant. In its first proposal the Commission had provided that:

> the producer of an article shall be liable for damage caused by a defect in the article, whether or not he knew or could have known of the defect. The producer shall be liable even if the article could not have been regarded as defective in the light of the scientific and technological development at the time when he put the article into circulation.

The development risks defence was introduced against the wishes of the Commission in response to concerns by some Member States about the liability exposure of high-risk industries. The defence was, however, made optional. Only Finland and Luxemburg chose to drop the defence, but in Spain and Germany it does not apply to certain categories of products – ironically these are high-risk products!

This background to the defence's adoption in the Directive might justify a fairly narrow construction of the defence. Indeed the presence of the defence has been said to justify a strict assessment of defect as development risks considerations are moved from the general assessment and considered in the context of the tightly drawn defence.[130]

127 Art. 3(3)(e).
128 Art. 3(3)(f).
129 Art. 6(1)(c).
130 *A v National Blood Authority* [2001] 3 All ER 289. Although arguably some of the same issues might have been addressed through assessing what reasonable expectations of safety were.

The defence applies where 'the state of scientific and technical knowledge at the time when he put the product into circulation was not such as to enable the existence of the defect to be discovered.'[131]

The scope of the defence has been considered by the CJEU in *Commission v United Kingdom.*[132] This involved a challenge brought by the Commission who argued that the United Kingdom's implementation was overgenerous to defendants. The Consumer Protection Act 1987 provided for a defence where 'the state of scientific and technical knowledge at the relevant time was not such that a producer of products of the same description as the product in question might be expected to have discovered the defect if it had existed in his products while they were under his control'.[133] This seemed overgenerous by introducing the concept of expectation of discoverability (rather than mere discoverability) and by linking the standard to categories of producers. The challenge was unsuccessful, partly because the CJEU felt the Commission should give more time for the courts to determine the scope of the defence. This seems unrealistic given the paucity of product liability case law in general and on development risks in particular. This in turn is explained by the high costs of bringing cases where scientific evidence is in question. Nevertheless, this was an interesting opportunity to test out competing theories of liability. As Mildred nicely puts it, the opposing camps in essence were fighting over whether the defence required 'absolute undiscoverability' or 'undiscoverabilty by reasonable means.'[134]

The CJEU gave some interesting comments on the scope of the defence. One aspect is pro-defendant by introducing the accessibility of knowledge requirement; the other, pro-claimant by defining knowledge to include discoveries not yet necessarily accepted by the majority of the scientific community.

The decision was favourable to defendants by introducing the requirement that the knowledge must have been accessible.[135] The Advocate-General gave the infamous example of an academic paper from Manchuria published in a local scientific journal in Chinese that could not be expected to be known about in the West.[136] This is highly problematic. Accessibility is not mentioned on the face of the Directive. Burton J in *A v National Blood Authority*[137] noted that the Manchuria example may not always work. If the product concerned was one for which

131 Art. 7(1)(e).

132 Case 300/95 *Commission v United Kingdom* [1997] ECR I-2649. See C.Hodges, 'Development risks: Unanswered questions' (1998) 61 *Modern Law Review* p.560, M Mildred and G Howells, "Comment on 'Development risks: Unanswered questions'" (1998) 61 *Modern Law Review* p.570 and G Howells and M Mildred, 'Is European product liability more protective than the Restatement (Third) of Torts: Product liability?' (1998) 65 *Tennessee Law Review* p.9, J Stapleton, 'Products liability in the United Kingdom: The myths of reform' 34 (1999) *Texas International Law Journal* p.45 and C Pugh and M Pilgerstorfer, 'The development risks defence – knowledge, discoverability and creative leaps' (2004) *Journal of Personal Injury Law* p.258.

133 S. 4(1)(e) of the Consumer Protection Act 1987.

134 M Mildred, 'The development risks defence' in D.Fairgrieve (ed) *Product Liability in Comparative Perspective* (Cambridge University Press, 2005), p.170.

135 Paragraphs 28–29.

136 Paragraphs 23.

137 [2001] 3 All ER 289 at 326.

Manchuria was renowned then research in that country might be highly relevant. He preferred the example of an unpublished document or unpublished research not available to the general public. However, that in itself raises the thorny issue of internal research. Especially in the pharmaceutical industry, producers are most likely to be the ones at the forefront of discoveries about the substances they use. Can they take advantage of the defence by simply keeping their research inaccessible to the public? In such circumstances they may well be liable in negligence, but it seems irrational not also to hold them liable under the Directive.

The CJEU decision was more favourable to claimants by holding that the Directive is concerned with the most advanced level of knowledge.[138] It followed the lead of the Advocate-General, who was clear that although scientific discoveries may at first be criticised and viewed as being unreliable, they should nevertheless remove the defence even though the goods were supplied before this knowledge had become generally accepted. He stressed that one isolated opinion can prevent a defendant from facing an unforeseeable risk. It was then for the defendant to decide how to react to that risk.[139] Stapleton has criticised this aspect of the judgment as she believes that to qualify as knowledge it should be tested against consideration of whose ideas are relevant and the weight to be afforded. She seems to suggest that at least a respectable minority opinion is needed.[140] Pugh and Pilgerstorfer criticise Stapleton's approach and suggest she is attempting to read common-law values into the judgment and prefer to place emphasis on the Advocate-General's desire to include all quantifiable risks, which they stress he did not require to be reasonably quantifiable.[141] However, this leaves the question of what is quantifiable? The concept of expert in the field might be used and it is not unrealistic to use this as a measure of whether something was knowledge, even if its value was not fully recognised at the time. Normally this would defeat the defence once a credible source had introduced new knowledge, but would assuage the fears of Stapleton that producers might have liability imposed simply because they had not taken account of the random musings of a discredited mystic.[142] This would not prevent the defence being defeated in most cases once some questions had been raised in the scientific literature.

Once knowledge is available the defence is removed. That is why the development risks defence is not available for manufacturing defects. The German Supreme Court[143] rejected the application of the defence to manufacturing defects in a case concerning a refillable mineral water bottle that exploded. Burton J in *A v National Blood Authority*[144] thought the only exception might

138 Para 26.
139 Tesauro AG at paras 21–22.
140 J Stapleton, 'Products liability in the United Kingdom: The myths of reform' (1999) 34 *Texas International Law Journal* p.59.
141 C Pugh and M Pilgerstorfer, 'The development risks defence – knowledge, discoverability and creative leaps' (2004) *Journal of Personal Injury Law* p.258.
142 J Stapleton, 'Products liability in the United Kingdom: The myths of reform' (1999) 34 *Texas International Law Journal* p.61.
143 (1995) NJW 2162.
144 (2001) 3 All ER 289 at para 77.

be for the first time such a defect arose. The rationale for not providing the defence for manufacturing defects, even where quality control systems do not exist of sufficient quality to detect the defect, is arguably that such failures are generally calculable and therefore represent the sort of socialisation of risk that strict product liability was intended to embrace. This approach is likely to prevail, but it does highlight the clumsy wording of the defence, which talks about enabling the existence of the defect to be discovered rather than just the defect *per se*. It also explains why the defence does not apply in situations such as in *A v National Blood Authority*, where the risk of a defect is known, but cannot be detected. By contrast, the Dutch decision in *Scholten v The Foundation Sanquin of Blood Supply*[145] held blood was not defective, because there was no way of ascertaining if it contained a known risk. The Australian decision of *Graham Barclay Oysters Pty v Ryan*[146] had also required the defect to be discoverable in the particular product (oysters), but was based on the different wording of the Australian law, which made it clear it had to be discoverable in the particular product.

A Commission study by the Fondazione Rosselli concluded that the defence should be maintained as an important contribution to balancing the interests of producers and consumers. It proposed developing alternative compensation schemes for victims of development risks.[147] There has clearly been concern at the differing interpretations given to the defence in national courts. Many of the decisions have restricted its scope, but some including one by the French Court of Appeal have been more lenient and allowed the defence even for a known risk where there was no consensus on whether it should be warned against.[148]

Enforcement

Product liability

Product liability is private law and is enforced through individual or collective consumer claims before the courts. There has been some increase in legal cases being brought, but the level varies widely across Europe with Austria perhaps leading the way due to the support its consumer organisation gives to bring claims. It has been relevant to high-profile scandals like infected blood[149] and PIP

145 Rb Amsterdam 3 February 1999, NJ 1999, 621.

146 102 FCR 307.

147 *Analysis of the Economic Impact of the Development Risks Clause as Provided by Directive 85/374/EEC on Liability for Defective Products* (2004) available at http://ec.europa.eu/enterprise/regulation/goods/docs/liability/2004–06-dev-risk-clause-study_en.pdf.

148 Cour d'Appel (Court of Appeal) Paris, 23 September 2004L No 02/16712 (2005) D 1012. This decision seems wrong and was in any event was overturned by the Cour de Cassation Cass civ 1e, 15 May 2007, No 05-10.234 (2007) D 1592 because the defence did not apply as the Directive had not been implemented in France at the relevant time.

149 G Howells and M Mildred, 'Infected blood: Defect and discoverability a first exposition of the EC Product Liability Directive' (2002) 65 *Modern Law Review* p.95.

breast implant litigation.[150] Often strict product liability is only one element of the litigation given the continued existence of alternative national laws[151] and the need to engage with other issues such as potential liability of regulators. There has also been some substantial litigation in the field of pharmaceuticals, but it has been argued that many of the claims brought on a regular basis are for small value.[152] Strict product liability seems to have become accepted, possibly, because it has not impacted too seriously on business risks. Having struck a balance in a politically sensitive area the Commission seems willing to leave well alone with its reports on the topic being fairly brief and essentially noting issues but preferring simply to monitor them.[153] It forms part of tort law and on a daily basis it is now a matter for personal injury lawyers. The development of a Community class action procedure that makes more product liability litigation viable when large numbers of consumers are affected may be a higher priority for the private practice lawyers.

Product safety

The General Product Safety Directive has been very important in promoting a more consistent approach to product safety. States are charged with ensuring that only safe products are on the market and are required to have a responsible authority to ensure compliance.[154] Regulation (EC) No 765/2008[155] was adopted partly to strengthen the controls on consumer products posing serious risks. It includes rules on the organisation of market surveillance and co-operation both between national bodies and between them and the Commission,[156] the market surveillance measures they should take,[157] how serous product risks should be addressed[158] and rules on restrictive measures taken[159] and exchange of information.[160] The Regulation does not prevent more specific measures being taken under the General Product Safety Directive.[161] It is proposed that the Commission should have a stronger role in monitoring the funding of national authorities and

150 B Van Leeuwen, 'PIP breast implants, the EU's new approach for goods and market surveillance by notified bodies' (2013) 5 *European Journal of Risk Regulation* p.338.

151 Lovells, *Product Liability in the European Union: A Report for the European Commission*, February 2003, Markt/2001/11/D.

152 T Fox, *Questioning the Social Desirability of Product Liability Claims*, Phd 2015 University of Exeter available at https://ore.exeter.ac.uk/repository/handle/10871/18742; accessed 22 July 2016.

153 Several official reports on the Directive have been issued: *First Report*: COM (95) 617 final; *Second Report*: COM (2000) 893 final; *Third Report*: COM (2006) 496 final. *Fourth Report*: COM (2011) 547 final.

154 Art. 6.

155 OJ 2008 L 218/30.

156 Arts 17–18 and 23–26.

157 Art. 19.

158 Art. 20.

159 Art. 21.

160 Arts. 22–23.

161 Art. 15(3).

work plans to ensure that enforcement is at an effective level throughout the Community.[162] This is important so that harmonisation is effective in practice as well as in theory.

States are required to give authorities a range of powers to both monitor the market and to take action with respect to products that pose risks.[163] Products can be subject to a duty to warn if they pose risks in certain conditions [164] or for certain persons.[165] Other prior conditions can also be imposed if the product poses risks in certain conditions.[166] Potentially dangerous products can be banned temporarily.[167] Dangerous products can be banned,[168] those on the market ordered to be withdrawn[169] and those already in the hands of consumers recalled.[170] Authorities are required to act in a proportionate manner taking due account of the precautionary principle and to encourage and promote voluntary action by producers and distributors.[171]

The 1992 and 2001 Directives had adopted a bifurcated notification procedure. Serious risks are notified under the Community Rapid Information System (RAPEX) procedure.[172] Less serious or localised actions taken by enforcement authorities are handled under a separate procedure. Under the Market Surveillance Regulation Proposal 2013 RAPEX will become the sole notification procedure for all risks, but it will not cover situations where the effects of risk do not go beyond the Member State.

Possibly the most important change in the relationship between regulator and industry arose from the duty imposed by the 2001 Directive on producers and distributors to notify enforcement authorities of any of their products that pose risks to consumers because they are incompatible with the general safety requirement.[173] The Commission developed Guidelines on when notification is necessary and how it should be made.[174] The current rules include an 'isolated circumstances' exemption. Under the reform package this will be replaced by exemptions where only a limited number of well-identified products are not safe; it can be demonstrated that the risk has been fully controlled and cannot any more endanger the health and safety of persons or the cause of the risk is such that knowledge of it does not represent useful information for the authorities or public.[175]

162 COM (2013) 78 final.
163 Art. 8–9.
164 Art. 8(1)(b)(i).
165 Art. 8(1)(c).
166 Art. 81(b)(ii).
167 Art. 8(1)(d).
168 Art. 8(1)(e).
169 Art. 8(1)(f)(i).
170 Art. 8 (1)(f) (ii).
171 Art. 8(2).
172 In 2001 Directive see Arts. 11 and 12 and Annex 2.
173 Art. 5(3) and Annex I.
174 Available at http://europa.eu.int/comm/consumers/cons_safe/prod_safe/gpsd/notification_dang_en.pdf.
175 Art. 13(1).

The 1992 and 2001 Directives provided a procedure for Community decisions valid for up to a year to be made where there were serious risks and Member States took different approaches.[176] This time limit has, however, proven problematic.[177] The Market Surveillance Regulation Proposal 2013 would provide the means to act against products presenting a serious risk.

Enforcement is currently spread across three instruments: (i) the General Product Safety Directive, (ii) Regulation (EC) No 765/2008[178] setting out the requirements for accreditation and market surveillance relating to the marketing of products, and (ii) sector-specific legislation (which increasingly refers to Decision No 768/2008/EC 2008 on a common framework for the marketing of products).[179] This tripartite system was criticised by the Schaldemose EU Parliament *Report on the Revision of the General Product Safety Directive and Market Surveillance*.[180]

The Market Surveillance Regulation Proposal 2013 is the EU's response. It seeks to ensure that as far as possible the same controls are applied to all products whether consumer or non-consumer, harmonised or non-harmonised. The Market Surveillance Regulation Proposal 2013 is mainly aimed at public authorities. It sets out the duties of market surveillance authorities, the powers they should have to require economic operators to take action and the power they should have to act themselves. It provides the Union with the power to assess measures taken at national level with regard to harmonised legislation in order to decide whether the measure is justified and therefore should be applied throughout the Union or unjustified and in need of being withdrawn. The RAPEX provisions will be included in this measure.[181] It also provides for maintaining an information and communication system for market surveillance (ICMS)[182] and for exchange of confidential information with third countries and international organisations.[183] There are provisions for co-operation and mutual assistance[184] central to which is the European Market Surveillance Forum.[185] The Commission can also assist by designating Union reference laboratories for specific products, categories or groups of products.[186] It also has powers to finance activities assisting enforcement.[187]

176 Germany unsuccessfully challenged this: *Germany v Council*, Case C-359/92 (1994) ECR I-3681.

177 European Commission, *More Product Safety and Better Market Surveillance in the Single Market for Products*, COM (2013) 74 final.

178 OJ 2008 L 218/30.

179 OJ 2008 L 218/82.

180 24 Feb 2011, A7-0033/2011. See G Howells, 'Product safety - a model for EU legislation and reform'. in K Purnhagen and P Rott (eds), *Varieties of European Economic Law and Regulation*, (Springer, 2014).

181 Arts. 19 and 20.

182 Art. 21.

183 Art. 22.

184 Arts 23–24.

185 Art. 25.

186 Art. 28.

187 Art. 29.

Way forward

It is noticeable that the General Product Safety Directive has been revised substantially, whereas there has been a lack of enthusiasm to engage with Product Liability Directive reform that is marked. The Commission has recently put forward a further package of reforms in the product safety field aimed at ensuring a more harmonised and coherent approach to market surveillance generally. The inclusion of a country of origin requirement has proven to be devisive and has stalled the reform's progress. It is not directly related to safety and should be less necessary if overall the controls are strengthened in practice across the Community. Member States should press forward with the proposed reforms that relate to safety and enforcement.

The reluctance to address product liability reform may be understandable given the lack of vocal criticism of the regime, which can be seen as relatively protective by international standards. Nevertheless, the Directive is built on a compromise and there is a need for guidance on how the balance of apportioning risk should be carried out. The parties are operating in the shadow of the law and that often gives business tactical advantages as they can decide which cases to test to the full in the courts. There needs to be some way in which a consensus can develop about the about the way risk is apportioned and the role of socialisation of risk in that apportionment. Many issues are also left open by the wording of the directive and are not answered authoritatively by the case law or else are answered in different ways by the courts of the various Member States. The ambiguity is not merely around the core defectiveness concept. Some of the unsettled issues can be very technical; such as whether the first 500 euro threshold for property damage is a deduction or threshold allowing full recovery once exceeded. National legislation give different interpretations. Core concepts such as 'being put into circulation' have also caused problems. Elsewhere it has been argued that such guidance might come from soft law.[188] The ongoing evaluation of the Directive may be an opportunity for some clarification to be provided, and it seems this may be driven by the need to adapt to the digital economy.[189]

This is an area where Europe has been able to export its legal ideas. Mainly this has been in the area of product liability, but also product safety rules have been taken up in many states. The CE marking is recognised in international trade as a symbol that represents the EU's commitment to ensure its products meet high technical standards. In specific sectors the EU rules have also had influence. For example, the Cosmetics Directive[190] was the model for the first step at harmonisation within ASEAN. It is noticeable that the EU is less well developed in relation to services. Service liability and safety is an area warranting more attention.

188 D Fairgrieve, G Howells and M Pilgerstorfer, 'The Product Liability Directive: Time to get soft?' (2013) 4 *Journal of European Tort Law* p.1.

189 Directive 76/768/EEC on the approximation of the laws of the Member States relating to cosmetic products (1976) OJ L 262/169, since replaced by Regulation 1223/2009 on cosmetic products (2009) OJ L 342/59.

190 Evaluation of the Directive 85/374/EEC concerning liability for defective products (http://ec.europa.eu/smart-regulation/roadmaps/docs/2016_grow_027_evaluation_defective_products_en.pdf) [accessed 24 May 2017].

8 EU consumer access to justice and enforcement

Introduction[1]

General introduction

As other chapters in this book demonstrate, recent decades have seen the development of a significant body of substantive consumer laws. A frequent complaint in many countries is the gap between the law in books and the law in practice. This arises where there are insufficient institutions, resources and powers to enforce the public laws regulating traders' conduct in the marketplace and individuals have the lack of capacity or motivation to invoke their private law rights through the courts. Consumer protection regimes tend to rely on a complex web of public regulation, private regulation and self-regulation.

Attention is now turning to how these consumer rights can be made effective given the particular problems facing consumers, notably their typical lack of expertise and the low value of their claims making them reluctant to engage professionals or venture much effort or expense in seeking to remedy the problem. However, given mass consumption, small individual losses can represent significant gains to traders and those behaving badly can gain an unfair advantage over traders who comply with their legal obligations. Within the EU Member States there are various mixes of public, private and regulatory redress mechanisms. EU policy itself adopts a pluralist approach building on different traditions. The EU has taken some steps to promote certain key elements of reform at the national level, e.g. supporting public law enforcement, developing injunctions as a form of redress and promoting alternative dispute resolution (ADR). For the most part though it has concentrated on ameliorating the additional barriers consumers and the enforcers of consumer law face in the cross-border context.

1 Parts of this chapter are based on 'Consumer Law Enforcement and Access to Justice' in C Twigg-Flesner (ed), *Research Handbook on EU Consumer and Contract Law* (Edward Elgar, 2017).

Chapter themes

New emphasis on enforcement

A central theme of the book is that the EU is giving more emphasis to enforcement.[2] This chapter concentrates on that theme. In contrast to many areas of substantive law where domestic and cross-border transactions are normally subject to the same rules, the EU has often created parallel regimes specifically to address cross-border aspects of access to justice and enforcement. This has been justified by the need to address practical features of cross-border disputes e.g. the desire for clarity in rules of private international law or the need for special procedures not to impose unduly on national procedural autonomy.

Use of soft law

Soft-law instruments have been frequently used in this area. The EU Recommendation on collective redress[3] is aimed at prompting national-level reflection on good practice. There are also examples in this area of the EU using soft law to develop consensus and as a precursor to binding legislation. In the ADR field, for instance, there were first recommendations[4] prior to the EU adopting binding legislation.[5]

Cross-border dimension

Ironically, the need for special cross-border rules on access to justice and enforcement has been created by the push to increase cross-border trade. The risks of more difficult enforcement of consumer law in the cross-border context is not something the EU always focuses on as it can detract from its goal of promoting the internal market. Yet there is certainly a downside in terms of enforcement and access to justice from increased cross-border trade. This has been recognised by the EU increasing its emphasis on developing redress and enforcement mechanisms. Many of the EU measures have focused on cross-border disputes. This has meant there has been a lot of regulatory activity in this field at the EU level in comparison to the very small number of actual cross-border sales that are problematic. This makes an assessment of these initiatives difficult given the marginal impact they will have in any event due to the limited scale of the problem they are addressing.

2 See Chapter 1 at pp.10–11.
3 Commission Recommendation on common principles for injunctive and compensatory collective redress mechanisms in the Member States concerning violations of rights granted under Union Law (2013) OJ L201/60.
4 Commission Recommendation on the principles for out-of-court bodies involved in the consensual resolution of consumer disputes (2001) OJ L109/2001; Commission Recommendation 98/257/EC on the principles applicable to the bodies responsible for out-of-court settlement of consumer disputes (1998) OJ L115/31.
5 Directive 2013/11/EU on alternative dispute resolution for consumer (2013) OJ L165/63.

No one-size-fits-all European model

There has, to date, not been the development of a particular European brand of consumer protection enforcement and redress. National consumer regimes are a mix of regulation, private law and self-regulation; with the exact mix varying from state to state. At the EU level the same elements are present.

Market regulation is seen as important by the EU, with an important development being the requirement for Member States to establish consumer protection agencies[6] and to furnish them with effective powers. The use of injunctions (and associated undertakings) is probably the most distinctive contribution of the EU legislature to consumer enforcement. Private enforcement is also seen as having a role to play, but the EU has failed fully to grasp the nettle on collective redress,[7] and has favoured alternative dispute resolution/on-line dispute resolution (ADR/ODR).[8] Europe has not created new ADR mechanisms, but has sought to build a framework around existing national bodies. It has for example established an ODR platform.[9] ODR is an obvious choice for resolving disputes in the e-commerce cross-border context. However, it may be useful to reflect that not all cross-border solutions may be models for the domestic context. For example, traditional forms of ADR or small claims courts might be more effective in some circumstances.

Consumer enforcement – general points

The access to justice movement

Most of this book has been about the substantive EU consumer law *acquis.* This is fairly well developed. However, unless there is to be a cavern between the law in the books and the law in practice, consumers, consumer groups and regulators must be able to make use of the law. The EU has for some time recognised the importance of effective consumer redress and enforcement.[10] In recent times, this has been given an increased emphasis and we anticipate work in this area will continue to be a major focus of EU activity going forward.[11] The EU identified at an early stage that consumer redress needed a range of solutions. This is in line with the famous 1970s study of Cappelletti and Garth, who described three waves of the access to justice movement: first, providing access to the law to the poor i.e. the legal-aid movement; second, protecting collective 'diffuse interests'; and

6 Below, p.322.
7 Below, pp.308–310.
8 Below, pp.311–318.
9 Below, pp.315–318.
10 European Commission, *Access of Consumers to Justice and the Settlements of Consumer Disputes in the Single Market* COM (93) 576 final; Commission, *Action Plan on Consumer Access to Justice and the Settlement of Consumer Disputes in the Internal Market* COM (96) 13 final.
11 European Commission, *A European Consumer Agenda – Boosting Confidence and Growth* COM (2012) 225 final, sections 3.4 and 4.3; and Regulation 254/2014/EU on a multi-annual consumer programme for the years 2014–2020 (2014) OJ L 84/42, Art. 3(1)(c).

the third 'access to justice approach' that adopts alternatives such as small claims procedures and ADR.[12] The EU has considered or adopted measures that can be linked to each of these three waves.

Special nature of consumer problems

A Eurobarometer in 2004 showed that over three-quarters of consumers never complained or only did so rarely.[13] Many consumer claims are for small value and are fairly straightforward. They are normally resolved by the consumer simply complaining and obtaining redress directly from the trader.[14] Legal instruments like commercial guarantees can play a role in promoting such informal dispute resolution,[15] but the law plays a limited role in such private negotiations. For many consumer disputes the transactions costs involved compared to the amounts at stake make litigation (at least by traditional means) impracticable.[16] The 2004 Eurobarometer survey found, that of the minority of consumers who complained, a very small minority (13%) actually took a case to court. This can be considered a rational attitude, because it has even been said that to litigate a consumer needs to have 'super-spite'.[17]

Consumers with cross-border disputes face additional problems. They may need to negotiate with traders at a distance, operate in foreign languages and be subject to foreign laws and the jurisdiction of the trader's courts. Private international law is meant to address the last set of issues, but the difficulties faced by consumers in dealing with private international law serves to highlight the vulnerability of their position. Private international law is very complex and expensive to litigate. The mere raising of a private international law issue probably makes most consumer claims too expensive to justify litigating. A 1995 study had found that 10% of cross-border consumers had been dissatisfied and of these a third had successfully complained. However, it was not considered reasonable to pursue a claim for only 2000 ECU at that time (some three decades ago).[18] Lawyers might advise consumers to bring claims if the dispute was for over 50,000 ECU, but up to that level costs may still equal the amount claimed.[19]

12 M Cappelletti and B Garth, *Access to Justice* (Sijthoff and Noordhoff, 1978–1979).

13 European Opinion Research Group, *European Union Citizens and Access to Justice – Special Eurobarometer 195* (Commission 2004), p.9, http://medsos.gr/medsos/images/stories/PDF/eurobarometer_11-04_en.pdf [accessed 1 March 2016].

14 Ibid., p.11.

15 C Twigg-Flesner, *Consumer Product Guarantees* (Ashgate, 2003).

16 M Olson, *The Logic of Collective Action* (Harvard UP, 1971).

17 A Leff, 'Injury, Ignorance and spite – the dynamics of coercive collection'. *Yale LJ* 80 (1970), p.1.

18 H von Freyhold, V Gessner, EL Vial and H Wagner (eds), *Cost of Judicial Barriers for Consumers in the Single Market* (Zentrum für Europaïsche Rechtspolitik an der Universität Bremen, 1995) at pp.392–393, http://aei.pitt.edu/37274/1/A3244.pdf [accessed 30 November 2015].

19 B Feldtmann, H von Freyhold and EL Vial, *The Cost of Legal Obstacles to the Disadvantage of Consumers in the Single Market* (von Freyhold, Vial & Partner Consultants, June 1998), pp.2 and 276, http://www.freyvial.de/Publications/egii-42.pd [accessed 30 November 2015].

Public enforcement and private redress

Consumer law enforcement is further complicated as it serves two distinct functions – providing individual consumers with remedies when things go wrong and regulating the market to prevent harm by removing rogue traders and bad practices. The former, often called consumer redress, is often associated with the access to justice agenda; the latter deals with public consumer regulation. However, the two are intertwined. Litigation (especially collective litigation), although primarily about compensation can affect the conduct of traders. Judgments can set standards of behaviour and the threat of costly litigation can deter traders from infringing the law. Equally, public enforcement can pave the way for redress. This may be through a formal procedure, as with the French *action civile*, where parties can join criminal actions, or by regulators seeking redress for consumers. This may also be by a follow-on civil action as often occurs in competition law. Equally, regulatory action can simply provide the evidence for consumers to bring claims or provide political muscle to bring about settlements.

Philosophy of access to justice – courts, ADR and regulatory enforcement

There have been attempts in many national legal systems to make courts and their procedures more consumer friendly and to reduce the costs to consumers of accessing the courts through the introduction of small claims procedures for claims below certain monetary limits.[20] Their success has varied. Even though there has been a small claims scheme introduced for cross-border disputes at the EU level the practical difficulties of suing across borders remain. This has concentrated attention on ADR[21] and ODR, the latter having obvious potential in the cross-border context and the on-line selling environment. However, the risk with ADR is that the individual problems may be resolved, but the law's formal development remains immune from the real-world problems. These are resolved in private and confidential fora. Some ADR schemes have sought to redress this problem by publicising decisions. Some ADR schemes have even been able to deal with class claims.

The largest philosophical difference is between those legal systems where the private law (taken to include ADR) is used to resolve both individual problems and to regulate the market and those systems where regulators have prime responsibility to ensure fair market practices. The former is typified by the US where due to punitive damages and class actions, public interest litigation plays an

20 J Stuyck, E Terryn, V Colaert, T Van Dyck, N Peretz, N Hoekx and P Tereszkiewicz, *An Analysis and Evaluation of Alternative Means of Consumer Redress Other than Redress through Ordinary Judicial Proceedings* (The Study Centre for Consumer Law – Centre for European Economic Law, 2007) http://www.eurofinas.org/uploads/documents/policies/OTHER%20POLICY%20ISSUES/comparative_report_en.pdf [accessed 12 July 2016].

21 For a survey of schemes see: Stuyck et al. (above), and C Hodges, I Benöhr, and N Creutzfeldt-Banda, *Consumer ADR in Europe* (Hart/Beck, 2012).

important role.[22] Although some European states have forms of collective redress procedures, none have as strong a private litigation culture as the US. Such litigation has at times been encouraged by the Commission, but in the consumer protection field, progress has been cautious and legislative measures have been restricted to soft-law measures.

In many EU states regulators have played an important role in market surveillance. The EU has sought to strengthen the role of national regulators, not least to ensure the Commission has contact points to perform the various co-ordination tasks required by EU law.

However, the regulatory traditions vary between states. In many of the new Member States there were limited regulatory structures, or more accurately regulators that were poorly financed so that they were unable to cope with the workload. By contrast, some of the richer European states have strong relatively well-resourced regulators. Here one thinks in particular of the Nordic Ombudsmen, the UK's Consumer Markets Authority, which superseded the Office of Fair Trading, and the DGCCRF in France. These all have different flavours and indeed in some systems like the UK have complex internal relationships with local or regional regulators, such as trading standards officers. In Germany, the main enforcement is carried out by local regulators in the Länder, but state-financed consumer organisations also play an important role.

Consumer organisations have also been given a role in enforcing consumer laws at the EU level. Their nature varies.[23] In Austria and Germany they have government funding and are central to the state's regulatory structures as they enforce the laws by bringing injunction actions. In other states they are well-funded, large-membership organisations.[24] In some states they can be numerous small consumer groups. The task is to find criteria to ensure only those with a sufficient general public role have standing to engage in enforcement. Consumer organisations also need to consider how best to co-operate and co-ordinate with government regulators.

State regulation might seem to imply use of the criminal and administrative law. There are certainly many instances when breach of consumer law in many states will lead to criminal sanctions or administrative fines.[25] Particularly for serious and/or deliberate breaches of the law this may be justified, but often the authorities prefer to find softer ways of educating traders about their obligations. Braithwaite's regulatory pyramid model has become popular. It counsels in favour of initial interventions being at the base level of education and persuasion

22 G Howells and T Wilhelmsson, 'EC and US approaches to consumer protection – should the gap be bridged?' (1997) *Yearbook of European Law* p.207.

23 The European Consumers Organisation (BEUC) is the umbrella organisation http://www.beuc.eu/topics [accessed 12 July 2016].

24 Such as *Which?* in the UK; UFC Que Choisir in France, Test-Achats in Belgium and Consumentenbond in the Netherlands.

25 See e.g. P Cartwright, *Consumer Protection and Criminal Law* (Cambridge University Press, 2001).

to comply with the law and only a gradual escalation to more serious sanctions.[26] The Nordic Ombudsmen, for example, often work with traders to find self-regulatory solutions and many regulators (including the European Commission) issue guidance notes[27] and rely on undertakings to curb bad practices. Undertakings may be used as part of procedures that can lead to injunctions. The use of the injunction as a regulatory tool has been a key feature of EU law; and of course consumer organisations have to rely on it as they cannot invoke administrative or criminal sanctions. Injunctions are civil law remedies and they blur the private law/regulatory divide. In some countries injunctions might be seen as the typical armoury of the state, even if they are available in the civil courts. The same blurring of lines is true about moves to promote restorative justice by giving powers to regulators and the courts to provide redress to consumers when they have suffered harm from breach of regulatory law.

The debates about the balance and relationship between private redress and public regulation, how best to reflect the collective dimension of many consumer disputes, and frequent lack of incentive for individual consumers to litigate have been intensely debated at the national level in recent years. The EU dimension adds an added layer of complication.

Cross-border solutions

In most areas of consumer law the impact of EU law has been to prompt law reform, which has applied to national and cross-border disputes alike. In parts of the substantive law, notably in relation to sales law, a gradual shift of focus has taken place with recent proposals specifically addressing on-line or cross-border transactions.[28] By contrast many EU initiatives on redress and enforcement have restricted themselves to providing parallel regimes addressing the particular problems caused when seeking redress or enforcement across borders. However, in recent times, there has been some movement in favour of access to justice solutions that apply to all transactions whether domestic or cross-border. The ADR Directive,[29] for

26 The model was first put forward in J Braithwaite, *To Punish or Persuade: Enforcement of Coal Mine Safety* (State University of New York Press, 1985). See important work of I Ayres and J Braithwaite, *Responsive Regulation: Transcending the Deregulation Debate*, (Oxford University Press, 1992).

27 See e.g. Commission, *Guidance on the Implementation/Application of Directive 2005/29/EC on Unfair Commercial Practices* SEC (2009) 1666; Directorate General Health and Consumer Protection, *Guidance Document on the Relationship Between the General Product Safety Directive (GPSD) and Certain Sector Directives with Provisions on Product Safety* (November 2003) http://ec.europa.eu/consumers/cons_safe/prod_safe/gpsd/guidance_gpsd_en.pdf [accessed 1 March 2016]; Directorate General Health and Consumer Protection, *Guidance Document on the Relationship between the General Product Safety Directive (GPSD) and Certain Sector Directives with Provisions on Product Safety* (DG SANCO, November 2005) http://ec.europa.eu/consumers/cons_safe/prod_safe/gpsd/gpsd_2ndchapiter_en.pdf [accessed 1 March 2016].

28 See Chapter 1, pp.9–10 and Chapter 5, pp.201–206.

29 Directive 2013/11/EU.

example, requires ADR be available for any dispute with a trader established in the state's territory. ADR stands to some extent outside the core of national procedural law. The EU is conscious of the procedural autonomy afforded to national legal orders and this explains its hesitant approach to matters touching purely national court procedures. Whilst the consistent development of law for domestic and cross-border disputes is generally to be preferred, these special rules for access to justice measures are not particularly problematic. For the most part, they simply seek to overcome the problems caused by the cross-border element.

The recognition that cross-border trade poses unique challenges for consumers that need specific remedial measures is an important concession by the EU. The Commission is well aware that the lack of effective means of redress is one of the most telling reasons why consumers are unwilling to shop across borders. It can do little directly about language barriers or distance, but it can seek to ameliorate the impact of disputes occurring across legal and national boundaries. It seeks to adopt measures that allow consumers to gain access to justice easier and ensure regulators and consumer organisations can control errant traders from exploiting national boundaries as barriers to effective regulatory control. Parallel national and cross-border substantive law regimes can be criticised for making the law over-complex. This is often not the case with parallel enforcement and access to justice rules. Very often these procedural rules simply make the process simpler for those seeking to enforce the law across borders. However, there are issues relating to the awareness of such rules. As there are in practice so few instances when the rules have been invoked, participants in the procedures – including court staff, ADR system administrators and regulators – may well not be conversant with the special characteristics of the procedures.

Ensuring effective redress and enforcement procedures take account of the needs of cross-border consumers is important as a means of giving consumers the confidence to shop across borders. However, it is necessary to recognise that the best these rules can do is ameliorate the problems caused by shopping across borders. Rationally, consumers should factor this detriment into any decision to shop in other Member States. All things being equal, shopping closer to home must be preferable and of course more environmentally friendly.

One disadvantage of the EU approach of grafting on special rules for cross-border consumers is that it can leave untouched national systems of varying effectiveness. However, effective redress and enforcement at the domestic level is also important if businesses across Europe are to have a level playing field. Of course the law should be applied without discrimination to all parties regardless of nationality. However, beyond that the impact of consumer law depends upon a combination of factors relating to the strength of the substantive law: the likelihood that breach will be detected and enforcement action taken or that consumers will seek and obtain redress, and the sanctions available. Strong laws, which are hardly ever invoked, or which only lead to mild sanctions, will have less impact than the same laws in states where consumers and regulators can easily invoke the laws and obtain effective redress and sanctions. Court systems that are expensive or take a long time to deliver justice can effectively deny justice.[30] Equally if regulators have few powers or resources regulation is fairly meaningless.

EU soft-law initiatives may have an impact on Member States and cause them to also develop better solutions in the domestic context. The establishment of consumer-friendly, cross-border regimes might also inspire domestic reform. Hence, for instance, if a small claims procedure is introduced for cross-border disputes, one would hope that within the national legal order there would be a debate about whether domestic procedures should offer at-least-as-good solutions for purely domestic disputes. The proposal in the proposed Market Surveillance Regulation 2013 in the context of product safety is that authorities draw up enforcement plans, including details on resources, so that the Commission can monitor the level of practical enforcement. This is a very positive move that should help ensure higher minimum standards.

Legal basis

The EU is aware of the need for judicial co-operation. Art. 2 of the Treaty on European Union and Art. 67 of the Treaty on the Functioning of the European Union provides that the Union shall constitute an area of freedom, security and justice with respect for fundamental rights and the different legal systems and traditions of the Member States. As regards civil matters, Art. 81 of the Treaty on the Functioning of the European Union provides for judicial co-operation in civil matters having cross-border implications. Many of the measures adopted by the EU are related to ensuring the mutual recognition of judgments and extra-judicial decisions and the surrounding procedures. But the Treaty also mentions promoting effective access to justice and the development of alternative methods of dispute resolution.[31] Where criminal matters are involved there are similar powers to promote co-operation.[32] Article 47 of the Charter of Fundamental Rights of the European Union provides there should be access to a remedy, a fair trial and in appropriate cases legal aid. Article 2 of the Treaty on European Union also provides that Member States shall provide remedies sufficient to ensure effective legal protection in the fields covered by Union law. Many of the measures discussed below draw upon these provisions as their legal base instead of or in addition to internal market or consumer protection Treaty provisions. However, some important measures such as the ADR Directive and ODR Regulation base themselves on Art. 114 the internal market provision and the support of consumer protection rather than on the civil justice provisions.

30 Lord Dyson, *Delay Too Often Defeats Justice* (The Law Society, Magna Carta Event, 22 April 2015), pp.6–10, https://www.judiciary.gov.uk/wp-content/uploads/2015/04/law-society-magna-carta-lecture.pdf [accessed 23 March 2016].

31 Arts. 81(e) and (g) TFEU.

32 Art. 82 TFEU.

Choice of legal instrument

The choices of legal instrument in this area have been interesting. Directives have been used sometimes, but frequently Regulations have been preferred either in the private international law field, presumably to provide increased certainty, or because distinct free-standing procedures or institutions have been set up – such as those for European small claims[33] and the ODR platform.[34] In some areas the EU has hesitated to go beyond issuing Recommendations, for instance, as regards consumer collective redress. With respect to ADR, the Commission treaded tentatively: first, adopting soft-law measures before moving on to legislation. This can be a useful model for other areas of law so that a greater consensus can be developed around principles before Member States are forced to comply with them.

General principles of equivalence and effectiveness

Our focus is on the EU laws establishing mechanisms for promoting consumer redress and enhancing enforcement. However, the importance of the general principles requiring national law to provide equivalent protection for EU laws as for national laws and ensuring effective protection should be remembered.[35]

The *Alassini*[36] case involved the review of a provision of Italian telecommunications law requiring users first to use a mandatory ADR procedure before being allowed access to courts. The CJEU noted that the principle of effectiveness might be impeded by this requirement, but noted restrictions could be allowed if they pursued the general objective of promoting out-of-court settlement of disputes and were not disproportionate. It noted that the procedure was non-binding, involved no fee, suspended any time-bars and did not involve substantive delay as it was required to be completed within 30 days. However, it required the national court to investigate whether complaints could only be submitted by electronic means and whether interim measures were possible, as the absence of non-electronic procedures and interim measures might allow the mandatory procedure to be challenged.

In *Aziz*,[37] national law was found to breach the effectiveness principle. The national procedural rules for enforcing mortgages did not allow a court handling the issues of unfairness of the mortgage terms to provide interim relief. Thus the law was helpless to prevent the debtor from being evicted whilst the matter was being resolved.[38]

33 See Regulation 861/2007/EC establishing a European Small Claims Procedure (2007) OJ L199/1.

34 See Regulation 524/2013/EU on on-line dispute resolution for consumer disputes (2013) L165/2013.

35 N Reich, 'Legal protection of individual and collective consumer interests' in N Reich and others, *European Consumer Law* (Intersentia, 2014).

36 C-317/08 *Rosalba Alassini v Telecom Italia SpA* (*The Alassini*) [2010] ECR I-2213.

37 C-415/11 *Aziz v Caixa d'Estalvis de Catalunya* [2013] 3 CMLR 5.

38 For other cases in this vein, see Chapter 4, pp.154–162.

The principle of effectiveness also lies behind why EU competition law gives harmed parties the right to seek damages.[39] Consumers may be able to take advantage of such claims, most likely by bringing follow-on damages actions when a substantive breach of competition law has been established. However, most of the substantive consumer rules provide for their own methods of redress and enforcement. It is unlikely, for instance, that a damages claim for unfair commercial practices will be required to make the Unfair Commercial Practices Directive's protection effective. The Directive itself foresees other means of providing effective enforcement. To be truly effective, consumer remedies will require a collective redress mechanism, as most consumer losses will be small. It is unlikely a class action procedure will not be found necessary in Europe to fulfil the effectiveness principle.

The effectiveness principle can also give consumers remedies when states have failed to implement EU law or have failed adapt their laws properly. A famous case where consumers benefitted from this rule was *Dillenkofer*.[40] The German government was held liable to compensate consumers of an insolvent holiday company, because it had failed, by the required date, to adopt rules requiring such businesses to have the means to refund and repatriate consumers in the event of insolvency.

These rules of effectiveness have also been used by businesses to restrict the means of enforcement to those prescribed in maximum harmonisation measures. Thus in *AGM COS.MET*[41] the Finnish government was made potentially liable to pay damages to the manufacturer of a vehicle lift because of public statements made by an official about his concern for the safety of the lift. The permitted actions by a Member State on discovery of a defect had been fully harmonised by the relevant Machinery Directive[42] and such public statements were not allowed. However, liability of the state will be relatively rare as the law must have been intended to confer individual rights and many duties of states will be considered of a more general supervisory nature.[43] Equally, liability will only be paid if national courts assess the breach to have been 'sufficiently serious'. These same limiting factors are likely to protect the Union from many claims.[44]

39 C-453/99 *Courage v Crehan* [2000] ECR I-6298; Joined Cases C-295/04 to C-298/04 *Vincenzo Manfredi and Others v Lloyd Adriatico Assicurazioni SpA* [2006] ECR I-6619; Directive 2014/104/EU of the European Parliament and of the Council of 26 November 2014 on certain rules governing actions for damages under national law for infringements of the competition law provisions of the Member States and of the European Union Text with EEA relevance [2014] OJ L349/1.

40 Joined cases C-178/94, C-179/94, C-188/94 and C-190-94 *Erich Dillenkofer & Others v Bundesrepublik Deutschland* [1996] ECR I-4845.

41 C-470/03 *A.G.M.-COS.MET Srl v Suomen valtio and Tarmo Lehtinen* [2007] ECR I-2749.

42 Directive 98/37/EC on the approximation of the laws of the Member States relating to machinery (1998) OJ L207/1.

43 C-222/02 *Peter Paul and Others v Bundesrepublik Deutschland* [2004] ECR I-9425.

44 See the failed claim in in respect of Community liability for failing to take action against adulterated wine: Joined Cases 326/86 and 66/88 *Benito Francesconi and Others v Commission of the European Communities* [1989] ECR 2087.

Court-based private redress

Private international law

Jurisdiction

The cross-border dimension of a dispute adds an extra layer of complication to consumer dispute resolution. Consumers do not like litigating in foreign courts. Consumers face the cost and inconvenience of travel to a foreign court. This can be expensive, unless the court is just across the border near the consumer's home. Going to court is stressful for most consumers, but having to use a foreign system and possibly a foreign language makes this worse. A consumer might be able to navigate their own system in their own language, without a lawyer, but this is more difficult in a foreign jurisdiction. Consumers prefer the rules of private international law to allow them to sue in their home state. Businesses equally fear being exposed to litigation in foreign jurisdictions and want to defend actions where they are established. The benefits of substantive harmonisation based on full harmonisation seems to be undermined by the reality that a business will be concerned by any action brought against it in a foreign court regardless of which legal rules apply. The compromise struck by Council Regulation (EC) No. 1215/2012 on jurisdiction and the recognition and enforcement of judgments in civil and commercial matters (Brussels I)[45] (replacing Regulation 44/2001) is to allow the cross-border consumer to have the right to litigate at home in particular circumstances, such as when they have been targeted by the foreign trader or goods have been sold on credit. Brussels I provides a general rule for contract disputes under which jurisdiction is linked to the place of performance of the obligation. In the case of sale of goods, this is where the goods were delivered or should have been delivered.[46] In the case of services it is where the service was or should have been provided.[47] The CJEU has established that where the contract does not expressly state the place for delivery, then the place for delivery is 'the place where the physical transfer of the goods took place, as a result of which the purchaser obtained, or should have obtained, actual power of disposal over those goods at the final destination of the sales transaction.'[48] This is different from the default position under many domestic sales-law regimes, and the effect is that a consumer will generally be able to sue in the courts of his jurisdiction.

Special protection is afforded to consumers in order to allow them to sue and only be sued in their own home jurisdiction where the consumer has had goods supplied with the assistance of credit[49] and most contentiously in cross-border

45 Regulation 1215/2012/EC on jurisdiction and the recognition and enforcement of judgments in civil and commercial matters (2012) OJ L351/1.

46 On the autonomous meaning of 'delivery' for these purposes, see C-386/05 *Color Drack GmBH v Lexx International Vetriebs GmBH* ECLI:EU:C:2007:262 and C-381/08 *Car Trim GmbH v KeySafety Systems Srl* ECLI:EU:C:2010:90.

47 Art. 7.

48 C-381/08 *Car Trim GmbH v KeySafety Systems Srl* ECLI:EU:C:2010:90.

49 Brussels I, Art. 17(1)(a) and (b).

situations where the contract has been concluded with a person who pursues commercial or professional activities in the Member State of the consumer's domicile[50] or, by any means, directs such activities to that Member State or to several states including that Member State, and the contract falls within the scope of such activities.[51] For the special rules to apply the goods need not have been bought using a distant means of communication. It would cover a consumer travelling to another state to make a purchase following such targeted marketing.[52] The complex task is to define what is understood by 'directing activities'. Where the trader uses mailshots it is normally rather easy to determine whether consumers are being targeted in a particular state, as the act of posting to a particular address is sufficient proof. It is more complex to make such an assessment of websites.[53] The CJEU has considered[54] that mere access to a website in the consumer's domicile was insufficient, as was mere mention of an e-mail or other contact address or the use of a language or currency generally used in the trader's state. Nevertheless, the Regulation was intended to be more protective of consumers than the former Convention[55] and the CJEU held the test was:

> whether, before the conclusion of any contract with the consumer, it is apparent from those websites and the trader's overall activity that the trader was envisaging doing business with consumers domiciled in one or more Member States, including the Member State of that consumer's domicile, in the sense that it was minded to conclude a contract with them.[56]

A non-exhaustive list of relevant evidence included 'the international nature of the activity, mention of itineraries from other Member States for going to the place where the trader is established, use of a language or a currency other than the language or currency generally used in the Member State in which the trader is established with the possibility of making and confirming the reservation in that other language, mention of telephone numbers with an international code, outlay of expenditure on an internet referencing service in order to facilitate access to the trader's site or that of its intermediary by consumers domiciled in other Member States, use of a top-level domain name other than that of the Member

50 Or has a branch, agency or other establishment in such Member State; Brussels I, Art. 15(2).

51 Brussels I, Art. 17(1)(c).

52 C–190/11 *Mühlleitner v Yusufi* ECLI:EU:C:2012:542.

53 The 'directing activities' test bears some comparison with the 'Zippo test' in the United States: see *Zippo Manufacturing Co. v. Zippo Dot Com, Inc.*, 952 F. Supp. 1119 (W.D. Pa. 1997).

54 Joined Cases C–585/08 and C–144/09 *Pammer v Reederei Karl Schluter GmbH & Co KG* and *Hotel Alpenhof GmbH v Heller* [2010] ECR I-12527.

55 Convention on the law applicable to contractual obligations (1980) OJ L266/1.

56 Joined Cases C-585/08 and C-144/09 *Peter Pammer v Reederei Karl Schlüter GmbH & Co. KG and Hotel Alpenhof GesmbH v Oliver Heller* [2010] ECR I-12527, para 92.

State in which the trader is established, and mention of an international clientele composed of customers domiciled in various Member States.'[57]

Consumer are restricted as to their freedom to contract out of these rules before a dispute has arisen. [58] They can only do so if the rules are more generous to consumers by allowing then to bring the dispute before the courts of another state, or give jurisdiction to the court of a state where both parties reside or are habitually resident.

For torts, jurisdiction lies with the courts of the place where the harmful event occurred or may occur.[59] In the product liability context this has been held to be the place of manufacture, with the need for certainty presiding over consumer protection issues.[60]

Applicable law

A court with jurisdiction still needs to determine the applicable law. Regulation 593/2008 on the law applicable to contractual obligations[61] (Rome I) deals with choice of law in contract. This has a general principle of freedom of contract,[62] but in the absence of choice applies the contract law of the state of habitual residence of the seller of goods or the supplier of a service.[63]

There are special rules for consumers that apply where the trader either '(a) pursues his commercial or professional activities in the country where the consumer has his habitual residence, or (b) by any means, directs such activities to that country or to several countries including that country.'[64]

The function of Art. 6 Rome I Regulation is not to override the parties' freedom of choice entirely. Where the consumer provisions apply, then, absent a choice of law by the parties, the contract will be governed be the law of the consumer's habitual residence. The parties retain the freedom to choose which law applies, but this cannot deprive the consumer 'of the protection afforded to him by provisions that cannot be derogated from by agreement by virtue of the law which, in the absence of choice, would have been applicable.'[65]

57 Ibid. For a critical assessment, see C Bisping, 'Mandatorily protected: The consumer in the European conflict of laws' (2014) 22 *European Review of Private Law* p.513.

58 Brussels I, Art. 17.

59 Brussels I, Art. 7(2).

60 C-45/13 *Kainz v Pantherwerke AG* [2010] ECR I-12527. Indeed the court noted consumer protection was not the motivation for the provision and that the place of damage may not in any event be the consumer's domicile.

61 (2008) OJ L177/6.

62 Rome I, Art. 3.

63 Ibid., Art. 4.

64 Ibid., Art. 6(1). There are some exceptions, where the consumer rules do not apply: e.g. in a contract for the supply of services where the services are to be supplied to the consumer exclusively in a country other than that in which he has his habitual residence; contracts of carriage other than package holidays; property and tenancy contracts and certain securities contracts, Art. 6(4).

65 Ibid., Art. 6(2).

For the most part this provision means that consumers targeted in their home state can benefit from their mandatory national law, which in some cases may offer higher protection than the level required in minimal harmonisation directives. In some rare cases it may also be possible to argue that some consumer laws are 'overriding mandatory provisions' i.e. they are laws 'the respect for which is regarded as crucial by a country for safeguarding its public interests, such as its political, social or economic organization, to such an extent that they are applicable to any situation falling within their scope'[66] and which should be applied in every contract. However, the courts are unlikely to classify many consumer rules in this way.

Tort law applicable law is governed by of Regulation 864/2007 on the law applicable to non-contractual obligations (Rome II).[67] Art. 5 is of particular interest as it has rules on the applicable law for product liability. The applicable law is that of the country in which the person sustaining the damage had his or her habitual residence when the damage occurred, if the product was marketed in that country; or, failing that the law of the country in which the product was acquired, if the product was marketed in that country; or, failing that the law of the country in which the damage occurred, if the product was marketed in that country. However, the applicable law will still be that of the defendant if he could not reasonably foresee the marketing of the product or a product of the same type in that country.[68] These special rules do not displace the general rule that if the defendant and injured party have the same habitual residence when the damage occurs the law of that country applies.[69] The tort law of another country will apply if it is manifestly more closely connected.[70]

Substantive EU consumer laws frequently contain rules preventing European law being applied by the choice of a law of a state outside the EU.

Enforcement

Once a judgment is handed down the Brussels I Regulation has provisions requiring it to be recognised without any special procedure;[71] though there are exceptions and that concerning whether the judgment is manifestly contrary to public policy[72] may be relevant in countries that have concerns about class actions. There is also a procedure for courts to make judgments enforceable on application.[73]

66 Ibid., Art. 9.
67 (2007) OJ L199/40.
68 Rome II, Art. 5(1).
69 Rome II, Art. 4(2).
70 Rome II, Art. 5(2). A manifestly closer connection with another country might be based in particular on a pre-existing relationship between the parties, such as a contract, that is closely connected with the tort/delict in question.
71 Brussels I, Art. 36.
72 Ibid., Art. 45(1).
73 Ibid., Arts. 39–44.

This intermediate step is removed in the European small claims procedure[74] and also under certain conditions for uncontested monetary claims under the European Enforcement Order.[75]

Legal aid

Consumers are likely to need legal assistance in cross-border disputes. This is due to the cases often involving private international law, foreign law and procedures and possibly being undertaken in a foreign language and potentially being some physical distance from the consumer's residence. Directive 2002/8/EC places obligations on Member States to provide legal aid for cross-border civil disputes.[76] This can cover pre-litigation advice, legal representation and assistance at court, exemption or assistance with court fees and the covering of costs orders against the applicant to the same extent as under national law. It also can extend to interpretation and translation costs and travel costs if the legally aided party has to attend court in the other state. The procedure is not well known. There have only been two occasions in which a Member State has processed more than 100 applications in a year.[77]

Simplified procedures

Simplified court procedures are one response to the costs of traditional litigation being prohibitive in many consumer cases. Reformed procedures might, *inter alia*, remove the requirement for the parties to be physically present at the court, thus avoiding travel costs. The use of lawyers can be made optional.

Payment orders

The European payment order procedure[78] applies to cross-border uncontested pecuniary claims and allows for a paper-based procedure under which representation is not mandatory and costs are limited to what they would be for national

74 Regulation 861/2007/EC establishing a European Small Claims Procedure (2007) OJ L199/1.

75 Regulation 805/2004/EC creating a European Enforcement Order for Uncontested Claims (2004) OJ L143/15.

76 Directive 2002/8/EC to improve access to justice in cross-border disputes by establishing minimum common rules relating to legal aid for such disputes (2002) OJ L26/41.

77 Commission, *Report from the Commission on the Application of Directive 2003/8/EC to Improve Access to Justice in Cross-border Disputes by Establishing Minimum Common Rules Relating to Legal Aid for Such Disputes* COM (2012) 71 final.

78 Regulation 1896/2006/EC creating a European order for payment procedure (2006) OJ L399/1; X Kramer, 'Enhancing enforcement in the European Union: The European order for payment procedure and its implementation in the Member States, particularly in Germany, The Netherlands and England' in CH van Rhee and A Uzelac (eds), *Enforcement and Enforceability. Tradition and Reform* (Intersentia, 2010).

claims. This procedure is most likely to be used against consumers for typically they are the party that will owe the money. Nevertheless, it can still be a worthwhile procedure from the consumer perspective. Debtors normally have to pay any debt-recovery costs. If this procedure keeps those costs down they will indirectly benefit.

Small claims[79]

Consumers are more likely to take advantage of the European small claims procedure.[80] This provides a simplified regime for cross-border claims for less than 2000 euro, excluding interest, expenses and disbursements.[81] This covers cross-border claims where one party is domiciled or habitually resident in a Member State other than that of the court or tribunal seized of the case.[82] The limitation to cross-border disputes has been criticised because the cross-border element may not be revealed until the enforcement phase. These claims would not benefit from the simplified enforcement procedures for orders made under the European procedure.[83] The original Commission proposal intended it to apply also to domestic claims.[84] There are a number of exceptions from the procedure. Those most relevant to consumer claims concern matters relating to the status or legal capacity of natural persons, bankruptcy, arbitration, tenancies in immovable property apart from monetary claims and violations of privacy or rights to personality.

This is a novel procedure. There is a lack of knowledge about it by many local court staff. This can be problematic, especially as the staff are intended to assist parties. One solution might be that Member States should designate special courts whose staff are trained in the procedure. European Consumer Centres[85] could then direct consumers to these courts or national courts could redirect

79 A Fiorini, 'Facilitating cross-border debt recovery – the European payment order and small claims regulations' (2008) 57 *International and Comparative Law Quarterly* p.449; X Kramer, 'A major step in the harmonization of procedural law in Europe: The European small claims procedure. Accomplishments, new features and some fundamental questions of European harmonization' in A Jongbloed (ed), *The XIIIth World Congress of Procedural Law: The Belgian and Dutch Reports* (Intersentia, 2008); X Kramer, 'The European small claims procedure: Striking the balance between simplicity and fairness in European litigation' (2008) *Zeitschrift für Europäisches Privatrecht* p.355.

80 Regulation 861/2007/EC establishing a European small claims procedure (2007) OJ L199/1 (Small Claims Procedure Regulation); X Kramer, 'Small claim, simple recovery? The European small claims procedure and its implementation in the Member States'. *ERA Forum* 12 (2011), p.119.

81 Small Claims Procedure Regulation, Art. 2(1).

82 Ibid., Art. 3(1).

83 P Cortés, *Online Dispute Resolution for Consumers in the European Union* (Routledge, 2011), p.100.

84 Commission, *Proposal for a Regulation of the European Parliament and of the Council Establishing a European Small Claims Procedure* COM (2005) 87 final.

85 *European Consumer Centres* (European Commission, 10 February 2016) http://ec.europa.eu/consumers/solving_consumer_disputes/non-judicial_redress/ecc-net/index_en.htm [accessed 10 March 2016].

claims. This may ensure more even implementation of the obligation courts have to assist parties in filling in forms.[86]

The procedure is commenced by completing a standard claim form, which is submitted with a description of any evidence and supporting documentation. Service is facilitated by a provision allowing this to be made by post attested by an acknowledgment of receipt.[87] Any national fees have to be paid on the same basis as in domestic proceedings. This may make access to justice more difficult in some states, though the relatively high fees in the United Kingdom do not seem to have deterred consumers' applications relative to other states. Indeed, the United Kingdom has received the highest number of such actions.[88] If there are any errors in the paperwork, then unless the application is clearly unfounded or inadmissible the court will give the claimant the opportunity to complete or rectify the form. The procedure is intended to be written. Oral hearings are only held when the court considers it necessary or a party so requests. A court can refuse such a request if a hearing is obviously not necessary for the fair conduct of the hearing. If an oral hearing is necessary positive encouragement is given to using technology such as video conferencing[89] and a flexible approach to the taking of evidence is also promoted.[90] The written documentation should be in the language of the court, though the court may, in practice, not always require documents to be translated. A party can, however, require translation if the document is not in the language of the court or one he understands.[91] Strict and relatively short timetables are laid down so that straightforward claims should be dealt with within 88 days.[92] In practice the courts seem to take a pragmatic approach as regards language, service and time limits.[93]

The Regulation provides that, whenever appropriate, the court or tribunal shall seek to reach a settlement between the parties. However, in many small claims procedures the restricted time allowed to deal with a case limits the practical scope for the judge to act as a mediator or conciliator. Legal representation is not mandatory,[94] but most consumers tend to be legally represented in cross-border claims. In many small claims schemes consumers are given confidence to bring claims by an exception being made to the 'loser pays' rules. The European procedure, however, provides that the unsuccessful party should bear the cost of

86 Small Claims Procedure Regulation, Art. 11.
87 Ibid., Art. 13.
88 A 2011 IMCO study placed the UK at the top (233 applications in 2010) see F Alleweldt and others, *Cross-border Alternative Dispute Resolution in the European Union* (European Parliament, 2011), p.55, http://www.europarl.europa.eu/meetdocs/2009_2014/documents/imco/dv/adr_study_/adr_study_en.pdf [accessed 10 March 2016].
89 Small Claims Procedure Regulation, Art. 8.
90 Ibid., Art. 9.
91 Ibid., Art. 6.
92 Ibid., Art. 5. Evidence from the Netherlands suggest in practice time limits are not adhered to but claims are dealt with relatively efficiently: X Kramer and E Ontanu, 'The functioning of the European small claims procedure in the Netherlands: normative and empirical reflections' (2013) 3 *Nederlands Internationaal Privaatrecht* p.324.
93 Ibid., p.327.
94 Small Claims Procedure Regulation Art. 10.

the proceedings, albeit subject to controls against unnecessary or disproportionate costs.[95] This may be justified because of the added complexity of cross-border claims, but only serves to underline the risks faced by cross-border consumers.

There are only limited grounds for defendants to seek review. These are based on procedural irregularities with the service of documents or their having been prevented from objecting by *force majeure* or extraordinary circumstances.[96] Appeals are a matter for national law, subject to the Commission being informed of what appeal process if any is available.

Any judgment becomes immediately enforceable in other Member States without the need for a declaration of enforceability and without any possibility of opposing its recognition if it has been properly certified by the court.[97]

This procedure has a relatively low profile. The scheme is under-used. Some problems have also been revealed, such as those involving language issues.[98] Perhaps surprisingly, given its fairly high court fees for small claims, the United Kingdom is the leader in accepting such claims. In many other states this procedure is less well used. This is perhaps not unexpected for consumers have few economic incentives to engage in litigation for small claims even at the national level and the cross-border element adds additional costs, barriers and stress that can only ever be partially mitigated by this novel and potentially helpful procedure.

The Commission has made proposals to improve the scheme.[99] These include raising the threshold to include claims up to 10,000 euro; broadening the definition of cross-border disputes to cover more claims; making more of the procedures electronic including the use of video-conferencing, when a hearing is needed: placing caps on court fees; and, only requiring the substance of the judgment to be translated when seeking enforcement (as the rest of the form is available in the different languages).

Collective redress[100]

Class or group actions procedures aim to deal with mass claims involving individuals with similar claims. They can be complex and require lawyers to run them, but can also be valuable in making litigation more accessible to consumers.

95 Ibid., Art. 16.
96 Ibid., Art. 18.
97 Small Claims Procedure Regulation, Art. 20.
98 X Kramer, 'The European small claims procedure: Striking the balance between simplicity and fairness in European litigation' (2008) *Zeitschrift für Europäisches Privatrecht* p.369.
99 Proposal for a Regulation of the European Parliament and of the Council amending Regulation (EC) No 861/2007 of the European Parliament and the Council of 11 July 2007 establishing a European small claims procedure and Regulation 1896/2006/EC creating a European order for payment procedure COM (2013) 794 final.
100 C Hodges, *The Reform of Class and Representative Actions in European Legal Systems: A New Framework for Collective Redress in Europe* (Hart, 2008); F Caffagi and HW Micklitz, *New Frontiers of Consumer Protection – the Interplay between Private and Public Enforcement* (Intersentia, 2009); J Steele and W van Boom (eds), *Mass Justice – Challenges of Representation and Distribution* (Edward Elgar, 2011); C Hodges and A Stadler, *Resolving Mass Disputes – ADR and Settlement of Mass Claims* (Edward Elgar, 2013).

Combining small individual claims can make them viable to litigate. Collective redress procedures can also be useful in high-value complex claims as legal and expert costs can be shared. Collective litigation can also be helpful to courts that otherwise would be overwhelmed with litigation on particular issues. In Germany a collective mechanism was adopted when the Frankfurt courts were inundated with investment claims.[101] ADR schemes can also have similar needs for collective solutions when facing major incidents affecting large numbers.[102]

At the EU level, collective redress proposals in the competition field[103] prompted discussion of the similar need for collective redress in the consumer field. Indeed in the consumer field, factors like calculation of damages would be simpler to assess for a claim based on unfair competition or use of unfair terms than in the competition cases. Following a public consultation in 2011, *Towards a More Coherent European Approach to Collective Redress*,[104] and EU Parliament Resolution[105] the Commission published its Communication, *Towards a European Horizontal Framework for Collective Redress.*[106] The intensity of debate can be gauged from the 19,000 responses to the 2011 consultation.[107] The result was Recommendation of 11 June 2013 on common principles for injunctive and compensatory redress mechanisms in the Member States concerning violations of rights granted under EU law.[108] It recommended Member States to have both injunctive and compensatory collective mechanisms in line with its principles. However, the Recommendation was also careful to propose safeguards against abuse. These include only allowing representative entities meeting strict criteria to bring representative actions; having early verification of claims; adoption of the 'loser pays' principle; controls on third-party funding; contingency fees being

101 This led to the Kapitalanleger-Musterverfahrensgesetz (KapMuG) (the law governing test cases in capital investment) coming into effect in 2005.

102 Payment protection insurance under the United Kingdom's Financial Ombudsman scheme is a good example of this. However, even with some guidance being given on collective general principles the Ombudsman's official site notes the numbers mean it will take years rather than months to deal with the claims, see '*PPI – Your Case with Us...*' (*Financial Ombudsman Service Limited*, 8 Mar 2016) http://www.financial-ombudsman.org.uk/contact/PPI-your-case.html [accessed 10 March 2016].

103 See Commission, *Damages Actions for Breach of the EC Antitrust Rules* COM (2005) 672 final; Commission, *Damages Actions for Breach of Anti-trust Rules* COM (2008) 16. See also Commission, *Public Consultation: Towards a Coherent European Approach to Collective Redress* SEC (2011) 173 final.

104 SEC (2011) 173 final.

105 European Parliament, *Towards a Coherent European Approach to Collective Redress* (2011/2089(INI)).

106 Commission, *Towards a European Horizontal Framework for Collective Redress* COM (2013) 401 final.

107 X Kramer, 'Enforcing mass settlements in the European Judicial Area: EU policy and the strange case of Dutch collective settlements (WCAM)' in C Hodges and A Stadler, *Resolving Mass Disputes – ADR and Settlement of Mass Claims* (Edward Elgar, 2013).

108 Commission, *Recommendation of 11 June 2013 on Common Principles for Injunctive and Compensatory Collective Redress Mechanisms in the Member States Concerning Violations of Rights Granted under Union Law* (2013) OJ L201/60.

viewed as exceptional and where allowed not creating incentives for unnecessary litigation and respecting the right to full compensation;[109] and, a prohibition on punitive damages. Encouragement is also given to the use of ADR for collective settlements.

Europe has been frightened off anything approaching a US-style class action, by stories of abuse of the system by plaintiff lawyers and large awards affecting the business environment.[110] Instead, Europe seems to favour promoting ADR as a means of individual redress and ensuring a stronger regulatory enforcement environment. Regulation may be valuable to promote a better-functioning market and ADR may be helpful in securing individual redress at affordable costs.[111] They are both considered below. However, class actions have a role to play both as a deterrent and a practical means of managing floods of cases. It also helps to socialise risk as the collective dimension of consumer issues is exposed when the claims are combined. The Recommendation provides a framework to promote collective redress and given the need to integrate such procedures into national civil procedure this is probably the most Europe could do. The right approach is for the EU to nudge Member States to adopt such solutions, rather than to impose an EU model. This seems akin to the open method of co-operation that promotes Member States' voluntary convergence and such an approach is to be applauded.

Alternative dispute resolution[112]

ADR – general considerations

ADR is a popular technique to promote consumer access to justice. Court-based litigation has traditionally been seen as the model form of dispute resolution. However, its high costs and formality make it impractical and even inappropriate for low-value consumer claims, even, some might argue, in the slimmed-down small claims procedures. ADR, using arbitrators who are often familiar with the sector, can also produce better-informed decisions. Of course the impartiality of the third party must be secured. Some ADR schemes can also base decisions on fairness as well as the law thereby reflecting good practices which may be ahead of the formal law.

Some ADR schemes hand down binding decisions. In others the decisions only bind the trader. Yet others might be mediation schemes which try to conciliate

109 If the right to full compensation is to be respected then conditional fees ('no win no fee') should be favoured as opposed to contingency fees where traditionally this assumes the success fee comes out of the claimant's award.

110 The extent to which these claims are true matters less than the perception of the US experience.

111 C Hodges and A Stadler, *Resolving Mass Disputes – ADR and Settlement of Mass Claims* (Edward Elgar, 2013).

112 N Reich, 'Legal protection of individual and collective consumer interests' in N Reich and others, *European Consumer Law* (Intersentia, 2014).

between the parties and encourage settlement. As schemes move away from application of the law towards encouraging settlement, there is clearly an issue of the consumer risking relinquishing rights as the price of settlement. Power may be exerted on the consumer in the face of practical realities and protecting his or her interest in a practical manner may be more important that fighting for full satisfaction of legal rights. Consumer dispute resolution is to some extent a compromise to ensure some redress where the value of claims would not justify full-blown litigation. Some sacrifice of the pursuit of perfect justice may be justified, but the important factor is to ensure the schemes preserve minimum procedural standards to protect the consumer interest.

Mandatory arbitration clauses, as used in US, can be problematic as they force consumers out of the legal system's protection. By contrast, giving consumers the option of using ADR can allow them a cheaper and more flexible way to seek redress. It typically does not require or encourage legal representation. It is now clear that in Europe consumers cannot be bound to ADR before a dispute arises and if they agree to submit a claim to ADR they must be informed in advance if such a clause is binding and have 'specifically accepted' it.[113]

EU law promoting ADR

Many versions of ADR have bloomed across Europe. Prior to the ADR Directive, EU law had only required out-of-court dispute resolution systems in the telecoms,[114] energy,[115] consumer credit[116] and payment services[117] sectors. However, its use had been encouraged in several other directives.[118] Those forms of ADR most favourable to consumers are free or low cost and only binding on the trader. But there are many variants. The Commission has welcomed the development

113 Directive 2013/11/EU, Art. 10.

114 Directive 2009/136/EC amending Directive 2002/22/EC on universal service and users' rights relating to electronic communications networks and services, Directive 2002/58/EC concerning the processing of personal data and the protection of privacy in the electronic communications sector and Regulation (EC) No 2006/2004 on cooperation between national authorities responsible for the enforcement of consumer protection laws (2009) OJ L337/11, Art. 34(1).

115 Directive 2009/72/EC on common rules for the internal market in electricity (2009) OJ L211/55, Art. 13.

116 Directive 2008/48/EC on credit agreements for consumers (2008) OJ L133/66, Art. 24.

117 Directive 2007/64/EC on payment services in the internal market (2007) OJ L319/1, Art. 83.

118 Directive 2002/65/EC on the distance marketing of consumer financial services (2002) OJ L271/16, Art. 14; Directive 2008/122/EC on the protection of consumers in respect of certain aspects of timeshare, long-term holiday product, resale and exchange contracts (2009) OJ L33/10, Art. 14; Directive 2000/31/EC on certain legal aspects of information society services, in particular electronic commerce, in the Internal Market (2000) OJ L178/1, Art. 17; Directive 2008/6/EC with regard to the full accomplishment of the internal market of Community postal services (2008) OJ L52/3, Art. 19; Directive 2002/92/EC on insurance mediation (2003) OJ L9/3, Art. 11; Directive 2004/39/EC on markets in financial instruments, Art. 53.

of ADR, but has also sought to ensure minimum safeguards are in place. It adopted two recommendations on this topic: one for bodies providing out-of-court settlement[119] and another where the bodies seek to encourage consensual resolution of disputes.[120] The CJEU has also supported ADR by not precluding national laws which make access to the courts dependent on first having tried to use ADR mechanisms.[121]

Subsequently the EU has adopted binding legislation. First, there was a directive promoting mediation and subsequently a package on ADR and on-line dispute resolution (ODR). The ADR Directive imposes a requirement that ADR schemes are available for all consumer disputes, whilst the ODR Regulation[122] establishes a platform to place consumers in touch with ADR schemes in other states and provides an infrastructure for the problem to be resolved using technology, if the ADR schemes allow for such ODR.

Mediation Directive[123]

The EU has encouraged mediation through the Mediation Directive.[124] This requires national courts to be allowed to recommend the use of mediation or at least invite parties to attend an information session on mediation.[125] It reinforces the principle of confidentiality for the mediation procedure,[126] ensures use of mediation does not prevent claims subsequently being brought due to limitation or prescription periods,[127] and enables parties to obtain an agreement equal to a court judgment.[128] These rules only apply to cross-border civil and commercial matters,[129] but Member States are not prevented from applying them to internal mediation processes. The Mediation Directive is facilitative and does not require the imposition of a duty to attempt mediation.

119 Commission Recommendation 98/257/EC on the principles applicable to the bodies responsible for out-of-court settlement of consumer disputes (1998) OJ L115/31 This also had a European complaint form attached to it.
120 Commission Recommendation 2001/310 on the principles for out-of-court bodies involved in the consensual resolution of consumer disputes [2001] OJ L109/56.
121 C-317/08 *Rosalba Alassini v Telecom Italia SpA* (*The Alassini*) [2010] ECR I-2213.
122 Regulation 524/2013/EU on online dispute resolution for consumer disputes (2013) OJ L165/1.
123 Directive 2008/52/EC on certain aspects of mediation in civil and commercial matters (Mediation Directive) (2008) OJ L136/3.
124 Ibid. In 2004 a voluntary Code of Conduct for Mediators had been promoted by the European Commission. See I Benöhr, 'Alternative dispute resolution for consumers in the European Union' in C Hodges, I Benöhr and N Creutzfeldt-Banda, *Consumer ADR in Europe* (Hart, 2012), pp.8–10. The Mediation Directive does not establish an accreditation procedure for mediators. Some trainers do offer special on-line mediation training: P Cortés, *Online Dispute Resolution for Consumers in the European Union* (Routledge, 2011), p.158.
125 Mediation Directive, Art. 5.
126 Ibid., Art. 7.
127 Ibid., Art. 8.
128 Ibid., Art. 6.
129 Ibid., Art. 1(2).

ADR Directive

The ADR Directive has at its core the obligation on Member States to ensure there is an ADR procedure available for *every* consumer dispute.[130] In countries that do not have one single consumer ADR procedure, but rather a patchwork of ADR procedures this is likely to be achieved by having a residual body. However, financing such a body may be problematic.[131]

The ADR Directive is one EU access-to-justice law that covers both purely domestic and cross-border disputes. However, the general duty to provide assistance to consumers is restricted to cross-border disputes.[132]

ADR schemes are broadly interpreted to include schemes which either propose or impose a solution, as well as those that only bring the parties together with the aim of facilitating an amicable solution.[133] In-house company schemes can be included, but have to satisfy additional criteria.[134] No business is required to use ADR. The Directive merely ensures there is an available ADR body to use should they want to. ADR bodies may refuse cases for various reasons, such as the claim being frivolous or vexatious; the claimant not first attempting to contact the trader to resolve the dispute; previous consideration of dispute by another ADR entity; delay in bringing the claim or the claim being outside prescribed monetary limits.[135]

The Directive requires ADR entities that want to be recognised have (i) expertise, independence and impartiality; (ii) transparency; (iii) effectiveness, including resolving disputes within 90 days; (iv) fairness; (v) liberty i.e. any decision being non-binding on the consumer if the use of procedure was agreed to in advance of dispute and only binding, in any event, if the consumer specifically accepted this and (vi) legality i.e. ensuring that the consumer is not deprived of protection that cannot be derogated from by agreement or that conflict of laws do not deprive the consumer of his mandatory protection.[136] The legality criterion has been fiercely defended by many consumer advocates, but it can pose practical problems to many ADR schemes who may not have the knowledge or resources

130 ADR Directive, Art. 5. N Reich, 'Legal protection of individual and collective consumer interests' in N Reich and others, *European Consumer Law* (Intersentia, 2014) takes a contrary view, though noting the ambiguous wording of Art. 5 suggests that to require Member States to set up such entities would go against the facilitative nature of the Directive, which should only require its rules are followed if there is an ADR body.

131 Department for Business Innovation and Skills (BIS), *Alternative Dispute Resolution for Consumers: Implementing the Alternative Dispute Resolution Directive and Online Dispute Resolution Regulation* (BIS, March 2014) https://www.gov.uk/government/uploads/system/uploads/attachment_data/file/288199/bis-14-575-implementing-alternative-dispute-resolution-directive-and-online-dispute-resolution-regulation-consultation.pdf [accessed 11 March 2016].

132 ADR Directive, Art. 14.

133 Ibid., Art. 2 (1).

134 Ibid., Arts. 2(2) and 6(3).

135 Art. 5(4).

136 Ibid., Arts. 6–11.

to apply the conflict rules, nor the wherewithal to discover and apply foreign law if that is required.

ADR entities that comply with the above criteria can provide specified information to the designated national competent authority which will provide a list to the Commission. There is no requirement that entities meet these criteria. Failure to do so simply means they cannot be on the list and so will not get referrals though the European system. There is no prohibition on schemes that do not meet the minimum criteria.

Information is used as a tool to promote the use of ADR. First, traders must inform consumers if they are obliged or committed to using ADR. This includes giving notice on any website and in general terms and conditions.[137] If a trader cannot settle a dispute it must again provide the consumer with this information and explain whether it will make use of ADR. It seems strange that there is a duty on a trader to mention an ADR entity, but then be free to decline to use it. The UK's BIS explains this as being driven by a desire to encourage traders to use ADR by hoping they will not want to look bad by disclosing an option they will not use.[138]

Cross-border ADR

Only a few schemes have historically aimed specifically to address cross-border disputes by ADR. The Austrian Internet Ombudsman was one example. It assisted consumers, but only from Austria, to complain against businesses established within the EU.[139] The EU had funded a pilot project – the Electronic Consumer Dispute Resolution (ECODIR) – run by UCD Dublin and Namur University, Belgium, that operated a staged approach of negotiation, mediation and finally recommendation. There was low awareness of the scheme and it could not continue without further funding.[140] It seems clear that such schemes need a subsidy from the trade or state and cannot rely on charges alone. The European Car Rental Conciliation Service and Seldia, the European Direct Selling Association, which has a European Code Administrator,[141] are two sector schemes that attempt some form of cross-border ADR. There are also trader sponsored trustmark schemes such as Euro-label (run by the European co-operation of national suppliers of Internet trustmarks[142]), Trusted Shops[143] and EMOTA - European E-Commerce

137 Ibid., Art. 13(1).

138 BIS (n 135) 28.

139 'Volksanwaltschaft' (*The Austrian Ombudsman Board*), http://volksanwaltschaft.gv.at/ [accessed 11 March 2016]; see J Hörnle, *Cross-border Internet Dispute Resolution* (CUP, 2009), p.78.

140 C Hodges, I Benöhr and N Creutzfeldt-Banda, 'Cross-border consumer ADR' in C Hodges, I Benöhr and N Creutzfeldt-Banda, *Consumer ADR in Europe* (Hart, 2012), p.364.

141 Ibid., pp.355–358.

142 'Shop securely in verified online shops with the Euro-Label' (*Euro-Label*), http://www.euro-label.com/en/about-us/index.html [accessed 11 March 2016].

143 'Shop across Europe with peace of mind' (*Trusted Shops*), http://www.trustedshops.eu/ [accessed 11 March 2016].

Association (the association representing distance and multi-channel selling).[144] However, these are struggling for wide-scale adoption in all Member States and for public recognition.

Assisting cross-border ODR – the ODR Regulation

Cross-border ADR is supported by the EU network of advice centres (European Consumer Centres) that assist consumer with cross-border disputes (ECC-Net[145]). In 2014 this network received 93,741 contacts from consumers and handled 37,601 complaints.[146] There is also a financial services network (Fin-Net[147]). An important function they have is to channel consumers to appropriate national ADR bodies. This will be assisted by a new Online Dispute Resolution (ODR) platform the Commission has established under Regulation (EU) No 524/2013 on on-line dispute resolution for consumer disputes.[148] Although on-line dispute resolution can cover a wide range of redress mechanisms including court-based schemes, this ODR Regulation is concerned with facilitating out-of-court dispute resolution. It essentially establishes a clearing house providing a complaint form, which is then transmitted to relevant ADR bodies. It is modelled after the Belgian *Belmed* scheme, which is an abbreviation for *Belgian Mediation*.[149] The ODR platform also will make available translation tools and a free-of-charge electronic case management tool.[150] Each Member State must have one ODR contact point, which provides support to and facilitates communication between the parties including advising on alternative means if the dispute cannot be resolved through the platform. The contact point also liaises with the Commission.[151] This structure is linked to the promotion of ADR by Directive 2013/11/EU on alternative dispute resolution for consumer disputes (ADR Directive). However, in the past, most ADR bodies did not offer ODR, and there is no requirement for them to adopt IT-based processes. In some instances the ODR Regulation may simply be an IT means of transferring disputes into traditional national procedures.

144 'EMOTA European Trustmark for e-Commerce' (*The European eCommerce & Omni-Channel Trade Association*), http://www.emota.eu/#!european-trustmark-/c1f52 [accessed 11 March 2016].
145 'European Consumer Centres' (n 87). This network was formed in 2005 by the merger of the EEJ-NET, a clearing house that assisted consumers with cross-border problems to find ADR providers and European Consumer Centres 'Euroguichets' that provide information and assistance on cross-border issues.
146 Ibid., (2015).
147 'Welcome to FIN-NET' (*Financial Dispute Resolution* Network) http://ec.europa.eu/internal_market/fin-net/ [accessed 11 March 2016].
148 (2013) OJ L 165/1.
149 S Voet, 'Public enforcement and A(ODR) as mechanisms for resolving mass problems: A Belgian perspective' in C Hodges and A Stadler, *Resolving Mass Disputes – ADR and Settlement of Mass Claims* (Edward Elgar, 2013).
150 ODR Regulation, Art. 6.
151 Ibid., Art. 7.

A criticism of the ODR Regulation is that it is not ambitious enough. The platform is too much of a mere conduit restricted to finding partners and providing technological assistance. ADR bodies cannot be required to participate or be made to use technology. The ODR Regulation fails to include any measure that encourages mediation (for example, the ODR platform might have had a function to seek conciliation between the trader and consumer[152]) or give sufficient incentives to use the scheme.

ODR – the pros and cons

ODR is itself a contentious issue.[153] Besides the general debate about the pros and cons of traditional litigation versus arbitration and mediation there are some specific issues relating to ODR. ODR has some obvious advantages over ADR. When purchases are made on the internet resolving them through IT seems an appropriate solution. It can help address the issue of distance between the parties that is involved in most cross-border disputes. There are obvious cost savings if parties do not need to travel. Time savings can be made as parties can respond to electronic communications according to their own schedule 24/7. Asynchronous messages can allow parties to reflect on their responses carefully and may have the effect of taking the heat out of disputes. The use of text messages may reduce the risk of discrimination and bias.

However, there are also downsides to ODR. Lack of face-to-face contact can be a problem as parties cannot benefit from body language signals. At the very least neutral third parties may need different training. As Cortés states, technology is not neutral as computer-mediated technology 'emphasizes some aspects of communications and minimizes or eliminates others.'[154] Not everyone may have access to the required technology and so based on the view of the CJEU making the use of ODR mandatory may mean the redress mechanism breaches the effectiveness principle.[155] ODR is still in its infancy and, as with all IT projects, there are risks of technological problems. Particularly where sensitive data is involved, security may be a concern. However, many consumer claims will not involve serious confidentiality issues.[156] Language barriers are still a major problem, where English (or another language) is not common to all parties. Translation technology needs to improve to be sufficiently reliable to be used in dispute resolution.

152 P Cortés, *Online Dispute Resolution for Consumers in the European Union* (Routledge, 2011), p.220.

153 See J Hörnle, *Cross-border Internet Dispute Resolution* (CUP, 2009), pp.86–90; P Cortés, *Online Dispute Resolution for Consumers in the European Union* (Routledge, 2011), pp. 56–59.

154 P Cortés, *Online Dispute Resolution for Consumers in the European Union* (Routledge, 2011), pp.56–59.

155 C-317/08 *Rosalba Alassini v Telecom Italia SpA* (*The Alassini*) [2010] ECR I-2213.

156 P Cortés, *Online Dispute Resolution for Consumers in the European Union* (Routledge, 2011), p.156.

There are a wide range of ODR bodies and consumers need to have confidence in their quality, but it may be difficult for consumers to assess the quality of ODR entities. Increasing confidence in such entities is the intention behind the ADR Directive. These bodies administering low-cost ODR, however, are likely to struggle fully to implement a principle of legality that requires accurate application of private international law on jurisdiction and applicable law and possible research into foreign law. There are also debates about the enforceability of ODR arbitral decisions under Art. V of the New York Convention on the Recognition and Enforcement of Foreign Arbitral Awards 1958, with the advice being to print off a copy and have it signed.[157]

ODR can include several innovative features such as automated negotiation, whereby, blind offers are mediated to produce potential settlements. CyberSettle was a front-runner with such schemes. Parties in such schemes can usually make three offers and if they fall within a range then the settlement would be proposed at the midpoint. There has been discussion of the fairness of this scheme which might favour repeat players. Its main value seems to be in insurance and commercial disputes where parties want to settle without openly revealing their bottom line. It was most successful in the US, but never established itself in UK as lawyers at the time could not be remunerated out of proceeds.[158] Obviously in any event a consumer claim would have to have a certain value to make such a scheme a viable option. Even in ODR, the economics of consumer dispute resolution for small amounts can be problematic. The more complex ODR schemes may also simply be too expensive for resolving low-value consumer claims.

The IT has been described as the fourth party in ODR, assisting or even replacing the neutral third party. Its performance can make or break an ODR system. Many schemes use assisted negotiation, where disputes are categorised and attempted to be matched with previous settlements. SquareTrade operated a scheme for eBay until 2008,[159] which had software-match solutions to problems and provided an on-line mediator with asynchronous email and web communications.[160] It was widely praised for its innovative use of technology, but part of its success was explained by its concentration on a limited number of issues.[161]

157 Ibid., p.112. Art. V requires the presentation of an authenticated original or certified copy of the award, which presupposes a hard-copy document. The UN Convention on the Use of Electronic Communications 2005 has not been sufficiently ratified to allow the use of electronic means to comply with Art. V of the New York Convention.

158 C Hodges, I Benöhr and N Creutzfeldt-Banda, 'Cross-border consumer ADR' in C Hodges, I Benöhr and N Creutzfeldt-Banda, *Consumer ADR in Europe* (Hart, 2012), p.360; P Cortés, *Online Dispute Resolution for Consumers in the European Union* (Routledge, 2011), p.65.

159 Until changes in the eBay feedback system meant it was removed: see P Cortés, *Online Dispute Resolution for Consumers in the European Union* (Routledge, 2011), p.148.

160 C Hodges, I Benöhr and N Creutzfeldt-Banda, 'Cross-border consumer ADR' in C Hodges, I Benöhr and N Creutzfeldt-Banda, *Consumer ADR in Europe* (Hart, 2012), p.360.

161 P Cortés, *Online Dispute Resolution for Consumers in the European Union* (Routledge, 2011), p.68.

On-line businesses such as eBay,[162] PayPal[163] and Amazon[164] use ODR, often involving assisted negotiation, which can also be advantageous for businesses if it reduces negative feedback. It has been estimated that, after PayPal launched its dispute resolution centre, buyers' claims decreased by 50% and chargebacks by 20%.[165] In practice in some countries help may also be provided through charge, credit and debit card holders' chargeback schemes based on contract or statutory rules.[166]

Assessment of EU ADR policy in an international context

The European ADR/ODR structure is really a clearing house directing consumers to schemes that meet minimum criteria. Member States must provide the trader with the option of offering ADR, but it is for traders to decide whether to participate. Equally, it is left to ADR providers to determine the extent to which they adapt their procedures to ODR norms. European law is nevertheless concerned to protect consumers and is based on ensuring mandatory European consumer law is applied.

By contrast work going on at the international level by the United Nations Commission on International Trade Law (UNCITRAL) is far more concerned with finding routes to resolve low-value claims through ODR and less concerned with the niceties of national consumer law. It is likely to provide a framework for negotiation (within the ODR framework), followed by facilitation and then arbitration or another form of adjudication. UNCITRAL is likely to establish (i) minimum standards for ODR providers, (ii) guidelines for neutral third parties, (iii) substantive legal principles for resolving disputes, and (iv) an enforcement protocol. The extent to which this is embraced by Europe depends upon how a trade-off is struck between achieving practical justice and protecting existing levels of consumer protection. Though many common problems can easily be resolved through a rough-and-ready ODR scheme, there is value in ensuring EU consumer law minimum standards are maintained, or else the substantive protection built up will be sacrificed on the altar of commercial and technological convenience.[167]

162 It has an eBay Moneyback Guarantee and also eBay Motors Vehicle Purchase Protection (VPP), see 'Shop on eBay with complete confidence' (*eBay*), http://pages.ebay.com/ebay-money-back-guarantee/ [accessed on 11 March 2016].

163 Buyer Protection Programme, see 'We're on your side' (*PayPal*), https://www.paypal.com/hk/webapps/mpp/paypal-buyer-protection?locale.x=en_HK&utm_source=owned-homepage&utm_medium=onsite&utm_campaign=2015-jul&utm_content=buyerprotection [accessed 11 March 2016].

164 'A-to-Z guarantee protection for buyers' (*Amazon Payments*), https://payments.amazon.co.uk/help/201212340 [accessed 11 March 2016].

165 P Cortés, *Online Dispute Resolution for Consumers in the European Union* (Routledge, 2011), p.60.

166 E.g. s.75 of the UK's Consumer Credit Act 1974, which makes credit card suppliers jointly liable with traders, has been held to apply when the card was used outside the UK.

167 J Hörnle, 'Online dispute resolution in the EU and beyond – keeping costs low or standards high?' (*Queen Mary School of Law Legal Studies*, 2011) Research Paper No. 122/2012, http://papers.ssrn.com/sol3/papers.cfm?abstract_id=2154214 [accessed 11 March 2016]; Hodges and Stadler (n 105); P Cortés, 'A new regulatory framework for extra-judicial consumer redress: Where we are and how to move forward' (2015) 35 *Legal Studies* p.114.

Public enforcement

Introduction

Many states have strong traditions of public enforcement of consumer law in order to promote a strong market and in recognition that consumers will often not take action frequently enough to be an effective control on bad practices and rogue traders. In some countries there is a tradition of state agencies enforcing consumer law e.g. the Scandinavian Ombudsmen and UK Consumer and Markets Authority (previously Office of Fair Trading). In others, private consumer organizations have played a major role e.g. France, Spain and Italy. In Austria and Germany consumer organizations play a major role, but are heavily financed by the state to perform this function. The resources put into enforcement varies widely between states. Several of the new Member States do not finance their consumer protection authorities well. Some regulators also have dual functions as banking regulators or competition authorities and there are debates as to whether this strengthens their power or dilutes their focus on protecting consumers.

State agencies typically use administrative and criminal law sanctions. These must, under general principles of EU law and according to formula found in most secondary laws, be sufficiently effective so as to be dissuasive.[168] The extent to which they have powers, or seek to use powers, to compensate consumers affected by breach of the laws varies. It does not seem to be an issue frequently discussed at the EU level. EU law seems to separate private rights concerned with individual redress and public law rules concerned with general market regulation[169]

Injunctions – a European enforcement mechanism

The remedy of injunction has been a favourite tool of the EU. This is in line with modern regulatory theory that believes in a hierarchy of actions, with criminal sanction being reserved for the most severe transgressions.[170] In practice most breaches will be dealt with by negotiation or the obtaining of undertakings from traders. The injunction is a civil law remedy directing a party to cease conduct that breaks the law. However, it also has a public-law character when invoked by the state.

Many of the directives that provide for injunctive powers leave it to national law to decide which entities can bring legal actions: state authorities or consumer organisations.[171] Though in the United Kingdom, *Which?* successfully used the

168 As included in e.g. Directive 93/13/EEC on unfair terms in consumer contracts (1993) OJ L95/29, Art. 7(1); Directive 2002/65/EC on distance marketing of financial services (2002) OJ L217/16, Art. 11; Directive 2011/83/EU on Consumer Rights (2011) OJ L304/64, Art. 24(1).

169 See discussion above, pp.294–296.

170 I Ayres and J Braithwaite, *Responsible Regulation: Transcending the Deregulation Debate* (OUP, 1992).

171 Directive 2009/22/EC on injunctions for the protection of consumers' interests (2009) OJ L110/30.

wording of the EU laws to push for it to be given new rights of standing to challenge unfair terms and to be a designated enforcer under Part 8 of the Enterprise Act 2008.

Consumer Injunctions Directive[172]

Powers to seek injunctions had been included in several directives, but there was no coherent approach. Moreover, it became apparent that it was harder to use injunctions under national law to stop practices that harmed consumers in another state.[173] National authorities or consumer organizations in the place where the trader was based may have lacked the motivation or even powers to bring such actions, whilst relevant bodies in the country affected normally lacked standing in the courts of other Member States. To protect the interests of consumers in the internal market and to ensure the injunction was available even if the trader was operating from another Member State, Directive 98/27/EC on injunctions for the protection of consumers' interests[174] was adopted. This was replaced by Directive 2009/22/EC on injunctions for the protection of consumers' interests[175] which extended its scope, but kept the same basic structure.

The Directive leaves it to the discretion of Member States whether independent public bodies or private organizations, or both, should be qualified entities so long as they aim to protect the collective interests of consumers in relation to the 13 directives listed in the Directive's annex.[176] A Member State's list of qualified entities is communicated to the Commission and then published in the Official Journal by the Commission. For intra-Community infringements i.e. where an infringement originating in a Member State affects the interests protected by a qualified entity in another Member State,[177] the courts or administrative authorities must accept this as proof of the legal capacity of the qualified entity to act before the courts or administrative tribunals it has designated for this purpose.

The United Kingdom's Office of Fair Trading (now replaced by the Competition and Markets Authority) used these powers to bring an action in the Belgium courts against the mail order company Duchesne.[178] Although an injunction was eventually obtained, the litigation had a complex history involving expense and many technical legal arguments. The OFT used the power again in 2008 to seek

172 S Wrbka, *European Consumer Access to Justice Revisited* (Cambridge University Press, 2014), pp.40–53; P Rott, 'The protection of consumers' interests after the implementation of the EC Injunctions Directive Into German and English Law'. (2001) 24 *JCP* p.399; H Schulte-Nölke, C Twigg-Flesner and M Ebers, *EU Consumer Law Compendium* (Sellier, 2008).

173 H Micklitz, 'Cross-border consumer conflicts – A French-German experience' in N Reich and G Woodroffe (eds), *European Consumer Policy after Maastricht* (Springer, 1994).

174 (1998) OJ L166/51.

175 (2009) OJ L110/30.

176 Ibid., Art. 3.

177 Ibid., Art. 4(1).

178 *Duchesne SA v Office of Fair Trading*, Cass, 2.11.2007, No C.06.0201.F/1.

an injunction against the Dutch distance-selling company, Best Sales.[179] However, the 2008 Injunctions Directive Report[180] made disappointing reading. Only two cases had been brought using the Directive's provisions. The 2012 Injunction Directive Report[181] seemed to show an improvement with 70 cases, but Wrbka sounds a cautionary note by commenting that in practice these were often not true intra-Community infringements, but rather cases being brought by bodies in their own courts against overseas firms.[182] There was also an example of a co-ordinated action with France's UFC-Que Choisir and Belgium's Test-Achats co-ordinating and obtaining a judgment in the Belgium courts obliging three airlines to stop using a number of contract terms regarded as unfair.[183]

It was noticeable that most of the cases were brought by entities with professional staff. As there are no minimum requirements for such entities or duties to undertake such work there is an obvious risk of uneven application given that the level of staff varies between the Member States. The gap is particularly obvious between the professional consumer organisations that exist in some states and the volunteer organisations that operate in others. However, variations in resources for this type of work also exist between Member States' public authorities due to the varying levels of funding.

Qualified entities often still prefer to use their own language and legal systems. In many cases, as private international law rules may lead to the application of the substantive law of the state where consumers are affected, their home state is a natural forum. The intra-Community infringement proceeding also suffers from being expensive, lengthy[184] and complex. No standardised procedure is set down. Injunctions in many states are limited to the case at hand and had no *erga omnes* effect and could even be limited to the territory of the state. Once obtained there may still be difficulties in enforcing injunctions.[185]

179 S Wrbka, *European Consumer Access to Justice Revisited* (Cambridge University Press, 2014), p.44.
180 Report from the Commission concerning the application of Directive 98/27/EC of the European Parliament and of the Council on injunctions for the protection of consumers' interest COM (2008) 756 final.
181 Report from the Commission concerning the application of Directive 2009/22/EC of the European Parliament and of the Council on injunctions for the protection of consumers' interest COM (2012) 635 final.
182 S Wrbka, *European Consumer Access to Justice Revisited* (Cambridge University Press, 2014), p.50.
183 Injunction Directives Report 2012 COM (2012) 635 final, para 2.5.
184 A study by J Stuyck and others, *An Analysis and Evaluation of Alternative Means of Consumer Redress Other than Redress through Ordinary Judicial Proceedings – Final Report* (*Leuven*, 17 Jan 2007) http://www.eurofinas.org/uploads/documents/policies/OTHER%20POLICY%20ISSUES/comparative_report_en.pdf [accessed 11 March 2016], p.324 found the proceedings could last from a few months to several years depending on which state they were brought in. The Injunctions Directive Report 2012 (COM (2012) 635 final) para 4.2 noted it could take more than five years in some states.
185 See S Wrbka, *European Consumer Access to Justice Revisited* (Cambridge University Press, 2014), pp.45–51; Report from the Commission concerning the application of Directive 98/27/EC of the European Parliament and of the Council on injunctions for the protection of consumers' interest COM (2008) 756 final, para 17–27; Injunctions Directive Report 2012 COM (2012) 635 final, paras 4.1–5.

The Commission has been positive about states going beyond the minimum requirements to extend the injunctions to other fields.[186] This is a rare recent endorsement from Brussels of the value of minimum harmonisation for consumers.

It is fair to conclude that the EU has managed to make the injunction a pervasive method of addressing breaches of consumer law in order to strengthen the regulation of the market. It was not so easy to make it effective in cross-border contexts.

Consumer Protection Co-operation Regulation

The practical difficulties of obtaining cross-border injunctions persuaded the Commission to change course and in the Regulation on consumer protection co-operation[187] instead requires the authorities in the state where the trader is located to take action. This has proven to be a helpful measure even if there has been a need to propose some modifications.[188]

Each Member State has to produce a list of National Competent Authorities (NCAs) with specific responsibilities for enforcing consumer law, as well as a Single Liaison Office (SLO) which plays a co-ordinating role. These NCAs must be equipped with minimum powers to investigate and take action against intra-Community infringements.[189] Intra-Community infringements cover acts or omissions that affect the collective interest of consumers in states other than the state where the act of omission occurred, or where the seller or supplier is established, or, where evidence or assets pertaining to the act or omission are.[190] The annex lists 19 EU directives or regulations to which the Regulation applies.

One authority can request from another information on whether an intra-Community infringement has occurred or may occur.[191] There can also be a request that a national authority take all necessary enforcement measures to bring about the cessation or prohibition of the intra-Community infringement without delay.[192] One potential gap in the legislation is that it does not cover action to prosecute infringements which have already ceased. There is a proposal to amend the Regulation in this respect.[193] There may be good reasons for bringing actions against those who have behaved poorly in the past based on the impact and seriousness of the infringement or the recidivist nature of the perpetrator.

Member States should notify competent authorities and the Commission of actions taken as well as any knowledge they have of other intra-Community

186 Injunctions Directive Report 2012 (COM (2012) 635 final), para 2.3.

187 Regulation 2006/2004/EC of the European Parliament and of the Council of 27 October 2004 on cooperation between national authorities responsible for the enforcement of consumer protection laws (2004) OJ L364/1.

188 See COM (2016) 283 final.

189 Reg 2006/2004, Art. 4(6).

190 Ibid., Art. 3(b).

191 Ibid., Art. 6.

192 Ibid., Art. 8.

193 See COM (2016) 283 final.

infringements.[194] These together with any details of co-ordinated actions[195] should be sent to Commission and are kept on its CPC IT System database.[196] Revised surveillance mechanisms are being proposed.[197]

Co-ordinated actions have been organised. These have involved sweeps against targeted bad practices. They have been some of the most high profile and successful achievements of the Regulation.

On the whole the Regulation seems to be welcomed by national authorities. However, it often serves as a stop-gap measure as many of these activities would take place in any event through bilateral arrangements. Nevertheless, the Consumer Protection Cooperation Network (CPC Network) provides a good framework for co-operation.

There has been a debate as to whether the Commission should have a more prominent role, either to nudge authorities to give proper resources and engage fully with the Regulation or in some instances to take on enforcement of EU-level infringements. Recent reform proposals suggest the Commission should have the power in the case of widespread infringements to adopt a common action by decision.[198] As recent litigation around the Apple contract shows, there is a need to ensure that European law is not only applied across the Union, but is applied evenly and the Commission might have a role to play in this regard.[199] It is also being proposed that the minimum powers of national authorities be increased.[200] It would also be helpful if the Commission was given the power to monitor the resources Member States invest in consumer enforcement, such as those in the Market Surveillance Regulation Proposal 2013. Some problems extend beyond resources and are harder to address as they go to the heart of national traditions. For example, delays are sometimes caused due to national rules requiring authorities to go to court before taking action and there are differences in the range and extent of sanctions imposed.

Conclusions

The EU has attempted to raise the general level of market surveillance by requiring agencies be established at the national level. In the context of product safety it was noted that it has proposed that their work programmes and resourcing be monitored. Further efforts in this direction are to be welcomed to promote a more consistent enforcement of EU law across the Member States.

194 Reg 2006/2004, Art. 7.
195 Ibid., Art. 9.
196 Ibid., Art. 10.
197 See COM (2016) 283 final.
198 See COM (2016) 283 final.
199 M Djurovic, 'The Apple case: The commencement of pan-European battle against unfair commercial practices' (2013) 9 *European Review of Contract Law* p.253.
200 See COM (2016) 283 final.

The EU has promoted the use of the injunction as a tool for remedying market failure. EU policy favours effective public regulation of the market, but leaves Member States to determine which agents should be responsible for ensuring compliance. Traditional private law plays a more marginal role in market regulation. The request, rather than demand, for Member States to consider introducing collective redress perhaps underlines this. However, ADR is emphasised for individual redress and these mechanisms often operate at least in the shadow of private law. Private law has an indirect effect on market conduct of traders.

Often, EU initiatives in this area have focused on the Single Market dimension, with some EU legislation in this field also covering domestic matters (notably as regards promotion of ADR). In the field of collective redress, it has been left to national systems to consider devising their own procedures based on recommendations. In this context, this approach should be welcomed as it respects the need for diversity within Europe based on national traditions and cultures. This is particularly prized in civil procedure where respect for national procedural autonomy is widely recognised as a guiding principle. It is nevertheless helpful to encourage states to converge voluntarily.

Even at the national level consumers and regulators face problems in accessing or securing justice. However, the internal market creates additional problems for enforcers and consumers seeking redress. The EU is working to find enhanced solutions. Europe has realised that good laws need good enforcement. This is an area in which one might expect to see increased activity. This may not involve too many new laws, but rather practical initiatives promoting action on the ground.

National traditions will continue to have important influences on the exact contours of Member States' procedures and preferences on forms of redress and manner of enforcement. Nevertheless, the EU Commission has an important role to play in providing a viable framework for consumer enforcement and redress. This should not be restricted to ensuring only cross-border disputes can be handled effectively. It needs to monitor the practical application of EU law within Member States to ensure it is being effectively enforced. Consumers and traders need to be assured that consumer law will be applied and enforced equally throughout the Union. This is in practice an even more demanding and longer-term project than harmonising the substantive *acquis*.

9 To boldly go where EU consumer law has not gone before

Conclusions

In this final chapter, we seek to draw together our main conclusions which emerge from the detailed consideration of the various areas of EU consumer law surveyed in this book. Having considered the current state of EU consumer law, we look ahead at how things could develop in the future. At the time of writing, a number of initiatives are on the horizon, a sure sign that the field of EU consumer law continues to be an 'incoming tide'.[1] However, whilst we can already see a number of initiatives, we will take this opportunity to reflect on the lessons that can be drawn from our analysis of current EU consumer law to put forward a number of theses as to how we think EU consumer law *should* develop in the future.

The current state of EU consumer law

In our opening chapter, we set our six aspects which have shaped our discussion in this book. Having considered a number of areas of EU consumer law in detail, we return to these to set out how our analysis has substantiated those points:

The balance between internal market and consumer protection objectives has swung too much in favour of market integration by the overstatement of the case for maximum harmonisation

Over the preceding chapters, the tension between the EU Commission's desire to pursue full, or maximum, harmonisation across all aspects of EU consumer law and the reluctance by (at least some of) the Member States to accept this has been a recurring theme. There can be no doubt that maximum harmonisation does have a role to play: for example with regard to technical standards for goods and services to ensure parity across the Single Market. One might even accept full harmonisation for rules governing individual contractual relationships where these are of an essentially technical nature, such as the right of

1 A phrase famously used by Lord Denning MR in *H.P. Bulmer Ltd v J. Bollinger SA* [1974] Ch.401 in describing the effect of the United Kingdom becoming a member of the then-European Economic Community. At the time of writing, the flow of the tide seems to be reversing in view of the UK's vote to leave the EU.

withdrawal or information duties. We can observe some success in this respect in the context of the Consumer Credit Directive,[2] for example – as well as the rules on pre-contractual information and the right of withdrawal in other measures.[3]

However, with substantive rules of consumer law such as unfair terms or consumer sales law, this has proven much more difficult, not least because the heterogeneous nature of European consumers in an EU of (still) 28 Member States does require some regional adjustment for the regulation of consumer contracts. Moreover, the experience with the Unfair Commercial Practices Directive has demonstrated that the implications of a maximum harmonisation approach may not always be appreciated fully at the time the Member States agree to a directive. The surprise this can cause was seen when the CJEU held that the Product Liability Directive was a maximum harmonisation measure – the Member States responded with a resolution calling on the Commission to mitigate the effects of this ruling (without success).[4]

A significant proportion of the CJEU's case law in respect of the UCPD is concerned with national provisions which have been found to be incompatible with the UCPD's maximum harmonisation standard.[5] The experience here shows in its starkest terms the effect of maximum harmonisation in removing any possibility for a Member State to deal with matters which might only affect that particular country or to deal with local peculiarities. The CJEU has time and again held that any commercial practices not included in Annex I to the UCPD cannot be prohibited outright.[6] Instead, enforcement bodies have to challenge traders on the basis of the criteria in Arts. 5–8 UCPD. Ultimately, this will necessitate court action, including the possibility of appeals and preliminary ruling requests, which could make this a process which is prohibitive both in terms of time and cost. The justification for removing the power of Member States to take any form of unilateral action once a field has become subject to maximum harmonisation is that permitting Member States to take unilateral action would adversely affected the level playing-field of the Single Market. Consumer protection concerns are brushed aside. The real problem here is the failure of the EU to recognise that there might be good reasons for national variations which outweigh any potential negative effect on the uniformity of the EU's legal rules. Maximum harmonisation has created an imbalance in the ability of Member States to regulate, to the detriment of consumer protection (to mis-quote Art. 3 of the Unfair Contract Terms Directive). However, a better balance could have been struck by providing for some mechanism by which Member States could take action unilaterally where specific domestic concerns so require. This could have taken a form similar to the safeguard procedure

2 See Chapter 6.
3 See Chapter 3.
4 See Chapter 7, p.265.
5 See Chapter 2.
6 See the discussion at pp.75–80.

in the General Product Safety Directive,[7] or notification procedures with the Commission providing temporary authorisation for action within one Member State.[8]

As things stand, the absence of a general safeguard procedure that would allow a Member State to derogate from maximum harmonisation standards in circumstances where there is a consumer protection problem particular to that Member State is regrettable. Article 114 TFEU, the basis for most EU consumer law directives, provides a treaty-based derogation[9] only in respect of the major needs referred to in Article 36 TFEU[10] or 'new scientific evidence relating to the protection of the environment or the working environment on grounds of a problem specific to that Member State'[11] – but not consumer protection. Moreover, it is not permissible to introduce safeguard procedures into measures adopted on the basis of Art. 114 TFEU except for the reasons mentioned in Art. 36 TFEU.[12] This leaves a binary choice when it comes to EU consumer law: minimum harmonisation or insufficient political support for a measure. Member States might be more willing to explore the potential for maximum harmonisation in respect of aspects of consumer law currently subject to minimum harmonisation if they had some reassurance that, if domestic circumstances so necessitated, they could derogate from this in particular instances.

In some areas of consumer law, minimum harmonisation was also seen as the only option for achieving any kind of common European set of rules, and this situation has not changed significantly over the decades. Particular examples of areas where minimum harmonisation was the only option are the directives dealing with rules on substantive aspects of contract law, notably the directives on unfair contract terms and consumer sales.[13] There is some variation as between the Member States in terms of the values and objectives of contract law. Broadly speaking, this ranges from the *laissez-faire* non-interventionist view in the common-law jurisdiction to the co-operative ethic championed by the Nordic countries, with other countries along the spectrum. The effect of three decades may have lessened the starkness of these variations, but they remain present in the fabric of domestic contract laws. Invariably, an attempt to introduce common EU rules on topics such as the regulation of unfair terms would clash with the range of different contract law philosophies, leaving minimum harmonisation as the only viable approach to achieve anything.

7 Art. 3(4), Directive 2001/95/EC.
8 Cf. Chapter 2, p.83.
9 See Art. 114(4)–(10) TFEU.
10 These are: 'public morality, public policy or public security; the protection of health and life of humans, animals or plants; the protection of national treasures possessing artistic, historic or archaeological value; or the protection of industrial and commercial property', but do not include consumer protection.
11 Art. 114 (5) TFEU.
12 See Art. 114(10) TFEU.
13 Cf. Recitals (2)–(5) of the Consumer Sales Directive (99/44/EC).

A high level of consumer protection is desirable not only for consumers but to enhance the international competitiveness of the 'European brand'

Our conception of a 'European consumer protection brand' is one which prioritises a high common level of consumer protection throughout the EU. An attempt to give this a clear branding was the 'blue button' idea for the abandoned Common European Sales Law.[14] A hallmark of this brand is the template function of the EU model of regulation for countries outside the EU.

A good example of the European brand is in the context of product safety regulation and the rules contained in the Product Liability Directive.[15] This has had beneficial effects both in respect of the legislation itself – which has served as a template for regulation in various non-EU countries as far as Australia – and also for the products made in the EU which demonstrate compliance with its high standards. Indeed, in order to be able to sell goods into the EU market, compliance with its technical standards (as evidenced by the widely-used 'CE' marking[16]) is essential. As a corollary, the EU's safety standards can contribute to improving safety standards elsewhere in the world, because producers wishing to sell their goods to the EU have to meet the EU's strict safety requirements.

Similarly, EU consumer legislation has served as a template for law reform in other jurisdictions. The Product Liability Directive[17] has been influential in the Asia-Pacific region.[18] Similarly, the Unfair Contract Terms Directive has served as a benchmark for the Australian rules on unfair terms.[19] The inspiration for countries outside the EU to align their consumer laws with the EU's rules seems, at least in part, to have been inspired by the legislation giving effect to the EU directives in the United Kingdom. Indeed, as a leading common-law jurisdiction, the UK's consumer legislation could have a much broader impact throughout the common law world. In this regard, the withdrawal of the UK from the EU could lessen the reach of the 'EU consumer protection brand' in those countries, especially if the UK will not continue to benchmark its consumer laws against those of the EU.

14 See Chapter 5, p.203, and H Schulte-Nölke, "EC Law on the formation of contract – from the Common Frame of Reference to the 'blue button'" (2007) *European Review of Contract Law* p.332.

15 Discussed in Chapter 7.

16 Although it has been noted that consumers might not fully appreciate the notion of this and other certification marks: see C Poncibo, 'Private certification schemes as consumer protection: A viable supplement to regulation in Europe?' (2007) 31 *International Journal of Consumer Studies* p.656.

17 Discussed in Chapter 7.

18 See J Kellam and L Nottage, 'Europeanisation of product liability in the Asia-Pacific region: A preliminary empirical benchmark' (2008) 31 *Journal of Consumer Policy* p.217.

19 See Schedule 2 of the Competition and Consumer Act 2010. Australian law does not have the same fairness test as that in the EU's Directive (discussed in Chapter 4) – there is no reference to 'good faith', although the significant imbalance criterion does feature.

Not every aspect of EU Consumer Law reflects the 'EU consumer protection brand', however. For example, the provision and regulation of consumer credit might work within the Single Market, but it is not something that could be offered beyond. There is limited cross-border provision of consumer credit and there is likely to be even less outside the EU's borders. On the other hand, developments such as the increased focus on responsible lending[20] could have beneficial effects in setting a trend for taking this into account elsewhere.

Moreover, the EU brand lacks coherence, which is in no small measure due to the piecemeal development of EU consumer law, particularly because this occurred without clear agreement on the broader principles which should underpin the various directives. There is room for strengthening the brand. At the end of this chapter, we will suggest a number of broader principles on which a more coherent brand could be built – indeed, we strongly argue for a debate about what those principles should be.

The EU approach to consumer protection risks being viewed as insufficiently protective due to its adoption of the average consumer standard and an information-based protection model which has not been developed in a sophisticated manner taking into account the lessons of behavioural economics

At various points in this book, the focus on the normative (and rather unrealistic) concept of the 'average consumer' was criticised.[21] The CJEU and the Commission have continued to invoke the 'average consumer' who is supposed to be reasonably well-informed and reasonably observant and circumspect. This is despite the fact that there is a considerable amount of research which reveals that most consumers have none of these characteristics. Much can be learned from behavioural economics and consumer psychology in developing an entirely new consumer concept.

Already, there is a partial recognition that there are some groups of consumers which do not fit the norm, and whose interests do nevertheless need to be protected in particular situations. EU consumer law does protect the needs of particular groups of consumers in some instances, although it lacks a coherent approach in this regard. For example, in several areas, there is an obligation to take into account the needs of certain vulnerable groups.[22] In the context of product safety, this is done by requiring that account of is taken of categories of consumers who might be at particular risk when using a potentially dangerous product.[23] Similarly, the Unfair Commercial Practices Directive provides for consideration of the impact of commercial practices on targeted groups of consumers, as well as particular categories of vulnerable consumers.[24] However,

20 See Chapter 6, p.218.
21 See e.g. Chapter 1, pp.27–31 and Chapter 2, pp.66–73.
22 Notably in the UCPD, Art. 5(2) and (3).
23 See Chapter 7, p.277.
24 See Chapter 2, p.72.

these approaches lack a coherent and consistent approach; in particular, the criteria for establishing whether a consumer should be regarded as vulnerable seem rather basic.[25]

Linked to the notion of the 'average consumer' is the importance of information, reflected in many rules of EU consumer law which mandate the provision of information to consumers. After all, in order to be a 'reasonably well-informed' consumer, a consumer must be given a lot of information! The information-based approach filters through not only in the overt provision of information to consumers in various contexts, but also in the way that information is used to adjust the potential liability of a trader towards a consumer. For example, in the context of product safety and product liability, information about risks conveyed through warnings and instructions can reduce the exposure of a trader towards a consumer.[26] Time and again, the preference of the EU's legislature has been the promotion of information-based rules over substantive regulation, however. This may be in part the result of the emphasis put on the value of information over regulation in early rulings by the CJEU on the free movement of goods.[27] However, whilst there is clearly a place for rules requiring the provision of information, insufficient thought has been given to research findings about an individual's ability to comprehend and process information which have emerged from the field of behavioural economics. Taking full account of these would necessitate a careful review of the rules in EU consumer law on the provision of information. This is particularly apparent e.g. in the context of consumer credit.[28] It is not enough simply to require that consumers are furnished with a lot of information unless due account is taken of the personal context of each individual consumer. At present, information is insufficiently tailored towards an individual consumer's particular requirements. Indeed, consumer credit is an example where too much information might not only undermine the ability of the consumer to make an informed choice but increase the risk of poor choices being made. Similarly, the volume of information routinely to be provided to a consumer when buying online is unlikely to make a difference to many consumers. One solution for using information more effectively would be to find ways of personalising this so it becomes more relevant to an individual consumer.[29]

It is worth noting that in the context of unfair contract terms, the CJEU seems to want to lessen the rigour of the principle of the supposed circumspectness of the consumer. Although the average consumer test is also now applied in this context, the CJEU's interpretation of the transparency test is done in a more consumer-friendly way. This is seen in particular in its focus on ensuring a term is

25 See Chapter 2, p.71.
26 See Chapter 7, p.260.
27 Seminally, Case 120/78 *Rewe v Bundesmonopolverwaltung für Branntwein (Cassis de Dijon)* [1979] ECR 649; see also e.g. C Mak, 'Free movement and contract law' in C Twigg-Flesner (ed), *Research Handbook on EU Consumer and Contract Law* (Elgar, 2016).
28 See Chapter 6.
29 Cf. Chapter 3, p.112.

economically understandable for the consumer, rather than on pure grammatical intelligibility.[30]

Overall, however, the consumer image deployed in EU consumer law is in need of an overhaul and needs to be based on the rich evidence about human behaviour which is now available.

EU consumer law should be more explicit in recognising that it has a social welfare function of redistributing risk

An implicit feature of many consumer law rules is that they have the effect of distributing the risks associated with transactions across all consumers using the trader as the mediator and insurer of risk.

The risk-distribution function can be seen clearly with the Product Liability Directive, which spreads the risk of harm caused by defective products among all consumers. It does so by imposing strict liability on the producer of goods, who is likely to spread the risk of having to compensate some injured consumers among all consumers through the price charged for the product. In a similar vein, a minimum legal quality standard such as the conformity requirement in consumer sales has an insurance function. These functions have been recognised in business models which offer insurance going beyond the legal requirements, e.g. through the sale of so-called 'extended warranties'.[31]

It is equally evident with the regulation of consumer credit – the risk of default of a proportion of consumer borrowers is factored into the cost a lender will impose on all its customers. Although that cost itself is not regulated in legislation, transparency about this cost is relevant e.g. in stating the APR.[32] It is also possible to identify a risk-distribution function with the regulation of unfair contract terms. In providing that unfair standard terms are not binding on a consumer, there is less of a burden on individual consumers to check contract terms carefully before they conclude a contract. A consumer can rely on the unfair terms rules subsequently if a trader relies on a term which would not withstand scrutiny. This risk-sharing function is reinforced by the strong public enforcement approach taken in the unfair contract terms directive.

In addition to the risk-distribution perspective, one should also employ a transaction cost perspective to the issue. The time used for studying the contract terms is a transaction cost for the consumer which is often forgotten in the consumer policy discussions. If consumers would really study all the terms they are confronted with, both in traditional contracting and nowadays in particular in digital contracting, this might take several weeks of the year.[33]

30 See Chapter 4, p.152.

31 These have been a particular issue in the UK, but are also an issue elsewhere in the EU. Cf. C Twigg-Flesner.'Dissatisfaction guaranteed? The legal issues of extended warranties explored' (2002) 4 *Web Journal of Current Legal Issues.* (archived at http://www.bailii.org/uk/other/journals/WebJCLI/2002/issue4/twigg-flesner4.html)

32 Chapter 6, p.232.

33 As evidenced by the publicity exercise by the Norwegian Consumer Council in May 2016, when it read out all the terms and conditions of 33 smartphone apps. This took more than 30 hours. See http://www.bbc.co.uk/news/world-europe-36378215 [last accessed 30 December 2016].

However, whilst it is possible to identify the risk-distribution effect of consumer law when analysing particular directives, it is rarely set out as a function or effect of these directives during the legislative process, nor is this acknowledged explicitly in the recitals. Nevertheless, it is important to highlight the inherent risk-distribution effect of much of EU consumer law.[34] This draws out the fact that risk-distribution is already a feature of EU consumer law, so when it comes to considering future developments in this field, lawmakers should not be afraid to make this characteristic more visible and, indeed, expressly develop rules on the basis of this.

EU legislation should be in a form which allows the EU rules to be integrated into national regimes and parallel regimes for cross-border sales should only be introduced where there are good justifications

Consumer protection should be seen as a matter of general importance for the EU, which means that there should be a pursuit of a common high base-line throughout the EU. However, the focus on the Single Market and the drive for maximum harmonisation have had the upper hand over consumer protection. Maximum harmonisation is justified as the best means of ensuring that traders can operate throughout the Single Market without having to deal with variations in legal rules. From that perspective, a regime on cross-border transactions might seem more logical.[35] However, consumer protection should not be concerned with stark uniformity. There may be instances where specific rules for cross-border situations might seem desirable and should be adopted. One criticism that could be levelled at the Commission in this regard is that it has not been bold enough in identifying and tackling aspects of the substantive law which could specifically support cross-border transactions. A key example here is the continuing reluctance to develop proposals for the direct liability of a producer for the quality of goods (and digital content) or the even bolder idea of network liability.[36] Much of the harmonisation work of substantive consumer law has primarily been concerned with establishing a set of common rules on the assumption that this would facilitate consumer transactions in the Single Market.[37] However, there has not been a consistent focus on considering whether the harmonised rules could really have this effect in practical terms.

On the other hand, in the context of redress and access to justice, more has been done to focus on cross-border issues.[38] In particular, the ODR

34 This extends beyond the topics considered in this book. Consider e.g. Regulation 261/2004/EC establishing common rules on compensation and assistance to passengers in the event of denied boarding and of cancellation or long delay of flights (2004) OJ L46/1.

35 C Twigg-Flesner, *A Cross-Border-Only Regulation for Consumer Transactions in the EU – A New Approach to EU Consumer Law* (Springer, 2012).

36 See Chapter 5, p.202, and R Bradgate and C Twigg-Flesner, 'Expanding the boundaries of liability for quality defects' (2002) 25 *Journal of Consumer Policy* p.345.

37 For example, Recital 5 to the Consumer Sales Directive (99/44/EC) states that 'the creation of a common set of minimum rules of consumer law, valid no matter where goods are purchased within the Community, will strengthen consumer confidence and enable consumers to make the most of the internal market'.

38 See Chapter 8.

regulation[39] has introduced a procedure which should make it easier for consumers who have bought something in another Member State to raise a complaint and seek redress. Similarly, mechanisms to ensure co-operation between national consumer protection authorities[40] are welcome from a cross-border perspective.

The overall impression is that the tension between consumer protection and the Single Market objective remains as present as ever. There is a need to ensure common levels of consumer protection throughout the Single Market, but that alone will not make it easier, nor encourage, consumers to source goods, services or digital content from suppliers in another Member State. Procedures for easier redress should help to reassure consumers that it will not be too difficult to deal with subsequent complaints, and considerable progress on this has been made. However, if the legal rights of consumers are not suited to the particular difficulties associated with cross-border transactions, then the impact of these procedures will be limited. There is still a need to consider how a common standard of consumer protection can combine the issues associated with local face-to-face transactions and on-line cross-border transactions in a coherent and clear set of legal rules.

The EU needs to ensure laws are effectively enforced

As Chapter 8 on access to justice has demonstrated, the EU has developed a broad portfolio of initiatives to support the enforcement of EU consumer law, ranging from out-of-court procedures to litigation to public enforcement. The EU has covered the full spectrum of possible approaches. Yet, one cannot help but feel that despite the best of intentions, the EU has been fairly unsuccessful in making a real difference, at least as far as enforcement across jurisdictional boundaries is concerned – utilisation of the various procedures seems to be rather low.

However, looking beyond the obvious attempts of the EU to promote the enforcement of EU consumer law by various means, there has been a more indirect effect of some aspects on enforcement. The clearest example of this is the extensive body of case law developed by the CJEU in respect of the '*ex officio* doctrine', i.e. the obligation of national courts to raise the unfairness of a contract term of their own motion. This is perhaps the strongest instance of the 'Jack-in-the-box' effect of EU consumer law – few anticipated the emergence of strong procedural requirements out of a basic duty to ensure the enforcement of the Directive. Indeed, this doctrine has developed beyond the area of unfair contract terms to apply to most areas of consumer law now. Although there are still areas of EU consumer law in respect of which the CJEU has not (yet) been asked to rule on the obligations of national courts

39 See p.315.
40 See p.322.

to apply consumer law rules of their own motion, it may be assumed that this doctrine now applies across the board. The extent to which this should be welcomed is linked to the onus put on national courts – are they permitted or obliged to raise consumer law of their own motion? This is also linked to questions of legal tradition which will influence the ability or willingness of national courts in a particular jurisdiction to respond. Many of the references to the CJEU which have resulted in the body of case law defining the scope of the *ex officio* doctrine originated in southern and eastern EU countries. Those might be more prepared to take this obligation seriously. In an adversarial system such as that in the UK, it might take more for judges to act in line with an *ex officio* obligation.[41]

Future developments

The picture of EU consumer law presented in this book is inevitably only a snapshot of the state-of-affairs at the beginning of 2017. A number of future developments are already on the horizon, and a few words on these are appropriate here. In particular, the EU's current focus is on the digital environment and the possible legal challenges this creates. Alongside various initiatives in that context, there is also an ongoing review exercise into the current state of EU consumer law ('REFIT'). However, these developments have a distinct flavour of 'more of the same' in terms of the techniques and approaches to EU consumer law discussed throughout this book, as the following overview demonstrates.

The digital agenda

The EU has decided that the main focus of its activities in the near term should be on facilitating the development of a digital Single Market, i.e. to support the rapidly-evolving use of the internet and smart-technology. Invariably, this will mean considering new legislation on a range of issues, including consumer law. The Commission has set out its thinking in the *Digital Single Market Strategy*,[42] and has since followed this up with a range of proposals.

Of immediate interest to us are the proposals for two new directives which were made in December 2015. The first would introduce maximum harmonisation rules for the on-line and distance sale of consumer goods,[43] and the second,

41 Although note that as far as the UK legislation on unfair terms is concerned, there is now a statutory duty on a court to consider the fairness of a term without this being raised by the parties, provided the court has sufficient factual and legal material to consider the term's fairness: see s.70 of the Consumer Rights Act 2015.

42 The cornerstone document is the European Commission's communication *A Digital Single Market for Europe*, COM (2015) 192 final, 6 May 2015.

43 *Proposal for a Directive of the European Parliament and of the Council on certain Aspects Concerning Contracts for the Online and Other Distance Sales of Goods* COM (2015) 635 final, 9 December 2015.

new rules for the supply of digital content.[44] At the time of writing, neither directive had progressed significantly through the legislative process, although it seems that priority has been given to the proposal on digital content. This is not altogether surprising: the proposal for the on-line and distance sales of goods overlaps with the Consumer Rights Directive (2011/83/EU) and the Consumer Sales Directive (99/44/EC), and there seems to be no real need to introduce a new set of rules which deals with one particular means of selling goods. It seems that this proposal was only made in anticipation of the outcome of the REFIT exercise.[45]

The proposal on digital content is likely to fare better, not least because there are few Member States which currently have legislation on digital content in place.[46] Developing legislation at the EU level in respect of matters which are not already widely regulated domestically is likely to fare better because there are fewer existing positions to be balanced. The proposal primarily focuses on establishing a conformity standard for digital content and remedies for instances when there is a lack of conformity of the digital content. However, there are concerns about the substance of these rules in the original proposal. For example, the test for establishing whether digital content is in 'conformity with the contract' in draft Article 6 takes as its starting point the subjective agreement of the parties,[47] and 'fitness for normal use' is merely a default requirement in the absence of any agreement. In the context of the sale of goods,[48] there is a stronger objective element in the presumption of conformity, and traders are less able to manipulate these elements to lower the overall standard of quality. The approach taken in the digital content proposal is surprising, not least because the idea of party agreement on which it is based, particularly in the supply of digital content, seems to be even more of a fiction than it is in the context of the sale of goods. Generally, acquiring digital content is an automated process and there is no room for negotiation between the parties. With the absence of human intervention on the trader's side, how can there be said to be any real agreement between the parties?[49] This proposal, wedded as it is to old ideas of what constitutes a contract and how it is formed, is a clear illustration of one of the central problems with EU consumer law: a conception of law which is insufficiently forward-looking.

44 *Proposal for a Directive of the European Parliament and of the Council on Certain Aspects Concerning Contracts for the Supply of Digital Content* COM (2015) 634 final, 9 December 2015.

45 See below.

46 The UK's Consumer Rights Act 2015 contains a dedicated chapter on the quality and fitness for purpose of digital content and remedies. There is also specific legislation in place in the Netherlands.

47 See also Recital 25 of the proposal.

48 See Chapter 5, p.179.

49 Cf. J Smits, *The New EU Proposal for Harmonised Rules for the Online Sales of Tangible Goods: Conformity, Lack of Conformity and Remedies*, Study for the JURI Committee of the European Parliament (February 2016), p.9.

We can also raise a more general question, taking us back to one of our main themes: the 'European brand of consumer protection'. There needs to be clarity as to what the purpose of a 'conformity' requirement is. Historically, it served as a default rule for instances when the parties to a contract had not specified what qualities they had agreed on with regard to the goods supplied. However, in the modern consumer context, a conformity requirement increasingly fulfils the role of laying down a clear legal standard which goods – and therefore any digital content – supplied to consumers must meet. The EU would be best advised to think about how it can really create a clear legal framework in support of digital content.

By way of contrast, it is also interesting to see that the Commission appears to have adopted a slightly more cautious attitude to the need for further legislation as regards online platforms that are central to many digital transactions, not least because the digital environment is one where new business models are still emerging. A particular area of difficulty is how the various types of on-line platforms should be regulated, if at all.[50] The Commission's approach seems to be not to rush towards adopting regulatory measures for on-line platforms. In its *Communication on Online Platforms*, it has indicated that it would adopt a two-stage approach to creating a regulatory environment for on-line platforms:[51] first, prior to any action being taken, it will identify what problems will need to be tackled, and any regulatory action will be in response to identified problems; and second, instead of introducing new legislation, it will first be considered whether existing laws can be applied to deal with any specific problems which are discovered.

This is further reflected in the separate *Communication on the Collaborative Economy*,[52] where the European Commission considers whether sharing-economy platforms should be subject to specific regulation. It is already the case that these platforms are covered by the restrictive liability provisions of the E-Commerce Directive, at least to the extent that they provide an 'information society service'. However, many collaborative-economy platforms go further and could be regarded as providing the underlying service, particularly where they rely on a strong brand-image. Where that is the case, additional obligations such as licencing requirements must be complied with by the platform.[53] Whether this applies to any particular platform requires a case-by-case analysis. The Commission has suggested that relevant factors include the extent to which the platform sets the final price and the key contract terms for the contractual relationship between

50 Cf. G Noto La Diega, 'Uber law and awareness by design. An empirical study on online platforms and dehumanised negotiations' (2015) *European Journal of Consumer Law* p.383.

51 European Commission, *Communication on Online Platforms and the Digital Single Market – Opportunities and Challenges for Europe*, COM (2016) 288/2, p.5.

52 European Commission, *Communication on a European Agenda for the Collaborative Economy* COM (2016) 356 final.

53 One only needs to consider how the ride-sharing platform Uber has been treated in various EU countries.

recipient and provider, and whether the platform owns the key assets used in providing the service.[54] But this *Communication* also maintains a cautious approach. On the one hand, this is to be welcomed, because it avoids a rush towards new legislation. On the other, there is a real risk that some consumer issues might fall through the cracks of existing consumer laws, where it is not immediately possible to extend the reach of the current law to the specific matters which arise in the context of the on-line platform economy.

The various initiatives forming part of the digital agenda have yet to be adopted and, where required, implemented into national law, so it is too soon to say what the full extent of new legislation with a consumer protection focus and its likely impact will be. Maximum harmonisation is the Commission's preferred option, but we remain unconvinced that this is appropriate for substantive rules of consumer law for the reasons we have set out throughout this book. That aside, there is considerable room for improving the quality of substance of these proposals. It would be regrettable if the digital agenda were to suffer from the same problems affecting current EU consumer law. There is a window of opportunity for doing things differently and better but it will not be open forever.

The REFIT exercise

At the time of preparing this book, the European Commission was undertaking a review of some of the areas of EU consumer law discussed in this book: unfair commercial practices, unfair terms, consumer sales and injunctions.[55] This is part of a wider programme of review undertaken by the European Commission of a range of policy areas. The overall purpose is to 'analyse the effectiveness, efficiency, coherence, relevance and EU-added value'[56] of these directives in order to establish whether their objectives have been fully attained. The *Fitness Check Roadmap* document highlights a focus on whether these directives have contributed to the Single Market and the extent to which remaining minimum harmonisation standards create barriers to trade.[57] It seems that the Commission is seeking supporting evidence to justify a further attempt to push for maximum harmonisation in areas where Member States have hitherto shown reluctance to accept this. In addition, the *Fitness Check Roadmap* suggests that the relevance of these directives for new market trends and changes in consumer behaviour should be considered, as well as the fit of existing directives with the EU's overall legal landscape.[58] Furthermore, there is to be consideration of regulatory

54 Ibid., 6–8.

55 The review also includes the price indications directive (98/6/EC) and the (non-consumer) Misleading and Comparative Advertising Directive (2006/114/EC).

56 European Commission, *Evaluation and Fitness Check Roadmap* (hereafter *Fitness Check Roadmap*); available athttp://ec.europa.eu/smart-regulation/roadmaps/docs/2016_just_023_evaluation_consumer_law_en.pdf [last accessed 20 December 2016].

57 *Fitness Check Roadmap*, p.9.

58 Ibid.

simplification, e.g. through removing overlaps between different directives and improving overall consistency. The *Fitness Check Roadmap* even suggests that it would 'explore whether and to what extent a potential codification of EU consumer law into a single EU instrument could bring added clarity, remove overlaps, and fill any gaps'.[59]

To scholars who have been following EU consumer law for some time, this will provoke a sense of *deja-vu*: in the middle part of the first decade of the new millennium, the Commission undertook its '*acquis* review', which was a similar exercise also prompted by a concern over the impact of minimum harmonisation clauses in some directives.[60] At that time, the Commission proposed a 'horizontal instrument'[61] on EU consumer law. This would have brought together the unfair contract terms and sales directives with 'common issues' such as the right of withdrawal and information obligations, all with the objective of simplifying and rationalising the *acquis* in the interest of better regulation. It has been remarked at various points throughout this book that the Commission's subsequent attempt to implement this proposal through the Consumer Rights Directive was largely unsuccessful as far as the areas of unfair terms and sale of goods are concerned.

It is surprising that, barely a decade later, the European Commission is essentially repeating the same exercise – framed differently, but with a similar potential outcome, identified early on: maximum harmonisation, and a possible horizontal instrument/consumer code. This exercise could, undoubtedly, produce some benefits: streamlining of the legislation and ensuring that there is consistency between the various elements of the consumer law directives might improve the quality of the current legislation. The discussion in this book noted various instances where the relationship between the different directives was found to be unclear, e.g. the way the UCPD relates to the directives on unfair contract terms and the Consumer Rights Directive.[62] However, there is no indication that the REFIT review would involve a more fundamental reflection on the state of EU consumer law. Rather, the analysis undertaken by the Commission appears to focus primarily on the extent to which there already are standardised, and perhaps even uniform, legal rules in place as a result of the initiatives thus far. It will extend to questions of relevance, which has both a deregulatory element (asking whether there is still need for aspects of the directives) and a scope element (adding objectives in view of market trends and consumer behaviour).[63] There

59 Ibid.

60 An academic study analysed the variations between national laws remaining after the implementation of eight directives: H Schulte-Nölke, C Twigg-Flesner and M Ebers (eds), *EC Consumer Law Compendium* (Sellier, 2008). This resulted in a *Green Paper on the Review of the Consumer Acquis* COM (2006) 744 final. See B Heiderhoff and M Kenny, 'The Commission's 2007 Green Paper on the consumer *acquis*: Deliberate deliberation' (2007) 35 *European Law Review* p.740, and C Twigg-Flesner, 'No sense of purpose or direction?' (2007) 3 *European Review of Contract Law* p.198.

61 *Green Paper*, pp.8–9.

62 See p.49 and p.86.

63 *Fitness Check Roadmap*, p.10.

are also vague indications that the suitability of the rules from the various directives for B2B transactions (particularly involving SMEs) and C2C transactions (e.g. in the sharing economy) will be considered.[64] Any changes which might be made to the existing *acquis* are likely to be incremental and are unlikely to result in a revolutionary change to the substance of EU consumer law.[65] It would be regrettable if there was yet another attempt to push maximum harmonisation in areas where fairly recent experience has shown that there is reluctance on the part of the Member States to accept this. Both the passage of the Consumer Rights Directive and the failed proposal for a Common European Sales Law are a clear indication of where the lines are likely to be drawn. The straightjacket imposed by maximum harmonisation (as illustrated by the experience with the UCPD in particular[66]) is unlikely to prove popular politically.

Where *should* EU consumer law go in the future?

The analysis of the main areas of EU consumer law in this book has demonstrated that, despite its positive achievements in broadening the tools for consumer protection, there are considerable reservations about some of the fundamental features of this area of law. In seeking to adopt new legislation on aspects of the digital environment, the European Commission might be taking EU consumer law into a new territory which is as yet largely untouched by domestic legislation. This should have provided the EU with a golden opportunity for using the largely blank canvas of legislation on digital matters to rethink its approach and develop new means of legislating. Instead, the proposals put forward by the Commission cling on to familiar themes: legislation addressing selected aspects of a topic, proposed directives written in highly technical legal language, and a likely return to favouring a maximum harmonisation approach for many aspects of private law. It may be that these proposals will be adopted, and that they might have a positive practical effect. However, this is hardly revolutionary law-making, and the old adage that 'there is nothing new under the sun'[67] sums up the current and likely future state of EU consumer law.

This is disappointing. Both the digital agenda and the REFIT exercise should have provided the context for a debate about the role for EU consumer law in the future. Indeed, there is still a window of opportunity for this debate within the REFIT exercise: analytical reports are due in 2017, and despite the desire to push ahead with a reform proposal swiftly, perhaps the Commission could be persuaded to pause before it embarks on the next stage of this review process.

64 Ibid.
65 Of course, we may be proved wrong on this. Readers are encouraged to study the follow-up actions taken by the European Commission in the wake of the REFIT exercise.
66 See Chapter 2, pp.73–84.
67 Ecclesiastes 1:9.

In the hope that there is room for such a debate, a number of thoughts to be taken on board are offered here.

Establishing a proper 'European brand' of consumer protection

One of the themes in this book has been that EU consumer law has the potential for establishing a distinct brand of consumer protection which could be an international benchmark. However, the analysis of the specific topics in the preceding chapters has also shown that this potential has not been fully realised. There is a lot more that could be done to turn EU consumer law into a prototype for twenty-first century consumer protection.

At a basic level, there is the continuing failure at the European level to agree on and articulate clearly the fundamental principles and objectives on which EU consumer law should build. Most of the time, there is reference to the high level of consumer protection mandated by the Treaty, but no detailed exploration of what this might require. Alongside this is the economic imperative of supporting the functioning of the Single Market. There is a distinct lack of discussion about the principles which might underpin the development of a high level of consumer protection. A debate about what these principles might be needs to start with a better understanding of the nature of consumers. It is a trite observation that consumers are a heterogeneous group and that consumer law needs to operate with images of consumers which will invariably be a simplification. However, the rough-and-ready 'average consumer' test in EU consumer law is too much of a simplification and unrelated to real world experience (even if the CJEU has showed signs of a more realistic approach in some of its case law, especially on unfair contract terms[68]). Something more refined is needed. The consumer image describing a typical consumer should reflect pertinent research evidence from areas such as behavioural economics and consumer psychology which offer insights as to the characteristics of consumers generally. Indeed, it is crucial to take this learning into account throughout the field of EU consumer law (although not necessarily to be slavishly followed) – and this might not even be as revolutionary as might be feared.[69] It should also to an appropriate extent recognise the fact that the typical consumer image is partially culturally bound. Consumers in different parts of the EU show partially different behavioural patterns, and the proper rules should take these variations into account.[70] The typical consumer image should be the benchmark for the development of both fundamental principles of consumer law and subsequent detailed legal rules.

68 See Chapter 4.

69 AL Sibony and G Helleringer, 'EU consumer protection and behavioural sciences: Revolution or reform?' in A Alemanno and AL Sibony, *Nudge and the Law* (Hart, 2015).

70 Cf. T Wilhemsson, 'The average European consumer: A legal fiction?' in T Wilhelmsson, E Paunio and A Pohjolainen (eds), *Private Law and the Many Cultures of Europe* (Kluwer Law International, 2007).

Having determined the key characteristics of a typical consumer, it would then be necessary to determine the fundamental principles at the root of EU consumer law. Here, it is only possible to offer some tentative suggestions. One such principle might be the protection of fairness in all stages of consumer transactions. There is already a nascent EU vision of fairness inherent in existing directives, [71] and this could be developed into a coherent principle that would apply to the way transactions are concluded, the substance of the contract, and the way disputes are resolved. A second principle could be transparency and clarity, but developed in recognition of the fact that consumers are not fully rational in the pure economic sense. A third might be giving effect to the reasonable expectations of consumers. Other principles might flow from treating consumer protection rather than market integration as the dominant objective. Thus, the risk distribution/insurance function of consumer law, which was mentioned at various points in this book, should similarly be expressly recognised as a general principle – or at least be acknowledged as a legitimate objective. None of these principles is necessarily new; however, their substance would be developed afresh on the basis of a more realistic consumer image. In addition, these principles would be the foundation stones of EU consumer law, rather than identified as somehow underpinning diverse rules put into place over a period of time. Agreeing on these principles could also have the effect of promoting the elements of a common European consumer culture to complement national consumer cultures, which would provide more solid foundations for the development of substantive legal rules over time. This would provide the deep layers of the law for legal rules and case law which have thus far been lacking. [72]

The legal tools

Once the consumer image and fundamental principles of the 'EU consumer protection brand' have been determined, legal rules have to be developed and subsequently enacted through appropriate means. These legal rules would be developed on the basis of the foundations set out above. A crucial factor in developing these is to consider how one could achieve a balanced and pragmatic use of both private and public law to create the best legal framework for consumer transactions. EU consumer law has always been a combination of both – for example, the regulation of unfair commercial practices has been primarily via a public law approach, whereas consumer sales contracts have been dealt with through private law tools. The regulation of unfair contract terms has elements of both. However, the balance between private and public law, as well as the alignment between

71 Cf. C Willett, *Fairness in Consumer Contracts* (Ashgate, 2007).

72 K Tuori, 'EC Law: An independent legal order or a post-modern Jack-in-the-box?' in LD Eriksson and S Hurri (eds), *Dialectic of Law and Reality* (Helsinki Faculty of Law, 1999); T Wilhelmsson, 'Private law in the EU: Harmonised or fragmented Europeanisation?' (2002) 10 *European Review of Private Law* p.77

these spheres and resolution of possible overlaps is something that could be fine-tuned considerably.[73]

In terms of private law, many of these will relate to individual transactions between a consumer and a trader, and so will have to link with contract law. However, it would be important to stop approaching EU consumer (contract) law as a deviation from the general rules of contract law.[74] The paradigm transaction underpinning much of general contract law differs from most consumer contracts. With most consumer contracts, there is no equality of bargaining strength, nor is there true consent and agreement resulting from negotiation. Instead, there is heavy mandatory regulation of most aspects of a typical consumer transaction. Although one cannot ignore the relevance of the rules of general contract law as background, the substance of EU consumer law should be developed by taking a distinct approach.[75]

As for appropriate means, the choice of instruments in EU law is limited. The use of directives and regulations was discussed in the opening chapter.[76] Directives have the advantage of permitting the absorption of legal rules into their context of each domestic law, which has the advantage of ensuring that EU-based rules are connected properly with related aspects of domestic law. However, one important lesson that can be drawn from over three decades of using directives to harmonise aspects of consumer law is that the very technical nature of directives, with at times very detailed articles, has created many difficulties. If the desire for detailed legal rules which are to be applied consistently across the EU remains the dominant objective, then a directive might not be the best option. It has been argued that, if the Single Market objective of creating a single set of rules for consumer contracts is taken as the primary objective, the use of a detailed regulation setting out the relevant legal rules would be the more appropriate means of doing so.[77] However, it would put certainty about legal rules above ensuring suitable consumer protection. The problem of the current approach is that a set of legal rules determined at the European level are pushed into the national laws and the varying legal cultures of the Member States,[78] where they are likely to take on a

73 For example, consider the overlap between the UPCD and pre-contractual information duties (see Chapter 3, p.104), as well as that of the UCPD and national rules on harassment, duress and undue influence.

74 In this context, the combination of responsibilities for contract law and consumer law under the auspices of DG Just has been unfortunate.

75 R Brownsword, 'Regulating transactions: Good faith and fair dealing' in G Howells and R Schulze (eds), *Modernising and Harmonizing Consumer Contract Law* (Sellier, 2009); also R Brownsword, 'Contract, consent and civil society: Private governance and public imposition' in P Odell and C Willett, *Global Governance and the Quest for Justice – Civil Society* (Hart, 2008).

76 See Chapter 1, p.42.

77 C Twigg-Flesner, *A Cross-Border-Only Regulation for Consumer Transactions in the EU – A New Approach to EU Consumer Law* (Springer, 2012).

78 T Wilhelmsson, 'The Legal, the cultural and the political – conclusions from different perspectives on harmonisation of European contract law' (2002) *European Business Law Review* p.54.

life of their own.[79] As a result, the degree of actual convergence achieved might be lower than one might expect in view of the number of directives which have been adopted[80] – even if there has been *some* convergence.

Our argument is that consumer protection should be the primary objective for EU consumer law, rather than the demands of the Single Market. Whilst this could be effected through a regulation, it is preferable to rely on properly designed domestic law to achieve this in full. EU measures would continue to be used to improve domestic law, and this could best be done by using directives. However, it would seem appropriate to reconfigure the way directives are utilised: instead of detailed rules, directives could state broader objectives – more precise than fundamental principles, but less technical than is often the case currently. Article 288 TFEU reminds us that directives specify a result to be achieved, and so a less rigid approach to drafting might be more beneficial. This approach would adapt a similar, less formal approach found in the open method of co-ordination.[81] This operates at the policy level, rather than at the level of binding obligation, but a less rigid use of directives could provide a similar degree of flexibility whilst ensuring a common standard of consumer protection can be achieved across the EU. It would allow the principles associated with the 'EU consumer protection brand' to become more portable as a consequence of not being expressed in detailed technical rules.[82] Admittedly, there would be circumstances where more technical rules would not only be appropriate but essential. An obvious example is the area of technical standardisation which relies on precise and often quite detailed rules, and these, in turn, are relevant for the regulation of product safety.[83] However, not every aspect of EU consumer law needs to be expressed through precise rules, particularly if these then need to become part of domestic law.

General outlook

The key message which emerges from this book and our concluding thoughts is that EU consumer law could have an important role to play in ensuring effective consumer protection throughout the EU, and beyond. It could become a true 'European brand of consumer protection' and serve as a model for developing consumer law elsewhere in the world. However, for this to happen, the script

79 G. Teubner, 'Legal irritants: Good faith in British law or how unifying law ends up in new divergences' (1998) 61 *Modern Law Review* p.11.

80 P Legrand, 'European legal systems are not converging' (1996) 45 *International and Comparative Law Quarterly* p.52.

81 W van Gerven, 'Bringing (private) laws closer at the European level' in F Cafaggi (ed), *The Institutional Framework of European Private Law* (Oxford: Oxford University Press, 2006).

82 A detailed 'omnibus EU consumer law' might also help to sell the EU brand if it were to function as a model law, but it would almost certainly not be exhaustive and therefore still depend on how its rules would interact with domestic law. Overall integrity at national level is more important than at EU level.

83 See Chapter 7, p.259.

needs to be re-written. The current consumer image is too far removed from reality, maximum harmonisation is too concerned with a focus on the Single Market imperative, and there is insufficient room for legitimate national variations. Individual directives would benefit from improvements. Some of these would be necessary to clarify issues concerning their detailed rules, as discussed in the preceding chapters. This would be a task for the short-term and something which the REFIT exercise might provide.

One factor which might cause complications is the decision of the United Kingdom to leave the European Union. At the time of writing, the precise terms of the UK's departure were unknown, but it is inevitable that the UK will cease to be an active player in the future development of EU consumer law, once it has left the EU. It is impossible to anticipate what kind of impact the exit of the largest common-law jurisdiction will have on the future development of EU consumer law. The UK has always had strong consumer protection laws, and the loss of its voice in reforming existing measures and developing new ones will not go unnoticed.

In our view, there is more that needs to be done for the 'EU consumer protection brand', starting with a more fundamental overhaul of the purpose for which EU consumer law is required. In recent years, the focus on developing general contract law at the European level[84] has overshadowed discussions about EU consumer law, but with the contract law agenda fading into the background, there is a fresh opportunity to focus on consumer law. Our analysis and discussion will hopefully prompt scholars to join this debate that now needs to be had to secure a bright future for EU consumer law, both within the EU and beyond.

84 C Twigg-Flesner, *The Europeanisation of Contract Law*, 2nd ed (Routledge, 2013).

Index

For Product Safety Concerns and Information please contact our EU
representative GPSR@taylorandfrancis.com
Taylor & Francis Verlag GmbH, Kaufingerstraße 24, 80331 München, Germany

www.ingramcontent.com/pod-product-compliance
Ingram Content Group UK Ltd.
Pitfield, Milton Keynes, MK11 3LW, UK
UKHW020021200926
475702UK00014B/1993
* 9 7 8 0 3 6 7 2 7 9 3 5 6 *